C++ Primer

2nd Edition

Stanley B. Lippman
AT&T Bell Laboratories

ADDISON-WESLEY PUBLISHING COMPANY

Reading, Massachusetts • Menlo Park, California • New York • Don Mills, Ontario
Wokingham, England • Amsterdam • Bonn • Sydney • Singapore
Tokyo • Madrid • San Juan • Milan • Paris

Library of Congress Cataloging-in-Publication Data

Lippman, Stanley B.
  C++ Primer / by Stanley B. Lippman -- 2nd ed.
    p. cm.
  Includes index.
  ISBN 0-201-54848-8
  1. C++ (Computer program language) I. Title. II. Title: C plus
plus primer
QA76.73.C15L57 1991
005.13'3--dc20   91-18434
                                                          CIP

Reprinted with corrections April, 1992

This book was typeset in Palatino and Courier by the author, using a Linotron 100 phototypesetter and a DEC VAX 8550 computer running UNIX® System V, Release 2.

UNIX is a registered trademark of AT&T. MS-DOS is a registered trademark of Microsoft Corporation. DEC and VAX are trademarks of Digital Equipment Corporation. Ada is a trademark of the Ada Joint Program Office, Department of Defense, United States Government.

5 6 7 8 9 10-HA-95949392

To Beth,
who makes this,
and all things,
possible

--

To Daniel and Anna,
who contain
virtually
all possibilities

Preface

I was both pleasantly surprised and gratified to find the first edition of the *C++ Primer* enthusiastically received by the C++ community. When my editor suggested a second edition, my first reaction was, "What? Already?" However, the conditions seemed as propitious as those surrounding the first edition: my wife and I were expecting a child again (this time a girl, Anna Rachel); I was again working long hours trying to get out a new release of the compiler (this time, Release 3.0); and, again, the C++ language had significantly evolved (this time, the template facility and a published exception handling specification). Okay, then. "But I want it to be a better edition, not just an update," I told my editor, my wife, my colleagues at work, and just about anyone who would listen. "Oh," they said, their voice muted, eyes cast downward to the street, carpet, meal. "Well, don't ruin it," they advised.

Background on C++

The C++ programming language was developed at AT&T Bell Laboratories in the early 1980s by Bjarne Stroustrup. It is an evolution of the C programming language, which extends C in three important ways:

1. It provides support for creating and using data abstractions

2. It provides support for object-oriented design and programming

3. It provides various nice improvements over existing C constructs

all while retaining C's simplicity of expression and speed of execution.

C++ is already widely available and is in wide use for real application and systems development. Within six months of its initial release from AT&T in late 1985, there were commercial ports of C++ available on over 24 systems, ranging from PCs to large mainframes. Since then, more ports have been made, and C++ is now available directly from many computer vendors. In 1988 the first native compilers were produced for the PC and workstation markets. Additionally, large-scale libraries and program support environments have begun to appear. The maturation of the C++ language is attested to by two recent events: the formation of an ANSI C++ committee and the publication of *The Annotated C++ Reference Manual* by Ellis and Stroustrup,

v

which serves as the baseline document for the C++ ANSI committee. Papers documenting user experience with C++ have appeared in various conferences (there are now two annual conferences devoted exclusively to C++) and technical publications.

Structure of this Book

This book provides a comprehensive introduction to C++ as reflected in its latest release, Release 3.0, and the baseline ANSI C++ document, *The Annotated C++ Reference Manual* by Ellis and Stroustrup. Additionally, it provides a consciously tutorial approach to describing the C++ language. Knowledge of C is not assumed, although familiarity with some modern, block structured language is. This book is intended as a *first* book on C++; it is not intended as a *first* book on programming!

Much of the power of C++ comes from its support for new ways of programming and new ways of thinking about programming problems. Learning to use C++ effectively, therefore, requires more than simply learning a new set of syntax and semantics. To facilitate this larger learning, the book is organized around a series of extended examples. These examples are used both to introduce the details of various language features, and to motivate them as well. By learning language features in the context of a full example, it becomes clear why such features are useful, providing a sense of when and how one would make use of them for real world problem solving. Additionally, this focus on examples, which can and should be executed, allows early use of concepts that will be explained more fully as the reader's knowledge base is built up. Early examples can and do contain simple uses of fundamental C++ concepts, giving a flavor for the kinds of programming one can do in C++ without requiring complete understanding of the details of design and implementation.

Fundamental to C++ are various facilities that allow the user to extend the language itself by defining new data types that then can be used with the flexibility and simplicity of built-in data types. The first step to mastery is to understand the base language itself. Chapters 0 through 4 focus on the language at this level, while Chapters 5 through 9 extend the discussion of the facilities which support creation of user-defined types. Chapter 10 provides a tutorial illustration of the process of object-oriented design in C++.

Chapter 0 introduces the essential elements of a C++ program and the details of how to get a C++ program entered and executed. Data types, expressions and statements are the subject of Chapters 1 and 2. Chapter 1 includes a discussion and example of the C++ class introducing this fundamental notion that will be expanded on throughout the book. Chapter 3 introduces functions, the notion of program scope, and the run-time allocation of variables through the use of a program's *free store*. Proficient programmers — and especially C programmers — may be tempted to skip these chapters. Don't. New concepts are included throughout these sections and even the most experienced C programmer will benefit from skimming the material and working through the examples in the text and the exercises.

Chapter 4 extends the discussion to encompass function overloading and the definition and use of template functions. Overloading allows multiple function instances that provide a common operation (but require differing implementations) to share a common name. The programmer can write `put()` rather than `putc()` or `puts()`, for example, and trust the compiler to resolve the call to the intended instance. A template function provides a prescription for the automatic generation of an infinite set of function instances varying by type but whose implementation remains invariant.

Chapters 5 and 6 focus on the class mechanism and how it supports the design and implementation of abstract data types. By creating new types to describe the problem domain, C++ allows the programmer to write applications with much less concern for the various bookkeeping aspects that make programming tedious. The implementation of types fundamental to the application can be implemented once and reused, allowing the programmer to concentrate on the problem rather than the details of the implementation. Facilities for encapsulating the data can dramatically simplify subsequent maintenance and change.

Chapter 7 examines the definition and use of the template class facility. Template classes facilitate the development of extensive class libraries. As with a template function, a template class provides a prescription for the automatic generation of an infinite set of class instances varying by type but whose implementation remains invariant.

Object-oriented programming and the facilities in C++ that support it are the topics of Chapters 8 and 9. Chapter 8 introduces inheritance. Through inheritance, the programmer can capture type relationships that are interdependent. The classic example is that of shapes. All shapes share certain attributes: location on the plane, logic to rotate the shape, draw the shape, etc. Inheritance allows these common attributes to be shared from the application's viewpoint while the implementation of each specific shape need worry only about providing definitions for those attributes that actually differ from one shape to the next. Fundamental to object-oriented approaches is the ability to choose at run time which exact function will be invoked. For example, at run time we must be able to tell a shape to rotate and know that the appropriate logic for a circle or square will be invoked depending on the actual type of the shape that is being rotated. In C++ this is handled through the virtual function mechanism, which is the topic of Chapter 9. Chapter 9 also introduces the more complicated inheritance hierarchies that are made possible through virtual base classes. Chapter 10 provides a tutorial illustration of object-oriented design using C++.

Changes to the Second Edition

The changes to the second edition fall into four general categories:

1. Coverage of new features added to the language: the template facility and exception handling.

2. Adjustments in the existing text to reflect refinements, changes, and extensions in the existing language. An example of a refinement is the small change in the rules for the initialization of a reference. This in turn modified slightly the argument-matching algorithm for the resolution of a call of an overloaded function. An example of a large change in the language is the introduction of nested types within classes. (A discussion of how nested types were "reintroduced" into C++ can be found in my article "Nested Types in C++," published in the *C++ Journal*, Fall, 1990.) An example of a language extension is the ability for a class to overload both a prefix and postfix instance of the increment and decrement operators. Appendix D lists the changes between the Release 2.0 and Release 3.0 language definition.

3. Improvements in the treatment or organization of certain language features. When the *C++ Primer* was first published, the only significant C++ text available was Stroustrup's *The C++ Programming Language* and that did not reflect changes in the language since the original Release 1.0. The publishing landscape has since changed radically. Accordingly, in this second edition, I've shifted the focus in some cases to illustrate how best to use a feature and to point out some potential pitfalls to avoid.

4. New material focusing primarily on class and object-oriented design. This seemed to be on everyone's wish list for a second edition. A new Chapter 10 provides a tutorial illustration of the object-oriented design process. The implementation of a template facility within an existing C++ compiler is the motivating example.

Exception handling, which at the time of the first edition, was an internal design worked out by Bjarne Stroustrup and Andrew Koenig of Bell Laboratories, is now a formal part of the C++ language, voted upon by the ANSI C++ committee in November 1990. At the time of the writing of this second edition, no implementation is publically available. Therefore, I have decided to describe exception handling in Appendix B rather than in the body of the text. I have chosen this approach for two reasons:

1. Without an implementation against which to try the code, I cannot guarantee, as I have with the other examples in the body of the text, that the examples actually compile and execute as stated.

2. It has been my experience that a language specification undergoes at times considerable change during the process of implementation and first use. Although the exception handling specification is an excellent paper specification, I strongly suspect its actual use will cause certain refinements to its definition.

I would rather, therefore, handle it exceptionally in this edition. Were it thrown within the body of the text, exception handling would likely be caught as follows: in a separate section in Chapter 4 treating nonclass-specific exceptions; in a separate section in Chapter 6 treating class-specific exceptions; and in a separate section in Chapter 8 treating exceptions and class inheritance.

The Future of C++

The language is still undergoing some small changes — these will likely continue until the ANSI C++ committee completes its work. Our growing experience with templates, for example, has suggested some potential changes to the definition of the facility. Will they all be adopted as currently proposed? It won't be clear for a while yet. The ANSI C++ committee, however, in my opinion is doing a good job and we can be sure what changes are introduced will be well-considered.

Are there likely to be any further extensions? One that seems more likely than not is the idea of metaclasses. Metaclasses permit an object to be queried at run time about such things as its actual type. Object-oriented database systems feel the absence of a language-supported metaclass facility most strongly. A number of designs have been independently proposed, but nothing, as of this writing, has formally been submitted to the language extension subgroup of the ANSI C++ committee, headed by Stroustrup.

Implementation Notes

The programs in this book were directly taken from source files that were compiled on either (and sometimes both) an AT&T 6386 WGS running UNIX System V Release 3.2 and a Sun3/60 workstation running version 4.0.3c of that operating system. All programs and program fragments were compiled using internal versions of Release 3.0 of C++ currently under development at Bell Laboratories.

An early draft of this second edition served as the basis for a four-day "short course" in C++ that I presented under the sponsorship of the UCLA Extension Program in February of 1991. Portions of this book have also been used in tutorials I've presented both at professional conferences and seminars. Drafts of the manuscript have served as both start-up and reference material for internal Bell Laboratories projects beginning to program in C++. Many of the programs and program fragments in this book have been used as part of the verification suite during the development of Releases 2.0 and 3.0. Additionally, many of the programs in this text are included with Releases 2.0 and 3.0 as demonstration programs of the various language features.

Acknowledgments

This book is the result of many invisible hands helping to keep its author on course. My most heartfelt thanks go to Barbara Moo. Her encouragement, advice, and close reading of innumerable drafts of the manuscript have been invaluable. Special thanks go to Bjarne Stroustrup for his continued help and encouragement, and for the wonderful language he has given us; to Stephen Dewhurst, who provided much early support as I was *first* learning C++; and to Nancy Wilkinson, another swashbuckling *cfront* coder and supplier of gummi bears.

Dag Bruck, Martin Carroll, William Hopkins, Brian Kernighan, Andrew Koenig, Alexis Layton, and Barbara Moo provided especially detailed and perceptive comments. Their reviews have improved this book considerably. Andy Baily, Phil Brown, James Coplien, Elizabeth Flanagan, David Jordan, Don Kretsch, Craig Rubin, Jonathan Shopiro, Judy Ward, Nancy Wilkinson, and Clay Wilson reviewed various drafts of the manuscript and provided many helpful comments. David Prosser clarified many ANSI C questions. Jerry Schwarz, who implemented the iostream package, provided the original documentation on which Appendix A is based. His detailed and thoughtful review of that appendix is much appreciated. Grateful thanks go to the other members of the Release 3.0 development team: Laura Eaves, George Logothetis, Judy Ward, and Nancy Wilkinson.

The following provided reviews of the manuscript for Addison-Wesley: James Adcock, Steven Bellovin, Jon Forrest, Maurice Herlihy, Norman Kerth, Darrell Long, Victor Milenkovic, and Justin Smith.

The following have pointed out errors in various printings of the first edition: David Beckedorff, Dag Bruck, John Eldridge, Jim Humelsine, Dave Jordan, Ami Kleinman, Andy Koenig, Tim O'Konski, Clovis Tondo, and Steve Vinoski.

I am *deeply* appreciative to Brian Kernighan and Andrew Koenig for making available a number of typesetting tools.

References

Two fine publications that focus exclusively on C++ are *The C++ Report*, edited by Robert Murray, and *The C++ Journal*, edited by Livleen Singh. Both are highly recommended. Another rich source of information about C++ is the delightful column Andrew Koenig writes for each issue of the *Journal of Object-Oriented Programming*.

[1] Alfred V. Aho, Ravi Sethi, and Jeffrey D. Ullman, *Compilers — Principles, Techniques, and Tools*, Addison-Wesley, Reading, MA, 1986.

[2] Grady Booch: *Object-Oriented Design*, The Benjamin/Cummings Publishing Company, Inc., CA, 1991.

[3] Martin Carroll: *Problems with Non-invasive Inheritance in C++*, Proceedings of the USENIX C++ Conference, Washington, D.C., April 22-25, 1991.

[4] Margaret Ellis and Bjarne Stroustrup: *The Annotated C++ Reference Manual*, Addison-Wesley, Reading, MA, 1990.

[5] Carlo Ghezzi and Mehdi Jazayeri: *Programming Language Concepts*, John Wiley & Sons, NY, 1982.

[6] Adele Goldberg and David Robson: *SMALLTALK-80: The Language and Its Implementation*, Addison-Wesley, Reading, MA, 1983.

[7] Samuel P. Harbison and Guy L. Steele, Jr.: *C: A Reference Manual*, 2nd edition, Prentice-Hall, Englewood Cliffs, NJ, 1987.

[8] Brian W. Kernighan and Dennis M. Ritchie: *The C Programming Language*, 2nd edition, Prentice-Hall, Englewood Cliffs, NJ, 1988.

[9] Andrew Koenig: *C Traps and PitFalls*, Addison-Wesley, Reading, MA, 1989.

[10] Andrew Koenig and Stanley Lippman: Optimizing Virtual Tables in C++ Release 2.0, *The C++ Report*, March 1990.

[11] Stanley Lippman: Nested Types in C++, *The C++ Journal*, Fall 1990.

[12] Barbara Liskov and John Guttag: *Abstraction and Specification in Program Development*, McGraw-Hill, NY, 1986.

[13] Ravi Sethi: *Programming Languages Concepts and Constructs*, Addison-Wesley, Reading, MA, 1989.

[14] Bjarne Stroustrup: *The C++ Programming Language*, 2nd Edition, Addison-Wesley, Reading, MA, 1991.

CONTENTS

Chapter 0: **Getting Started**

For the individual first learning C++, two questions naturally arise:

1. What is a C++ program, anyway? How is one written?

2. Once it is written, how do you get the program to run?

This chapter presents the basic knowledge and procedures for turning C++ source code into executable programs.

0.1 Problem Solving

Programs often are written in response to some problem or task to be solved. Let's look at an example. A bookstore enters into a file the title and publisher of each book it sells. The information is entered in the order the books are sold. Every two weeks the owner by hand computes the number of copies of each title sold and the number sold from each publisher. The list is alphabetized by publisher and used for purposes of reordering. You have been asked to supply a program to do this work.

One method of solving a big problem is to break it down into a number of smaller problems. Hopefully, these smaller problems are easier to solve. Our bookstore problem divides nicely into four subproblems, or tasks:

1. Read in the sales file.

2. Count the sales by title and by publisher.

3. Sort the titles by publisher.

4. Write out the results.

Items 1, 3, and 4 represent problems we know how to solve; they do not need to be broken down further. Item 2, however, is still a little more than we know how to do. So we reapply our method to this item:

2a. Sort the sales by publisher.

2b. Within each publisher, sort the sales by title.

2c. Compare adjacent titles within each publisher group. For each matching pair, increment an occurrence count of the first and delete the second.

1

Items 2a, 2b, and 2c also now represent problems that we know how to solve. Since we can solve all the subproblems that we have generated, we have in effect solved the original, bigger problem. Moreover, we see that the original order of tasks was incorrect. The sequence of actions required is the following:

1. Read in the sales file.

2. Sort the sales file — first, by publisher, then, by title within publisher.

3. Compact duplicate titles.

4. Write out the results into a new file.

The resulting sequence of actions is referred to as an *algorithm*. The next step is to translate our algorithm into a particular programming language — in this case, C++.

0.2 The C++ Program

In C++, an action is referred to as an *expression*. An expression terminated by a semicolon is referred to as a *statement*. The smallest independent unit in a C++ program is a statement. In natural language, an analogous construct is the sentence. The following, for example, are statements in C++:

```
int value;
value = 7 + 1;
cout << value;
```

The first statement is referred to as a *declaration* statement. It defines an area of computer memory associated with the name value that can hold integer values. The second statement is referred to as an *assignment* statement. It places in the area of computer memory associated with the name value the result of adding together 7 and 1. The third statement is an *output* statement. cout is the output destination associated with the user's terminal. << is the output operator. The statement writes to cout — that is, the user's terminal, the value stored in the area of computer memory associated with the name value.

Statements are logically grouped into named units referred to as *functions*. For example, all the statements necessary to read in the sales file are organized into a function called readIn(). Similarly, we organize a sort(), compact(), and print() function.

In C++, every program must contain a function called main(), supplied by the programmer, before the program can be run. Here is how main() might be defined for the preceding algorithm:

```
int main()
{
    readIn();
    sort();
    compact();
    print();
    return 0;

}
```

A C++ program begins execution with the first statement of main(). In this case, the program begins by executing the function readIn(). Program execution continues by sequentially executing the statements within main(). A program terminates normally following execution of the last statement of main().

A function consists of four parts: a return type, the function name, an argument list, and the function body. The first three parts are collectively referred to as the *function prototype*. The argument list, enclosed within parentheses, contains a comma-separated list of zero or more arguments. The function body is enclosed within a pair of braces ("{}"). It consists of a sequence of program statements.

In this instance, the body of main() *calls* for execution the functions readIn(), sort(), compact(), and print(). When these have completed, the statement return 0; is executed. return, a predefined C++ statement, provides a method of terminating the execution of a function. When supplied with a value such as 0, that value becomes the *return value* of the function. In this case, a return value of 0 indicates the successful completion of main().

Let's turn now to how the program is made ready for execution. First we must provide definitions of readIn(), sort(), compact(), and print(). At this point, the following dummy instances are good enough:

```
void readIn() { cout << "readIn()\n"; }
void sort() { cout << "sort()\n"; }
void compact() { cout << "compact()\n"; }
void print() { cout << "print()\n"; }
```

void is used to specify a function that does not provide a return value. As defined, each function will simply announce its presence on the user's terminal when invoked by main(). Later, we can replace these dummy instances with the actual functions as they are implemented. This sort of incremental method of building programs provides a useful measure of control over the programming errors we inevitably make. Trying to get a program to work all at once is simply too complicated and confusing.

A program source file consists of two parts — a file name and a file suffix. The file suffix serves to identify the contents of the file. This suffix will vary among the different implementations of C++. Under the UNIX operating system, the C++ file may end either with ".c" or ".C". The lowercase ".c" reflects the very close ties between the C++ and C programming languages. (All C program source files must end with ".c".) To distinguish a C++ source file, use the ".C" file suffix.†

Enter the following complete program into a C++ source file.

```
#include <iostream.h>

void read() { cout << "read()\n"; }
void sort() { cout << "sort()\n"; }
void compact() { cout << "compact()\n"; }
void write() { cout << "write()\n"; }

int main() {
    read();
    sort();
    compact();
    write();
    return 0;
}
```

iostream.h is referred to as a *header file*. It contains information about cout that is necessary to our program. #include is referred to as a preprocessor directive. It causes the contents of iostream.h to be read into our text file. Section 0.5 (page 13) discusses preprocessor directives.

Once the program has been entered into a file, the next step is to compile it. This is done as follows ($ is the system prompt):

```
$ CC prog1.C
```

The command name used to invoke the C++ compiler will vary among different implementations. CC is the command name for the C++ compiler developed within AT&T Bell Laboratories. Check the reference manual or ask your system administrator for the C++ command name on your system.

Part of the compiler's job is to analyze the program text for "correctness." A compiler cannot detect if the meaning of a program is correct, but it can detect errors in the *form* of the program. Two common forms of program error are the following:

†Under MS-DOS, however, the ".C" suffix is not available — MS-DOS does not distinguish between lower- and uppercase letters. Implementations of C++ under MS-DOS support the following file suffixes:

• cxx (x is a "+" rotated 45 degrees).

• cpp (p stands for "plus").

1. *Syntax errors.* The programmer has made a "grammatical" error in the C++ language. For example,

```
int main ( {     // error: missing ')'
     readIn():    // error: illegal character ':'
     sort();
     compact();
     print();
     return 0    // error: missing ';'
}
```

2. *Type errors.* Data in C++ has an associated type. The value 10, for example, is an integer. The word "hello" surrounded by double quotation marks is a string. If a function expecting an integer argument is given a string, a type error is signaled by the compiler.

An error message will contain a line number and a brief description of what the compiler believes that you have done wrong. It is a good practice to correct errors in the sequence they are reported. Often a single error can have a cascading effect and cause a compiler to report more errors than actually are present. Once you have corrected your program text, the program should be recompiled.

A second part of the compiler's job is to translate formally correct program text. This translation, referred to as *code generation*, typically generates object or assembly instruction text understood by the computer on which the program is to be run.

The result of a successful compilation is an executable file. By default, on the author's system, this file is called a.out. It can be executed as follows:

```
$ a.out
```

Output of the program looks like this:

```
readIn()
sort()
compact()
print()
```

The command option -o name allows the programmer to specify a name for the program file other than a.out. For example, the command line

```
$ CC -o prog1 prog1.C
```

will create the executable file prog1. To run the program, the user will write

```
$ prog1
```

In addition to the language compiler and C++ command, a C++ implementation provides a set of standard libraries. Program libraries are a collection of precompiled functions. In C++, for example, input and output are supported within the C++ standard library. Programmers can use library functions within their programs in the same way they use functions they themselves have written.

At its best, a program library allows an expert to package his or her knowledge for use by the general programmer. Few of us, for example, know how electricity works; most of us, however, know how to turn on a switch. A good library can be as easy to use as a light switch. In the next section, we look at the C++ input/output library.

0.3   A First Look at Input/Output

Input and output are not part of the C++ language, but are supported by a library written in C++ known as the *iostream* library. Appendix A looks at this library in detail.† In this section, enough information is introduced to get the reader started.

Input coming from the user's terminal, referred to as *standard input*, is "tied" to the predefined iostream cin (pronounced "see-in"). Output directed to the user's terminal, referred to as *standard output*, is tied to the predefined iostream cout (pronounced "see-out").

The output operator ("<<") is used to direct a value to standard output. For example,

```
cout << "The sum of 7 + 3 = ";
cout << 7 + 3;
cout << "\n";
```

The two-character sequence \n represents the *newline* character. When written, the newline character causes the output to be directed to the next line. Rather than explicitly writing the newline character, one can apply the predefined iostream manipulator endl. endl inserts a newline character into the output stream, then *flushes* the output buffer. Rather than writing

```
cout << "\n";
```

one writes

```
cout << endl;
```

Successive occurrences of the output operator can be concatenated. For example,

---

†Those readers with a C++ implementation not based on either Release 2.0 or 3.0 may have an earlier version of the library called the *stream* library. Users of this library should substitute the stream.h header file for each occurrence of the iostream.h header file within this text.

```
cout << "The sum of 7 + 3 = " << 7 + 3 << endl;
```

Each successive output operator is applied in turn to cout. For readability, the concatenated output statement may span several lines. The following three lines make up a single output statement:

```
cout << "The sum of "
     << v1 << " + "
     << v2 << " = " << v1 + v2 << endl;
```

Similarly, the input operator (">>") is used to read a value from standard input. For example, the following program implements a simple algorithm to read in two values, determine the larger of the two values, and write out the value that is largest.

```
#include <iostream.h>

void read2( int&, int& );
int max( int, int );
void writeMax( int );


main() {
   int val1, val2;

   read2( val1, val2 );
   int maxVal = max( val1, val2 );
   writeMax( maxVal );
   return 0;
}


void read2(int& v1, int& v2)
{
   cout << "Please enter two numeric values: ";
   cin >> v1 >> v2;
}


int max(int v1, int v2)
{
    if ( v1 > v2 )
          return v1;
    else
          return v2;
}
```

```
void writeMax(int val)
{
    cout << val
         << " is the largest value.\n";
}
```

A few remarks should be made about this program. The three function names are listed before the definition of main() . The initial listing, referred to as a *forward declaration*, informs the program that these functions exist and that their definition occurs somewhere else in the program, either later in this file or in a separate file. A function must always be declared to the program before it can be called. A forward declaration is one way to do this.

val1 and val2 are referred to as *symbolic variables*. The statement

```
int val1, val2;
```

defines these variables to the program. Variables must also be made known to the program before they can be used. Variables are discussed in detail in Chapter 1.

v1 and v2, referred to as *formal arguments*, make up the argument list of both read2() and max(). val is the single formal argument of writeMax(). The significance of their declaration is looked at in Section 3.6 (page 125) in the discussion of how arguments are passed to functions.

The reader may have noticed that main() is declared slightly differently this time. It does not explicitly specify a return type. This is permissible in C++: a function that does not indicate a return type is presumed to return an integer value.

When compiled and executed, the program outputs the following (the user entered the values 17 and 124):

```
Please enter two numeric values: 17 124
124 is the largest value.
```

The two values entered by the user, 17 and 124, are separated by a blank. Blanks, tabs and newlines are referred to as *white space* in C++. The statement

```
cin >> v1 >> v2;
```

correctly reads in the two values because the input operator ("`>>`") discards all white space that it encounters.

Declarations of cin and cout are contained within iostream.h. If the programmer should forget to include this file, each reference to either cin or cout will be flagged as a type error by the compiler. The storage of forward declarations is the primary use of header files. Section 4.4 (page 210) considers header files in detail.

A third predefined iostream, cerr (pronounced "see-err"), referred to as *standard error*, is also "tied" to the user's terminal. cerr is used to alert the user to some exceptional condition occurring in the program during execution. For example, the following code segment alerts the programmer to an attempt to divide by zero:

```
if ( v2 == 0 ) {
    cerr << "error: attempt to divide by zero";
    return;
}
v3 = v1/v2;
```

The following program reads a character at a time from standard input until *end-of-file* is encountered. It keeps a count of both the number of characters and the number of lines it reads. Its output is of the following form:

```
lineCount characterCount
```

Here is the implementation:

```
#include <iostream.h>

main() {
    char ch;
    int lineCnt=0, charCnt=0;

    while ( cin.get(ch) )
    {
        switch ( ch )
        {
          case '\t':
          case ' ':
                break;
          case '\n':
                ++lineCnt;
                break;
          default:
                ++charCnt;
                break;
        }
    }
    cout << lineCnt << " " << charCnt << endl;
    return 0;
}
```

get() is an iostream function which reads one character at a time, placing that character in its argument — in this case, ch. The two-character sequence \t represents the *tab* character.

The switch statement provides a form of conditional testing on a value. If the value matches an explicit case, the statements following that case are executed. If there is no match, the statements following `default` are exe-cuted. Each newline character that is read increments by 1 the value of `lineCnt`. `charCnt` is incremented by 1 each time a character is read that is not a tab, blank, or newline. The `while` statement, referred to as a *loop*, pro-vides for the repeated execution of a set of statements as long as some condi-tion holds true. In this case, the `switch` statement is executed for as long as `get()` reads in another character from standard input. (The `while` and `switch` statements are discussed in Chapter 2.)

Exercise 0-1. Enter the program in the file `prog2.<some-suffix>` and com-pile it into an executable file named `prog2`.

☐

Exercise 0-2. Run the program against the text of the previous exercise. Run it against the text of its own program source file. Run it against text consist-ing only of white space. Run it against text consisting only of end-of-file.

☐

Exercise 0-3. Modify the the program to keep a separate count of tabs (`tabCnt`) and blank lines (`blankCnt`). The output should look as follows:

```
            Total Characters: xx

    Lines:   x
    Chars:   x
    Tabs:    x
    Blanks: x
```

☐

0.4 A Word About Comments

Comments serve as an aid to the human readers of our programs; they are a form of engineering etiquette. They may summarize a function's algorithm, identify the purpose of a variable, or clarify an otherwise obscure segment of code. Comments do not increase the size of the executable program. They are stripped from the program by the compiler before code generation.

There are two comment delimiters in C++. The comment pair ("/* */") is the same comment delimiter used in the C language. The beginning of a comment is indicated by a "/*". The compiler will treat everything that falls between the "/*" and a matching "*/" as part of the comment. A comment pair can be placed anywhere a tab, space, or newline is permitted and can span multiple lines of a program. For example,

```
/*
 * This is a first look at a C++ class definition.
 * Classes are used both in data abstraction and
 * object-oriented programming.  An implementation
 * of the Screen class is presented in Chapter 5.
 */

class Screen {
/* This is referred to as the class body */
public:
     void home();         /* move cursor to 0,0 */
     void refresh();      /* redraw Screen       */
private:
/* Classes support ''information hiding''.    */
/* Information hiding restricts a program's   */
/* access to the internal representation of   */
/* a class (its data).  This is done through  */
/* use of the ''private:'' label              */
     char *cursor; /* current Screen position  */
};
```

Too many comments intermixed with the program code can obscure the code. Surrounded as it is by comments, for example, the declaration of cursor is very nearly hidden. In general, it is preferable to place a comment block above the text that it is explaining.

Comment pairs do not nest. That is, one comment pair cannot occur within a second pair. Try the following program, which will generate many compiler errors, on your system. How would you fix it?

```
#include <iostream.h>

/*
 * comment pairs /* */ do not nest.
 * "do not nest" is considered source code,
 * as are both these lines and the next.
 */

main() {
     cout << "hello, world\n";
}
```

The second comment delimiter, indicated by a double slash ("//"), serves to delimit a single line comment. Everything on the program line to the right of the delimiter is treated as a comment and ignored by the compiler. For example,

```
#include <iostream.h>
#include "my_io.h"
int isOdd(int);

main() {
    int v1, v2;          // hold values from user

    read2(v1, v2); // declared in my_io.h

    if (isOdd(v1) == 1)
        cout << v1
            << " is odd\n";

    if (isOdd(v2) == 1)
        cout << v2
            << " is odd\n";

    return 0;
}

isOdd(int val) {
/* return 1 if val is odd; otherwise, return 0
 * % is the modulus operator: 3 % 2 yields 1. */

    return(val % 2 != 0);
}
```

This program determines whether values are even or odd. It reuses the read2() function defined in the previous section; the read2() function prototype has been stored in a header file named my_io.h. When the program is compiled and executed, its output looks as follows (the values 497 and –25 are entered by the user):

```
Please enter two numeric values: 497 -25
497 is odd
-25 is odd
```

The two characters of either comment delimiter must not be separated by white space. The following two lines, for example, are *not* treated as comments, but, rather, as program text:

```
/ * not a comment: white space not allowed */
/ / also not a comment: must be //
```

Programs typically contain a mixture of both comment forms. Multiline explanations are generally set off between comment pairs. Half-line and single-line remarks are more often delineated by the double slash.

0.5 Preprocessor Directives

Provided with the standard libraries are a set of standard header files, such as `iostream.h`. These header files contain all the information a user requires in order to make use of these libraries. In order to access a variable or function defined within the standard libraries, we must include the associated header file into our program.

Header files are made a part of our program by the include *directive*. Directives are specified by placing a pound sign ("#") in the very first column of a line in our program. Directives are processed prior to the invocation of the language compiler. The program that handles directives is referred to as the *preprocessor*.

The `#include` directive reads in the contents of the named file. It takes one of two forms:

```
#include <iostream.h>
#include "my_io.h"
```

If the file name is enclosed by angle brackets ("<>") the file is presumed to be a predefined, or *standard*, header file. The search to find it will examine a predefined set of locations, which can be modified by specifying the −I option to the CC command.† For example,

```
$ CC -I incl -I/usr/local/include prog1.c
```

tells the preprocessor to look first in the directory `incl` and then in the directory `/usr/local/include` before looking in the predefined set of locations. The first located instance of the file terminates the search.

If the file name is enclosed by a pair of quotation marks, the file is presumed to be a user-supplied header file. The search to find it begins in the current directory. If it is not found, then the predefined set of locations is examined. The −I option also works with user-supplied header files.

The included file may itself contain a `#include` directive. Because of nested include files, a header file may sometimes be pulled in multiple times for a single source file. Conditional directives can be used to guard against the multiple processing of a header file. For example,

```
#ifndef STRING_H
#define STRING_H
/* String.h contents go here */
#endif
```

The conditional directive `#ifndef` evaluates as true if the name that follows

---

†Those using other implementations should refer to the reference guide for their C++ command to find the name of the analogous command option.

it is not yet defined. When a conditional directive evaluates as true, the subsequent lines until a #endif is encountered are included. If the conditional directive evaluates as false, the lines between it and the #endif directive are ignored.

The #define directive defines the name that follows it. In this case, it defines STRING_H. If the String.h header file is included again, the #ifndef directive will evaluate to false; the contents of String.h will not be included a second time.

The #ifdef directive evaluates as true if the name that follows it is defined. For example,

```
#ifdef u3b2
/* system specific code
 * for AT&T 3B computers goes here */
#endif

#ifdef sun3
/* system specific code
 * for Sun3/60 Workstations goes here */
#endif
```

C++ predefines the name __cplusplus (two underscores). A user who wishes to mix C and C++ program code might write the following:

```
#ifdef __cplusplus
extern min( int, int );
int *pi = new int;
#else
extern min();
int *pi;
#endif
```

The statements between the #else directive and the #endif directive will be included if the #ifdef or #ifndef directive evaluates to false.

The preprocessor is closely tied to the C language (and is often called *cpp*, the C preprocessor). Many implementations simply use the underlying C preprocessor and therefore do not recognize the C++ single-line comment delimiter. If you wish to include a comment on a #define directive line, it is safest to use the C comment pair notation:

```
#ifdef u3b2
#define SYSV     /* UNIX System V */
#endif
```

Chapter 1: **The C++ Data Types**

C++ provides a predefined set of data types, operators to manipulate those types, and a small set of statements for program flow control. These elements form an alphabet with which many large, complex real-world systems can be written. At this basic level, C++ is a simple language. Its expressive power arises from its support for mechanisms that allow the programmer to define new data abstractions.

The first step in mastering C++ — understanding the basic language — is the topic of this chapter and the next one. This chapter discusses the predefined data types and looks at the mechanisms for constructing new types, while Chapter 2 examines the predefined operators and statements.

The program text we write and program data we manipulate are stored as a sequence of bits in the memory of the computer. A *bit* is a single cell, holding a value of 0 or 1. In physical terms this value is an electrical charge which is either "off" or "on." A typical segment of computer memory might look as follows:

...00011011011100010110010000111011...

This collection of bits at this level is without structure. It is difficult to speak of this bit stream in any meaningful way.

Structure is imposed on the bit stream by considering the bits in aggregates referred to as *bytes* and *words*. Generally, a byte is composed of 8 bits. A word is typically composed of either 16 or 32 bits. Byte and word sizes vary from one computer to the next. We speak of these values as being *machine dependent*. Figure 1.1 illustrates our bit stream organized into four addressable byte rows.

The organization of memory allows us to refer to a particular collection of bits. Thus, it is possible to speak of the word at address 1024 or the byte at address 1040, allowing us to say, for example, that the byte at address 1032 is not equal to the byte at address 1048.

It is still not possible, however, to speak meaningfully of the content of the byte at address 1032. Why? Because we do not know how to interpret its bit sequence. To speak of the meaning of the byte at address 1032, we must know the type of the value being represented.

Type abstraction allows for a meaningful interpretation of fixed-length bit sequences at a particular address. Characters, integers, and floating point

1024	0	0	0	1	1	0	1	1
1032	0	1	1	1	0	0	0	1
1040	0	1	1	0	0	1	0	0
1048	0	0	1	1	1	0	1	1

Figure 1.1 Addressable Machine Memory

numbers are examples of data types. Other types include memory addresses and the machine instructions that drive the workings of the computer.

C++ provides a predefined set of data types, which allow the representation of integers and floating point numbers and of individual characters.

- The type char can be used to represent individual characters or small integers. A char is represented in a machine byte.

- The type int can be used to represent integer values. Typically, an int is represented in a machine word.

C++ also provides short and long integer types. The actual size of these types is machine dependent. char, short, int, and long are referred to collectively as the *integral types*. Integral types may be either signed or unsigned. The difference is in the interpretation of the type's left-most bit. In a signed type, the left-most bit serves as the *sign bit*, while the remaining bits represent the value. In an unsigned type, all the bits represent the value. If the sign bit is set to 1, the value is interpreted as negative; if 0, positive. An 8 bit signed char may represent the values -128 through 127; an unsigned char, 0 through 255.

The types float, double, and long double represent floating point single, double, and extended precision values. Typically, floats are represented in one word; doubles, in two words, and long double in either three or four words. The actual sizes are machine dependent. The choice of a data type is determined by the range of values that it is expected to hold. For example, if the values are guaranteed never to exceed 255 or to be negative, then an unsigned char provides sufficient representation. Were the values to also include -1, however, then the smallest sufficient data type would be that of a short.

1.1 Constant Values

When a value such as 1 occurs in a program, it is referred to as a *literal constant*: literal because we can speak of it only in terms of its value; constant because its value cannot be changed.

Every literal has an associated type. 0, for example, is of type int. 3.14159 is a literal constant of type double. We refer to a literal constant as *nonaddressable*; although its value is stored somewhere in the computer's memory, we have no means of accessing that address.

Literal integer constants can be written in decimal, octal, or hexadecimal notation. (This does not change the bit representation of the value.) The value 20, for example, can be written in any of the following three ways:

```
20     // decimal
024    // octal
0x14   // hexadecimal
```

Prepending a 0 (zero) to a literal integer constant will cause it to be interpreted as being octal notation. Prepending either 0x or 0X will cause a literal integer constant to be interpreted as being hexadecimal notation. (Appendix A discusses printing values in octal or hexadecimal notation.)

By default, literal integer constants are treated as signed values of type int. A literal integer constant can be specified as being of type long by following its value with either L or l (the letter "ell" in either uppercase or lowercase). Using the lowercase letter in general should be avoided since it is easily mistaken for the number 1. In a similar manner, a literal integer constant can be specified as being unsigned by following its value with either a U or u. An unsigned long literal constant can also be specified. For example,

```
128u     1024UL     1L     8Lu
```

A floating point literal constant can be written in either scientific or common decimal notation. Using scientific notation, the exponent can be written as either E or e. By default, literal floating point constants are treated as double precision values. A single precision literal constant is indicated by following the value with either an F or f. Similarly, extended precision is indicated by following the value with either an L or l (again, use of the lowercase instance is discouraged). For example:

```
3.14159F        0.1f        12.345L        0.0
3e1             1.0E-3      2.             1.0L
```

A printable literal character constant can be written by enclosing the character within single quotation marks. For example,

```
'a'           '2'            ','            ' '  (blank)
```

Selected nonprintable characters, the single and double quotation marks, and
the backslash can be represented by the following escape sequences:

```
newline             \n
horizontal tab      \t
vertical tab        \v
backspace           \b
carriage return     \r
formfeed            \f
alert (bell)        \a
backslash           \\
question mark       \?
single quote        \'
double quote        \"
```

A generalized escape sequence can also be used. It takes the form

```
\ooo
```

where ooo represents a sequence of up to three octal digits. The value of the
octal digits represents the numerical value of the character in the machine's
character set. The following examples are representations of literal constants
using the ASCII character set:

```
\7 (bell)          \12 (newline)
\0 (null)          \062 ('2')
```

A string literal constant is composed of zero or more characters enclosed in
double quotation marks. Nonprintable characters can be represented by their
escape sequence. A string literal can extend across multiple source program
lines. A backslash as the last character on a line indicates that the string literal is continued on the next line. The following are examples of string literal
constants:

```
"" (null string)
"a"
"\nCC\toptions\tfile:[cC]\n"
"a multi-line \
string literal signals its \
continuation with a backslash"
```

A string literal is of type *array of characters*. It consists of both the string literal and a terminating null character added by the compiler. For example,
while 'a' represents the single character a, "a" represents the single character a followed by the null character. The null character is used to signal the
end of the string.

1.2 Symbolic Variables

Imagine that we are given the problem of computing 2 to the power of 10. Our first attempt might look as follows:

```
#include <iostream.h>

main() {
    // a first solution
    cout << "2 raised to the power of 10: ";
    cout << 2 * 2 * 2 * 2 * 2 * 2 * 2 * 2 * 2 * 2;
    cout << endl;
    return 0;
}
```

This works, although we might double or triple check to make sure that exactly 10 literal instances of 2 are being multiplied. Otherwise we're satisfied. Our program correctly generates the answer 1024.

We're next asked to compute 2 raised to the power of 17 and then to the power of 23. Changing our program each time is a nuisance. Worse, it proves to be a remarkably error-prone process. All too often the modified program produces an answer with one too few or too many instances of 2.

Finally we are asked to produce a table listing the powers of 2 from 0 through 15. Using literal constants in a straight code sequence requires 32 lines of the following form:

```
cout << "2 raised to the power of X\t";
cout << 2 * ... * 2;
```

where X will increase by one with each code pair.

At this point, if not earlier, we realize that there must be a better way. And indeed there is. The solution involves two program capabilities that we have not yet formally introduced:

1. Symbolic — that is, named — variables, which allow for the storage and retrieval of values.

2. Flow of control statements, which allow for the repeated execution of a segment of code.

For example, here is a second method of computing 2 raised to the power of 10:

```
#include <iostream.h>

main()
{
    // a second more general solution

    int value = 2;
    int pow = 10;

    cout << value
         << " raised to the power of "
         << pow << ": \t";

    for (int i=1, res=1; i <= pow; ++i) {
        res = res * value;
    }

    cout << res << endl;
    return 0;
}
```

The statement beginning with for is referred to as a *loop*: as long as i is less than or equal to pow, the body of the for loop (enclosed by braces) is executed. The for loop is referred to as a *flow of control* statement. (Program statements are discussed in detail in Chapter 2.)

value, pow, res, and i are symbolic variables that allow for the storage, modification, and retrieval of values. They are the topic of the following subsections. First, however, let's apply another level of generalization to the program by factoring out the portion of the program that computes the exponential value and defining it as a separate function:

```
unsigned int
pow( int val, int exp )
{
    // general function for computing
    // val raised to exp power

    for ( unsigned int res = 1; exp > 0; --exp )
        res = res * val;

    return res;
}
```

Now, each program that requires computing an exponential value can use this instance of pow() rather than reimplementing it each time. Generating a table of the powers of 2 can be done as follows:

```
#include <iostream.h>

extern unsigned int pow(int,int);
main()
{
    int val = 2;
    int exp = 15;

    cout << "The Powers of 2\n";
    for (int i=0; i <= exp; ++i)
        cout << i << ": "
                << pow(val,i) << endl;
    return 0;
}
```

The output of this program is presented in Table 1.1.

The Powers of 2

0: 1
1: 2
2: 4
3: 8
4: 16
5: 32
6: 64
7: 128
8: 256
9: 512
10: 1024
11: 2048
12: 4096
13: 8192
14: 16384
15: 32768

Table 1.1 Powers of 2

This implementation of pow() does not handle a number of special conditions, including negative exponents and resulting values that are very large.

Exercise 1-1. What would happen if pow() were passed a negative second argument? How might pow() be modified to handle this?

☐

Exercise 1-2. Every data type has an upper and lower bound to the range of values it can hold. These bounds are determined by the size in bits of its type representation. How might this affect the implementation of pow()? For example, how would you modify pow() to handle a call such as pow(2,48)? □

What Is a Variable?

A symbolic variable is identified by a user-supplied name. Each variable is of a particular data type. For example, the following statement declares a variable ch of the data type char:

```
char ch;
```

char is a *type specifier*. short, int, long, float, and double also serve as type specifiers. In general, any declaration must begin with a type specifier. The data type determines the amount of storage allocated to the variable and the set of operations that can be performed on the variable. (For our purposes, a char will be a byte of size 8 bits.)

Both a symbolic variable and a literal constant maintain storage and have an associated type. The difference is that a symbolic variable is *addressable*. That is, there are two values associated with a symbolic variable:

1. Its data value, stored at some location in memory. This is sometimes referred to as a variable's *rvalue* (pronounced "are-value").

2. Its location value; that is, the address in memory at which its data value is stored. This is sometimes referred to as a variable's *lvalue* (pronounced "ell-value").

In the expression

```
ch = ch - '0';
```

the symbolic variable ch appears on both the right- and left-hand sides of the assignment operator. The right-hand instance is *read*. Its data value is fetched from its memory location. The character literal '0' is then subtracted from that value. The term rvalue is derived from the variable's position to the right of the assignment operator. An rvalue may be read but not altered. You might think of rvalue as meaning *read value*.

The left-hand instance is *written*. The result of the subtraction operation is stored at the location value of ch; its previous value is overwritten. The term lvalue is derived from the variable's position to the left of the assignment operator. You might think of lvalue as meaning *location value*.

ch is referred to as an *object*. An object represents a region of memory. ch represents a region of memory of size 1 byte.

The *definition* of a variable causes storage to be allocated. A definition introduces the variable's name and its type. Optionally, an initial value for the variable may also be introduced. There must be one and only one definition of a variable in a program.

The *declaration* of a variable announces that the variable exists and is defined somewhere else. It consists of the variable's name and its type preceded by the keyword extern. (For a full discussion, see Section 3.9 (page 133) on program scope.) A declaration is *not* a definition. A declaration does not result in an allocation of storage. Rather, it is an assertion that a definition of the variable exists elsewhere in the program. A variable can be declared multiple times in a program.

In C++, a variable must be defined or declared to the program before it is used.

The Name of a Variable

The name of a variable, its *identifier*, can be composed of letters, digits, and the underscore character. It must begin with either a letter or an underscore. Upper- and lowercase letters are distinct. There is no language-imposed limit on the permissible length of a name, which varies among implementations.

C++ reserves a set of words for use within the language as keywords. The predefined type specifiers, for example, are all reserved keywords. The keyword identifiers may not be reused as program identifiers. Table 1.2 lists the reserved keywords in C++.

There are a number of generally accepted conventions in naming identifiers, most concerning the human readability of programs:

- An identifier is normally written in lowercase letters. For example, one writes index, not Index or INDEX.

- An identifier is provided with a mnemonic name; that is, a name which gives some indication of its use in a program, such as the word index or salary.

- A multiword identifier either places an underscore between each word or capitalizes the first letter of each embedded word. For example, one writes is_empty or isEmpty, not isempty.

C++ Keywords				
asm	delete	if	return	try
auto	do	inline	short	typedef
break	double	int	signed	union
case	else	long	sizeof	unsigned
catch	enum	new	static	virtual
char	extern	operator	struct	void
class	float	private	switch	volatile
const	for	protected	template	while
continue	friend	public	this	
default	goto	register	throw	

Table 1.2 C++ Keywords

Variable Definitions

A simple definition consists of a type specifier followed by a name. The definition is terminated by a semicolon. Examples of simple definitions follow:

```
double salary;
double wage;
int month;
int day;
int year;
unsigned long distance;
```

When more than one identifier of a type is being defined, a comma-separated list of identifiers may follow the type specifier. The list may span multiple lines. It is terminated by a semicolon. For example, the preceding definitions can be rewritten as follows:

```
double salary, wage;
int month,
    day, year;
unsigned long distance;
```

A simple definition specifies the type and identifier of a variable. It does not provide a first value. A variable without a first value is spoken of as *uninitialized*. An uninitialized variable is not without a value; rather, its value is said to be *undefined*. This is because the memory storage allocated for the variable is not swept clean. Whatever was stored there by the previous use of the memory remains. When an uninitialized variable is read, its arbitrary bit pattern is interpreted as its value. This value may vary from one execution of a program to another.

For example, here is the output of a series of executions of a function that contains two uninitialized identifers, `value1` and `value2`. In each case, the associated values represent the arbitrary remains of the memory allocated for each identifier. Section 3.10 (page 143) contains the actual program that generates this output.

```
value1: 0          value2: 74924    sum:      74924
value1: 0          value2: 68748    sum:      68748
value1: 0          value2: 68756    sum:      68756
value1: 148620     value2: 2350     sum:      150970
value1: 2147479844         value2: 671088640
           sum:     -1476398812
value1: 0          value2: 68756    sum:      68756
```

A first value may be specified in the definition of a variable. A variable with a declared first value is spoken of as an *initialized* variable. C++ supports two forms of variable initialization, an explicit syntax using the assignment operator:

```
int ival = 1024;
```

and an implicit form in which the first value is placed within parentheses:

```
int ival( 1024 );
```

In both cases, `ival` is initialized with a first value of `1024`. Examples of initialized variables include the following:

```
#include <math.h>

double price = 109.99, discount = 0.16;
double sale_price ( price * discount );

int val = get_value();
unsigned abs_val = abs( val );
```

`abs()`, a predefined function stored in the math library, returns the absolute value of its argument. `get_value()` is a user-defined function that returns a random integer value. A variable may be initialized with an arbitrarily complex expression.

1.3 Pointer Types

A pointer variable holds values that are the addresses of objects in memory. Through a pointer, an object can be referenced indirectly. Typical uses of pointers are the creation of linked lists and the management of objects allocated during program execution.

Every pointer has an associated type. The data type specifies the type of data object the pointer will address. A pointer of type `int`, for example, will point to an object of type `int`. In order to point to an object of type `double`, a pointer of type `double` is defined.

The storage allocated a pointer is the size necessary to hold a memory address. This means that a pointer of type `int` and a pointer of type `double` are usually the same size. The pointer's associated type specifies how the contents and size of the memory it addresses should be interpreted. The following are examples of pointer variable definitions:

```
int *ip1, *ip2;
unsigned char *ucp;
double *dp;
```

A pointer definition is specified by prefixing the identifier with the dereference operator ("*"). In a comma-separated definition list, the dereference operator must precede each identifier intended to serve as a pointer. In the following example, `lp` is interpreted as a pointer to a `long` and `lp2` is interpreted as a data object of type `long` and not as a pointer type:

```
long *lp, lp2;
```

In this next example, `fp` is interpreted as a data object of type `float` and `fp2` is interpreted as a pointer to a `float`:

```
float fp, *fp2;
```

For clarity, it is preferable to write

```
char *cp;
```

rather than

```
char* cp;
```

Too often, a programmer, later wishing to define a second character pointer, will incorrectly modify this definition as follows:

```
char* cp, cp2;
```

A pointer may be initialized with the lvalue of a data object of the same type. Recall that an object appearing on the right-hand side of the assignment operator yields its rvalue. To obtain an object's lvalue, a special operator must be applied. This operator is referred to as the *address-of* operator; its symbol is the ampersand ("&"). For example,

```
int i = 1024;
int *ip = &i; // assign ip the address of i
```

A pointer may also be initialized with another pointer of the same type.

```
// ok: now ip2 also addresses i
int *ip2 = ip;
```

In this case, the application of the address-of operator would be wrong.

```
int *ip3 = &ip; // error
```

Applying the address-of operator to ip returns the address of a pointer to an integer. ip3, however, is a pointer to an integer variable, not a pointer to a pointer to an integer. The initialization is therefore flagged as an error during compilation. A correct declaration is the following:

```
int **ip3 = &ip; // ok
```

ip3 is now a pointer to a pointer to an integer.

It is always an error to initialize a pointer to a data object's rvalue. The following declaration will be flagged as illegal during compilation:

```
int i = 1024;
int *ip = i; // error
```

It is also an error to initialize a pointer to an lvalue of an object of a different type. The following definitions of uip and uip2 will be flagged as illegal during compilation:

```
int i = 1024, *ip = &i;  // ok
unsigned int *uip = &i,   // error
              *uip2 = ip; // error
```

C++ is a *strongly typed* language. All initializations and assignments of values are checked at compile time to be sure the types of these values are correctly matched. If they are not and if a rule exists for matching them, the compiler will apply that rule. This rule is referred to as a *type conversion*. (See Section 2.11 (page 86) for a discussion.) If there is no rule, the statement is flagged as an error. This is the desirable action since initialization or assignment without a conversion rule is unsafe and will likely result in a program error during execution.

The assignment of an object's rvalue to a pointer is unsafe because the pointer will assume the value is a memory address. An attempt to either read or write to that "address" is likely to be disastrous.

The danger in assigning to a pointer the lvalue of an object of a different type is more subtle. It goes back to the idea that a pointer's type specifies how the addressed memory should be interpreted.

For example, although an int pointer and a double pointer can each hold the same memory address, the size of the memory read and written through the two pointers will differ by the different sizes of an int and a double. Additionally, the organization and meaning of the bit sequences may differ between data types.

This is not to say that the programmer cannot convert a pointer of one type to a pointer to another type. Since this is potentially unsafe, however, the programmer must do it explicitly. Section 2.11 (page 89) discusses explicit type conversions, referred to as *casts*.

A pointer of any type may be assigned a value of 0, indicating that a pointer is not currently addressing a data object. A value of 0, when used as a pointer value, is sometimes referred to as *NULL*. There is also a special pointer type, `void*`, which may be assigned the address of an object of any data type. Section 2.11 (page 89) discusses the `void*` pointer type.

In order to access the object a pointer addresses, the dereference operator must be applied. For example,

```
int i = 1024;
int *ip = &i; // ip now points to i
int k = *ip;  // k now contains 1024
```

Were the dereference operator not applied, k would be initialized to the address of i and not to i's value, resulting in a compile time error:

```
int *ip = &i; // ip now points to i
int k = ip;   // error
```

In order to assign a value to the object a pointer addresses, the dereference operator must be applied to the pointer. For example,

```
int *ip = &i; // ip now points to i

*ip = k;             // i = k
*ip = abs( *ip ); // i = abs(i);
*ip = *ip + 1;       // i = i + 1;
```

The following two assignment statements have very different results, although both are legal. The first statement increases the value of the data object that ip addresses; the second increases the address that the pointer ip contains.

```
int i, j, k;
int *ip = &i;

*ip = *ip + 2; // add two to i (i = i + 2)
ip = ip + 2;   // add to the address ip contains
```

A pointer may have its address value added to or subtracted by an integral value. This sort of pointer manipulation, referred to as *pointer arithmetic*, may at first appear slightly nonintuitive until we realize that the addition is of data objects and not of discrete decimal values. That is, the addition of 2 to a pointer increases the value of the address it contains by the size of two objects of its type. For example, allowing that a char is 1 byte, an int is 4 bytes, and a double is 8, the addition of 2 to a pointer increases its address value by 2, 8, or 16 depending on whether the pointer is of type char, int, or double.

Exercise 1-3. Given the following definitions:

```
int ival = 1024;
int *iptr;
double *dptr;
```

which of the following assignments, if any, are illegal? Explain why.

```
(a) ival = *iptr;        (e) ival = iptr;
(b) *iptr = ival;        (f) iptr = ival;
(c) *iptr = &ival;       (g) iptr = &ival;
(d) dptr = iptr;         (h) dptr = *iptr;
```

☐

Exercise 1-4. A variable is assigned one of only three possible values: 0, 128, and 255. Discuss the advantages and disadvantages of declaring the variable to be of the following data types:

```
(a) double          (c) unsigned char
(b) int             (d) char
```

☐

String Pointers

The most frequently defined pointer to a predefined data type is char*. This is because all string manipulation in C++ is done through character pointers. This subsection considers the use of char* in detail. In Chapter 6, we will define a String class type.

The type of a literal string constant is a pointer to the first character of the string. This means that every string constant is of type char*. We may declare a variable of type char* and initialize it to a string, as follows:

```
char *st = "The expense of spirit\n";
```

The following program, which is intended to compute the length of st, uses pointer arithmetic to advance through the string. The idea is to terminate the loop statement when the null character the compiler places at the end of every literal string constant is encountered. Unfortunately, we have coded the program incorrectly. Can you see the error?

```
#include <iostream.h>
char *st = "The expense of spirit\n";

main() {
    int len = 0;
    while (st++ != '\0') ++len;

    cout << len << ": " << st;
    return 0;
}
```

This program fails because `st` is not dereferenced. That is,

```
st++ != '\0'
```

tests whether or not the address `st` contains is the null character, not whether the character that it addresses is null. The condition will always evaluate as true since each iteration of the loop adds one to the address in `st`. The program will execute forever, or until the system stops it. A loop such as this is referred to as an *infinite loop*.

Our second version of the program corrects this mistake. It runs to completion. Unfortunately, its output is in error. Can you see the mistake we've made this time?

```
#include <iostream.h>
char *st = "The expense of spirit\n";

main()
{
    int len = 0;
    while (*st++ != '\0') ++len;

    cout << len << ": " << st;
    return 0;
}
```

The mistake in this case is that `st` no longer addresses the string literal constant. It has been advanced one character beyond the terminating null character. (The output of the program depends on the contents of the addressed memory.) Here is one possible solution:

```
st -= len;
cout << len << ": " << st;
```

The program is compiled and executed. Its output, however, is still incorrect. It now generates the following:

```
22: he expense of spirit
```

This reflects something of the nature of programming. Can you see the mistake we've made this time?

The terminating null character of the string is not being taken into account. st must be repositioned the length of the string *plus one*. The following line is correct:

```
st -= len + 1;
```

When compiled and executed, the program correctly outputs the following:

```
22: The expense of spirit
```

The program is now correct. In terms of program style, however, it is still less than perfect. The statement

```
st -= len + 1;
```

has been added to correct the error introduced by directly incrementing st. The reassignment of st does not fit into the original logic of the program, however, and the program is now somewhat more difficult to understand.

In a program this small, of course, one obscure statement may not seem very serious. Consider, however, that this statement represents 20% of the executable statements in our program. Extrapolate that to a program of 10,000 lines and the problem is no longer trivial. A program correction like this is often referred to as a *patch* — something stretched over a hole in an existing program.

We patched our program by compensating for a logic error in the original design. A better solution is to correct the original design flaw. One solution is to define a second character pointer and initialize it with st. For example,

```
char *p = st;
```

p can now be used in our computation of the length of st, while st is left unchanged:

```
while ( *p++ != '\0' )
```

Let's look at another improvement to our program — one that permits our work to be used by others. As it is coded now, there is no way for another program to calculate the length of a string except by rewriting or copying our work. Either alternative is wasteful.

A more productive alternative is to factor out the code that calculates the length of a string. By placing that code in a separate function, it becomes available to any programmer on our system. Here is how we might define stringLength():

```
#include <stream.h>

void stringLength( char *st )
{ // calculate length of st
    int len = 0;
    char *p = st;

    while ( *p++ )
        ++len;

    cout << len << ": " << st ;
}
```

The definition

```
    char *p = st;
```

corrects the design flaw of the original program. The statement

```
    while ( *p++ )
```

is a shorthand notation for

```
    while ( *p++ != '\0' )
```

Now we can modify main() to take advantage of the stringLength()
function:

```
    extern void stringLength( char* );
    char *st = "The expense of spirit\n";

    main() {
        stringLength( st );
        return 0;
    }
```

stringLength() is stored in the file string.C. Compiling and executing
this program is done as follows:

```
    $ CC main.C string.C
    $ a.out
    22: The expense of spirit
    $
```

The design of stringLength() reflects the needs of our original program too closely. It is not general enough to serve most other programs. For
example, imagine that we are asked to write a function that determines
whether two strings are equal. We might design our algorithm as follows:

- Test whether the two pointers address the same string. If they do, the
  strings are equal.

- Otherwise, test whether the lengths of the two strings are the same. If they are not, the two strings are unequal.

- Otherwise, test whether the characters of the two strings are equal. If they are, the two strings are equal. Otherwise, the two strings are unequal.

`stringLength()`, as we have designed it, cannot be used with this new function. A more general design would have it simply return the length of the string. Any display of that string should be left to the program that calls `stringLength()`. Here is our new implementation:

```
int stringLength( char *st ) {
    int len = 0;
    while ( *st++ ) ++len;
    return len;
}
```

It may surprise the reader to see that this version of `stringLength()` again directly increments `st`. This does not present a problem in this new implementation for the following two reasons:

1. Unlike those earlier versions, this `stringLength()` implementation does not access `st` after `st` has been modified, and so the change to `st` does not matter.

2. Any changes made to the value of `st` within `stringLength()` disappear when `stringLength()` completes execution. `st` is said to be *passed-by-value* to the `stringLength()` function. This means, in effect, that `stringLength()` manipulates only a copy of `st`. Section 3.6 (page 125) discusses pass-by-value in detail.

`stringLength()` can now be called by any program wishing to calculate the length of a string. For the purposes of our program, the `main()` function must be reimplemented:

```
    ...
    main() {
        int len = stringLength( st );
        cout << len << ": " << st;
        return 0;
    }
```

`stringLength()` performs the same service that the `strlen()` library function performs. By including the standard header file `string.h`, the programmer can utilize a large number of useful string functions, including the following:

```
// copy src into dst
char *strcpy( char *dst, const char *src );

// compare two strings.  return 0 if equal.
int strcmp( const char *s1, const char *s2 );

// return the length of st
int strlen( const char *st );
```

For more details and a full list of the string library functions, refer to your
library reference manual.

Exercise 1-5. Explain the difference between 0, '0', '\0', and "0".

☐

Exercise 1-6. Given the following set of variable definitions,

```
int *ip1, ip2;
char ch, *cp;
```

which of the following assignments are type violations? Explain why.

```
(a) ip1 = "All happy families are alike";
(b) cp = 0;                    (f) cp = '\0';
(c) ip1 = 0;                   (g) ip1 = '\0';
(d) cp = &'a';                 (h) cp = &ch;
(e) ip1 = ip2;                 (i) *ip1 = ip2;
```

☐

1.4 Constant Types

There are two problems with the following `for` loop statement, both concerning the use of 512 as an upper bound.

```
for (int i = 0; i < 512; ++i );
```

The first problem is readability. What does it mean to test i against 512?
What is the loop doing — that is, that makes 512 matter? (In this example,
512 is referred to as a *magic number*, one whose significance is not evident
within the context of its use. It's as if the number had been plucked from thin
air.)

The second problem is maintainability. Imagine that the program is
10,000 lines. This `for` loop header appears in 4% of the code. The value 512
must now be doubled to 1024. The 400 occurrences of 512 must be found
and converted. Overlooking even one instance breaks the program.

The solution to both problems is the use of an identifier initialized to 512. By choosing a mnemonic name, perhaps bufSize, we make the program more readable. The test is now against the identifier rather than the literal constant:

```
i < bufSize
```

The 400 occurrences no longer need to be touched in the case where bufSize is changed. Rather, only the one line that initializes bufSize requires change. Not only is this significantly less work, but the likelihood of making an error is reduced significantly. The cost of the solution is one additional variable. The value 512 is now said to be *localized*.

```
int bufSize = 512; // input buffer size
// ...

for ( int i = 0; i < bufSize; ++i )
// ...
```

The problem with this solution is that bufSize is an lvalue. It is possible for bufSize to be accidentally changed from within the program. For example, here is a common error made by a programmer coming to C++ from a Pascal-derived language:

```
// accidentally changes the value of bufSize
if ( bufSize = 1 )
    // ...
```

In C++, "=" is the assignment operator and "==" is the equality operator. Pascal and languages derived from it use "=" as the equality operator. The programmer has accidentally changed bufSize's value to 1, which will result in a difficult-to-trace program error. (Often such an error is difficult to find because the programmer does not *see* the code as being wrong — the reason many compilers issue a warning for this type of assignment.)

The const type modifier provides a solution. It transforms a symbolic variable into a *symbolic constant*. For example,

```
const int bufSize = 512; // input buffer size
```

defines bufSize to be a symbolic constant initialized with the value 512. Any attempt to change that value from within the program will result in a compile-time error. A symbolic constant is referred to as a *read-only* variable.

Since a const variable may not be modified once it has been defined, it *must* be initialized. The definition of an uninitialized symbolic constant will result in a compile-time error. For example,

```
const double pi; // error: uninitialized const
```

It is also a compile-time error to assign the address of a symbolic constant to a pointer. Otherwise, the constant value could be changed indirectly through the pointer. For example,

```
const double minWage = 3.60;
double *p = &minWage; // error

*p += 1.40;
```

The programmer, however, may declare a pointer that addresses a constant. For example,

```
const double *pc;
```

pc is a pointer to a const object of type double. pc, itself, however, is not a constant. This means the following:

1. pc can be changed to address a different variable of type double at any time within the program.

2. The value of the object addressed by pc cannot be modified through pc.

For example,

```
pc = &minWage; // ok
double d;
pc = &d; // ok
d = 3.14159; // ok
*pc = 3.14159; // error
```

The address of a const variable can only be assigned to a pointer to a constant, such as pc. A pointer to a constant, however, can also be assigned the address of an ordinary variable, such as

```
pc = &d;
```

Although d is not a constant, the programmer is assured that its value cannot be modified through pc. Pointers to const objects are most often defined as the formal arguments of a function. Section 3.7 (page 128) examines this use of pointers to constants.

The programmer may also define a const pointer. For example,

```
int errNumb; // possible error status of program
int *const curErr = &errNumb; // constant pointer
```

curErr is a constant pointer to an object of type int. The programmer can modify the value of the object curErr addresses:

```
    if ( *curErr ) {
        errorHandler();
        *curErr = 0;
    }
```

but cannot modify the address that curErr contains:

```
    curErr = &myErrNumb; // error
```

A constant pointer to a const object may also be defined:

```
    const int pass = 1;
    const int *const true = &pass;
```

In this case, neither the value of the object addressed by true nor the address itself can be changed.

Note that the type of a literal character string such as *"hello, world\n"* is char*, not const char*. Were it the latter, an assignment such as the following would be illegal:

```
    // ok: "ok" is char*, not const char*
    char *str = "ok";
```

Exercise 1-7. Explain the meaning of the following five definitions. Identify any illegal definitions.

(a) `int i;`   (d) `int *const cpi;`
(b) `const int ic;`   (e) `const int *const cpic;`
(c) `const int *pic;`

☐

Exercise 1-8. Which of the following initializations are legal? Explain why.

(a) `int i = 'a';`
(b) `const int ic = i;`
(c) `const int *pic = &ic;`
(d) `int *const cpi = &ic;`
(e) `const int *const cpic = &ic;`

☐

Exercise 1-9. Based on the definitions in the previous exercise, which of the following assignments are legal? Explain why.

(a) `i = ic;`   (d) `pic = cpic;`
(b) `pic = &ic;`   (e) `cpic = &ic;`
(c) `cpi = pic;`   (f) `ic = *cpic;`

☐

1.5 Reference Types

A reference type is defined by following the type specifier with the address-of operator. A reference object, like a constant, must be initialized.

```
int val = 10;
int &refVal = val; // ok
int &refVal2;       // error: uninitialized
```

A reference type, sometimes referred to as an *alias*, serves as an alternative name for the object with which it has been initialized. All operations applied to the reference act on the object to which it refers. For example,

```
refVal += 2;
```

adds 2 to val, setting it to 12.

```
int ii = refVal;
```

assigns ii the value currently associated with val, while

```
int *pi = &refVal;
```

initializes pi with the address of val.

A reference can be thought of as a special kind of pointer — one to which object syntax may be applied. For example,

```
( *pi == refVal && pi == &refVal )
```

is always true if both pi and refVal address the same object. Unlike a pointer, however, a reference must be initialized and, once initialized, a reference cannot be made to alias another object. It is never necessary to explicitly declare a constant reference — for example,

```
int &const refVal = val; // unnecessary
```

since this is the implicit meaning of each reference definition.

A declaration list of two or more reference objects must precede each identifier with an address-of operator. For example,

```
int i;

// one reference, r1; one object, r2
int &r1 = i, r2 = i;

// one object, r1; one reference, r2
int r1, &r2 = i;

// two references, r1 and r2
int &r1 = i, &r2 = i;
```

A nonconstant reference can only be initialized with an lvalue of its exact type. Each of the three following initializations, for example, are illegal:

```
unsigned char uc;
double d1, d2;

int &ir = 1024; // error: not an lvalue
char &cr = uc;  // error: inexact types
double &dr = d1+d2; // error: not an lvalue
```

Only a reference to a constant object or pointer can be initialized either with an rvalue, such as 1024, or lvalue not of its exact type. Each of the above declarations can be redeclared as follows:

```
const int &ir = 1024; // ok
const char &cr = uc;   // ok
const double &dr = d1+d2; // ok
```

The primary use of a reference type is as an argument or return type of a function, especially when applied to user-defined class types. Section 3.7 (page 127) discusses how reference types are used in this manner.

1.6 Enumeration Types

An enumeration type declares a set of symbolic integral constants. The elements of an enumeration, referred to as *enumerators*, differ from their equivalent const declarations in that there is no addressable storage associated with each enumerator. Therefore, it is an error to apply the address-of operator to an enumerator.

An enumeration is declared with the enum keyword and a comma-separated list of enumerators enclosed in braces. By default, the first enumerator is assigned the value 0. Each subsequent enumerator is assigned a value one greater than the value of the enumerator that immediately precedes it. For example, the following enumeration associates false with 0 and true with 1.

```
enum { false, true }; // false == 0, true == 1
```

A value may also be explicitly assigned to an enumerator. This value need not be unique. As before, in the absence of an explicit assignment, the value assigned to an enumerator is one greater than its immediately preceding element. In the following example, false and fail are assigned the value 0, while pass and true are assigned the value 1:

```
enum { false, fail = 0, pass, true = 1 };
```

An enumeration may optionally be provided with a *tag name*. Each named enumeration defines a unique type and can be used as a type specifier for declaring identifiers. For example,

```
// declares two distinct Enumeration types
enum TestStatus { not_run=-1, fail, pass };
enum Boolean { false, true };

main()
{
    const testSize = 100;
    TestStatus testSuite[ testSize ];
    Boolean found = false;

    for ( int i = 0; i < testSize; ++i )
            testSuite[ i ] = not_run;

    return 0;
}
```

Each named enumeration defines a unique integral type. The associated set of enumerators are the only values that can legally be assigned to objects of an enumeration. For example,

```
main()
{
    TestStatus test = not_run;
    Boolean found = false;

    test = -1; // error: TestStatus = int
    test = 10; // error: TestStatus = int

    test = found; // error: TestStatus = Boolean
    test = false; // error: TestStatus = const Boolean

    int st = test; // ok: implicit conversion
    return 0;
}
```

By declaring test to be of the TestStatus enumeration type, the programmer enlists the compiler's help in making sure that test is only assigned one of its three valid enumerator values. In addition, the use of an enumeration tag name provides a helpful form of program documentation.

1.7 Array Types

An array is a collection of objects of a single data type. The individual objects are not named; rather, each one is accessed by its position in the array. This form of access is referred to as *indexing* or *subscripting*. For example,

```
int i;
```

declares a single integer object, while

```
int ia[ 10 ];
```

declares an array of 10 integer objects. Each object is referred to as an *element* of ia. Thus

```
i = ia[ 2 ];
```

assigns i the value stored in the element of ia indexed by 2. Similarly,

```
ia[ 7 ] = i;
```

assigns the element of ia indexed by 7 the value of i.

An array definition consists of a type specifier, an identifier, and a *dimension*. The dimension, which specifies the number of elements contained in the array, is enclosed in a bracket pair ("[]"). An array must be given a dimension size greater than or equal to one. The dimension value must be a constant expression; that is, it must be possible to compute the value of the dimension at compile time. This means that a variable may not be used to specify the dimension of an array. The following are examples of both legal and illegal array definitions:

```
extern int get_size();
const int buf_size = 512, max_files = 20;
int staff_size = 27;

char input_buffer[ buf_size ]; // ok
char *fileTable[ max_files - 3 ]; // ok

double salaries[ staff_size ]; // error
int test_scores[ get_size() ]; // error
```

Note that the elements of an array are numbered beginning with 0. For an array of 10 elements, the correct index values are 0 through 9, not 1 through 10. This is a common source of program error, often referred to as the *off by one* error. For example, the following for loop *steps through* the 10 elements of an array, initializing each to the value of its index:

```
main () {
     const array_size = 10;
     int ia[array_size];

     for (int ix = 0; ix < array_size; ++ix )
          ia[ ix ] = ix;
}
```

An array may be initialized explicitly by specifying a comma-separated list of values enclosed in braces. For example,

```
const array_size = 3;
int ia[ array_size ] = { 0, 1, 2 };
```

An explicitly initialized array need not specify a dimension value. The compiler will determine the array size by the number of elements listed:

```
// an array of dimension 3
int ia[] = { 0, 1, 2 };
```

If the dimension size is specified, the number of elements provided must not exceed that size. Otherwise, a compile-time error results. If the dimension size is greater than the number of listed elements, the array elements not explicitly initialized are set to 0.

```
// ia ==> { 0, 1, 2, 0, 0 }
const array_size = 5;
int ia[ array_size ] = { 0, 1, 2 };
```

A character array may be initialized with either a list of comma-separated character literals enclosed in braces or a string constant. Note, however, that the two forms are *not* equivalent. The string constant contains the additional terminating null character. For example,

```
char ca1[] = { 'C', '+', '+' };
char ca2[] = "C++";
```

ca1 is of dimension 3; ca2 is of dimension 4. The following declaration will be flagged as an error:

```
// error: "Daniel" is 7 elements
char ch3[6] = "Daniel";
```

An array may not be initialized with another array, nor may one array be assigned to another. Additionally, it is not permitted to declare an array of references.

```
const int array_size = 3;
int ix, jx, kx;
int &iar[] = { ix, jx, kx }; // error

int ia[] = { 0, 1, 2 }; // ok
int ia2[] = ia; // error

main() {
    int ia3[ array_size ]; // ok
    ia3 = ia; // error
    return 0;
}
```

To copy one array into another, each element must be copied in turn. For example,

```
const int array_size = 7;
int ia1[] = { 0, 1, 2, 3, 4, 5, 6 };

main() {
    int ia2[ array_size ];
    for (int ix = 0; ix < array_size; ++ix )
        ia2[ ix ] = ia1[ ix ];
    return 0;
}
```

Any expression that results in an integral value can be used to index into an array. For example,

```
int someVal, get_index();
ia2[ get_index() ] = someVal;
```

Users should be aware, however, that the language provides no compile- or run-time range checking of the index. Nothing stops a programmer from stepping across an array boundary except his or her attention to detail and a thorough testing of the code. It is not inconceivable for a program to compile and execute and still be wrong.

Exercise 1-10. Which of the following array definitions are illegal? Explain why.

```
int get_size();
int buf_size = 1024;

(a) int ia[ buf_size ];       (c) int ia[ 4 * 7 - 14 ];
(b) int ia[ get_size() ];     (d) int ia[ 2 * 7 - 14 ];
```

☐

Exercise 1-11. Why is the following initialization an error?

```
char st[ 11 ] = "fundamental";
```

☐

Exercise 1-12. There are two indexing errors in the following code fragment. Identify them.

```
main() {
    const int array_size = 10;
    int ia[ array_size ];

    for ( int ix = 1; ix <= array_size; ++ix )
        ia[ ix ] = ix;
    // ...
}
```

☐

Multidimensional Arrays

Multidimensional arrays can also be defined. Each dimension is specified with its own bracket pair. For example,

```
int ia[ 4 ][ 3 ];
```

defines a two-dimensional array. The first dimension is referred to as the *row* dimension; the second, the *column* dimension. That is, ia is a two-dimensional array of four rows of three elements each. A two-dimensional array is also referred to as a matrix.

Multidimensional arrays may also be initialized.

```
int ia[ 4 ][ 3 ] = {
    { 0, 1, 2 },
    { 3, 4, 5 },
    { 6, 7, 8 },
    { 9, 10, 11 }
};
```

The nested braces, which indicate the intended row, are optional. The following initialization is equivalent, although less clear.

```
int ia[4][3] = { 0,1,2,3,4,5,6,7,8,9,10,11 };
```

The following definition initializes the first element of each row. The remaining elements are initialized to 0.

```
int ia[ 4 ][ 3 ] = { {0}, {3}, {6}, {9} };
```

Were the nested braces left off, the results would be very different. The following definition

```
int ia[ 4 ][ 3 ] = { 0, 1, 2, 3 };
```

initializes the first three elements of the first row and the first element of the second. The remaining elements are initialized to 0.

Indexing into a multidimensional array requires a bracket pair for each dimension. For example, the following pair of nested `for` loops initializes a two dimensional array.

```
main()
{
    const rowSize = 4;
    const colSize = 3;
    int ia[ rowSize ][ colSize ];

    for ( int i = 0; i < rowSize; ++i )
        for ( int j = 0; j < colSize; ++j )
            ia[ i ][ j ] = i + j;
    return 0;
}
```

In the Pascal or Ada programming language, a multidimensional array is indexed by a comma-separated list of values enclosed in either a bracket pair or set of parentheses. Although the expression

```
ia[ 1, 2 ]
```

is a legal construct in both C++ and Pascal, its meaning is very different in the two languages.

- In Pascal, the expression indexes the second element of the first row. It evaluates to the integer value of that element.

- In C++, the expression indexes the *third* row of `ia` (the rows and columns, recall, are indexed beginning with 0). It evaluates to a pointer of type `int*` addressing the zeroth element of that row. Why?

In C++, the expression

```
ia[ 1, 2 ]
```

is treated as a comma expression yielding a single integer value — in this case,

```
ia[ 2 ]
```

Multi-dimensional indexing requires a separate bracket pair for each index the programmer wishes to access.

Relationship of Array and Pointer Types

The definition of an array consists of four distinct elements: the type specifier, the identifier, the index operator ("[]"), and, within the operator, the
dimension. For example,

```
char buf[ 8 ] = "abcdefg";
```

defines buf to be an array of 8 elements of type char. In this case, the array
has been initialized. The first seven elements are the characters a through g.
The eighth character is that of null.

Subscripting occurs by applying the index operator to the array identifier.

```
buf[ 0 ];
```

returns the value of the initial element contained in buf.

What, however, if the index operator is omitted? What is the value of the
array identifier itself?

```
buf;
```

The array identifier evaluates to the *address* in memory of the first element
contained in buf. An alternative method of returning the value of the initial
element contained in buf, therefore, is to write

```
*buf;
```

That is,

```
buf[ 0 ] == *buf == 'a';
```

The pointer and array notation are equivalent. To address the second element of the array, the programmer can write either of the following:

```
// equivalent modes of addressing the second element
*(buf + 1);
buf[ 1 ];
```

Both expressions yield the value 'b'. More generally, either of the following
notations can be used to traverse the array:

```
// equivalent modes of traversing the array
// represented by buf

for (int ix = 0; ix < 8; ++ix)
     if ( buf[ ix ] != *(buf + ix) )
          error( "something is very wrong" );
```

It is more convenient, of course, to use the array subscript notation when
addressing the elements of an array. The two methods, however, are equivalent.

Writing

```
buf;
```

is the equivalent of writing

```
&buf[ 0 ];
```

Both return the address of the initial element in the array. The address-of operator, when applied to a data object, returns a pointer of that object's type. In this case, the object is of type `char`. This means that `buf` must also return a value of type `char*`. The following initialization of the pointer pBuf, therefore, must be legal:

```
char *pBuf = buf; // ok
```

pBuf and buf now point to the initial element of the array. Therefore, it must be possible to apply the two methods of addressing array elements to pBuf. For example,

```
for (int ix = 0; ix < 8; ++ix)
    if ( pBuf[ ix ] != *(buf + ix) ||
       ( buf[ ix ] != *(pBuf + ix))
           error( "something is very wrong" );
```

The equivalence between a pointer and an array identifier has to do with the access, or addressing, of a contiguous block of memory. The methods by which the array identifier and pointer come to address that memory, however, are very different.

- An array definition causes a block of storage to be allocated sufficient to contain the specified number of elements. The size of `buf`, for example, on a machine where each character is represented as a single byte, is 8 bytes. The array identifier is initialized with the address of this storage, which cannot be changed within the program. In effect, the array identifier is the equivalent of a constant pointer. An attempt to increment `buf`, for example, is illegal and is flagged as a compile-time error. The following three forms of indexing within the array represented by `buf` are equivalent.

```
for (int ix = 0; ix < 8; ++ix ) {
    cout << *buf++;        // error: cannot change buf
    cout << *(buf+ix);     // ok
    cout << buf[ ix ];     // ok and preferred
}
```

- The definition of a pointer provides it with the storage sufficient to hold the value of a memory address. The size of pBuf, for example, on a Sun3/60 workstation, is 4 bytes. The programmer must first set a pointer to address some previously allocated object or chunk of storage before it may be safely used. This can be done either by assigning it the address of a previously defined identifier or by assigning it memory allocated during program execution through use of operator new. A pointer, unlike an array identifier, can have its address directly incremented. The following three forms of indexing within the array addressed by pBuf are equivalent.

```
pBuf = buf;
for (int ix = 0; ix < 8; ++ix ) {
        cout << *pBuf++;      // ok
        cout << *(pBuf+ix);   // ok
        cout << pBuf[ ix ];   // ok
}
```

Exercise 1-13. Although the following program compiles without either a warning or an error message, there is something seriously wrong. What is the problem? How might you fix it?

```
char buf[] = "fiddleferns";

main() {
    char *ptr = 0;
    for (int i=0; buf[i] != '\0'; ++i)
            ptr[i] = buf[i];
    return 0;
}
```

☐

1.8 Class Types

A user-defined data type in C++, referred to as a *class*, is an aggregate of named data elements, possibly of different types, and a set of operations designed to manipulate that data. Typically, a class is used to introduce a new data type into the program; a well-designed class can be used as easily as a predefined data type. Classes are discussed in detail in Chapters 5 through 9. Because they are the central concept in C++, this section introduces them through an extended example — the design of an integer array class.

Four of the more irritating aspects of a predefined array type are the following:

1. The size of an array must be a constant expression. The programmer, however, does not always know at compile time how large an array is

necessary. A more flexible array type would permit the programmer to specify (or modify) the array dimension during the execution of the program.

2. There is no range-checking of an array index. The following program fragment, for example, uses the wrong upper bounds constant for the array it is initializing. Although the program runs to completion, its results will likely prove incorrect because of its modification of memory outside the boundary of the array.

```
const int size = 25;
const int sz = 10;
int ia[ sz ];

main()
{
    // array boundary overflow error -- this
    // is not caught during program execution
    for ( int i = 1; i < size; ++i )
        ia[ i ] = i;

    void do_something( ia );
    return 0;
}
```

3. There is no way to know the size of the array from an examination of the array itself. It therefore becomes necessary to pass the size of an array to a function along with the array. Array arguments would be easier to use if an array knew its size.

4. It would be nice to be able to copy one array to another in a single statement. For example,

```
int ia[ sz ];

int ia2[ sz ] = ia; // error: not supported
ia = ia2; // error: not supported
```

In this section, a class is defined which supports these four additional characteristics of an array. Moreover, the syntax for using objects of the array class will be as simple as that for "ordinary" arrays. The design of an Array class type is presented in detail in Chapter 6. At this point, we will simply present the definition of the Array class and discuss its implementation. Here is what it looks like:

```
    const int ArraySize = 12; // default size

    class IntArray {
    public:
    // operations performed on arrays
        IntArray( int sz = ArraySize );
        IntArray( const int*, int );
        IntArray( const IntArray& );
        ~IntArray() { delete [] ia; }
        IntArray& operator=( const IntArray& );
        int& operator[]( int );
        int getSize() { return size; }
    protected:
        void init( const int*, int );

    //   internal data representation
        int size;
        int *ia;
    };
```

A class definition consists of two parts: the *class head*, composed of the keyword class and a tag name, and the *class body*, enclosed by braces and terminated with a semicolon.

A class tag name represents a new data type. It serves as a type specifier in the same way as do the built-in type specifiers. The following are examples of how variables of the IntArray class may be defined:

```
    const int sz = 10;
    int mySize = 1024;
    int ia[sz];
    IntArray myArray( mySize ), iA( sz );   // ok
    IntArray *pA = &myArray;                 // ok
    IntArray iA2;                            // ok
```

The class body contains the member definitions. The class members consist of both the operations that can be performed by the class, and the data necessary to represent the class abstraction. In our case, an integer array is represented by two data members:

1. size, which holds the number of elements represented by the array.

2. ia, which addresses the memory in which the elements are contained.

The protected and public keywords control access to the class members. Members that occur in a public section of the class body can be accessed from anywhere within the general program. Members that occur in a protected (or private) section can be accessed only by the member functions of the IntArray class. This access restriction is referred to as *information hiding*. Information hiding provides two primary benefits:

1. Should the data representation of the class change, only the class member functions, not user programs, need to be modified.

2. Should there be an error in the manipulation of a class data member, only the small set of class member functions, not an entire program, need to be examined.

Four member functions of IntArray — special initialization and dealloca-tion functions — use the class tag name as their name. Although defined by the class designer, they are invoked automatically by the compiler. The func-tion preceded by the tilde ("~"), the deallocation function, is referred to as a *destructor*. The other three are initialization functions; they are referred to as *constructors*. The constructor

```
IntArray( int sz = ArraySize );
```

is referred to as a *default constructor*. This means that it can be invoked with-out requiring the programmer to supply an argument. sz represents the array size requested by the user. If the user does not care to represent a size, by default the array is given ArraySize elements. A default value repre-sents a value that may not apply to any particular instance but is on average applicable to all. The following definition of iA2, for example, is initialized by the default constructor:

```
IntArray iA2;
```

Here is an implementation of this instance of IntArray ():

```
#include <assert.h>
IntArray::IntArray( int sz )
{
    /* allocate an integer array of 'size' elements
     * new returns a pointer to this array or 0
     * 0 indicates the program has exhausted its
     * available memory: a generally fatal error
     */
    size = sz;
    ia = new int[size];
    assert( ia != 0 );

    for ( int ix=0; ix < sz; ++ix )
        ia[ix] = 0;
}
```

The double colon ("::") operator is referred to as the scope operator. It tells the compiler that the IntArray function being defined is a member of the

IntArray class. A class member function can access its own class members directly. When we write

```
size = sz;
```

`size` refers to the data member of the class variable for which the member function has been invoked. In our example, `size` is the data member of `iA2`.

Operator `new` provides a method of *dynamic memory allocation*. The expression

```
new int[size];
```

is a request by the programmer for the allocation during execution of the program of an integer array of `size` elements. Operator `new` returns a pointer addressing the first element of the array. If it cannot allocate the amount of requested memory, it returns a value of 0. The potential failure of operator `new` is referred to as a *program exception*.

C++ has introduced an exception handling mechanism to provide for the uniform handling of program exceptions. Making use of this mechanism, we would write something like the following:

```
if (ia == 0)
    throw memExhaust;
```

where memExhaust is a predefined exception indicating the failure of operator `new`. There is no current implementation of the exception handling mechanism available, however. A reasonable alternative until then is the `assert()` macro facility. The statement

```
assert( ia != 0 );
```

asserts a truth condition of a correct program; that is, that `ia` is never set to 0 after a call of operator `new`. Should that assertion evaluate as false, the program immediately terminates with an error message. In order to make use of assertions, the `assert.h` system header file must be included in your program. A general discussion of the exception handling mechanism can be found in Appendix B.

A second constructor for the IntArray class initializes the new IntArray class object with a built-in integer array. It requires two arguments, the actual array, and a second argument indicating the size of the array.

```
int ia[10] = {0,1,2,3,4,5,6,7,8,9};
IntArray iA3(ia,10);
```

The implementation of this constructor is almost identical to that of the first constructor. Rather than duplicate this code, it can be factored out into a separate function that both constructors can share. Let's call the function `init()`.

```
#include <assert.h>

void IntArray::init(const int *array, int sz)
{
    ia = new int[size=sz];
    assert( ia != 0 );

    for (int ix = 0; ix < size; ++ix)
        ia[ix] = (array!=0) ? array[ix] : 0;
}
```

Both constructors can now share this code without unnecessary duplication. Here is the definition of our second constructor:

```
IntArray::IntArray(const int *array, int sz) {
    init( array, sz );
}
```

The default constructor is redefined as follows:

```
IntArray::IntArray(int sz) {
    init( 0, sz );
}
```

The peculiar expresssion

```
(array!=0) ? array[ix] : 0;
```

is referred to as the *arithmetic if* operator. It tests if the value of `array` is *not* equal to 0. A nonzero value indicates that an array has actually been passed to `init()`; its values can be used to initialize the new IntArray class object. If no array is provided, each element of the new array is initialized to 0.

The final instance of `IntArray()` handles initialization of one IntArray object with another. It is invoked automatically whenever a definition of the following form occurs:

```
IntArray iA4 = myArray;
```

Here is its implementation:

```
IntArray::IntArray( const IntArray &iA ) {
    init( iA.ia, iA.size );
}
```

In order to access the class members of a particular class variable, a member selector operator must be used:

1. The dot operator (".") is used whenever the programmer wishes to access either a data member or member function of a particular class object.

2. The arrow operator ("–>") is used whenever the programmer wishes to access a member of a particular class object through a class pointer.

For example,

```
iA.size;
```

is read as meaning the following: *Select the* `size` *data member of the class object* `iA`.

The assignment of one array object with another is handled by

```
IntArray& operator=( const IntArray& );
```

The odd-looking function name is part of the mechanism that allows a class to overload the C++ operators to have meaning when applied to class objects. Section 6.3 (page 302) discusses class operator overloading in detail. Here is an implementation of this function. Notice that it resizes the target array to be the same size as the array to be copied.

```
IntArray& IntArray::operator=( const IntArray &iA )
{
    // test for assignment to itself: iA = iA
    if (this == &iA) return *this;

    delete [] ia; // free up existing memory
    init( iA.ia, iA.size );
    return *this;
}
```

The overloaded assignment operator will be invoked automatically whenever one IntArray object is assigned to another. For example,

```
ia2 = myArray;
```

The identifier `this` is a pointer through which the programmer can access the class object invoking the member function. For example, in the assignment of `ia2`, above, the `this` pointer addresses `ia2`. Section 5.4 (page 235) discusses the rationale and use of the `this` pointer.

The array class will not be of much practical interest unless users can easily index into a class object. The following loop construct must be supported:

```
int upperBound = myArray.getSize();
for ( int ix = 0; ix < upperBound; ++ix )
    myArray[ ix ] = myArray[ ix ] + ix;
```

`getSize()` provides read access to the nonpublic IntArray class member `size`. This is necessary since an attempt by the program to directly access `size` violates information hiding. The expression `myArray.size` in the following code fragment

```
main() {
    IntArray myArray;
    int upperBound = myArray.size;
    // ...
}
```

generates the following error message from the compiler:

```
error:  main() cannot access
        IntArray::size: protected  member
```

In order that information hiding not be prohibitively expensive to the run-time efficiency of a program, C++ provides a mechanism for the "in line" expansion of a function. By defining getSize() within the class definition of IntArray, it is automatically treated as an *inline* function. Each call of getSize() is replaced by the expansion of its body "in line." Section 3.2 (page 115) discusses inline functions in detail.

Indexing into an IntArray class object is supported by an overloaded subscript class operator. The subscript operator function must support *both* read and write capabilities. The read portion is simple: accept an index value and return the appropriate element. This provides for a statement of the following form:

```
int ix = myArray[ someValue ];
```

The subscript operator must also provide for a statement of the form:

```
myArray[ ix ] = someValue;
```

In order for myArray[ix] to appear on the left-hand side of the assignment operator, it must evaluate to an lvalue. This is done by specifying its return value as a reference type. A reference, recall, serves as an alias for another variable — Section 3.7 (page 130) discusses a reference return value. Here is an implementation of the subscript operator. For efficiency, it is declared to be an inline function.

```
inline int&
IntArray::operator[](int index) {
    return ia[ index ];
}
```

Typically, the class definition and any associated constant values or typedef names are stored in a header file. The header file is named with the class tag name. In this case, the header file is called IntArray.h. All programs wishing to use the IntArray class will include this header file. Similarly, the member functions of a class are typically stored in a program text file named with the class tag name. In this case, the member functions will be placed in the file IntArray.C. To use these functions, a program must link them into its executable. Rather than require that these functions be recompiled with each program wishing to utilize the IntArray class, we can precompile the functions and store them in a library. This is done as follows:

```
$ CC -c IntArray.C
$ ar cr IntArray.a IntArray.o
```

ar is a command to create an *ar*chive library provided on the UNIX system. The characters cr that follow it represent two command line options. IntArray.o, an object file, contains the machine language representation of the C++ program code. It is generated when the compiler is given the command-line option -c. IntArray.a is the name we wish given to the IntArray class library we are about to create. To use this library, the programmer can place its name explicitly on the command line when compiling a program:

```
$ CC main.c IntArray.a
```

This will cause the IntArray member functions to be included in the executable version of the program.

Exercise 1-14. The IntArray class illustrated here provides a minimum number of operations. List some additional functionality that you believe an array class should provide for its users.

☐

Exercise 1-15. One useful capability would be the ability to assign an IntArray object with a built-in integer array. Unfortunately, use of an assignment operator such as

```
IntArray::operator=( const int *ia, int size );
```

does not work in supporting the following:

```
IntArray myIA( 2 );
int ia[ 4 ] = { 0, 1, 2, 3 };

myIA = ia; // error: does not work
```

Describe what the problem is. ☐

    IntArray represents one important use of the C++ class mechanism. IntArray is referred to as an *abstract data type*. Programmers can use the IntArray class in much the same way that they can use the predefined C++ data types. This aspect of classes is considered in detail in Chapters 5 and 6.

Inheritance and Subtyping

A second important use of the class mechanism is to define subtype relationships. For example, IntArrayRC is a type of integer array class that also provides range checking of its subscript values. It is implemented through a mechanism referred to as *inheritance*. Here is the definition of IntArrayRC:

```
#include "IntArray.h"

class IntArrayRC : public IntArray {
public:
    IntArrayRC( int = ArraySize );
    IntArrayRC( const int*, int );
    int& operator[]( int );
};
```

IntArrayRC needs to define only those aspects of its implementation that are different or in addition to the implementation of IntArray:

1. It must provide its own instance of the subscript operator, one that provides range checking.

2. It must provide an operation to do the actual range checking.

3. It must provide its own set of automatic initialization functions — that is, its own set of constructors.

The data members and member functions of IntArray are all available to IntArrayRC as if IntArrayRC had explicitly defined them itself. This is the meaning of

```
class IntArrayRC : public IntArray
```

The colon (":") defines IntArrayRC to be *derived* from IntArray. A derived class inherits (that is, shares) the members of the class it is derived from. IntArrayRC can be thought of as extending the IntArray class by providing the additional feature of subscript range checking. The subscript operator is implemented as follows:

```
#include <assert.h>

int&
IntArrayRC::operator[]( int index ) {
    assert( index >= 0 && index < size );
    return ia[ index ];
}
```

Constructors are not inherited since they serve as class-specific initialization functions. IntArrayRC defines the following two constructors:

```
IntArrayRC::IntArrayRC(int sz)
    : IntArray( sz ) {}

IntArrayRC::IntArrayRC(const int *iar, int sz)
    : IntArray( iar, sz ) {}
```

The portion of the constructor marked off by the colon is referred to as a *member initialization list*. It provides the mechanism by which the IntArray constructor is passed its argument. The body of the IntArrayRC constructors are null since their job is only to pass their arguments to the associated IntArray constructor. Here is an example of using an IntArrayRC object:

```
#include "IntArrayRC.h"

main()
{
    IntArrayRC ia;

    // subscript error: 1 .. size
    for ( int ix = 1; ix <= ia.getSize(); ++ix )
        ia[ ix ] = ix;
    return 0;
}
```

This program incorrectly indexes ia from 1 to size rather than from 0 to size−1. When compiled and executed, the program results in the following output (slightly prettified):

```
Assertion failed:  index >= 0 && index < size
```

As this program example illustrates, range checking can provide an important safeguard in the use of an array type. Range checking, however, also incurs run-time overhead. An application might wish to combine IntArray and IntArrayRC class types in different portions of its code. Class inheritance supports this in two ways:

1. The class derived from, referred to as a *base class*, can be assigned objects of a derived class. For example,

```
#include "IntArray.h"

void swap( IntArray &ia, int i, int j )
{
    int tmp = ia[ i ];
    ia[ i ] = ia[ j ];
    ia[ j ] = tmp;
}
```

swap() can be passed arguments of an IntArray class or arguments of any class derived from IntArray, such as IntArrayRC. For example, given the following two class objects:

```
IntArray ia1;
IntArrayRC ia2;
```

the following two calls of swap() are legal:

```
swap( ia1, 4, 7 );
swap( ia2, 4, 7 );
```

This ability of assigning derived class objects to objects of a base class allows inherited classes to be used interchangeably.

There is one problem, however. The subscript operator is implemented differently in the two integer array classes. When we call

```
swap( ia1, 4, 7 );
```

the IntArray subscript operator must be used. When, however, we call

```
swap( ia2, 4, 7 );
```

the IntArrayRC subscript operator must be used. The subscript operator to be used by swap() must change with each call, depending on the actual class type of its argument. This is resolved automatically by the language compiler in C++ through a mechanism referred to as *class virtual functions*.

2. Virtual class member functions are inherited members, such as the subscript operator, whose implementation is dependent on its class type.

To make the subscript operator virtual, we must modify its declaration in the IntArray class body:

```
class IntArray {
public:
    virtual int& operator[]( int );
    ...
};
```

Each invocation of swap() now calls the appropriate subscript operator as determined by the actual class type with which swap() is called. There is a trade-off involved in a virtual function call: Because the function is resolved at run time, it is not inline expanded. Here is an example:

```
#include <iostream.h>
#include "IntArray.h"
#include "IntArrayRC.h"

void swap(IntArray&,int,int);

main() {
    IntArray ia1;
    IntArrayRC ia2;

    // error: should be size-1
    cout << "swap() with IntArray ia1\n";
    swap( ia1, 1, ia1.getSize() );

    cout << "swap() with IntArrayRC ia2\n";
    swap( ia2, 1, ia2.getSize() );

    return 0;
}
```

When compiled and executed, the program generates the following results:

```
swap() with IntArray ia1
swap() with IntArrayRC ia2
Assertion failed:  index >= 0 && index < size
```

Exercise 1-16. List another possible specialized instance of an IntArray class. What additional operations or data does it require? Is it necessary to replace any of the IntArray operations? Which ones? □

Templates

The IntArray class provides a useful alternative to the predefined integer array type. But what about users wishing to use an Array class of type double or short? What differs between the implementation of an Array class of type double and the IntArray class is simply the type of the elements it needs to contain; the code itself remains invariant. Templates provide a mechanism for indicating those types that need to change with each class instance. This is done by *parameterizing* the types within a template class definition. These parameters serve as place-holders in otherwise invariant code; later, they are bound to actual types such as int, double, or short. Here is a simplified parameterized version of the Array class (a full template implementation of an Array class is presented in Chapter 7):

```
#ifndef ARRAY_H
#define ARRAY_H

const int ArraySize = 12;

template <class Type>
class Array {
public:
    Array(int sz=ArraySize)
        { size=sz; ia=new Type[ size ]; }
    virtual ~Array() { delete [] ia; }

    int getSize() { return size; }
    virtual Type&
        operator[](int index) { return ia[index]; }
protected:
    int size;
    Type *ia;
};

#endif
```

The parameterized type, in our example called Type, is placed within both the class template and the member functions of the class wherever the type specifier will need to vary with each individual instantiation of the class. This occurs three times in our example:

```
ia = new Type[size];
Type& operator[](int index);
Type *ia;
```

With each instantiation of the Array class — to either int, double, short, etc. — the actual type of the instantiation is substituted for the generic Type. Here is an example of how the Array class template might be used:

```
#include <iostream.h>
#include "Array.h"

main()
{
    // instantiate particular template instances
    Array<int> ia(4);       // integer instance
    Array<double> da(4);    // double instance
    Array<char> ca(4);      // char instance
```

```
        int ix;
        for ( ix = 0; ix < ia.getSize(); ++ix ) {
            ia[ix] = ix;
            da[ix] = ix * 1.75;
            ca[ix] = ia[ix] + 97;
        }

        for ( ix = 0; ix < ia.getSize(); ++ix )
            cout << "[ " << ix << " ]    ia: "  << ia[ix]
                    << " ca: "  << ca[ix]
                    << " da: "  << da[ix] << endl;

        return 0;
    }
```

In this example, there are three individual instances of the Array class template: int, double, and char. These are declared by following the class template name by a list of the actual types enclosed in angle brackets (<actual-type, ...>). The instantiated classes behave exactly the same as non-template classes. When compiled and executed, this program produces the following output:

```
    [ 0 ]   ia: 0     ca: a    da: 0
    [ 1 ]   ia: 1     ca: b    da: 1.75
    [ 2 ]   ia: 2     ca: c    da: 3.5
    [ 3 ]   ia: 3     ca: d    da: 5.25
```

What about the specialized range-checking array subtype? A template class can serve as both a base and a derived class. Here is the definition of a template range-checking array class:

```
    #ifndef ARRAYRC_H
    #define ARRAYRC_H
    #include <assert.h>
    #include "Array.h"

    template <class Type>
    class ArrayRC : public Array<Type> {
    public:
        ArrayRC(int sz = ArraySize) : Array<Type>( sz ){};
        Type& operator[](int index) {
            assert( index >= 0 && index < size );
            return ia[ index ];
        }
    };

    #endif
```

Each instantiation of the ArrayRC class generates the associated Array class instance. For example, the declaration

```
ArrayRC<int> ia_rc(10);
```

causes an integer instance of both an Array class and an ArrayRC class to be generated. ia_rc behaves exactly the same as the previous nontemplate instance of the range-checking Array subtype. To illustrate this, let's rewrite the earlier program to exercise the Array and ArrayRC template class types. First, in order to support the statement

```
// swap() now must also be a template
swap( ia1, 1, ia1.getSize() );
```

we must define swap() to be a template function:

```
#include "Array.h"

template <class Type>
void swap( Array<Type> &array, int i, int j )
{
       Type tmp = array[ i ];
       array[ i ] = array[ j ];
       array[ j ] = tmp;
}
```

Each call of swap() will now generate the appropriate instance depending on the type of ia1. Here is the rewritten instance of main() using the template Array and ArrayRC classes:

```
#include <iostream.h>

#include "Array.h"
#include "ArrayRC.h"

template <class Type>
void swap( Array<Type> &array, int i, int j )
{
       Type tmp = array[ i ];
       array[ i ] = array[ j ];
       array[ j ] = tmp;
}
```

```
main() {
    Array<int> ia1;
    ArrayRC<int> ia2;

    cout << "swap() with IntArray<int> ia1\n";
    int size = ia1.getSize();
    swap( ia1, 1, size );

    cout << "swap() with IntArrayRC<int> ia2\n";
    size = ia2.getSize();
    swap( ia2, 1, size );

    return 0;
}
```

The results of this program are the same as for the nontemplate IntArray class implementation.

Inheritance and virtual functions are the two primary components of *object-oriented programming*. They are considered at length in Chapters 8 and 9. Template functions are examined in detail in Chapter 4. Template classes are looked at in Chapters 7 and 9.

1.9 Typedef Names

Arrays, references, and pointers are sometimes spoken of as *derived types*. They are constructed from other types by applying the subscript, address-of, or dereference operators to the definition of a particular variable; these operators can be thought of as type constructors. The derived type may then be further derived, such as in the declaration of a reference to a pointer

```
void foo( int *&p_ref );
```

or in the definition of an array of pointers

```
char *winter[ 3 ];
char *spring[] = { "March", "April", "May" };
```

winter and spring are arrays. Each contains three elements of type char*. spring is initialized. The statement

```
char *cruellestMonth = spring[ 1 ];
```

initializes cruellestMonth to "April", the character string addressed by the second element of spring.

The following two output statements are equivalent:

```
main() {
  cout << "Lilacs breed in " << spring[ 1 ];
  cout << "Lilacs breed in "
       << cruellestMonth;
}
```

The `typedef` mechanism provides a general facility for introducing mnemonic synonyms for existing predefined, derived, and user-defined data types. For example,

```
template <class Type> class Array;

typedef double wages;
typedef Array<int> IntArray;
typedef IntArray testScores;
typedef unsigned int bit_vector;
typedef char *string;
typedef string monthTable[3];
```

These typedef names can serve as type specifiers within the program:

```
const classSize = 93;

string myName = "stan";
wages hourly, weekly;
testScores finalExam( classSize );
monthTable summer, fall = {
            "September", "October", "November"
};
```

A typedef definition begins with the keyword `typedef`, followed by the data type and identifier. The identifier, or typedef name, does not introduce a new type, but rather a synonym for the existing data type. A typedef name may appear anywhere in a program that a type name may appear.

A typedef name can serve as a program documentation aid. It can also reduce the notational complexity of a declaration. Typedef names, for example, are typically used to improve the readability of definitions of pointers to functions and pointers to class member functions. (These pointer types are discussed in Chapters 4 and 5.)

A typedef name can also be used to encapsulate machine-dependent aspects of a program. On some machines, for example, an `int` may be large enough to contain a set of values; on others, a `long` may be required. By replacing the explicit type with a typedef, only one statement will require change when the program is *ported* from one machine to another.

Here is a question almost everyone answers incorrectly once. The mistake is in conceptualizing the typedef as a textual macro expansion. Given the following typedef

```
typedef char *string;
```

what is the type of cstring in the following declaration?

```
extern const string cstring;
```

The first answer is almost always

```
const char *cstring
```

That is, a pointer to a constant character. But that is incorrect. string is a pointer to a character. Therefore, a const string must be a *constant* pointer to a character; that is,

```
char *const cstring;
```

1.10 Volatile Objects

An object is declared volatile when its value can possibly be changed in ways outside either the control or detection of the compiler. Certain optimizations ordinarily performed by a compiler should therefore not be applied to objects the programmer specifies as volatile.

The volatile specifier is used in much the same way as is the const specifier — as an additional modifier to a type. For example,

```
volatile display_register;
volatile Task *curr_task;
volatile int ixa[ max_size ];
volatile Screen bitmap_buf;
```

display_register is a volatile object of type int. If an additional type specifier is absent, the default "base" type of the object is int. curr_task is a pointer to a volatile task class object. ixa is a volatile array of integers. Each element of the array is considered to be volatile. bitmap_buf is a volatile Screen class object. Each of its data members are considered to be volatile.

The essential purpose of the volatile modifier is to notify the compiler that the object can change in ways undetectable by the compiler. The compiler, therefore, should not aggressively optimize code containing the object.

Chapter 2: **Expressions and Statements**

Data types were the focus of Chapter 1. We looked at the predefined data types, methods of defining new data types, and how to define data objects. In this chapter we look at the predefined operations that can be used to manipulate that data. These operations consist of a predefined set of operators and a set of statements with which to organize these operators and to direct the flow of program execution. In Chapter 3 the focus will be the function, a mechanism through which the user can define his or her own set of operations.

2.1 What Is an Expression?

An expression is composed of one or more *operations*. The objects of the operation(s) are referred to as *operands*. The operations are represented by *operators*. For example, in C++ the test for equality is represented by the operator "==".

Operators that act on one operand are referred to as *unary* operators, while operators that act on two operands are referred to as *binary* operators. The operands of a binary operator are distinguished as the *left* or *right* operand. Some operators represent both a unary and binary operation. For example,

```
*ptr
```

represents the unary dereference operator. It returns the value stored in the object `ptr` addresses. However,

```
var1 * var2
```

represents the binary multiplication operator. It computes the product of its two operands, `var1` and `var2`.

The evaluation of an expression performs one or more operations, yielding a result. Except when noted otherwise, the result of an expression is an rvalue. The data type of the result of an expression is in general determined by the data type of the operand(s). When more than one data type is present, type conversions take place following a predefined set of rules. Section 2.11 (page 86) considers type conversions in some detail.

When two or more operators are combined, the expression is referred to as a *compound expression*. The order of operator evaluation is determined by the *precedence* and *associativity* of the operators. (This will be explained after we look at the predefined set of operators.)

The simplest form of an expression consists of a single literal constant or variable. This "operand" is without an operator. The result is the operand's rvalue. For example, here are three simple expressions:

```
3.14159
"melancholia"
upperBound
```

The result of 3.14159 is 3.14159. Its type is double. The result of melancholia is the address in memory of the first element of the string. Its type is char*. The result of upperBound is its rvalue. Its type is determined by its definition.

The following sections discuss the predefined C++ operators, presented in their presumed order of familiarity.

2.2 Arithmetic Operators

Operator	Function	Use
*	multiplication	expr * expr
/	division	expr / expr
%	modulus (remainder)	expr % expr
+	addition	expr + expr
–	subtraction	expr – expr

Table 2.1 Arithmetic Operators

Division between integers results in an integer. If the quotient contains a fractional part, it is truncated. For example,

```
21 / 6;
21 / 7;
```

both result in a value of 3.

The modulus operator ("%") computes the remainder of division between two values. It can be applied only to operands of the integral types. The left operand of the modulus operator is the dividend. The divisor is the operator's right operand. Both operands must be of an integral data type. The following are examples of both legal and illegal expressions using the modulus operator:

```
3.14 % 3 // error: floating point operand
21 % 6   // ok: result is 3
21 % 7   // ok: result is 0

int i;
double f;

i % 2    // ok: non-zero result indicates i is odd
i % f    // error: floating point operand
```

In certain instances, the evaluation of an arithmetic expression will result in an incorrect or undefined value. These occurrences are referred to as *arithmetic exceptions*. An exception may be due to the nature of mathematics — such as division by zero — or due to the nature of computers — such as *overflow*. For example, an unsigned char of 8 bits can hold the range of values 0 through 255. The following multiplication assigns an unsigned char the value 256.

```
unsigned char uc = 32;
int i = 8;
uc = i * uc; // overflow
```

To represent 256, 9 bits are required. The assignment of 256 to uc, therefore, results in an overflow of the memory allocated for its data type. The actual value uc contains is undefined and will vary across different machines.

2.3 Equality, Relational, and Logical Operators

The equality, relational, and logical operators evaluate to either true or false. A truth condition yields 1; a false condition yields 0.

The logical AND ("&&") operator evaluates to true only if both its operands evaluate to true. The logical OR ("||") operator evaluates to true if either of its operands evaluate to true. The operands are guaranteed to be evaluated from left to right. Evaluation stops as soon as the truth or falsity of the expression is determined. Given the forms

```
expr1 && expr2
expr1 || expr2
```

expr2 is guaranteed not to be evaluated if either of the following is true:

- In a logical AND expression, expr1 evaluates to false, or

- In a logical OR expression, expr1 evaluates to true.

A valuable use of the logical AND operator is to have expr1 evaluate to

oper	function	use
!	logical NOT	!expr
<	less than	expr < expr
<=	less than or equal	expr <= expr
>	greater than	expr > expr
>=	greater than or equal	expr >= expr
==	equality	expr == expr
!=	inequality	expr != expr
&&	logical AND	expr && expr
||	logical OR	expr || expr

Table 2.2 Equality, Relational, and Logical Operators

false in the presence of some boundary condition that would make the evaluation of expr2 dangerous. For example,

```
while ( ptr != 0 &&
        ptr->value < upperBound &&
        notFound( ia[ ptr->value ] ))
```

A pointer with a value of 0 is not addressing an object. Applying the member selection operator to a 0–valued pointer is always trouble. The first logical AND operand prevents that possibility. Equally troublesome is an out-of-bounds array index. The second operand guards against that possibility. The third operand is safe to evaluate only when the first two operands return true.

The logical NOT operator ("!") evaluates to true if its operand has a value of zero; otherwise, it evaluates to false. For example,

```
int found = 0;
while ( !found ) {
    found = lookup( *ptr++ );
    if ( ptr == endPtr ) // at end
        return 0;
}
return ptr;
```

The expression

```
( !found )
```

returns true as long as found is equal to 0.

Use of the logical NOT is in part a question of style. For example,

```
( !found )
```

is clear in its meaning: *not found*. Is it as clear, however, what the following condition tests?

```
!strcmp( string1, string2 )
```

`strcmp()` is a C library routine that compares its two string arguments for equality. A return value of 0 indicates that the two strings are equal. Use of the logical NOT notation in this case may actually obscure the condition under test. This is better written as

```
if ( strcmp( string1, string2 ) == 0 ) // ...
```

2.4 Assignment Operators

The left operand of the assignment operator ("=") must be an lvalue. The effect of an assignment is to store a new value in the left operand's associated storage. For example, given the following three definitions:

```
int i;
int *ip;
int ia[ 4 ];
```

the following are all legal assignments:

```
ip = &i;
i = ia[ 0 ] + 1;
ia[ *ip ] = 1024;
*ip = i * 2 + ia[ i ];
```

The result of an assignment operator is the value of the expression that is assigned to its left operand. The data type of its result is the type of its left operand.

Assignment operators can be concatenated provided that each of the operands being assigned is of the same general data type. For example,

```
main()
{
    int i, j;
    i = j = 0; // ok: each assigned 0
    // ...
}
```

`i` and `j` are each assigned 0. The order of evaluation is right to left.

Assignment operator concatenation also allows for notational compaction, as in the following conditional test of the value assigned to the character variable ch:

```
char ch;
char next_char();

if ((ch = next_char()) != '\n') /* ... */ ;
```

Use of this notation is a matter of personal style. Be careful, however, that compactness does not slip over the edge into obscurity.

The compound assignment operator also provides a measure of notational compactness. For example,

```
int arraySum( int ia[], int sz ) {
    int sum = 0;
    for ( int i = 0; i < sz; ++i )
        sum += ia[ i ];
    return sum;
}
```

The general syntactic form of the compound assignment operator is

```
a op= b;
```

where op= may be one of the following ten operators: +=, -=, *=, /=, %=, <<=, >>=, &=, ^=, |=. Each compound operator is equivalent to the following "longhand" assignment:

```
a = a op b;
```

The longhand notation for summing a vector, for example, is

```
sum = sum + ia[ i ];
```

Exercise 2-1. The following is illegal. Why? How would you correct it?

```
main() {
    int i = j = k = 0;
}
```

☐

Exercise 2-2. The following is also illegal. Why? How would you correct it?

```
main() {
    int i, j;
    int *ip;

    i = j = ip = 0;
}
```

☐

2.5　Increment and Decrement Operators

The increment ("++") and decrement ("−−") operators provide a convenient notational compaction for adding or subtracting 1 from a variable. Both operators should be thought of as assignment operators; the operand must be an lvalue. Each operator has a *prefix* and *postfix* form. For example,

```
main() {
    int c;
        ++c; // prefix increment
        c++; // postfix increment
}
```

Let's illustrate the use of the post- and prefix forms of the operators by defining a Stack class. A Stack will perform two operations:

1. `push(value)`, which places a value at the top of the stack.

2. `pop()`, which returns the value stored at the top of the stack.

In addition, there are two possible exception conditions:

1. *overflow*: attempting to `push()` onto a stack which is full.

2. *underflow*: attempting to `pop()` a stack which is empty.

The internal representation of the stack will be implemented as an array. The following members are therefore required:

1. `size`: the size of the allocated array.

2. `array`: the actual array to implement the stack.

3. `top`: an index to the top element of the stack. An empty stack will set `top` equal to −1. (The values of the stack are held in elements 0 through `size-1`.) A full stack is indicated by `top` having the value `size-1`.

The predicate functions `is_empty()` and `is_full()` are trivial to write:

```
const int BOS = -1; // Bottom Of Stack

is_empty() { return (top == BOS ); }
is_full()  { return (top == size-1); }
```

The implementation of `push()` illustrates the prefix form of the increment operator. Recall that `top` points to the current stack top. The new item must be placed in the element one greater than the current value of `top`:

```
// push some_value onto stack
{
      if ( is_full() )
            // report error and exit
            ;

      array[ ++top ] = some_value;
}
```

The prefix form of ++ increments the value of top *before* that value is used as an index into array. It is a compact notation for the following two statements:

```
top = top + 1;
array[ top ] = v;
```

The implementation of pop() illustrates the postfix form of the decrement operator. Recall again that top points to the current stack top. After the stack is popped, top must be decremented.

```
// pop the topmost element of the stack
{
      if ( is_empty() )
            ; // report error and exit()
      return array[ top-- ];
}
```

The postfix form of -- decrements the value of top *after* that value is used as an index into array. It is a compact notation for the following statement pair:

```
array[ top ];
top = top - 1;
```

The execution of the return statement follows the decrement of top.

All that remains now is to define the internal representation of the stack. Ultimately, what we would like is to define a template Stack class that can contain any element type. For the moment, let us instead implement a Stack to contain integers. After the reader completes the discussion of template classes in Chapter 7, he or she should then try reimplementing Stack as a template class.

First, let us encapsulate the type-dependent information through the use of a typedef:

```
typedef int Type;
```

Next, let us fill in the class definition, placing it in a header file we will name Stack.h.

```
#ifndef STACK_H
#define STACK_H

typedef int Type;
const int BOS = -1; // Bottom Of Stack
const int stack_size = 24;

class Stack {
public:
    Stack( int sz = stack_size );
    ~Stack();
    is_empty() { return top == BOS; }
    is_full() { return top == size-1; }
    void push( Type value );
    Type pop();
private:
    int top;
    int size;
    Type *array;
};

#endif
```

The initialization of a Stack requires the run-time allocation of memory to be addressed by array. This is done through operator new. In addition, top must be set to BOS and size must be set to either the user-specified or default Stack value. The "deinitialization" of a Stack requires that we return the memory originally allocated back to what is referred to as the *program's free store*. This is done through the use of operator delete. Here is an implementation of both the Stack constructor and destructor:

```
#include <assert.h>
#include "Stack.h"

Stack::Stack( int sz )
{
    array = new Type[ sz ];
    assert( array != 0 );
    top = BOS;
    size = sz;
}

Stack::~Stack() {
    delete array;
}
```

These functions are placed in a file we name Stack.C. push() and pop() are also placed here:

```
#include <iostream.h>
#include <stdlib.h>

void Stack::push( Type value )
{
    if ( is_full() ) {
        cerr << "?? push on full stack" << endl;
        exit( -1 );
    }
    array[++top] = value;
}

Type Stack::pop() {
    if ( is_empty() ) {
        cerr << "?? pop on empty stack" << endl;
        exit( -1 );
    }
    return array[top--];
}
```

Here is a program example testing our Stack class implementation:

```
#include <iostream.h>
#include "Stack.h"

main() {
    const int size = 1000;
    Stack stack( size );

    // fill up the stack: 0...999
    for (int ix = 0; ix < size; ++ix)
        stack.push(ix);

    int error_cnt = 0;
    // check for sanity of stack
    for (ix = size-1; ix >= 0; --ix)
        if (stack.pop() != ix)
            ++error_cnt;

    // report results and return
    cerr << "Stack class test errors: ("
            << error_cnt << ")\n";
    return error_cnt;
}
```

To compile and execute it, type the following UNIX command:

```
$ CC main_stack.c Stack.c && a.out
```

Exercise 2-3. Modify the program to cause an underflow. Modify it to cause an overflow. □

Exercise 2-4. Add a function to return the index of the last item entered. Test it. □

Exercise 2-5. Add a function to return the number of items that can still be pushed onto the Stack without overflow. Test it. □

Exercise 2-6. Why do you think C++ wasn't named ++C? □

2.6 The sizeof Operator

The `sizeof` operator returns the size, in bytes, of an expression or type specifier. It may occur in either of two forms:

```
sizeof (type-specifier);
sizeof expr;
```

Here is an example of how both forms of the `sizeof` operator are used:

```
int ia[] = { 0, 1, 2 };
const sz = sizeof ia / sizeof( int );
```

This next program illustrates the use of the `sizeof` operator on a variety of type specifiers.

```
#include <iostream.h>
#include "Stack.h"

main() {
    cout << "short :\t\t" << sizeof(short) << endl;
    cout << "short* :\t" << sizeof(short*) << endl;
    cout << "short& :\t" << sizeof(short&) << endl;
    cout << "short[3] :\t" << sizeof(short[3]) << endl;

    cout << endl;   // to separate output

    cout << "Stack :\t\t" << sizeof(Stack) << endl;
    cout << "Stack* :\t" << sizeof(Stack*) << endl;
    cout << "Stack& :\t" << sizeof(Stack&) << endl;
    cout << "Stack[3] :\t" << sizeof(Stack[3]) << endl;
    return 0;
}
```

When compiled and executed, the program generates the following output on a Sun3/60 workstation:

```
short :           2
short* :          4
short& :          2
short[3] :        6

Stack :           12
Stack* :          4
Stack& :          12
Stack[3] :        36
```

Application of the `sizeof` operator on a pointer type returns the size of the memory necessary to contain an address of that type. On a Sun3/60 workstation, a pointer to type `short` and a pointer to a Stack class are both contained in 4 bytes of memory — a machine word.

Application of the `sizeof` operator on a reference type, however, returns the size of the memory necessary to contain the referenced object, not the memory necessary to contain the reference type itself.

2.7 The Arithmetic if Operator

The arithmetic `if` operator, the only ternary operator in C++, has the following syntactic form:

```
expr1 ? expr2 : expr3;
```

`expr1` is always evaluated. If it evaluates to a true condition — that is, any nonzero value — `expr2` is evaluated; otherwise, `expr3` is evaluated. The following program illustrates how the arithmetic if operator might be used.

```
#include <iostream.h>

main() {
    int i = 10, j = 20, k = 30;

    cout << "The larger value of "
         << i << " and " << j << " is "
         << ( i > j ? i : j ) << endl;

    cout << "The value of " << i << " is"
         << ( i % 2 ? " " : " not " )
         << "odd" << endl;
```

```
/* the arithmetic if can be nested,
 * but a deep nesting is difficult to read
 * in this example,
 * max is set to the largest of 3 variables */

int max = ( (i > j)
        ? (( i > k) ? i : k)
        : ( j > k ) ? j : k);

cout << "The larger value of "
        << i << ", " << j << " and " << k
        << " is " << max << endl;
return 0;
}
```

When compiled and executed, the program generates the following output:

```
The larger value of 10 and 20 is 20
The value of 10 is not odd
The larger value of 10, 20 and 30 is 30
```

2.8 Comma Operator

A comma expression is a series of expressions separated by a comma. These expressions are evaluated from left to right. The result of a comma expression is the value of the right-most expression. In the following example, each side of the arithmetic if operator is a comma expression. The value of the first comma expression is 1; the value of the second is 0.

```
main() {
    // examples of a comma expression
    int ival = (ia != 0)
                ? ix=get_index(), ia[ix]=ix, 1
                : set_array(ia), 0;
    // ...
}
```

2.9 The Bitwise Operators

A bitwise operator interprets its operand(s) as an ordered collection of bits. Each bit may contain either a 0 (off) or a 1 (on) value. A bitwise operator allows the programmer to test and set individual bits or bit subsets.

The operands of the bitwise operators must be of an integral type.

Operator	Function	Use
~	bitwise NOT	~expr
<<	left shift	expr1 << expr2
>>	right shift	expr1 >> expr2
&	bitwise AND	expr1 & expr2
^	bitwise XOR	expr1 ^ expr2
|	bitwise OR	expr1 | expr2

Table 2.3 Bitwise Operators

Although they may be either signed or unsigned, unsigned operands are recommended. How the "sign bit" is handled in a number of the bitwise operations may differ across implementations; programs that work under one
implementation may fail under another. Thus, the use of unsigned operands
makes for more portable programs.

First we will examine how each operator works. Then we will consider an
example of how bitwise operators might be used. In Section 6.4 (page 326)
we will implement a BitVector class.

The bitwise NOT operator ("~") flips the bits of its operand. Each 1 bit is
set to 0; each 0 bit is set to 1.

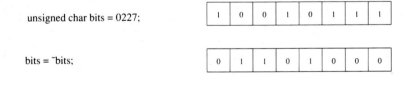

The bitwise shift operators ("<<, >>") shift the bits of the left operand some
number of positions either to the left or right.

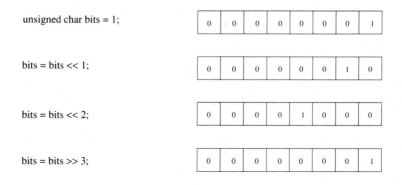

The operand's excess bits are discarded. The left shift operator ("<<") inserts 0-valued bits in from the right. The right shift operator (">>") inserts 0-valued bits in from the left if the operand is unsigned. If the operand is signed, it may either insert copies of the sign bit or insert 0-valued bits; this behavior is machine dependent.

The bitwise AND operator ("&") takes two integral operands. For each bit position, the result is a 1-bit if both operands contain 1-bits; otherwise, the result is a 0-bit. (This operator should not be confused with the logical AND operator ("&&").)

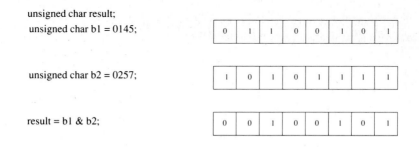

The bitwise XOR (exclusive or) operator ("^") takes two integral operands. For each bit position, the result is a 1-bit if either but not both operands contain a 1-bit; otherwise, the result is a 0-bit.

result = b1 ^ b2;

1	1	0	0	1	0	1	0

The bitwise OR (inclusive or) operator ("|") takes two integral operands. For each bit position, the result is a 1-bit if either or both operands contain a 1-bit; otherwise, the result is a 0-bit.

result = b1 | b2;

1	1	1	0	1	1	1	1

A variable utilized as a discrete collection of bits is referred to as a *bit vector*. Bit vectors are an efficient method of keeping *yes/no* information on a set of items or conditions.

Here is an example. A teacher has 30 students in a class. Each week the class is given a pass/fail quiz. A bit vector will be used to track the results of each quiz.

```
unsigned int quiz1 = 0;
```

The teacher must be able to turn on and off and to test individual bits. For example, student 27 has taken a make-up quiz and passed. The teacher must turn bit 27 on. The first step is to set the 27th bit of an integer to 1, while all the other bits remain 0. This can be done with the left shift operator ("<<") and the integer constant 1:

1

0	0	0	0	0	0	0	0
0	0	0	0	0	0	0	0
0	0	0	0	0	0	0	0
0	0	0	0	0	0	0	1

1 << 27

0	0	0	0	1	0	0	0
0	0	0	0	0	0	0	0
0	0	0	0	0	0	0	0
0	0	0	0	0	0	0	0

If this value is bitwise ORed with `quiz1`, all but the 27th bit will remain unchanged. The 27th bit is turned on:

```
quiz1 |= 1<<27;
```

Imagine that the teacher reexamined the quiz and discovered that student 27 actually had failed the make-up. The teacher must now turn off bit 27. This time the integer must have all the bits except the 27th turned on. Notice that this is the inverse of the previous integer. Applying the bitwise NOT to the previous integer will turn on every bit but the 27th:

~(1 << 27)

1	1	1	1	0	1	1	1
1	1	1	1	1	1	1	1
1	1	1	1	1	1	1	1
1	1	1	1	1	1	1	1

If this value is bitwise ANDed with `quiz1`, all but the 27th bit will remain unchanged. The 27th bit is turned off:

```
quiz1 &= ~(1<<27);
```

Here is how the teacher can determine the on or off status of a bit. Consider student 27 again. The first step is to set the 27th bit of an integer to 1. The bitwise AND of this value with `quiz1` will evaluate to true if bit 27 of `quiz1` is also on; otherwise, it will return 0 (false):

```
int hasPassed = quiz1 & (1<<27);
```

Exercise 2-7. Given the following two definitions:

```
unsigned int ui1 = 3, ui2 = 7;
```

What is the result of each of the following expressions?

    (a)   ui1 & ui2   (c)   ui1 | ui2

    (b)   ui1 && ui2   (d)   ui1 || ui2

□

Exercise 2-8. What is the effect of assigning 0377 to a variable of type unsigned char in terms of its bit pattern? Draw a picture.

□

Exercise 2-9. How might a programmer isolate the second byte of a variable of type int using the bitwise operators?

□

Exercise 2-10. There is a method of generating the powers of two using the left shift operator and the literal constant 1. Generate a table of the first 16 values. □

2.10 Precedence

Operator precedence — that is, the order in which operators are evaluated in a compound expression — is important to learn in order to avoid many common sources of program error. What, for example, is the result of the following arithmetic expression?

```
6 + 3 * 4 / 2 + 2
```

A purely left-to-right evaluation yields a value of 20. Other possible results include 9, 14, and 36. Which is correct? 14.

In C++, multiplication and division have a higher precedence than addition. This means that they are evaluated first. Multiplication and division have the same precedence, however. Operators that have the same precedence are evaluated from left to right. The order of expression evaluation is therefore the following:

```
1.  3 * 4 => 12
2.  12 / 2 => 6
3.  6 + 6 => 12
4.  12 + 2 => 14
```

Here is a compound expression insidiously in error. The problem is that the inequality operator ("!=") has a higher precedence than the assignment operator:

```
while ( ch = nextChar() != '\0' )
```

The programmer's intention is to assign ch the next character then test that character to see whether it is null. The behavior of the code, however, is to test the next character to see whether it is null. ch is then assigned the truth or false value of the test. The next character is never assigned.

Precedence can be overridden by the use of parentheses, which mark off subexpressions. In the evaluation of a compound expression, the first action is to evaluate all parenthetical subexpressions. Each subexpression is replaced by its result; evaluation continues. Innermost parentheses are evaluated before outer pairs. For example,

```
4 * 5 + 7 * 2 ==> 34
4 * ( 5 + 7 * 2 ) ==> 76
4 * ( (5 + 7) * 2 ) ==> 96
```

Here is the earlier compound expression properly parenthesized to reflect the programmer's intentions:

```
while ( (ch = nextChar()) != '\0' )
```

Table 2.4 presents the full set of C++ operators in order of precedence. 17R should be read as "precedence level 17, right to left associativity." Similarly, 7L should be read as "precedence level 7, left to right associativity." The higher the precedence level, the greater the precedence of the operator.

Exercise 2-11. Using Table 2.4, identify the order of evaluation of the following compound expressions:

```
(a)    ! ptr == ptr->next
(b)    ~ uc ^ 0377 & ui << 4
(c)    ch = buf[ bp++ ] != '\0'
```

☐

Exercise 2-12. The three expressions in the previous exercise all evaluate in an order contrary to the intentions of the programmer. Parenthesize them to evaluate in an order you imagine to be the intention of the programmer.

☐

Exercise 2-13. Why does the following fail to compile? How would you fix it?

```
    void doSomething();

    main() {
        int i = doSomething(), 0;
    }
```

☐

2.11 Type Conversion

At the machine level, all data types melt away into a contiguous stream of bits. Type information is a kind of prescription: "take x number of bits and interpret them using the following pattern...."

Converting one predefined type into another typically will change one or both properties of the type but not the underlying bit pattern. The size may widen or narrow, and of course the intepretation will change.

Some conversions are not safe; typically, a compiler will warn about these. Conversions from a wider data type to a narrower data type are one category of unsafe type conversion. Here are three examples of potentially unsafe conversions:

```
    long lval;
    unsigned char uc;

    int (3.14159);
    (signed char) uc;
    short (lval);
```

The following two notations,

```
    type (expr)
    (type) expr
```

are referred to as *casts*. They represent an explicit request by the programmer to convert expr into type.

The three cases illustrate the potential dangers of narrowing type conversions.

In the first case, the fractional part is lost. For example,

```
    // 3.14159 != 3.0
    3.14159 != double (int (3.14159) );
```

In the second case, for half the possible values of uc (128 - 255), the interpretation of the bit pattern has changed. The left-most bit is now the sign bit.

In the third case, for any value of lval which requires bits beyond the size of a short, the result of the conversion is undefined.

Level	Operator	Function
17R	: :	global scope (unary)
17L	: :	class scope (binary)
16L	->,.	member selectors
16L	[ ]	array index
16L	( )	function call
16L	( )	type construction
15R	sizeof	size in bytes
15R	++,--	increment,decrement
15R	~	bitwise NOT
15R	!	logical NOT
15R	+,-	unary minus, plus
15R	*,&	dereference, address-of
15R	( )	type conversion (cast)
15R	new,delete	free store management
14L	->*,.*	member pointer selectors
13L	*,/,%	multiplicative operators
12L	+,-	arithmetic operators
11L	<<,>>	bitwise shift
10L	<,<=,>,>=	relational operators
9L	==,!=	equality, inequality
8L	&	bitwise AND
7L	^	bitwise XOR
6L			bitwise OR
5L	&&	logical AND
4L	||	logical OR
3L	?:	arithmetic if
2R	=,*=,/=	assignment operators
2R	%=,+=,-=,<<=	
2R	>>=,&=,|=,^=	
1L	,	comma operator

Table 2.4 Operator Precedence and Associativity

Some conversions are safe on some machines but involve narrowing on others. On most machines, for example, an `int` is the same size as either a `short` or `long` but not both. One of the following conversions will be unsafe on any machine that does not implement `short`, `int`, and `long` as three distinct sizes:

```
unsigned short us;
unsigned int ui;

// one of these conversions is unsafe
int( us );
long( ui );
```

The whole issue of type conversion can be quite bewildering, but it is something of which programmers must be aware. The next two subsections look at implicit and explicit type conversions. Section 6.5 (page 334) discusses user-defined conversions for class types.

Implicit Type Conversions

An implicit type conversion is a conversion performed by the compiler without programmer intervention. An implicit conversion is applied generally whenever differing data types are intermixed. Such a conversion is performed following a set of predefined rules referred to as the *standard conversions*.

Assigning a value to an object converts the value to the type of the object. Passing a value to a call of a function converts the value to the type of the function argument. For example,

```
void ff( int );

int val = 3.14159; // conversion to int 3
ff( 3.14159 );     // conversion to int 3
```

In both cases, the double literal `3.14159` is implicitly converted to type `int` by the compiler. A warning is issued since the conversion involves a narrowing.

In an arithmetic expression, the widest data type present becomes the target conversion type. For example,

```
val + 3.14159;
```

The widest data type of this arithmetic expression is of type `double`. `val` is implicitly converted to `double` by widening (also referred to as *type promotion*). Its value 3 becomes `3.0` and is added to `3.14159`. The result of the expression is `6.14159`.

Note that the value of val remains 3. The type conversion is applied to a copy of val's value. A variable is not written in the process of type conversion.

```
val = val + 3.14159;
```

Two conversions occur. The value of val is promoted to double. The result, 6.14159, is then narrowed to type int. This narrowed value is then assigned to val. val now contains the value 6.

The behavior is exactly the same when this expression is written as

```
val += 3.14159;
```

For example, the resulting value of the following two statements is 23, not 20:

```
int i = 10;
i *= 2.3; // 23, not 20
```

The truncation of the double literal constant occurs after the multiplication.

Explicit Conversions

It is somewhat wasteful to perform two conversions for the compound expression

```
i = i + 3.14159;
```

Since the target data type is int, it seems more sensible to narrow the double operand rather than promote i to double, then narrow the sum to int.

One reason for an explicit cast is to override the usual standard conversions. For example,

```
i = i + int(3.14159);
```

3.14159 is now converted to int, yielding the value 3. This is added to and then assigned to i.

A predefined standard conversion allows a pointer of any nonconst data type to be assigned to a pointer of type void*. A void* pointer is used whenever the exact type of an object is either unknown or will vary under particular circumstances. A void* pointer is sometimes referred to as a *generic* pointer because of its ability to address objects of any data types. For example,

```
int ival;
int *pi = 0;
char *pc = 0;
void *pv;

pv = pi; // ok: implicit conversion
pv = pc; // ok: implicit conversion

const int *pci = &ival;
pv = pci; // error;
const void *pcv = pci; // ok
```

However, a void* pointer may not be dereferenced directly. (There is no
type information to guide the compiler in interpreting the underlying bit pattern.) Rather, a void* pointer must first be converted to a pointer to a particular type.

In C++, however, there is *no* predefined conversion of a void* pointer to
a pointer to a particular type since it is potentially unsafe. For example,
attempting to assign a void* pointer to a pointer to anything other than
void* will result in a compile-time error:

```
int ival;
void *pv;
int *pi = &ival;
char *pc;

pv = pi; // ok
pc = pv; // error: no standard conversion: unsafe
```

A second reason for an explicit cast is to override type checking. C++, in
general, permits a value to be explicitly cast to any data type. By providing
an explicit cast, the programmer assumes responsibility for the safety of the
type conversion. For example,

```
pc = (char*)pv; // ok: explicit cast
strcmp(pc,"Anna"); // trouble if pc addresses ival

// ok: explicit casting away of constness
pv = (void*) pci;
```

A third reason for an explicit cast is to disambiguate a situation in which
more than one conversion is possible. We will look at this case more closely
in Section 4.1 (page 176) in our discussion of overloading function names.

Given the following set of identifiers:

```
char ch;                    unsigned char unChar;
short sh;                   unsigned short unShort;
int intVal;                 unsigned int unInt;
long longVal;               float fl;
```

Exercise 2-14. Identify which of the following assignments are unsafe because of possible narrowing:

```
(a)  sh = intVal         (d)  longVal = unInt
(b)  intVal = longVal    (e)  unInt = fl
(c)  sh = unChar         (f)  intVal = unShort
```

☐

Exercise 2-15. Identify the data type of the following expressions:

```
(a)   'a' - 3
(b)   intVal * longVal - ch
(c)   fl + longVal / sh
(d)   unInt + (unsigned int) longVal
(e)   ch + unChar + longVal + unInt
```

☐

2.12 Statements

Statements form the smallest executable unit within a C++ program. Statements are terminated with a semicolon; their simplest form is the empty, or null, statement. It takes the following form:

```
; // null statement
```

A null statement is useful in those instances where the syntax of the language requires the presence of a statement but where the logic of the program does not. This is occasionally the case with the `while` and `for` loop statements. For example,

```
while ( *string++ = *inBuf++ ) ; // null statement
```

The presence of an unnecessary null statement will not generate a compile-time error. (The author once used an ALGOL68 compiler at Columbia University that flagged every null statement as a fatal error. Imagine being up at 3 A.M. waiting 40 minutes to compile a program, only to have an extraneous semicolon terminate the compilation.)

```
int val;; // additional null statement
```

is composed of two statements: the declaration statement `int val` and the null statement.

A declaration followed by a semicolon is a *declaration statement*, the only statement that can be specified outside a function. An expression followed by a semicolon is an *expression statement*.

Compound Statements and Blocks

A number of syntactic constructs in the language permit only a single statement to be specified. The logic of the program, however, may require that a sequence of two or more statements be executed. In these cases a compound statement can be used. For example,

```
if ( account.balance - withdrawal < 0 )
{ // compound statement
    issueNotice( account.number );
    chargePenalty( account.number );
}
```

A compound statement is a sequence of statements enclosed by a pair of braces. The compound statement is treated as a single unit and may appear anywhere in the program where a single statement may appear. A compound statement need not be terminated with a semicolon.

A compound statement containing one or more declaration statements is referred to as a *block*. Blocks are considered in detail in Section 3.10 (page 139) in the discussion of scope.

2.13   Statement Flow Control

The default flow of statement execution is sequential. Every C++ program begins with the first statement of `main()`. Each statement in turn is executed. When the final statement is executed, the program is done.

Except in the simplest programs, sequential program execution is inadequate to the problems we must solve. Through our program examples we have already seen the conditional `if` statement and the `while` and `for` loop statements. The following subsections review the entire C++ statement set.

2.14   The if Statement

An `if` statement tests a particular condition. Whenever that condition evaluates as true, an action or set of actions is executed. Otherwise, the action(s) are ignored.

The syntactic form of the `if` statement is the following:

```
if ( expression )
    statement;
```

The *expression* must be enclosed in parentheses. If it evaluates to a nonzero value, the condition is considered as true and the *statement* is executed.

Users of the Array class presented in Chapter 1 have requested a min() operation that returns the smallest value contained within the array. In addition, a count of the occurrence of the minimum value within the array is kept. The algorithm for implementing this operation requires the following steps:

* for each element in the array, do the following:

* compare the element to the current minimum value

* if it is less than the minimum value, reset the minimum value to this element, reset the counter to 1.

* if it is equal to the minimum value, increment the counter by 1.

* otherwise, do nothing

* after examining each element, return the value *and* the occurrence count to the user.

Two if statements are required:

```
if ( minVal > ia[ i ] ) ... // new minVal
if ( minVal == ia[ i ] ) ... // another occurrence
```

A somewhat common programmer error in the use of the if statement is to not provide a compound statement when multiple statements must be executed upon a condition evaluating as true. This can be a very difficult error to uncover since the text of the program looks correct. For example,

```
if ( minVal > ia[ i ] )
    minVal = ia[ i ];
    occurs = 1; // not part of if statement
```

Contrary to the indentation and intention of the programmer,

```
occurs = 1;
```

is not treated as part of the if statement but rather is executed unconditionally following evaluation of the if statement. Here is the if statement written correctly:

```
if ( minVal > ia[ i ] ) {
    minVal = ia[ i ];
    occurs = 1;
}
```

Our second if statement looks as follows:

```
if ( minVal == ia[ i ] )
    ++occurs;
```

Notice that the order of the if statements is significant. Our function will always be off by 1 if we place them in the following order:

```
if ( minVal > ia[ i ] ) {
    minVal = ia[ i ];
    occurs = 1;
}


// potential error if minVal
// has just been set to ia[i]
if ( minVal == ia[ i ] )
    ++occurs;
```

Not only is the execution of both if statements on the same value potentially dangerous, it is also unnecessary. The same element cannot be both less than minVal and equal to it. If one condition is true, the other condition can be ignored safely. The if statement allows for this kind of *either-or* condition by providing an else clause.

The syntactic form of the if-else statement is the following:

```
if ( expression )
    statement-1;
else
    statement-2;
```

If the *expression* evaluates to a nonzero value, the condition is considered to be true and *statement-1* is executed; otherwise, *statement-2* is executed. Note that if *statement-1* is not a compound statement, it must be terminated by a semicolon. Programmers familiar with either Pascal or Ada, in which the semicolon following *statement-1* is illegal, often fail to provide the necessary semicolon. For example,

```
if ( minVal == ia[ i ] )
    ++occurs; // terminating ';' required
else
if ( minVal > ia[ i ] ) {
    minVal = ia[ i ];
    occurs = 1;
}
```

In this example, *statement-2* is itself an `if` statement. If `minVal` is less than the element, no action is taken.

In the following example, one of the three statements is always executed:

```
if ( minVal < ia[ i ] )
    ; // null statement
else
if ( minVal > ia[ i ] ) {
    minVal = ia[ i ];
    occurs = 1;
}
else // minVal == ia[ i ]
    ++occurs;
```

The `if-else` statement introduces a source of potential ambiguity referred to as *the dangling-else* problem. This problem occurs when a statement contains more `if` than `else` clauses. The question then arises, with which `if` does the additional `else` clause properly match up? For example,

```
if ( minVal <= ia[ i ] )
    if ( minVal == ia[ i ]
        ++occurs;
else {
    minVal = ia[ i ];
    occurs = 1;
}
```

The indentation indicates the programmer's belief that the `else` should match up with the outer `if` clause. In C++, however, the dangling-else ambiguity is resolved by matching the `else` with the last occurring unmatched `if`. In this case, the actual evaluation of the `if-else` statement is as follows:

```
if ( minVal <= ia[ i ] ) {
    // effect of dangling-else resolution
    if ( minVal == ia[ i ]
        ++occurs;
    else
        { minVal = ia[ i ]; occurs = 1; }
}
```

One method of overriding the default dangling-else matching is to place the last occurring `if` in a compound statement:

```
if ( minVal <= ia[ i ] ) {
    if ( minVal == ia[ i ] )
        ++occurs;
}
else
    { minVal = ia[ i ]; occurs = 1; }
```

Some coding styles recommend *always* using compound statement braces to avoid possible confusion and error in later modifications of the code.

Here is a first cut at implementing our `min()` operation. `Array::min()` is to be read as indicating that the function `min()` occurs within the scope of the Array class. The question marks indicate that we don't as yet know what arguments or return type our function should take.

```
??? Array::min( ??? ) {
    int minVal = 0;
    occurs = 0;

    for ( int ix = 0; ix < size; ++ix ) {
        if ( minVal == ia[ ix ] )
            ++occurs;
        else
        if ( minVal > ia[ ix ] ) {
            minVal = ia[ ix ]; occurs = 1;
        }
    }
    return ???;
}
```

`occurs` is declared to be an `int` in order to handle the case where each element of the array is the same value. The maximum occurrence count of the smallest value, that is, is the size of the array itself. Therefore, the appropriate data type for `occurs` is the same as that for the data member `size` of the Array class. Similarly, `minVal`'s data type must be the same as the data type of the actual array of elements — in this case, `int`.

Our first implementation of `min()`, as we've coded it, is incorrect. Can you see what the problem is? If the smallest array value is a value greater than 0, our implementation in fact does not find it. A better first value for `minVal` is the first element of the array:

```
int minVal = ia[0];
```

Before we look at this further, let's resolve the issue of the function's return type and set of arguments.

By default, a function returns one value. `min()`, however, needs to return both a smallest value *and* an occurrence count of that value. Here are two possible solutions:

- Define a class to hold both values. For example,

```
class Occurs_count {
public:
    Occurs_count( int val, int cnt ) {
        value = val; count = cnt; }
    get_val() { return value; }
    get_cnt() { return count; }
private:
    int value, count;
};
```

The implementation of `min()` using this solution looks as follows:

```
#include "Array.h"
#include "Occurs_count.h"

Occurs_count Array::min()
{
    // body remains the same as previously
    return Occurs_count(minVal, occurs);
}
```

`Occurs_count.h` is a header file containing the definition of the `Occurs_count` class. The definition of `Array::min()` is placed in the `Array.C` file we created in Section 1.8.

- Pass an argument of a reference type to hold the occurrence count. For example,

```
#include "Array.h"

int Array::min( int &occurs )
{
    int minVal = ia[0];
    occurs = 0;

    // rest of function remains the same
    return minVal;
}
```

Section 3.7 (page 127) discusses the reference argument type in detail.

Before we try out each of these program solutions, let's provide one further refinement to our implementation of `min()`. Recall, the initial portion of the function now looks as follows:

```
// initial portion of min()
int minVal = ia[ 0 ];
occurs = 0;

for ( int i = 0; i < size; ++i ) {
    if ( minVal == ia[ i ] )
    // ...
```

The first iteration of the for loop — that is, i set to 0, always finds minVal equal to ia[i]. occurs is incremented to 1. This is correct but unnecessary. Our code could be modified to start *after* this step. For example,

```
// revised portion of min()
int minVal = ia[ 0 ];
occurs = 1; // it's been seen

// don't look at ia[0] again
for ( int i = 1; i < size; ++i ) {
    if ( minVal == ia[ i ] )
    // ...
```

It is a trivial refinement, to be sure, but the kind of small detail the practiced eye of a programmer should catch.

Here is an example of exercising our first implementation that returns a class Occurs_count object holding both values:

```
#include <iostream.h>
#include "Occurs_count.h"
#include "Array.h"

int ia[10] = { 9,4,8,3,7,2,6,1,5,1 };
main() {
    Array iA(ia,10);
    Occurs_count result = iA.min();
    cout << "Minimum value: " << result.get_val()
        << " occurs: " << result.get_cnt()
        << " times." << endl;
    return 0;
}
```

Here is the same program implemented to invoke our argument reference version of min():

```
#include <iostream.h>
#include "Array.h"

int ia[10] = { 9,4,8,3,7,2,6,1,5,1 };
main() {
    Array iA(ia,10);
    int occurs = 0;
    int minVal = iA.min(occurs);

    cout << "Minimum value: " << minVal
         << " occurs: " << occurs
         << " times." << endl;
    return 0;
}
```

Place one or the other implementation of `main()` in a file called `min_test.C`. Personally, I prefer the argument reference version. Under my UNIX system, to compile and execute the program, I write the following:

```
$ CC -o min_test min_test.C Array.C
$ min_test
```

Using either implementation, the program generates the following output:

```
Minimum value: 1 occurs: 2 times.
```

Exercise 2-16. Change the declaration of `occurs` in the argument list of `min()` to be a nonreference argument type and rerun the program. □

2.15 The switch Statement

Deeply nested `if-else` statements can often be correct syntactically and yet not express the intended logic of the programmer. Unintended `else-if` matchings are more likely to pass unnoticed, for example. Modifications to the statements are also much harder to get right. As an alternative method of choosing among a set of mutually exclusive choices, C++ provides the `switch` statement.

For example, suppose that we have been asked to count the number of occurrences of each of the five vowels in random segments of text. (The conventional wisdom is that e is the most frequently occurring vowel.) Our program logic is as follows:

- Read each character in turn until there are no more characters to read.

- Compare each character to the set of vowels.

- If the character matches one of the vowels, add 1 to that vowel's count;

- Display the results.

The program was used to analyze the previous section of this book. Here is the output, which verifies the conventional wisdom regarding the frequency of the vowel e:

```
aCnt:    394
eCnt:    721
iCnt:    461
oCnt:    349
uCnt:    186
```

The program is implemented as a five-way switch statement with a truth condition for each vowel. In a switch statement, the truth condition is implemented as a case label. The Vowels enumeration is used to enhance the readability of the program text. The program is implemented as follows:

```
#include <iostream.h>
enum Vowels { a='a', e='e', i='i', o='o', u='u' };

main() {
   char ch;
   int aCnt=0, eCnt=0, iCnt=0, oCnt=0, uCnt=0;

   while ( cin >> ch )
     switch ( ch ) {
         case a:
             ++aCnt;
             break;
         case e:
             ++eCnt;
             break;
         case i:
             ++iCnt;
             break;
         case o:
             ++oCnt;
             break;
         case u:
             ++uCnt;
             break;
     };
```

```
        cout << "aCnt: \t" << aCnt << endl;
        cout << "eCnt: \t" << eCnt << endl;
        cout << "iCnt: \t" << iCnt << endl;
        cout << "oCnt: \t" << oCnt << endl;
        cout << "uCnt: \t" << uCnt << endl;
        return 0;
    }
```

There is a problem in the logic of the program, however. For example, how does the program handle the following input?

```
    UNIX
```

The capital U and the capital I are not recognized as vowels. Our program fails to count vowels occurring as uppercase characters. Before we fix our program, however, let's look more closely at the switch statement.

The value following the case keyword, referred to as the *case label*, must be followed by a colon. Each case label must be a constant expression of an integral type. No two case labels may have the same value; if they do a compile-time error occurs.

When the switch statement is executed, its expression is evaluated and compared to each case label until either a match is successful or all labels have been examined. If the expression matches a case label, execution begins with the first statement following the case label. If there is no match between the expression and the set of case labels, no action is taken.

A common misconception is that only the statements defined for the matched case label are executed. Rather, execution begins there and continues across case boundaries until the end of the switch statement is encountered. Let's look more closely at this other common cause of program error. Here is our earlier switch statement, modified slightly:

```
    switch ( ch ) {
        case a: ++aCnt;
        case e: ++eCnt;
        case i: ++iCnt;
        case o: ++oCnt;
        case u: ++uCnt;
    };

    cout << ch << endl; // for illustration
```

If ch is set to i, execution begins following case i. iCnt is incremented. Execution, however, does not stop there, but continues across case boundaries until the closing brace of the switch statement. oCnt and uCnt are also both incremented. If ch is next set to e, eCnt, iCnt, oCnt, and uCnt are all incremented.

The programmer must explicitly tell the compiler to stop statement execution within the `switch` statement. This is done by specifying a `break` statement after each execution unit within the `switch` statement. Under most conditions, the last statement of a case label is `break`.

When a `break` statement is encountered, the `switch` statement is terminated. Control shifts to the statement immediately following the closing brace of the `switch`. In the example, this statement is

```
cout << ch << endl; // for illustration
```

A case label that deliberately omits a `break` statement should in most cases provide a comment stating that the omission is deliberate. If obvious from the context, however, the comment may be left out safely.

When might the programmer wish to omit a `break` statement from a case label? One circumstance is when a set of values are all to be handled by the same sequence of actions. Each element of the range must be provided with its own case label. For example, recall our earlier program that failed to read uppercase vowels. Here is a corrected implementation:

```
// of course, the enum Vowels needs to be updated
enum Vowels {
    a='a', e='e', i='i', o='o', u='u',
    A='A', E='E', I='I', O='O', U='U'
};

switch (ch ) {
    case A:
    case a:
        ++aCnt;
        break;
    // ...
    case U:
    case u:
        ++uCnt;
        break;
};
```

The `switch` statement provides the equivalent of an unconditional `else` clause. This is the `default` label. If no case label matches the value of the `switch` expression and the `default` label is present, the statements following the `default` label will be executed. For example, let's add a default case to our `switch` statement. The default case will count the number of consonants:

```
#include <ctype.h>

// ...
switch (ch) {
    case A:
    case a:
        ++aCnt;
        break;
    // ...
    case U:
    case u:
        ++uCnt;
        break;
    default:
        if isalpha( ch )
            ++conCnt;
        break;
};
```

isalpha() is a C library routine; it evaluates to true if its argument is a letter of the alphabet. To use it, the programmer must include the system
header file ctype.h.

   Although it is not strictly necessary to specify a break statement in the
last label of a switch statement, the safest course is to always provide one. If
an additional case label is added later to the bottom of the switch statement, the absence of the break statement may suddenly become significant.

Exercise 2-17. Modify the program so that it also counts the number of
spaces read.

☐

Exercise 2-18. Modify the program so that it counts the number of occurrences of the following two-character sequences: ff, fl, and fi. ☐

Iterative Statements

Many program activities involve performing a fixed set of statements against
a collection of similar objects. A bank program, for example, may be written
to process checks. For each check, the program must, among other actions,

- Read in the check,

- Verify that it has a correct account number,

- Verify that the account has funds sufficient to cover the amount of the
  check,

- Debit the account for the amount of the check, and

- Record the transaction.

To repeat this sequence of code for each check is hardly reasonable. Rather, the language provides iterative control statements, called *loops*, that allow the program to repeat execution of the single instance of the fixed set of statements.

A loop cycles over a body of code for as long as a specified condition remains true. The bank program would probably specify the following truth condition:

```
while there exists a check to be processed
```

This loop will terminate when the last check has been processed; that is, when the specified condition becomes false. This specified condition is sometimes referred to as a *loop control*.

C++ supports three loop constructs: the while, do, and for statements. The main distinction among them is the method of loop control. For all three statements, a true condition is any nonzero value. A zero value indicates a false condition.

2.16   The while Statement

The syntactic form of the while loop is as follows:

```
while ( expression )
    statement;
```

For as many iterations as the *expression* evaluates to a true condition, the *statement* (or compound statement) is executed. The sequence is as follows:

1. Evaluate the expression.

2. Execute the statement if the condition is true.

If the first evaluation of the expression tests false, the statement is never executed. For example, the algorithm to count vowels introduced in the earlier subsection on the switch statement requires that characters from the input stream be read in one character at a time until the end of the file is reached. The while loop is a perfect candidate for implementing this:

```
char ch;
while ( cin >> ch )
    switch( ch ) { ... }
```

Because the entire switch is considered a single statement, it does not need to be placed in a compound statement.

The while loop is particularly appropriate for manipulating strings and other pointer types. For example,

```
ff( const char *st )
{
    int len = 0;
    const char *tp = st;

    // compute length of st
    while ( *tp++ ) ++len;

    // now copy st
    char *s = new char[ len + 1];
    while ( *s++ = *st++ )
        ; // null statement

    // ... rest of function
}
```

Exercise 2-19. Implement a function to determine if two strings are equal.

□

Exercise 2-20. Implement a function which returns the number of occurrences of a character within a string.

□

Exercise 2-21. Implement a function which determines if a substring occurs within a string. □

2.17 The for Statement

A for loop is used most commonly to step through a fixed-length data structure such as an array. We have utilized it a number of times already. The syntactic form of the for loop is as follows:

```
for ( init-statement; expression-1; expression-2 )
      statement;
```

init-statement can be either a declaration or an expression. It is generally used to initialize or assign to one or a set of variables. It may be null. The following are all legal instances of the *init-statement*:

```
for ( int i = 0; ...
for ( ; /* null init-statement */ ...
for ( i = 0; ...
for ( int lo = 0, hi = max, mid = max/2; ...
for ( char *ptr = getStr(); ...
for ( i = 0, ptr = buf, dbl = 0.0; ...
```

expression-1 serves as the loop control. For as many iterations as *expression-1* evaluates as a true condition, *statement* is executed. *statement* may either be a single or a compound statement. If the first evaluation of *expression-1* evaluates to false, *statement* is never executed. The following are all legal instances of *expression-1*:

```
(...; index < arraySize; ... )
(...; ptr; ... )
(...; *st1++ = *st2++; ... )
(...; ch = getNextChar(); ... )
```

expression-2 is evaluated after each iteration of the loop. It is generally used to modify the variables initialized in *init-statement*. If the first evaluation of *expression-1* evaluates to false, *expression-2* is never executed. The following are all legal instances of *expression-2*:

```
( ...; ...; ++i )
( ...; ...; ptr = ptr->next )
( ...; ...; ++i, --j, ++cnt )
( ...; ...; ) // null instance
```

Given the following for loop,

```
const int sz = 24;
int ia[ sz ];

for ( int i = 0; i < sz; ++i )
    ia[ i ] = i;
```

the order of evaluation is as follows:

1. *init-statement* is executed once at the start of the loop. In this example, i is defined and initialized to 0.

2. *expression-1* is executed. A true condition, any value other than 0, causes execution of *statement*. A false condition terminates the loop. An initial false condition results in *statement* never being executed.

In this example, i is compared to sz. For as long as i is less than sz,

```
ia[ i ] = i;
```

is executed.

3. *expression-2* is executed. Typically, this modifies the variable(s) initialized in *init-statement*. In the example, i is incremented by 1.

This constitutes one complete iteration of the for loop. Step 2 is now repeated. This process can be modeled as the following equivalent while loop:

```
init-statement;
while ( expression-1 )
{
    statement;
    expression-2;
}
```

Exercise 2-22. Implement a function to compare two arrays for equality. Be sure to define what it means for two arrays to be equal.

□

Exercise 2-23. Implement a function to search an array for a particular value. If the value is found, return its array index. What should the function do if the value is not found? □

2.18 The do Statement

Imagine that we have been asked to write an interactive program that converts miles into kilometers. The outline of the program looks like this:

```
int more = 1;   // dummy value to start loop

while ( more ) {
    val = getValue();
    val = convertValue(val);
    printValue(val);
    more = doMore();
}
```

The problem here is that the loop control is set up within the loop body. With the for and while loop, however, unless the loop control evaluates to true, the loop body will never be executed. This means that the programmer must provide a first value to start the loop going. The do loop guarantees that its loop body is always executed at least once. It does not require a forced startup.

The syntactic form of the do loop is as follows:

```
do
    statement;
while ( expression );
```

statement is executed before *expression* is evaluated. If the condition evaluates
as false, the do loop terminates. Our program outline now looks as follows:

```
do {
    val = getValue();
    val = convertValue(val);
    printValue(val); }
while ( doMore() );
```

Jump Statements

Jump statements unconditionally transfer program control within a function.
Jump statements include the break, continue, and goto statements. The
following sections look at each jump statement in turn.

2.19   The break Statement

A break statement terminates the smallest enclosing while, do, for, or
switch statement. Execution resumes at the statement immediately following the terminated statement. For example, Array requires a member function that searches the array for the first occurrence of a particular value. If it
is found, the function returns its index; otherwise, the function returns −1.
This is implemented as follows:

```
#include "Array.h"

Array::search( Type val )
{ // val in ia? return index; otherwise, −1
    int loc = -1;
    for ( int ix = 0; ix < size; ++ix )
        if ( val == ia[ ix ] ) {
            loc = ix;
            break;
        }
    return loc;
}
```

If a match is found, there is no reason to continue looking. break terminates
the for loop. The return statement immediately following the for loop is
executed.

2.20 The continue Statement

A `continue` statement causes the current iteration of the nearest enclosing `while`, `do`, or `for` loop to terminate. In the case of the `while` and `do` loops, execution resumes with the loop control evaluation. In the case of the `for` loop, execution resumes with the evaluation of *expression-2*. Unlike the `break` statement, which terminates the loop, the `continue` statement terminates only the current iteration. For example, the following program fragment reads in a program text file one word at a time. Every word that begins with an underscore will be processed; otherwise, the current loop iteration is terminated:

```
while ( cin >> inBuf ) {
    if ( inBuf[0] != '_' )
        continue; // terminate iteration
    // ... process string ...
}
```

2.21 The goto Statement

If the `break` and `continue` statements did not exist, the programmer would need some way to jump out of a loop or `switch` statement. The `goto` statement provides just such a facility, one rarely used in programming today. The `goto` statement transfers program control unconditionally. The target destination of a `goto` is a label. The target label and `goto` must appear in the same function.

The syntactic form of the `goto` statement is

```
goto label;
```

where *label* is a user-supplied identifier. A label may be used only as the target of a `goto` and must be terminated by a colon.

A label may not immediately precede a closing right brace. A `null` statement following the label is the typical method of handling this constraint. For example,

```
    end: ; //null statement
}
```

A `goto` statement may not jump forward over a variable definition with an explicit initializer, such as

```
main() {
    goto end;
    // error: goto over initialized variable
    int ix = 10;
end: ;
}
```

or an implicit initializer — that is, a class object initialized by a constructor of
its class

```
#include "Array.h"
main() {
    goto end;
    // error: goto over implicit initialization
    Array ia;
end: ;
}
```

except if the initialized variable definition occurs in a block and the entire
block is jumped over. A backward jump over an initialized variable definition, however, is not constrained. For example,

```
#include "Array.h"
extern int getValue();
extern void processArray(Array&);

foo( int max_bound ) {
begin:
    int sz = getValue();
    if ( sz <= 0 )
        goto end;
    else
    if ( sz > max_bound )
        goto begin; // ok: backward jump

    { // ok: entire block jumped over
    Array myArray( sz );
    processArray( myArray );
    }
end: ;
}
```

Chapter 3: **Functions, Scope, and the Free Store**

A function can be thought of as a user-defined operation. In general, a function is represented by a name, not an operator. The operands of a function, referred to as its *arguments*, are specified in a comma-separated *argument list* enclosed in parentheses. The result of a function is referred to as its *return type*. A function that does not yield a value has a return type of void. The actual actions a function performs are specified in the *body* of the function. The function body is enclosed in braces ("{ }") and is sometimes referred to as a block. Here are some examples of functions:

```
inline int abs( int i )
{ // return the absolute value of i
    return( i < 0 ? -i : i );
}

inline int min( int v1, int v2 )
{ // return the smaller of two values
    return( v1 <= v2 ? v1 : v2 );
}

gcd( int v1, int v2 )
{ // return the greatest common denominator
    int temp;
    while ( v2 ) {
        temp = v2;
        v2 = v1 % v2;
        v1 = temp;
    }
    return v1;
}
```

A function is evaluated whenever the call operator ("()") is applied to the function's name. If the function expects to receive arguments, these arguments, referred to as the *actual arguments* of the call, are placed inside the call operator. Each argument is separated by a comma. This is referred to as *passing arguments* to a function. In the following example, main() calls abs() twice and min() and gcd() once each. It is defined in the file main.C.

111

```
#include <iostream.h>
#include "localMath.h"

main() {
  int i, j;

  // get values from standard input
  cout << "Value: "; cin >> i;
  cout << "Value: "; cin >> j;

  cout << "\nmin: " << min( i, j ) << endl;
  i = abs( i ); j = abs( j );
  cout << "gcd: " << gcd( i, j ) << endl;
  return 0;
}
```

A function call can cause one of two things to occur. If the function has been declared *inline*, the body of the function is expanded at the point of its call during compilation; otherwise, the function is invoked at run time. A function invocation causes program control to transfer to the function being invoked; execution of the currently active function is suspended. When evaluation of the called function is completed, the suspended function resumes execution at the point immediately following the call. Function invocation is managed on the program's *run-time stack*.

If a function is not declared to the program before it is used, a compile-time error will result.

The function definition, of course, serves as its declaration. However, a function may be defined only once in a program. Typically, the definition resides in its own program text file or in a text file containing it and other related functions. A function is usually used in files other than the one containing its definition. Therefore, an additional method of declaring a function is required.

The declaration of a function consists of its return type, name, and argument list. These three elements are referred to as the *function prototype*. A function prototype may appear multiple times in a file without penalty.

To compile main.C, abs(), min(), and gcd() must first be declared; otherwise, each of their calls within main() will generate a compile-time error. The three prototypes look as follows (the prototype need not specify an argument's name, only its type):

```
int abs( int );
int min( int, int );
int gcd( int, int );
```

Function prototypes (and the definition of inline functions) are best placed within header files. These header files can then be included whenever the declarations are required. This way, all files share a common declaration; should that declaration have to be modified, only that one instance need be changed.

The header file for our program might be defined as follows. Let's call it localMath.h.

```
int gcd( int, int );

inline int abs(int i) {
    return( i<0 ? -i : i );
}

inline int min(int v1,int v2) {
    return( v1<=v2 ? v1 : v2 );
}
```

ιpilation of the program is done as follows:

```
$ CC main.C gcd.C
```

ution of the program produces the following results:

```
Value: 15
Value: 123

in: 15
:d: 3
```

ιrsion

ι that calls itself, either directly or indirectly, is referred to as a *nction*. gcd(), for example, can be rewritten as a recursive func-

```
:d( int v1, int v2 )

  if (v2 == 0 )
      return v1;
  return rgcd( v2, v1%v2 );
```

function must always define a *stopping condition*; otherwise, the ll recur "forever." In the case of rgcd(), the stopping condition ler of 0.

d(15, 123);

3. Table 3.1 traces the execution.

v1	v2	return
15	123	rgcd(123, 15)
123	15	rgcd(15, 3)
15	3	rgcd(3, 0)
3	0	3

Table 3.1 Trace of rgcd(15,123)

The last call, rgcd(3,0), satisfies the stopping condition. It returns the greatest common denominator, 3. This value successively becomes the return value of each prior call. The value is said to *percolate* upward.

A recursive function is likely to run slower than its nonrecursive (or *itera- tive*) counterpart due to the overhead associated with the invocation of a function. The function code, however, is likely to be smaller and less com plex.

A factorial of a number is the product of its counting sequence beginnin with 1. The factorial of 5, for example, is 120; that is,

```
1 x 2 x 3 x 4 x 5 = 120
```

Computing the factorial of a number lends itself to a recursive solution:

```
unsigned long
factorial( int val ) {
    if ( val > 1 )
        return val * factorial( val-1 );
    return val;
}
```

The stopping condition in this case is when val contains a value of 1.

Exercise 3-1. Rewrite factorial() as an iterative function.

☐

Exercise 3-2. What would happen if the stopping condition were as follows

```
if ( val != 0 )
```

☐

Exercise 3-3. Why do you think the return value is specified as an unsigne long while the argument is of type int? ☐

3.2 Inline Functions

A question not as yet addressed directly is why min() was defined as a
function. The benefits include the following:

- It is generally easier to read a call of min() than an instance of the arithmetic if, especially when i and j are complex expressions.

- It is easier to change one localized instance than 300 occurrences within
  an application. For example, if it is decided the test should read

  ```
  i <= j
  ```

  finding every coded occurrence would be tedious and prone to error.

- There is a uniform semantics. Each test is guaranteed to be implemented
  the same.

- The function instance provides full type checking of its arguments. Type
  errors are caught at compile time.

- The function can be reused rather than rewritten by other applications.

There is, however, one serious drawback to making min() a function: It is
significantly slower. The two arguments must be copied, machine registers
must be saved, the program must branch to a new location. The handwritten
code is simply faster.

```
int minVal  =  i <= j  ? i : j;
int minVal2 = min( i, j );
```

Inline functions provide a solution. A function specified as inline is
expanded "in line" at each point in the program in which it is invoked. For
example,

```
int minVal2 = min( i, j );
```

is expanded during compilation into

```
int minVal2 = ( i <= j ) ? i : j;
```

The run-time overhead of making min() a function is removed.

min() is declared inline by specifying the inline keyword in its definition. Note, however, that the inline specification is only a recommendation
to the compiler. A recursive function, such as gcd(), for example, cannot be
completely expanded inline (although its first invocation may). A 1,200 line
function is also likely not to be expanded inline. In general, the inline mechanism is meant to optimize small, straight-line, frequently called functions. It
is of primary importance in its support of information hiding in the design of
abstract data types, such as the Array class introduced in Chapter 1.

3.3   Strong Type Checking

gcd() expects two arguments of type int. What happens if its arguments
are of type float or type char*? What happens if gcd() is passed only
one argument or more than two?

gcd()'s primary operation is performing modulo arithmetic on its two
values. Modulo arithmetic may not be applied to nonintegral operands.
Therefore the call

```
gcd( 3.14, 6.29 );
```

is likely to fail during execution. A worse result would be for it to return
some invalid value (worse because the invalid result may go unnoticed, or, if
found, may be quite difficult to trace). What could possibly be the result of
the following call?

```
gcd( "hello", "world" );
```

Or the accidental concatenation of two values in this call?

```
gcd( 24312 );
```

The only desirable result of attempting to compile either of the latter two
calls of gcd() is a compile-time error; any attempt to execute these calls
invites disaster. In C++, these two calls do result in compile-time error mes-
sages of the following general form:

```
// gcd( "hello", "world" )
error: invalid argument types (char*, char*) --
       expecting (int, int )

// gcd( 24312 )
error: missing value for argument two
```

What of the earlier call in which gcd() is passed two arguments of type
double? Flagging the call as a type error is correct but perhaps too severe.
Rather, the arguments are implicitly converted to int, fulfilling the type
requirements of the argument list. Because it is a narrowing conversion, a
warning is issued. The call becomes

```
gcd( 3, 6 );
```

which returns a value of 3.

C++ is a *strongly typed* language. Both the argument list and the return
type of every function call are *type checked* during compilation. If there is a
type mismatch between an actual type and a type declared in the function
prototype, an implicit conversion will be applied if possible. If an implicit
conversion is not possible or if the number of arguments is incorrect, a
compile-time error is issued.

The function prototype provides the compiler with the type information necessary for it to perform compile-time type checking. This is why a function may not be called until it has first been declared.†

3.4 Returning a Value

The return type of a function may be a predefined type, such as int or double, a derived type, such as int& or double*, a user-defined type, such as an enumeration or class, or void, signifying the absence of a return type. The following are examples of possible function return types:

```
class Date { /* definition */ };
enum Boolean { false, true };

Boolean look_up(int*,int);
double sqrt(double);
char *strcpy(char*, const char*);
Date &calendar(const char*);
void error(const char*, ...);
```

Neither an array nor a function can be specified as a return type. Rather, a pointer to either an array or a function is specified as a return type. For example,

```
// illegal: explicit array as return type
int[10] foo_bar();

// ok: pointer to an implicit array
int *foo_bar();
```

A function that does not return a value should declare a return type of void. A function without an explicit return value by default is assumed to return a value of type int.

The following two declarations of is_equal() are equivalent; both describe is_equal() as having a return type of int:

```
typedef unsigned long u_long;

int is_equal(u_long*,u_long*);
is_equal(u_long*,u_long*);
```

The return statement terminates the function currently executing. Program control is returned back to the function from which the now-terminated

---

†This type checking ability is considered so valuable, in fact, that the ANSI committee for the C language has adopted the C++ function prototype for the ANSI C language.

function was called. There are two forms of the return statement:

```
return;
return expression;
```

A return statement is not strictly necessary in a function that declares a return type of void. It is used primarily to effect a premature termination of the function. (This use of the return statement parallels the use of the break statement inside a loop.) An implicit return is effected upon completion of a function's final statement. For example,

```
void d_copy(double *src, double *dst, int sz)
{ /* copy ``src'' array into ``dst''
  * simplifying assumption: arrays are same size */

    // if either array pointer is empty, quit
    if (src == 0 || dst == 0) return;

    // if the two arrays are the same
    if (src == dst) return;

    // nothing to copy -- perhaps a warning
    // message or error is appropriate
    if (sz <= 0) return;

    // still here? then it's time to copy
    for (int ix = 0; ix < sz; ++ix)
            dst[ix] = src[ix];

    // no explicit return necessary
}
```

The second form of the return statement specifies the function result. It may be an arbitrarily complex expression; it may itself contain a function call. Implementation of factorial(), for example, contains the following return:

```
return val * factorial(val-1);
```

A value returning function — that is, a function not declared to have a return type of void— must return a value. The absence of a return value is a compile time error. (Some compilers — ours, for example — do not enforce this constraint on main().) Although the language cannot guarantee the correctness of a result, it does at least guarantee that a result is provided for each value returning function. The following program, for example, fails to compile because two of its exit points do not return a value.

```
enum Boolean {false, true};

Boolean is_equal(char *s1, char *s2)
{ /*
   * if s1 is equal to s2 and both
   * address memory, return true;
   * otherwise, return false
   */

   // program error: failure to return value
   if (s1==0 || s2==0) return;

   // same string: pointer equivalence
   if (s1 == s2) return true;

   // traverse string until either unequal
   // or terminating null is reached
   for ( ; *s1 && *s1 == *s2; ++s1, ++s2) ;

   // determine terminating condition of loop
   // if both equal, then null was reached
   if (*s1 == *s2) return true;

   // program error: failure to return value
   // when *s1 != *s2
}
```

If the type of the value returned does not exactly match the formal return type, an implicit conversion, if possible, is applied. If no implicit conversion is possible, an error is generated.

A function may return only one value. If the program's logic requires that multiple values be returned, the programmer might do any of the following:

- A variable defined outside a function is referred to as a *global variable*. A global variable is able to be accessed from within any function, provided it has been properly declared. The programmer can assign a second "return" value to a global variable. The advantage of this strategy is its simplicity. The disadvantage is that it is nonintuitive, by which is meant that it is unclear from a call of the function that this variable is being set. This makes it difficult for others programmers to understand or make changes to the code. This act of setting a global variable from within a function is referred to as a *side effect*.

- Return an aggregate data type that contains the multiple values. For this sort of use, a class in general is more flexible than an array. In addition, a programmer can return only a pointer to an array; the programmer may return a class object, pointer, or reference to a class.

- The formal arguments may be defined as either pointer or reference types. This will provide access to the lvalues of these arguments. They may then be directly set to contain some value. (Section 2.14 (page 97) presents a program example of using a reference argument to return a second value. Section 3.7 (page 127) presents a general discussion of reference arguments.)

3.5 The Function Argument List

The different functions of a program can communicate by two methods. (By *communicate* is meant a shared access to values.) One method makes use of global program variables; the second, of a function's formal argument list.

The general accessibility of a global variable from anywhere within the program is both its main benefit and its most significant liability. The visibility of a global variable makes it a convenient method of communication between the different parts of a program. The drawbacks to relying on global variables to communicate between functions are as follows:

- The functions that utilize the global variable depend on the existence and type of that global variable, making the reuse of that function in a different context much more difficult.

- If the program must be modified, global dependencies increase the likelihood of introducing bugs. Moreover, introducing local changes requires an understanding of the entire program.

- If a global variable gets an incorrect value, the entire program must be searched to determine where the error occurs; there is no localization.

- Recursion is more difficult to get right when the function makes use of a global variable.

The argument list provides an alternative method of communication between a function and the general program. The argument list, together with the function's return type, defines the *public interface* of the function. A program that limits its knowledge of a function to the function's public interface should not have to change if the function changes. Similarly, a function that is self-contained can be used across programs; it need not be limited to a specific application.

Omitting an argument or passing an argument of the wrong type are common sources of serious run-time program error in the pre-ANSI C language. With the introduction of strong type checking in C++, these interface errors are almost always caught at compile time.

The likelihood of error in passing arguments increases with the size of the argument list — some functions in FORTRAN take 32 arguments. As a general rule, eight arguments should be the maximum. If a function is written with larger argument lists, perhaps it is trying to do too much; a better design might be to divide it into two (or more) more specialized functions.

As an alternative to a large argument list, the programmer might define a class type to contain the argument values. This has two benefits:

1. The complexity of the argument list is significantly reduced.

2. Validity checks of the argument values can be performed by class member functions rather than inside the function. This reduces the size of the function and makes it easier to understand.

Argument List Syntax

The argument list of a function may not be omitted. A function that does not take any arguments can be represented either with an empty argument list or an argument list containing the single keyword void. For example, both of the following declarations of fork() are equivalent:

```
int fork();        // implicit void
int fork( void ); // equivalent declaration
```

The argument list is referred to as the *signature* of a function because the argument list is often used to distinguish one instance of a function from another. The name and signature of a function uniquely identify it. Section 4.1 (page 167) on overloading functions discusses this idea more fully.

The signature consists of a comma-separated list of argument types. A name may optionally follow each type specifier. The shorthand comma-separated type declaration syntax is an error within the signature. For example,

```
min( int v1, v2 ); // error
min( int v1, int v2 ); // ok
```

No two argument names appearing in a signature may be the same. The argument name allows the argument to be accessed from within the body of the function. Therefore the argument name is unnecessary in a function declaration. If present, its name should serve as a documentation aid. For example,

```
print( int *array, int size );
```

There is no language-imposed penalty for specifying a different name for an argument in the declaration(s) and definition of a function. The human reader of the program, however, may become confused.

A Special Signature: Ellipses ...

It is sometimes impossible to list the type and number of all the arguments that might be passed to a function. In these cases, ellipses ("...") can be specified within the function signature.

Ellipses suspend type checking. Their presence tells the compiler that zero or more arguments may follow and that the types of the arguments are unknown. Ellipses may take either of two forms:

```
foo( arg_list, ... );
foo( ... );
```

In the first form, the comma following the argument list is optional.

The standard C library output function `printf()` is an example in which ellipses are necessary. `printf()` always takes a character string as its first argument. Whether it takes additional arguments is determined by its first argument, referred to as a format string. Metacharacters, set off by %, indicate the presence of additional arguments. For example,

```
printf( "hello, world\n" );
```

takes a single string argument. However,

```
printf( "hello, %s\n", userName );
```

takes two arguments. The % indicates the presence of a second argument; the s indicates that the type of the argument is *string*.

`printf()` is declared in C++ as follows:

```
printf( const char* ... );
```

This requires that every call of `printf()` be passed a first argument of type `char*`. After that, anything goes.

The following two declarations are *not* equivalent:

```
void f();
void f( ... );
```

In the first instance, `f()` is declared as a function that takes no arguments; in the second, `f()` is declared as a function that may take zero arguments or more. The calls

```
f( someValue );
f( cnt, a, b, c );
```

are legal invocations of the second declaration only. The call

```
f();
```

is a legal invocation of both functions.

A Special Signature: Default Initializers

A default value is a value that, although not universally applicable, is judged to be appropriate in a majority of cases. A default value frees the individual from having to attend to every small detail. Under the UNIX system, for example, by default each text file created by the author has read and write permission for the author but only read permission for all others. If the author wishes to either loosen or tighten the permissions on his or her files, the UNIX system supports a simple mechanism by which the author can modify or replace the default values.

A function may specify a default value for one or more of its arguments using initialization syntax within the signature. A function to create and initialize a two-dimensional character array intended to simulate a terminal screen, for example, can provide default values for the height, width, and background character of the screen:

```
char * screenInit( int height = 24, int width = 80,
                   char background = ' ' );
```

A function that provides default argument initializers can be invoked with or without a corresponding actual argument. If an argument is provided, it overrides the default value; otherwise, the default value is used. Each of the following calls of screenInit() is correct:

```
char *cursor;

// equivalent to screenInit(24,80,' ')
cursor = screenInit();

// equivalent to screenInit(66,80,' ')
cursor = screenInit( 66 );

// equivalent to screenInit(66,256,' ')
cursor = screenInit(66, 256);

cursor = screenInit(66, 256, '#');
```

Note that it is impossible to supply a character value for background without also supplying height and width values. Arguments to the call are resolved *positionally*. Part of the work of designing a function with default initializers is the arrangement of arguments within the signature such that those most likely to take a user-specified value occur first. The design assumption within screenInit() (possibly arrived at through experimentation) is that height is the value most likely to be supplied by the user.

A function may specify default initializers for all or only a subset of its arguments. The rightmost uninitialized argument must be supplied with a default initializer before any argument to its left may be supplied. Again, this is because arguments to a call of the function are resolved positionally. A default argument initializer is not limited to a constant expression.

An argument can have its default initializer specified only once in a file. The following, for example, is illegal:

```
ff( int = 0 ); // in ff.h

#include "ff.h"
ff( int i = 0 ) { ... } // error
```

By convention, the default initializer is specified in the function declaration contained in the public header file, and not in the function definition.

Succeeding declarations of a function may specify additional default initializers — a useful method of customizing a general function for a specific application. The UNIX system library function chmod() changes the protection level of a file. Its function prototype is found in the system header file stdlib.h. It is declared as follows:

```
chmod( char *filePath, int protMode );
```

where protMode represents a file-protection mode and filePath represents the name and path location of the file. A particular application is always changing a file's protection mode to *read-only*. Rather than indicate that each time, chmod() is redeclared to supply the value by default:

```
#include <stdlib.h>
chmod( char *filePath, int protMode=0444 );
```

Given the following function prototype declared in a header file:

```
ff( int a, int b, int c = 0 ); // ff.h
```

how can we redeclare ff() in our file to provide b with a default initializer? The following is illegal — it respecifies c's default initializer:

```
#include "ff.h"
ff( int a, int b = 0, int c = 0 ); // error
```

The following also seems illegal, but in fact is the correct redeclaration:

```
#include "ff.h"
ff( int a, int b = 0, int c ); // ok
```

At the point of this redeclaration of ff(), b is the rightmost argument without a default initializer. Therefore, the rule that the default initializer be assigned positionally beginning with the rightmost argument has not been violated. In fact, we can now redeclare ff() a third time:

```
#include "ff.h"
ff( int a, int b = 0, int c ); // ok
ff( int a = 0, int b, int c ); // ok
```

3.6 Argument Passing

Functions are allocated storage on a structure referred to as the program's *run-time stack*. That storage remains on the stack until the function is terminated. At that point, the storage is automatically popped. The entire storage area of the function is referred to as the *activation record*.

The argument list of a function describes its *formal arguments*. Each formal argument is provided storage within the activation record. The storage size of an argument is determined by its type specifier. The expressions found between the parentheses of a function call are referred to as the *actual arguments* of the call. Argument passing is the process of initializing the storage of the formal arguments by the actual arguments.

The default initialization method of argument passing in C++ is to copy the rvalues of the actual arguments into the storage of the formal arguments. This is referred to as *pass-by-value*.

Under pass-by-value, the function never accesses the actual arguments of the call. The values the function manipulates are its own local copies; these are stored on the stack. In general, changes made to these values are not reflected in the values of the actual arguments. Once the function terminates and the stack of the function's activation record is popped, these local values are lost.

Under pass-by-value, the contents of the actual arguments are not changed. This means that a programmer need not save and restore argument values when making a function call. Without a pass-by-value mechanism, each formal argument not declared const would have to be considered potentially altered with each function call. Pass-by-value has the least potential for harm and requires the least work by the general user. Pass-by-value is a reasonable default mechanism for argument passing.

Pass-by-value, however, is not suitable for every function. Situations under which pass-by-value is unsuitable include the following:

- When a large class object must be passed as an argument. The time and space costs to allocate and copy the class object onto the stack are often too high for real-world program applications.

- When the values of the argument must be modified. The function swap() is an example of where the user wants to change the values of the actual arguments but cannot do so under pass-by-value.

```
void swap( int v1, int v2 ) {
    int tmp = v2;
    v2 = v1;
    v1 = tmp;
}
```

swap() exchanges the local copies of its arguments. The actual variables passed to swap() are unchanged. This is illustrated in the following program, which calls swap:

```
#include <iostream.h>
void swap(int,int);

main() {
    int i = 10;
    int j = 20;

    cout << "Before swap():\ti: "
         << i << "\tj: " << j << endl;

    swap( i, j );

    cout << "After swap():\ti: "
         << i << "\tj: " << j << endl;
    return 0;
}
```

Compiling and executing this program results in the following output:

```
Before swap():   i: 10    j: 20
After swap():    i: 10    j: 20
```

Two alternatives to pass-by-value are available to the programmer. In one instance, the formal arguments are declared as pointers. swap(), for example, could be rewritten as follows:

```
void pswap( int *v1, int *v2 ) {
    int tmp = *v2;
    *v2 = *v1;
    *v1 = tmp;
}
```

main() must be modified to declare and call pswap(). The programmer must now pass the address of the two objects, not the objects themselves:

```
pswap( &i, &j );
```

Compiling and executing this revised program shows the output to be correct:

```
// use of pointers allows programmer to
// access the actual arguments to the call

Before swap():   i: 10    j: 20
After swap():    i: 20    j: 10
```

The second alternative to pass-by-value is to declare the formal arguments to be type reference. swap(), for example, could be rewritten as follows:

```
void rswap( int &v1, int &v2 ) {
      int tmp = v2;
      v2 = v1;
      v1 = tmp;
}
```

The call of rswap() in main() looks the same as the original call of swap():

```
rswap( i, j );
```

Compiling and executing the program will show that the values of i and j are properly exchanged.

3.7 A Reference Argument

The declaration of an argument as a reference overrides the default pass-by-value argument passing mechanism. The function receives the lvalue of the actual argument rather than a copy of the argument itself. When is it appropriate to specify an argument as a reference? In a case such as rswap() where it is necessary to change the actual arguments. With pass-by-value, the function manipulates local copies of its arguments. A common situation for which references are used is to pass back additional results from the call of a function.

For example, look_up() is a function that searches for a particular value in an array. If found, look_up() returns the index into the array; otherwise, it returns −1 indicating that the value is not present. In the case of multiple occurrences, the index to the first occurrence is returned. In addition, making use of a reference argument, look_up() also returns a count of the number of occurrences.

```
// occurs is made a reference argument in order that
// it may contain a second return value of look_up

int look_up(const int *array, int size,
            int value,      // is value in array?
            int &occurs)    // how many times?
{
    int index = -1;
    occurs = 0;

    for ( int ix=0; ix < size; ++ix )
        if ( array[ix] == value )
        {
            if ( index == -1 )
                index = ix;
            ++occurs;
        }

    return index;
}
```

A second circumstance under which it makes sense to declare an argument as a reference is when passing large class objects to a function. Under pass-by-value, the entire object is copied with each call; as a reference, only the address of the argument is copied. For example,

```
class Huge { public: double stuff[1000]; };
extern int total( const Huge& );

main() {
    Huge table[ 1000 ];
    // ... initialize table

    int sum = 0;
    for ( int ix=0; ix < 1000; ++ix )
        sum += total( table[ix] );

    // ...
}
```

Whenever a reference (or pointer) argument is not intended to be modified within the function, it is a good practice to declare the argument as const. This allows the compiler to prevent unintentional changes from occurring, especially in a chain of function calls to which the argument is passed. For example, the following program fragment violates the *constness* of the argument to bar() and is flagged by the compiler as an error.

```
class X;
extern int foo_bar(X&);

int foo(const X& xx) {
    // error: const passed to nonconst
    return foo_bar(xx);
}

int bar(const X& x) {
    int ival = foo( x );
    // ...
    return ival;
}
```

For this program to compile, either the signature of foo_bar() must change — either of the following are acceptable:

```
extern int foo_bar(const X&);
extern int foo_bar(X); // pass-by-value
```

or the argument passed to it needs to be a copy of xx that foo_bar() is permitted to change:

```
int foo( const X &xx) {
    // ...
    X x2 = xx; // copy values
    return foo_bar(x2); // ok
};
```

A pointer argument can also be declared as a reference should the programmer wish to modify the pointer itself rather than the object addressed by the pointer. For example, here is a function to swap two pointers:

```
void prswap( int *&v1, int *&v2 ) {
    int *tmp = v2;
    v2 = v1;
    v1 = tmp;
}
```

The declaration

```
int *&p1;
```

should be read from right to left: p1 is a reference to a pointer to an object of type int. The modified implementation of main() will look as follows:

```
#include <iostream.h>
void prswap( int *&v1, int *&v2 );

main() {
    int i = 10;
    int j = 20;

    int *pi = &i;
    int *pj = &j;

    cout << "Before swap():\tpi: "
        << *pi << "\tpj: " << *pj << endl;

    prswap( pi, pj );
    cout << "After swap():\tpi: "
        << *pi << "\tpj: " << *pj << endl;
    return 0;
}
```

When compiled and executed, the program generates the following output:

```
Before swap():  pi: 10  pj: 20
After swap():   pi: 20  pj: 10
```

By default, the value returned by a function is also passed by value. For large class objects, a reference (or pointer) return type is more efficient. However, the programmer should be aware of the following two potential pitfalls:

1. Returning a reference to a local object. The local object goes out of scope with the termination of the function. The reference is left aliasing undefined memory. For example,

```
// problem: returning a reference to a local object
String& concat(const String &s1, const String &s2)
{
    String result = s1;
    result += s2;
    // oops: result exits scope after return
    return result;
}
```

In this case, the return type should be declared as a nonreference:

```
String concat( ...
```

2. The value returned is an actual lvalue. Any modification of it changes the actual object being returned. For example,

```
int &get_val(int *ia, int ix) {
    return ia[ix];
}

int ar[] = { 0, 1, 2, 3 };
main() {
    // increments ar[0] to 1
    get_val(ar,0)++;
    // ...
}
```

To prevent the unintended modification of a reference return value, the return value should be declared constant:

```
const int &get_val( ...
```

An example of returning an lvalue in order to modify the actual object being returned is presented in Chapter 6 in the discussion of overloading a class subscript operator.

3.8 An Array Argument

Arrays in C++ are never passed by value. Rather, an array is passed as a pointer to its zeroth element. For example,

```
void putValues( int[ 10 ] );
```

is treated by the compiler as having been declared as

```
void putValues( int* );
```

The array's size is not relevant to the declaration of the formal argument. The following three declarations are equivalent:

```
// three equivalent declarations of putValues
void putValues( int* );
void putValues( int[] );
void putValues( int[ 10 ] );
```

This has two implications for the programmer:

- The changes to an array argument within the called function are made to the actual array of the call, not to a local copy. In cases where the array of the call must remain unchanged, programmers will themselves need to simulate pass-by-value.

- The size of an array is not part of its argument type. The function being passed an array does not know its actual size and neither does the compiler. There is no checking of array sizes. For example,

```
void putValues ( int[ 10 ] ); // treated as int*
main() {
    int i, j[ 2 ];
    putValues ( &i ); // ok: int*; run-time error
    putValues ( j );  // ok: int*; run-time error
    return 0;
}
```

The extent of the argument type checking confirms that both calls of
putValues() are provided with an argument of type int*.

By convention, string character arrays encode their termination point
with a null character. All other array types, however, including character
arrays, which wish to handle embedded nulls, must in some way make their
size known when passed as formal arguments to a function. One common
method is to provide an additional argument that contains the array's size.

```
void putValues ( int[], int size );
main() {
    int i, j[ 2 ];
    putValues ( &i, 1 );
    putValues ( j , 2 );
    return 0;
}
```

putValues() prints out the values of an array in the following format:

```
( 10 )< 0, 1, 2, 3, 4, 5, 6, 7, 8, 9 >
```

where 10 represents the size of the array. Here is an implementation:

```
#include <iostream.h>

const lineLength = 12; // elements to a line
void putValues ( int *ia, int sz )
{
    cout << "( " << sz << " )< ";
    for ( int i = 0; i < sz; ++i ) {
        if ( i % lineLength == 0 && i )
            cout << "\n\t"; // line filled
        cout << ia[ i ];

        // separate all but last element
        if ( i % lineLength != lineLength-1 &&
            i != sz-1 )
                cout << ", ";
    }
    cout << " >\n";
}
```

Although this implementation works, it unfortunately works only for arrays of integers. A second function is needed to handle an array of doubles, a third for an array of longs. A better implementation of putValues() is to define it as a template function. A template function is one whose code remains invariant across a wide set of different argument types. Template functions are introduced in Chapter 4. In that discussion, a template implementation of putValues() is presented.

A multidimensional array declared as a formal argument must specify the size of all its dimensions beyond that of its first. For example,

```
void putValues( int matrix[][10], int rowSize );
```

declares matrix to be a two-dimensional array. Each matrix row consists of 10 column elements. matrix may equivalently be declared as

```
int (*matrix)[10];
```

This declares matrix to be a pointer to an array of 10 elements.

```
matrix += 1;
```

will advance matrix the size of its second dimension and point it to its next row — a reason why the size of the second dimension must be supplied. The parentheses around matrix are necessary because of the higher precedence of the index operator.

```
int *matrix[ 10 ];
```

declares matrix to be an array of 10 integer pointers.

3.9 Program Scope

Earlier it was stated that every identifier in a program must be unique. This does not mean, however, that a name can be used only once in a program: a name can be reused provided that there is some *context* by which to distinguish between the different instances. One context is the signature of a function. In the last section, for example, putValues() is used as the name of two functions. Each has a unique, distinguishing signature.

A second, more general context is *scope*. C++ supports three kinds of scope: *file* scope, *local* scope, and *class* scope. File scope is that portion of the program text that is not contained within either a function or a class definition. File scope is the outermost scope of a program. It is said to *enclose* both local and class scope.

In general, local scope is that portion of the program text contained within the definition of a function. Each function is considered to represent a distinct local scope. Within a function, each compound statement (or block) containing one or more declaration statements maintains an associated local scope. Local block scopes can be nested. The argument list is treated as being within the local scope of the function. The argument list is *not* considered to be within the enclosing file scope.

Section 5.8 (page 257) presents a full discussion of class scope. There are two salient points to make now:

1. Each class is considered to represent a distinct class scope.

2. Member functions are treated as being within the scope of their class.

A global variable without an explicit initializer is guaranteed by the language to have its storage initialized to 0. Thus, in the following two definitions, both i and j have an initial value of 0:

```
int i = 0;
int j;
```

The value of an uninitialized local variable is undefined.

A name may be reused in distinct scopes without penalty. In the following program fragment, for example, there are four unique instances of i a:

```
// swap element ix with jx in array ia
void swap( int *ia, int ix, int jx );

// sort array ia of size elements
void sort( int *ia, int size );

// display the array on standard output
void putValues( int *ia, int size );

const size = 10;
int ia[ size ] = { 4, 7, 0, 9, 2, 5, 8, 3, 6, 1 };

main()
{
    int ix, jx;

    // ... set ix, jx

    swap( ia, ix, jx );
    sort( ia, size );
    putValues( ia, size );
    return 0;
}
```

Every variable has an associated scope which, together with its name, uniquely identifies it. A variable is visible to the program only from within its scope. A local variable, for example, may be accessed only within the function within which it is defined — the reason why its name may be reused within other scopes without conflict.

A variable defined at file scope is visible to the entire program. There are three cases under which its visibility is constrained:

1. A local variable may reuse a global variable's name. The global variable is now said to be hidden by the local instance. What if the programmer must access the now-hidden global instance? The scope operator provides a solution.

2. A global variable is defined in one file but also used in a second file or multiple files. How does the programmer declare the variable in these other files? Use of the `extern` keyword provides a solution.

3. Two global variables defined in separate program files reuse the same name but are intended to refer to different program entities. Each by itself compiles cleanly. When compiled together, the variable is flagged as being multiply defined, and compilation stops. How does the programmer compile the program without having to change all the instances of one of the variables? Use of the `static` keyword provides a solution.

These three cases are the subject of the following three subsections.

The Scope Operator

The scope operator ("`::`") provides a solution to the problem of accessing a hidden global variable. An identifier prefixed with the scope operator will access the global instance. In the following example, contrived to illustrate how the scope operator may be used, the function computes a Fibonacci series. There are two definitions of the variable `max`. The global instance indicates the maximum value for the series. The local instance indicates the desired length of the series. (Recall, the formal arguments of a function occur within the function's local scope.) Both instances of `max` must be accessed within the function. Every unqualified reference to `max`, however, refers to the local instance. In order to access the global instance, the scope operator must be used — `::max`. Here is an implementation:

```
#include <iostream.h>
const max = 65000;
const lineLength = 12;

void fibonacci( int max )
{
    if ( max < 2 ) return;
    cout << "0 1 ";

    int v1 = 0, v2 = 1, cur;
    for ( int ix = 3; ix <= max; ++ix ) {
        cur = v1 + v2;
        if (cur > ::max) break;
        cout << cur << " ";
        v1 = v2;
        v2 = cur;
        if (ix % lineLength == 0) cout << endl;
    }
}
```

Here is an implementation of `main()` to exercise the function:

```
#include <iostream.h>
void fibonacci( int );

main() {
    cout << "Fibonacci Series: 16\n";
    fibonacci( 16 );
    return 0;
}
```

Compiling and executing the program produces the following output:

```
Fibonacci Series: 16
0 1 1 2 3 5 8 13 21 34 55 89
144 233 377 610
```

extern Variables

The `extern` keyword provides a method of declaring a variable without defining it. Similar in effect to the function prototype, it says that elsewhere in the program an identifier of this type is defined.

```
extern int i;
```

is a "pledge" to the program that elsewhere there exists the definition

```
int i;
```

The `extern` declaration does not cause storage to be allocated. It may appear multiple times within a program. Typically, however, it is declared once in a public header file to be included when necessary.

The `extern` keyword may also be specified in a function prototype. Its only effect is to make the implicit "defined elsewhere" nature of the prototype explicit. It takes the following form:

```
extern void putValues( int*, int );
```

The declaration of an extern variable with an explicit initializer is treated as a definition of that variable. Storage is allocated and any subsequent definitions of that variable in the same scope is flagged as an error. For example,

```
extern const bufSize = 512; // definition
```

static Global Variable

A global identifier preceded by the keyword `static` will be invisible outside the file in which it is defined. Variables and functions only of interest within the file in which they are defined are declared static. In this way, they cannot clash with global identifiers in other files that accidentally reuse the same names.

Static identifiers at file scope are spoken of as having *internal linkage*. (Nonstatic global identifiers are said to have *external linkage*.) By default, inline functions and `const` definitions have static linkage.

Here is an example of when a function might be declared static. The file is `sort.C`. It contains three functions: `bsort()`, `qsort()`, and `swap()`. `bsort()` and `qsort()` provide for sorting an array in ascending order. `swap()` is invoked by both functions but is not intended for general use. For our example, it is declared `static`. (It may alternatively be declared `inline`.)

`qsort()` is an implementation of C.A.R Hoare's *quicksort* algorithm. Let's look at the function in detail. `low` and `high` represent the lower and upper bounds of the array. `qsort()`, a recursive function, applies itself to progressively smaller subarrays. The stopping condition is when the lower bound is equal to (or greater than) the upper bound (line 3).

`elem` (line 6), is referred to as the *partition element*. All array elements less than `elem` are moved to the left of `elem`; all elements greater are moved to the right. The array is now partitioned into two subarrays. `qsort()` is recursively applied to each (lines 18 – 19).

The purpose of the `for(;;)` loop is to perform the partition (lines 8 – 15). At each iteration of the loop, `lo` is advanced to index the first element of `ia` greater than or equal to `elem` (line 9). Similarly, `hi` is decremented to

```
static void swap ( int *ia, int i, int j ) {
    int tmp = ia[ i ];
    ia[ i ] = ia[ j ];
    ia[ j ] = tmp;
}


void bsort( int* ia, int sz )
{ // bubble sort
    for ( int ix = 0; ix < sz; ix++ )
        for ( int j = ix+1; j < sz; j++ )
            if ( ia[ix] > ia[j] )
                swap( ia, ix, j );
}
```

```
1   void qsort( int *ia, int low, int high ) {
2   // stopping condition for recursion
3       if ( low < high ) {
4           int lo = low;
5           int hi = high + 1;
6           int elem = ia[ low ];
7
8           for (;;) {
9               while ( ia[ ++lo ] < elem ) ;
10              while ( ia[ --hi ] > elem ) ;
11
12              if ( lo < hi )
13                  swap( ia, lo, hi );
14              else break;
15          }  // end, for(;;)

16
17      swap( ia, low, hi );
18      qsort( ia, low, hi - 1 );
19      qsort( ia, hi + 1, high );
20      } // end, if ( low < high )
21  }
```

index the "endmost" element of ia equal to or less than elem (line 10). If lo is no longer less than hi, the elements have been partitioned and we break the loop; otherwise, the elements are swapped and the next loop iteration begins (lines 12 – 14).

Although the array has been partitioned, elem is still located at ia[low]. The swap() on line 17 places elem in its final position in the array. qsort() is then applied to the two subarrays.

The following implementation of main() to execute the two sorting functions utilizes putValues() to print the arrays.

```
#include <iostream.h>
#include "sort.h"  /* bsort(), qsort() */
#include "print.h" /* putValues() */

// for illustration, predefine arrays
int ia1 [10]={ 26, 5, 37, 1, 61, 11, 59, 15, 48, 19};
int ia2 [16]={ 503, 87, 512, 61, 908, 170, 897, 275,
        653, 426, 154, 509, 612, 677, 765, 703 };

main() {
  cout << "Bubblesort of first array" << endl;
  bsort( ia1, 10 );
  putValues( ia1, 10 );

  cout << "\nQuicksort of second array" << endl;
  qsort( ia2, 0, 15 );
  putValues( ia2, 16 );
  return 0;
}
```

When compiled and executed, the program produces the following output:

```
Bubblesort of first array
( 10 )< 1, 5, 11, 15, 19, 26, 37, 48
        59, 61 >

Quicksort of second array
( 16 )< 61, 87, 154, 170, 275, 426, 503, 509
        512, 612, 653, 677, 703, 765, 897, 908 >
```

3.10 Local Scope

In general, local variables are allocated storage at the time a function is invoked; they are said to *come into* or *enter scope*. This storage is allocated from the program's run-time stack and is part of the activation record of the function. An uninitialized local variable will contain a random bit pattern left over from a previous use of that storage. Its value is spoken of as *undefined*.

Upon termination of the function, its activation record is popped from the run-time stack. In effect, the storage associated with the local variables is deallocated. The variables are said to *go out of* or *exit scope* upon termination of the function. Any values they contain are lost.

Because the storage associated with local variables is deallocated upon termination of the function, the address of a local variable should never be passed outside its scope. Here is an example:

```
char *globalString;

char *trouble() {
    char localString[ 24 ];
    // ... do something

    return localString; // dangerous
}
```

```
main() { globalString = trouble(); ... }
```

globalString is set to the address of the local character array, localString. Unfortunately, localString's storage is deallocated on completion of trouble(). On the reentry into main(), globalString is addressing technically unallocated memory.

When the address of a local variable is passed outside its scope, it is referred to as a *dangling reference*. This is a serious programmer error because the contents of the addressed memory are unpredictable. If the bits at that address are somehow relevant, the program may run to completion but provide invalid results.

Local scopes may be nested. Any block that contains a declaration statement maintains its own local scope. For example, the following defines two levels of local scope, performing a binary search of a sorted array.

```
const notFound = -1; // global scope

int binSearch( int *ia, int sz, int val )
{ // local scope: level #1
    int low = 0;
    int high = sz - 1;

    while ( low <= high )
    { // local scope: level #2
        int mid = (low+high)/2;
        if (val == ia[ mid ]) return mid;
        if (val < ia[ mid ])
            high = mid-1;
        else low = mid+1;
    }
    return notFound; // local scope: level #1
}
```

The while loop of binSearch() defines a nested local scope. It contains one identifier, the integer mid, enclosed by binSearch()'s local scope. It contains the argument members ia, sz, and val, plus the local variables high and low. The global scope encloses both local scopes. It contains one identifier, the integer constant notFound.

When a reference is made to an identifier, the immediate scope in which the reference occurs is searched. If a definition is found, the reference is resolved; if not, the enclosing scope is searched. This process continues until either the reference is resolved or global scope has been exhausted. If the latter occurs, the reference is flagged as an error. Use of the scope operator ("::") limits the search to global scope.

A `for` loop permits the definition of variables within its control structure. For example,

```
for ( int i = 0; i < arrayBound; ++i )
```

Variables defined inside the `for` loop control are entered into the same scope as the `for` statement itself, as if the `for` statement were written like this:

```
int i;
for ( i = 0; i < arrayBound; ++i )
```

This permits the programmer to access the control variables after completion of the loop. For example,

```
const notFound = -1;

findElement ( int *ia, int sz, int val )
{
    for ( int ix = 0; ix < sz; ++ix )
        if ( ia[ ix ] == val ) break;

    if ( ix == sz ) return notFound;
    return ix;
}
```

This does not permit the programmer, however, to reuse the name of control variables within the same scope. For example,

```
fooBar ( int *ia, int sz ) {
    for (int i=0; i<sz; ++i) ... // defines i
    for (int i=0; i<sz; ++i) ... // error: i redefined
    for (i=0; i<sz; ++i) ...      // ok
}
```

static Local Variables

It is desirable to declare an identifier as a local variable whenever its use is confined to a function or a nested block. When the value of that variable must persist across invocations, however, an ordinary local variable cannot be used. Its value will be discarded each time it exits scope.

The solution in this case is to declare the identifier as static. A *static local variable* has permanent storage. Its value persists across invocations; its access remains limited to its local scope. For example, here is a version of gcd() that traces the depth of its recursion using a static local variable:

```
#include <iostream.h>

traceGcd( int v1, int v2 )
{
    static int depth = 1;
    cout << "depth #" << depth++ << endl;

    if (v2 == 0 ) {
        depth = 1;
        return v1;
    }
    return traceGcd( v2, v1%v2 );
}
```

The value associated with the static local variable depth persists across invocations of traceGcd(). The initialization is performed only once. The following small program exercises traceGcd():

```
#include <iostream.h>
extern traceGcd(int, int);

main() {
    int rslt = traceGcd( 15, 123 );
    cout << "gcd of (15,123): " << rslt << endl;
    return 0;
}
```

When compiled and executed, the program generates the following results:

```
depth #1
depth #2
depth #3
depth #4
gcd of (15,123): 3
```

The following program illustrates the danger of not initializing local variables. Section 1.2 (page 25) presents the output of its execution.

```
#include <iostream.h>

const iterations = 2;
void func() {
     int value1, value2; // uninitialized
     static int depth = 0;

     if ( depth < iterations )
          { ++depth; func(); }
     else depth = 0;

     cout << "\nvalue1:\t" << value1;
     cout << "\tvalue2:\t" << value2;
     cout << "\tsum:\t" << value1 + value2;
}

main() {
     for (int ix=0; ix<iterations; ++ix) func();
     return 0;
}
```

register Local Variables

Local variables heavily used within a function can be specified with the key-word `register`. If possible, the compiler will load the variable into a machine register. If it cannot, the variable remains in memory. Array indices and pointers occurring within a loop are good candidates for register variables.

```
for (register int ix=0; ix<sz; ++ix) ...
for (register char *p=str; p; ++p) ...
```

A formal argument can also be declared as a register variable:

```
int find( register char *str, char ch ) {
    while ( *str )
        if ( *str++ == ch ) return 1;
    return 0;
}
```

Register variables may increase the speed of a function if the variables selected are used heavily.

3.11   Free Store Allocation

Every program is provided with a pool of unallocated memory that it may utilize during execution. This pool of available memory is referred to as the program's *free store*, and by using it, the Array class can defer allocation of its array member until run time. Let's reexamine how this is done:

```
#include <assert.h>
IntArray::IntArray( int sz )
{
    /* allocate an integer array of 'size' elements
     * new returns a pointer to this array or 0
     * 0 indicates the program has exhausted its
     * available memory: a generally fatal error
     */
    size = sz;
    ia = new int[size];
    assert( ia != 0 );

    for ( int ix=0; ix < sz; ++ix )
        ia[ix] = 0;
}
```

Array has two data members, `size` and `ia`. `size` contains a count of the number of elements of the array. `ia`, an integer pointer, addresses the array allocated on the free store. One aspect of free store memory is that it is unnamed. Objects allocated on the free store are manipulated indirectly through pointers. A second aspect of the free store is that the allocated memory is uninitialized. The purpose of the `for` loop is to initialize each element of `ia` to 0.

Free store memory is allocated by applying operator `new` to a type specifier, including that of a class name. Either a single object or an array of objects can be allocated. For example,

```
int *pi = new int;
```

allocates one object of type `int`. Operator `new` returns a pointer to that object to which `pi` is initialized.

```
Array *pia = new Array( 1024 );
```

allocates an Array class object. After the memory for a class object is allocated, a class constructor, if defined, is automatically invoked to initialize that memory. The parentheses following the class name, if present, supply arguments to the class constructor. In this case, `pia` is initialized with the address of an Array class object of 1024 elements. If the parentheses are not present, as in

```
Array *pia2 = new Array;
```

then the class must either define a constructor that does not require arguments or else define no constructors at all.

An array is allocated from the free store by following the type specifier
with a bracket-enclosed dimension. The dimension can be an arbitrarily
complex expression. Operator new returns a pointer to the first element of
the array. For example,

```
#include <string.h>
char *copyStr( const char *s )
{
    char *ps = new char[ strlen(s) + 1 ];
    strcpy( ps, s );
    return ps;
}
```

Arrays of class objects can also be allocated. For example,

```
Array *pia = new Array[ someSize ];
```

allocates an array of Array objects of some size. (Arrays of class objects are
examined in detail in Chapter 6.)

The allocation of memory at run time is referred to as *dynamic memory
allocation*. We say that the array addressed by pia is allocated *dynamically*.
The storage of pia itself, however, is allocated during compilation — the
reason why pia can be a named object. Allocation that occurs during compilation is spoken of as *static memory allocation*. We say that the pointer pia is
allocated *statically*.

An object's lifetime — that period of time during program execution
when storage is bound to the object — is referred to as an object's *extent*.
Variables defined at file scope are spoken of as having *static extent*. Storage
is allocated before program start-up and remains bound to the variable
throughout program execution. Variables defined at local scope are spoken
of as having *local extent*. Storage is allocated at each entry into the local
scope; on exit, the storage is freed up. A static local variable exhibits static
extent.

Objects allocated on the free store are spoken of as having *dynamic extent*.
Storage allocated through the use of operator new remains bound to an
object until explicitly deallocated by the programmer. Explicit deallocation is
achieved by applying operator delete to a pointer addressing the dynamic
object. Let's look at an example.

Array::grow() expands the array ia addresses by half its size. First a
new, larger array is allocated. Then the values of the old array are copied and
the additional elements are initialized to 0. Finally, the old array is explicitly
deallocated by applying operator delete.

```
void Array::grow()
{
   Type *oldia = ia;
   int oldSize = size;

   size += size/2 + 1;
   ia = new Type[ size ];

   // copy elements of old array into new
   int ix = 0;
   for ( ; ix < oldSize; ++ix )
        ia[ ix ] = oldia[ ix ];

   // initialize remaining elements to 0
   for ( ; ix < size; ++ix ) ia[ ix ] = 0;

   delete oldia;
}
```

oldia has local extent; it is deallocated automatically upon termination of the function. The array oldia addresses, however, is not. Its extent is dynamic and persists across local scope boundaries. If the array oldia addresses is not explicitly deallocated using operator delete, the memory bound to the array is lost to the program.

```
   delete oldia;
```

returns the storage to the free store.

When deleting an array of class objects, an empty bracket pair ([]) must be placed between the delete operator and pointer to the array of class objects. For example, given the following array,

```
   Array *pia = new Array[ size ];
```

the delete operator applied to pia looks as follows:

```
   delete [] pia;
```

The empty bracket pair is necessary in order that the delete operator knows to apply the class destructor to each element of the array.

Operator delete must be applied only to memory that has been allocated by operator new. Applying the delete operator to memory not allocated on the free store is likely to result in undefined program behavior during execution. There is, however, no penalty for applying the delete operator to a pointer set to 0 — that is, a pointer that does not address an object. The following are examples of safe and unsafe applications of operator delete:

```
void f() {
    int i;
    char *str = "dwarves";
    int *pi = &i;
    Array *pia = 0;
    double *pd = new double;

    delete str;  // dangerous
    delete pi;   // dangerous
    delete pia;  // safe
    delete pd;   // safe
}
```

A const pointer cannot have the delete operator applied to it — that would after all change the value of the object the pointer addresses. The attempt to apply the delete operator results in a compile-time error. For example,

```
const int *pi = new int(1024);
foo() {
    delete pi; // error: const int* pointer
    // ...
}
```

The program's free store is not infinite; during the course of program execution it may become exhausted. (Failure to delete objects no longer needed, of course, will speed up exhaustion of the free store.) By default, operator new returns 0 when insufficient free store is available to satisfy its request.

The programmer cannot safely ignore the possibility that operator new has returned 0. Our grow() function, for example, will fail if operator new is unable to allocate the requested memory. Our code, recall, looks as follows:

```
ia = new int[ size ];

// trouble if new returns 0
for ( int i = 0; i < oldSize; ++i )
        ia[ i ] = oldia[ i ];
```

The programmer must prevent the execution of the for loop on a zero-valued ia. One current method of doing this is for the programmer to utilize the assert macro facility. For example,

```
#include <assert.h>
// ...
ia = new int[ size ];
assert( ia != 0 );
```

Alternatively, the programmer can explicitly insert a test on ia following the call of operator new:

```
ia = new int[ size ];
if ( ia == 0 ) {
      error("Array::grow(): free store exhausted");
}
```

where error() is a general function defined by the programmer to report errors and exit as gracefully as possible. The preferred method, once the C++ exception handling mechanism is available, is for the programmer to raise an exception using a *throw clause*:

```
if (ia == 0)
      throw memExhaust;
```

where memExhaust might be a predefined exception indicating the failure of operator new. (Alternatively, if operator new itself is implemented to raise an exception for the exhaustion of the program's free store, user code could then simply place calls of operator new within a *try block*:

```
try {
    ia = new int[ size ];
    // ...
}
catch ( memExhaust ) { /* ... */ }
```

(A general discussion of the exception handling mechanism can be found in Appendix B.)

Here is a small program that illustrates the use of grow():

```
#include <iostream.h>
#include "Array.h"

Array ia( 10 );
main() {
    cout << "size: " << ia.getSize() << endl;
    int ix = 0;
    for ( ; ix < ia.getSize(); ++ix )
          ia[ix] = ix*2;

    ia.grow();
    cout << "new size: " << ia.getSize() << endl;

    for (ix = 0; ix < ia.getSize(); ++ix )
          cout << ia[ix] << " ";
    cout << endl;
    return 0;
}
```

When compiled and executed, the program generates the following output:

```
size: 10
new size: 16
0 2 4 6 8 10 12 14 16 18 0 0 0 0 0 0
```

Here is a function designed to illustrate the exhaustion of free store. Implemented as a recursive function, its stopping condition is a return value of 0 from new.

```
#include <iostream.h>

void exhaustFreeStore( unsigned long chunk ) {
    static int depth = 1;
    static int reported = 0;

    ++depth; // keep track of invocations
    double *ptr = new double[ chunk ];
    if ( ptr )
        exhaustFreeStore( chunk );

    // free store exhausted
    delete ptr;
    if ( !reported++ )
        cout << "Free Store Exhausted:"
             << "\tchunk: " << chunk
             << "\tdepth: " << depth << endl;
}
```

Executing exhaustFreeStore() four times with different-sized arguments produced the following results:

```
Free Store Exhausted:    chunk: 1000000   depth: 4
Free Store Exhausted:    chunk: 100000    depth: 22
Free Store Exhausted:    chunk: 10000     depth: 209
Free Store Exhausted:    chunk: 1000      depth: 2072
```

The C++ library provides some help in keeping watch over the free store. The exception handler _new_handler is discussed in Section 4.3 (page 207) in the following chapter.

The programmer may place an object allocated from the free store at a specific address. The form of this invocation of operator new looks as follows:

```
new (place_address) type-specifier
```

where *place_address* must be a pointer. In order to use this instance of operator new, the header file new.h must be included. This facility allows the programmer to preallocate memory which at a later time will contain objects specified by this form of operator new. For example,

```
#include <iostream.h>
#include <new.h>

const Chunk = 16;
class Foo { public: int val; Foo(){ val = 0; }};

// preallocate memory, but no Foo objects
char *buf = new char[ sizeof(Foo) * Chunk ];

main() {
    // construct Chunk Foo objects in buf
    Foo *pb = new (buf) Foo[ Chunk ];

    // check that objects were placed in buf
    if ( (char*)pb == buf )
        cout << "Operator new worked!: pb: "
             << pb << " buf: " << (void*)buf << endl;
    return 0;
}
```

When compiled and executed, this program generates the following output:

```
Operator new worked!: pb: 0x234cc buf: 0x234cc
```

There is one possibly confusing aspect to this program. This is the cast of buf to void*. This is necessary because the output operator, when passed a char* operand, prints the "null terminated string" that it addresses. By casting buf to void*, the output operator knows to print the address value of buf. This is because the output operator is *overloaded* to take two different pointer argument types: char* and void*. Overloaded functions are discussed in Chapter 4.

3.12   A Linked List Example

In order to illustrate both pointer manipulation and the use of operators new and delete, this section implements a rudimentary list class. A list is a sequence of items, each of which contains a value of some type and the address, perhaps null, of the next item on the list. A list may be empty; that is, there can be a list of no items. A list cannot be full, although the attempt to create a new list item can fail if the program's free store is exhausted.

A first step in the design of a class is to enumerate the set of operations users of the class will need to perform. This set is referred to as the *public interface*. What might the public interface of a list class consist of?

A user needs to determine if a list is empty. This can be done by a query, or predicate, function. By convention, a predicate function returns 0 for false and a non-zero value for true. To make this clearer in our program, we can introduce an enumeration named Boolean:

```
enum Boolean { false = 0, true };
```

is_empty() might then be declared as follows:

```
Boolean is_empty();
```

Users need to add an item to a list. An item may be inserted at the beginning of the list:

```
void insert( someItem );
```

where someItem represents the value to be inserted, or appended to the end of the list:

```
void append( someItem );
```

A list may decrease by the removal of an item — provided, of course, that the list is not empty.

```
??? remove( someItem );
```

Should the operation to remove an item from a list return a value? What if the user attempts to remove an item that is not present on the list? A return value might indicate the success or failure of the operation. What if an item occurs multiple times within the list? Should the operation remove all instances or only the first? Or last? For our design, the operation removes all occurrences of an item. The return value provides a count of the items actually removed.

The user of the list class needs the ability to query the list for the presence of an item. This, too, is a predicate function returning the Boolean value of its search.

```
Boolean is_present( someItem );
```

Users also need to display the items of a list.

```
void display();
```

(Later, in Chapter 6, we'll see that class display functions can be overloaded to make use of the iostream output operator.) How should a list be displayed? Our class prints each item separated by a space. The entire set of items is enclosed within parentheses. For example,

```
( ) /* an empty list */
( 0 1 2 3 4 )
```

The public interface of a class is placed within a `public` section of the class definition. Here is our list class as we have currently defined it:

```
typedef int Type;
enum Boolean { false = 0, true };

class List {
public:
    void insert( Type someItem );
    void append( Type someItem );
    int remove( Type someItem );

    Boolean is_present( Type someItem );
    Boolean is_empty();
    void display();
};
```

Why have we introduced a typedef? In order to localize type-dependencies in our implementation. A list is a collection of items of some type. In a real-world implementation, a list class is defined to be a template class, allowing for the automatic generation of lists of integers, floating point values, etc. Since our purpose in discussing a list class is to illustrate pointer manipulation and the use of operators new and `delete`, we are limiting ourselves to a list class of integers. In order to make the eventual transition to a template list class easier, however, the integer type dependency is localized with the use of a `typedef`.

The next step in the design is to decide on a physical representation of the class. In our List class representation, list and item are treated as separate abstractions. A list serves as a header node addressing a singly-linked sequence of zero or more items. An item consists of a value and a link. A link is represented as a pointer addressing a next item. Here is our design:

```
class Item {
friend class List;
private:
    Type val;
    Item *next;
};

class List {
public:
    // public interface ...
private:
    Item *list;
};
```

A class such as Item is sometimes referred to as an auxiliary class — its purpose is to help in the implementation of our List class. Because it is not intended to be used by the general program, it does not provide a public interface. Rather, it declares the List class to be its friend. A friend can access the nonpublic members of the class it is a friend to. The Item class members val and next are effectively public members to the member functions of the List class. (Friendship, public and private access are discussed in detail in Chapter 5.)

Each time a list is created, we need to ensure that its pointer member is initialized to zero. This can be done automatically by defining a special class function member referred to as a *constructor*. A constructor is defined by giving it the name of its class. For example, here is the List class constructor:

```
List () { list = 0; }
```

Apart from its name, the only thing unusual about a constructor is that it must not specify a return type or return a value. Here is the Item class constructor:

```
Item( Type value, Item *item = 0 )
{
    val = value;
    next = item;
}
```

When the user declares a List object — for example,

```
List il;
```

the list constructor is automatically applied to il. Since the constructor is defined to be an inline function, it is as if the following statement sequence had been written:

```
List il;
il.list = 0; // inline expansion of constructor
```

Similarly, when a new item is added to the list, the Item constructor is invoked. For example, when the programmer writes

```
il.insert( 1024 );
```

the insert operation needs to generate a new Item node initialized to 1024. This is done as follows:

```
Item *pt = new Item( 1024 );
```

Operator new is invoked to allocate a new Item node from the program's free store. Once that is accomplished, the constructor is applied to the new Item node. Since the constructor is defined to be an inline function, it is as if the following statement sequence had been written:

```
Item *pt = new Item;

// inline expansion of Item constructor
pt->val = 1024;
pt->next = 0; // default value
```

Finally, when a List object goes out of scope, we need to insure that all its associated Item nodes are returned to the program's free store. This can be done automatically by defining a special class function member referred to as a *destructor*. A destructor is defined by giving it the name of its class preceded by a tilde (˜). A destructor is automatically invoked whenever a class object goes out of scope — or when operator delete is applied to a pointer to a class object. For example, here is the List class destructor:

```
˜List()
{
    remove();
}
```

The destructor invokes a second instance of the remove() operation. Unlike the first instance, this instance destroys *all* the Items within a list. The destructor, in effect, returns all the Items to the program's free store. Let's look at an example of the List destructor being applied.

```
List *plist = new List;
```

causes operator new to allocate a List object from the program's free store. Before any first use of that object, the List constructor is automatically applied. When the programmer writes

```
delete plist;
```

the List destructor is automatically applied to the object pointed to by plist prior to the invocation of operator delete. (If plist is set to zero, neither operation is invoked.) Since the destructor is defined to be an inline function, it is as if the following statement sequence had been written:

```
plist->remove(); // inline expansion of destructor
delete plist;
```

Here is the complete class definition for Item and List:

```
enum Boolean { false = 0, true };

typedef int Type;
class Item {
    friend class List;
private:
    Item(Type value, Item *item = 0) {
        val = value; next = item; }
    Type val;
    Item *next;
};

class List {
public:
    List() { list = 0; }
    ~List() { remove(); }

    void insert(Type);
    void append(Type);
    int remove(Type);
    void remove(); // remove all items

    Boolean is_present(Type);
    Boolean is_empty();
    void display();
private:
    Item *list;
};
```

The next step is that of implementing the List class public interface. The implementation of is_empty() is easy. If list is set to zero, the List object is empty.

```
Boolean List::is_empty() {
    return list == 0 ? true : false;
}
```

insert() places a new Item at the front of the list. It is implemented as follows:

```
#include <assert.h>

void List::insert(Type val) {
    Item *pt = new Item( val, list );
    assert( pt != 0 ); // catch free store exhaustion
    list = pt;
}
```

append() is slightly more complicated. It must add the new Item to the

end of the list. An auxiliary function, at_end(), returns a pointer to the last
Item on the list.

```
Item *List::at_end() {
    if (list == 0) return 0; // empty

    Item *prev, *curr;
    prev = curr = list;

    while ( curr ) { // find end of list
        prev = curr;
        curr = curr->next;
    }
    return prev;
}
```

append() must test for the special case of an empty list. Here is an implementation:

```
#include <assert.h>

void List::append( Type val )
{
    Item *pt = new Item( val );
    assert( pt != 0 );

    if ( list == 0 ) { // empty list
        list = pt; return;
    }

    Item *atEnd = at_end();
    atEnd->next = pt;
}
```

As we have implemented it, the cost of appending an item is considerably
greater than that of inserting an item. insert() places the new item at the
front of the list. append(), however, first iterates through the entire list
before appending the item. This can be quite expensive — unacceptably so
in a real-world application. The cost of the two operations should essentially
be equal.

The solution is to replace the at_end() function with an at_end data
member:

```
Item *at_end;
```

at_end supports our List class implementation rather than the actual List
class abstraction. append() can now be rewritten as follows:

```
#include <assert.h>

void List::append( Type val )
{
    Item *pt = new Item( val );
    assert( pt != 0 );

    if (list == 0)
        list = pt;
    else
        at_end->next = pt;

    at_end = pt;
}
```

The ability to replace at_end() with the at_end data member depends on having encapsulated the List class implementation from users. Programs that rely only on the List class public interface are unaffected (except that they will run faster) by the reimplementation of append().

insert() also needs to be revised:

```
#include <assert.h>

void List::insert(Type val) {
    Item *pt = new Item( val, list );
    assert (pt != 0);

    // this line added to handle at_end
    if ( list == 0 ) at_end = pt;

    list = pt;
}
```

Finally, the List constructor should be updated to set at_end to zero.

The reimplementation illustrates a benefit of making the physical representation of a class inaccessible to the general program. Because access to the list data member is restricted, the job of reengineering the List class is constrained to the reimplementation of the small set of List class member functions. Were access to the list scattered throughout user code, each portion of that code touching list would need to be identified, understood, and, possibly, modified. Were list accessed indirectly in user code through a pointer, the possibility of correctly reimplementing the nonencapsulated List class would be even more difficult.

display() simply prints out each Item separated by a space. The set of Items is enclosed within parentheses. For convenience, the operation is hard-coded to print to the user's terminal.

```
#include <iostream.h>

void List::display()
{
        cout << "( ";
        for (Item *pt=list; pt; pt=pt->next)
             cout << pt->val << " ";
        cout << ")" << endl;
}
```

The List destructor needs to be able to destroy an entire list. The remove() operation taking no arguments does just that. Here is its implementation:

```
void List::remove() {
    Item *pt = list;

    while ( pt ) {
         Item *tmp = pt;
         pt = pt->next;
         delete tmp;
    }
    list = at_end = 0;
}
```

If it should be determined that this instance of remove() is needed only as a helping function to the List class destructor, it can be placed within a private section of the List class. Both data and function members can be made inaccessible to the general program.

The second instance of remove() destroys all occurrences of a particular item within a list. It returns a count of the number of occurrences destroyed.

Finally, users may wish to know whether an Item is present within a list. is_present() returns the Boolean result of its search. Here is an implementation:

```
Boolean List::is_present( Type item ) {
    if ( list == 0 ) return false;
    if ( list->val == item || at_end->val == item )
         return true;

    Item *pt = list->next;
    for (; pt != at_end; pt = pt->next)
         if ( pt->val == item)
              return true;

    return false;
}
```

```
int List::remove( Type val ) {
    Item *pt=list;
    int cnt = 0;

    // while the first item on list equals val
    while ( pt && pt->val == val ) {
            Item *tmp = pt->next; // save pointer to next
            delete pt;
            ++cnt;
            pt = tmp;
    }

    if ((list = pt) == 0 ) {
        at_end = 0; // list is empty
        return cnt;
    }

    Item *prv = pt; pt = pt->next;
    while ( pt ) { // iterate through list
        if ( pt->val == val ) { // match
            prv->next = pt->next;
            if (at_end == pt)
                at_end = prv;
            delete pt;
            ++cnt;
            pt = prv->next;
        }
        else {
            prv = pt;
            pt = pt->next;
        }
    }
    return cnt;
}
```

The List class definition, together with the typedef definition of Type and the enumeration definition of Boolean, are placed in a header file named List.h. The member functions not defined in the class definition are collected together in a file named List.C. At the top of that file we add

```
#include "List.h"
```

A common error in the manipulation of pointers to class objects is that of dereferencing through a pointer that is set to zero. For example,

```
Boolean List::is_present( Type item ) {
    // error: what if list and at_end equal 0?
    if ( list->val == item || at_end->val == item )
    // ...
}
```

This code fails to consider the case when both list and at_end are set to zero — that is, when neither is pointing to an Item class object. Although the result of this code is incorrect on all machines, the run-time behavior of such code varies across machines. On a Sun3/60, for example, the program fails during execution because the memory space beginning at zero is reserved for the operating system's use. An attempt to read or write within that memory space during execution of the program results in a *segmentation violation*. The program dumps core. On a Vax/780 and the AT&T 6386 WGS, the memory space beginning at zero is unprotected. The expression

```
list->val == item || at_end->val == item
```

is evaluated but the result is wrong.

Figure 3.1 presents a small program with which to test the List class implementation. It is placed in a file named mlist.0.C. When the program is compiled and executed, it generates the following output:

```
ok: empty List class
( )
( 0 1 2 1 4 1 6 1 8 1 10 1 )
6 items of value 1 removed.
( 0 2 4 6 8 10 )
( 1 1 1 1 1 1 0 2 4 6 8 10 )
( )
```

Exercise 3-4. An alternative List class design places val and next within the List class definition rather than factoring them out into a separate Item class. Discuss the advantages and disadvantages of this design.

□

Exercise 3-5. The original implementation of the List class named the operation to remove an Item as

```
void List::delete( Type Item );
```

This does not compile, however. Explain why.

□

Exercise 3-6. Users of the List class would like an additional operation that returns the length() of a List — that is, a count of the number of Items.

```
#include <iostream.h>
#include "List.h"

main() {
    const int size = 12;
    const int odd = 1;
    List il;

    // sanity check: exercise empty list
    if ( il.is_empty() != true ||
        il.is_present(1024) != false )
            cerr << "List class internal error (1)\n";
    else cout << "ok: empty List class\n";

    il.remove(1024); // verify can handle this
    il.display();

    for (int ix=0; ix<size; ++ix)
            il.append(ix%2 ? odd : ix);
    il.display();

    if ( il.is_present(odd) != true )
        cerr << "List class internal error (2)\n";
    int odd_cnt = il.remove(odd);
    cout << odd_cnt << " items of value "
            << odd << " removed.\n";
    il.display();

    for ( ix=0; ix<odd_cnt; ++ix) il.insert( odd );
    il.display();
    il.remove(); // remove all items
    il.display();
    return 0;
}
```

Figure 3.1 List Class Test Program

Two alternative designs are (a) to compute the count of Items at each request, and (b) to add a length data member to hold a current count of the number of Items. Discuss the trade-offs of the two designs. Which would you choose to implement? Why?

□

Exercise 3-7. Implement a remove_last() operation for the List class. remove_last() destroys the last entry of an Item. Write a small program to exercise your implementation. □

A common operation on a list is the concatenation of one list with another. The operation is simple — the implementation is easy to get wrong. For example,

```
void List::concat(List &il) { // incorrect implementation
    if ( at_end == 0 )
        list = il.list;
    else
        at_end->next = il.list;
    at_end = il.at_end;
}
```

The problem is that two List objects now point to the same sequence of items. Changes to one list — such as an insertion or delete — incorrectly also happen to the other list. One strategy for correcting this problem is to copy each list item taking part in the concatenation.

```
void List::concat(List &il) {
    Item *pt = il.list;
    while ( pt ) {
        append( pt->val );
        pt = pt->next;
    }
}
```

A second common list operation is that of inversion. In this case, the sequence of list items is reversed — the end of the list is made the front; the front is made the end. Here is an implementation:

```
void List::reverse() {
    if (list==0 || list->next==0) return;

    Item *pt = list;
    Item *prv = 0;

    list = at_end;
    at_end = pt;

    while (pt != list) {
        Item *tmp = pt->next;
        pt->next = prv;
        prv = pt;
        pt = tmp;
    }
    list->next = prv;
}
```

The following small program exercises both concat() and reverse():

```
#include <iostream.h>
#include "List.h"

main() {
    int i;
    List il, il2;
    const int size = 8;

    for (i=0; i < size/2; ++i) il.append(i);
    for (i=size/2; i<size; ++i) il2.append(i);

    cout << "list il:\t";   il.display();
    cout << endl << "list il2:\t"; il2.display();

    cout << endl << "concat il il2:\t";
    il.concat(il2); il.display();

    cout << endl << "reverse il:\t";
    // il2.remove() must not affect il
    il2.remove(); il.reverse(); il.display();

    return 0;
}
```

When executed, the program generates the following output:

```
list il:          ( 0 1 2 3 )
list il2:         ( 4 5 6 7 )
concat il il2:    ( 0 1 2 3 4 5 6 7 )
reverse il:       ( 7 6 5 4 3 2 1 0 )
```

Exercise 3-8. Pointer manipulation is actually quite simple, but it does take some getting used to. Drawing a picture of the manipulations often helps in understanding what is going on. Draw a picture of the operations of `reverse()`.

☐

Exercise 3-9. Modify the List class implementation so that only one occurrence of each item is maintained.

☐

Exercise 3-10. Modify the List class implementation so that the list of Items is maintained in sorted order. ☐

Chapter 4: **Overloaded and Template Functions**

Function name overloading allows multiple function instances that provide a common operation on different argument types to share a common name. If you have written an arithmetic expression in a programming language, you have used a predefined overloaded function. In this chapter, we see how to define our own.

Template functions provide an "algorithm" for the automatic generation of particular instances of that function varying by type. A function is overloaded when its meaning remains invariant over a set of instances, each of which is implemented in a different way. A function is defined as a template when its implementation remains invariant over a set of instances, each of which handles a unique data type. In this chapter, we see how to define and use template functions.

4.1 Overloaded Function Names

A word is said to be overloaded when it has two or more distinct meanings. The intended meaning of any particular use is determined by its context. If we write

```
static int depth;
```

the meaning of static is determined by the scope in which it appears. It is either a local static variable or a static variable declared at file scope. (In the next chapter, we will introduce a third meaning for static, that of a static class member.)

In each case, the meaning of static is made clear by providing the context of its use. When that context is missing, we speak of the word as being *ambiguous*. An ambiguous word can have two or more meanings, each of them equally possible.

In natural language, ambiguity is often deliberate. In literature, for example, ambiguity can enrich our understanding of a book's characters or themes. An individual, perhaps, is described as *bound and determined*. One character might turn to another and say, "People are never *just*." The human mind can hold different meanings for a word simultaneously.

Ambiguity, however, does not sit well with a compiler. If the context in which an identifier or statement occurs is insufficient to make its meaning clear, the compiler will report an error. Ambiguity is an important issue in overloading function names, the topic of this section, and in class inheritance, the topic of Chapters 8 and 9.

Why Overload a Function Name?

In C++, two or more functions can be given the same name provided that each signature is unique, in either the number or the types of their arguments. For example,

```
int max( int, int );
int max( const int*, int );
int max( const List& );
```

A separate implementation of max() is required for each unique set of arguments. Each, however, performs the same general action; each returns the largest of its set of values.

From a user's viewpoint, there is only one operation, that of determining a maximum value. The implementation details of how that is accomplished are of little general interest. With function overloading, the user can simply write the following:

```
int ix = max( j, k );
int iy = max( i_array, 1024 );
```

The arithmetic operators provide an analogy. The expression

```
1 + 3
```

invokes the addition operation for integer operands, while the expression

```
1.0 + 3.0
```

invokes a different addition operation that handles floating-point operands.

The implementation is transparent to the user because the addition operator ("+") is overloaded to represent the different instances. It is the responsibility of the compiler, not the programmer, to distinguish between these different instances. Function-name overloading provides a similar transparency to user-defined functions.

Without the ability to overload a function name, each instance must be given its own unique name. For example, our set of max() functions becomes the following:

```
int i_max( int, int );
int ia_max( const int*, int );
int list_max( const List& );
```

This lexical complexity is not intrinsic to the problem of determining the larger of a set of objects, but rather reflects a limitation of the programming environment — each identifier occurring at the same scope must be unique. Such complexity presents a practical problem to the programmer, who must either remember or look up each name.

Function-name overloading relieves the programmer of this lexical complexity.

How to Overload a Function Name

When a function name is declared more than once in a program, the compiler will interpret the second (and subsequent) declarations as follows:

* If both the return type and signature of the two functions match exactly, the second is treated as a redeclaration of the first. For example,

```
// declares the same function
extern void print( int *ia, int sz );
void print( int *array, int size );
```

Argument names are irrelevant in signature comparisons.

* If the signatures of the two functions match exactly but the return types differ, the second declaration is treated as an erroneous redeclaration of the first and is flagged at compile time as an error. For example,

```
unsigned int max( int*, int sz );
extern int max( int *ia, int ); // error
```

A function's return type is not considered when distinguishing between overloaded instances.

* If the signatures of the two functions differ in either the number or type of their arguments, the two function instances are considered to be overloaded. For example,

```
extern void print( int *, int );
void print( double *da, int sz );
```

A typedef name provides an alternative name for an existing data type; it does not create a new data type. The following two instances of search() are treated as having exactly the same signature. The declaration of the second instance results in a compile-time error because, although it declares the same signature, it declares a different return type.

```
// typedef does not introduce a new type
typedef char *string;

// error: same signature, different return value
extern int search( string );
extern char *search( char* );
```

When Not to Overload a Function Name

Overloading allows a set of functions that perform a similar operation, such as print(), to be collected under a common mnemonic name. The resolution of which function instance is meant is transparent to the user, removing the lexical complexity of providing each function with a unique name, such as iPrint() and iaPrint().

When is it not beneficial to overload a function name? Whenever information that would make the program easier to understand is lost. Here are some examples.

The following set of functions operate on a common data abstraction. They may at first seem as likely candidates for overloading:

```
void setDate( Date&, int, int, int );
Date& convertDate( char* );
void printDate( const Date& );
```

These functions operate on the same data type but do not share the same operation. In this case the lexical complexity is a programmer convention that associates a set of functions with a common data type. The C++ class mechanism makes this sort of convention unnecessary. These functions should be made member functions of the Date class. For example,

```
class Date {
public:
    set( int, int, int );
    Date &convert( char* );
    void print();

    // ...
};
```

The following set of five member functions for a Screen class perform various move operations. Again, it might first be thought to overload this set under the name move().

```
Screen& moveHome ();
Screen& moveAbs ( int, int );
Screen& moveRel ( int, int, char *direction );
Screen& moveX ( int );
Screen& moveY ( int );
```

The last two instances cannot both be overloaded; their signatures are exactly the same. To provide a unique signature, we could compress the two functions into one:

```
Screen& move ( int, char xy );
```

Each function now has a unique signature, allowing the set to be overloaded with the name move. By our criteria, however, the overloading of these functions is a bad idea — information is lost; the program is obscured. Although cursor movement is a general operation shared by all these functions, the specific nature of that movement is unique among certain of these functions. moveHome (), for example, represents a special instance of cursor movement. Which of the two calls is the easier to understand as a reader of the program? Which of the two calls is easier to remember as a user of the Screen class?

```
myScreen.home ();
myScreen.move ();
```

Overloading at times can also be unncessary. In many cases, default arguments allow multiple instances of a function to be compressed into a single instance. For example, the two cursor functions

```
moveAbs (int,int);
moveAbs (int,int,char*);
```

are distinguished by the presence or absence of the char* third argument. If a default value for that argument can be found which, when passed to the function, has a meaning of no argument present, then these two functions can be merged into one. And there is just such a default value in this case — a pointer value of 0:

```
move ( int, int, char* = 0 );
```

Programmers are best served by not thinking of each language feature as the next mountain to climb. Use of a feature should follow from the logic of the application and not simply because it is there.

Resolving an Overloaded Function Call

The signature of a function distinguishes one instance from another in an overloaded function set. For example, here are four distinct instances of print():

```
extern void print( unsigned int );
extern void print( char* );
extern void print( char );
extern void print( int );
```

A call to an overloaded function is resolved to a particular instance through a process referred to as *argument matching*, which can be thought of as a process of disambiguation. Argument matching involves comparing the actual arguments of the call with the formal arguments of each declared instance. There are three possible outcomes of a call of an overloaded function:

1. A match. The call is resolved to a particular instance. For example, each of the following three calls of print() results in a match:

```
unsigned int a;

print( 'a' );      // matches print(char);
print( "a" );      // matches print(char*);
print( a );        // matches print(unsigned);
```

2. No match. The actual argument cannot be made to match an argument of the defined instances. Each of the following two calls of print() results in no match:

```
int *ip;
SmallInt si;

print( ip ); // error: no match
print( si ); // error: no match
```

3. Ambiguous match. The actual argument can match more than one defined instance. The following call, an example of an ambiguous match, can match each instance of print() except the one that takes an argument of type char*.

```
unsigned long ul;
print( ul ); // error: ambiguous
```

Matching can be achieved in one of three ways, in the following order of precedence:

1. An exact match. The type of the actual argument exactly matches the type of one defined instance. For example,

```
extern void ff( int );
extern void ff( char* );

f( 0 ); // matches ff(int)
```

0 is of type int. The call exactly matches ff (int) .

2. A match through promotion. If no exact match is found, an attempt is made to achieve a match through promotion of the actual argument. For example,

```
extern void ff(int);
extern void ff(char*);

ff('a'); // matches ff(int)
```

'a' is of type char. It is promoted to type int after no exact match is found.

3. A match through application of a standard conversion. If no exact match or match through a promotion is found, an attempt is made to achieve a match through a standard conversion of the actual argument. For example,

```
class X;
extern void ff( X& );
extern void ff( char* );

ff( 0 );   // matches ff(char*)
```

4. A match through application of a user-defined conversion. Finally, if no match has as yet been achieved, the application of a user-defined conversion on the actual argument is attempted. For example,

```
class SmallInt {
public:
    operator int();
    // ...
};

SmallInt si;
extern void ff( char* );
extern void ff( int );

ff( si ); // matches ff(int)
```

operator int () is referred to as a conversion operator. Conversion operators allow a class to define its own set of "standard" conversions. Section 6.5 (page 334) looks at these user-defined conversions in detail.

Details of an Exact Match

Argument matching can distinguish between constant and nonconstant pointer and reference arguments. For example,

```
extern void ff( const char* );
extern void ff( char* );

char *cp;
const char *pcc;

ff( pcc );    // ff( const char* )
ff( cp );     // ff( char* )
ff( 0 );      // error: ambiguous
```

The last call is ambiguous because zero is an exact match of type int. It can only match either pointer instance of ff() through application of a standard conversion. The conversion of zero to a pointer type, however, matches both instances of ff().

Which instance of ff(), above, do you think the following call resolves to?

```
// ff(char*) or ff(const char*)?
ff( "a string literal constant" );
```

Although a string literal is referred to as a constant, its type is that of a non-constant char*. If this were not the case, initializations such as the following would not be allowed:

```
// ok: each is of type char* not const char*
char *p = "a string literal constant";
char q[] = "another string literal constant";
```

const is not meaningful when applied to either an object

```
// error: cannot distinguish between instances
extern void f(int);
extern void f(const int);
```

or a constant pointer:

```
// error: cannot distinguish between instances
extern void f(int*);
extern void f(int *const);
```

In both cases, the argument is passed by value; the const specifier is superfluous.

Each named enumeration defines a unique type that matches exactly only its enumerated elements and identifiers of the enumeration type. For example,

```
enum Bool { False, True } found;
enum Stat { Fail, Pass };

extern void ff( Bool );
extern void ff( Stat );
extern void ff( int );

ff( Pass );   // ff( Stat )
ff( 0 );      // ff( int )
ff( found );  // ff( Bool )
```

An exact match can be overridden by the use of an explicit cast. For example, given the following set of overloaded functions,

```
extern void ff(int);
extern void ff(void *);
```

the call

```
ff( 0xffbc );
```

matches `ff(int)` exactly since `0xffbc` is a literal integer constant written in hexadecimal notation. The programmer can force the `void*` instance of `ff()` to be invoked, however, by providing an explicit cast. This is done as follows:

```
ff( (void *)0xffbc );  // ff(void*)
```

An explicit cast of an actual argument causes the argument to match the type of the cast exactly.

Given the following pair of overloaded functions

```
extern void ff(const int&);
extern void ff(long);
```

the following call is not strictly an exact match:

```
int ival;

// ok: no ambiguity: ff(const int&)
// trivial conversions take precedence
ff(ival);
```

`ival` is neither a constant nor a reference. However, conversions such as these, referred to as trivial conversions, are given precedence over all other conversions. Another trivial conversion is that between an array and a pointer of the same type. For example,

```
extern void ff( const void* );
extern void ff( const int* );
int ia[10] = { /* ... */ };
```

```
ff(ia); // ok: ff(const int*)
```

Argument matching can also distinguish between volatile and nonvolatile arguments.

Details of a Promotion

If there is no exact match on the first pass, the following promotions take place:

- An argument of type char, unsigned char, or short is promoted to type int. An argument of type unsigned short is promoted to type int if the machine size of an int is larger than that of a short; otherwise, it is promoted to type unsigned int.

- An argument of type float is promoted to type double.

- An argument of an enumeration is promoted to type int.
  In the second pass, an attempt is made to match the argument exactly in its promoted type. For example,

```
extern void ff( int );
extern void ff( short );
extern void ff( long );
```

```
ff( 'a' ); // ff(int);
```

The character constant exactly matches the overloaded instance that takes a formal argument of type int. The matching of either type short or type long requires application of a standard conversion. The search for a match is complete.

An actual argument of type int cannot match exactly a formal argument of either char or short. Similarly, a double does not match exactly an argument of type float. For example, given the following pair of overloaded functions,

```
extern void ff( long )
extern void ff( float );
```

the following call is ambiguous:

```
ff( 3.14 ); // error: ambiguous
```

The literal constant 3.14 is of type double. It matches neither instance exactly. A match is achieved with either instance by means of a standard conversion. Since there are two conversions possible, the call is flagged as ambiguous. No one standard conversion is given precedence over another. The programmer can resolve the ambiguity either by an explicit cast, such as the following

```
ff( long( 3.14 )); // ff( long )
```

or through use of the float constant suffix:

```
ff( 3.14F ); // ff( float )
```

In the following example, given the following declarations,

```
extern void ff( unsigned );
extern void ff( int );
extern void ff( char );
```

a call with an actual argument of type unsigned char matches the formal argument of type int. The other two instances both require application of a standard conversion.

```
unsigned char uc;
ff( uc ); // ff(int)
```

This last example illustrates the promotion of enumerations:

```
enum Bool { False, True } found;
enum Stat { Fail, Pass };

extern void ff( int );
extern void ff( char );

// ok: enumerations promoted to int
ff( Pass );  // ff( int )
ff( 0 );     // ff( int )
ff( found ); // ff( int )
```

Details of a Match by Standard Conversion

If there is no resolution of an overloaded function call by means of an exact match, a match is attempted by application of a standard type conversion. For example,

```
extern ff( char* );
extern ff( double );

ff( 'a' ); // ff( double );
```

Through the application of a standard type conversion to an actual argument of the function call,

1. any numeric type will match a formal argument of any other numeric type, including unsigned;

2. enumeration types will match a formal argument of numeric type;

3. zero will match both a formal argument of a pointer type and a formal argument of a numeric type; and,

4. a pointer of any type will match a formal argument of void*.
   Here are some examples:

```
extern void ff( char* );
extern void ff( void* );
extern void ff( double );

main() {          int i;
    ff( i );    // matches ff( double );
    ff( &i );   // matches ff( void* );
    ff( "a" );  // matches ff( char* );
    return 0;
}
```

All standard conversions are treated as requiring equal work. The conversion of a char to an unsigned char, for example, does not take precedence over the conversion of a char to a double. Closeness of type is not considered. If more than one match is possible by application of the standard conversions, the call is ambiguous and it is flagged at compile time as an error: For example, given the following pair of overloaded functions,

```
extern ff( unsigned int );
extern ff( float );
```

each of the following calls matches both instances. Each call is ambiguous and is flagged as an error.

```
// each call is ambiguous
ff( 'a' );
ff( 0 );
ff( 2uL );
ff( 3.14159 );
```

Ambiguity can be resolved by an explicit cast.

Multiple Argument Calls

A call with multiple arguments is resolved by applying the matching rules to each argument in turn. The function chosen is the one for which the resolution of each argument *is the same or better* than for all other functions in the overloaded set, and it is strictly better than all other functions for at least one argument. This matching algorithm for multiple arguments is referred to as the *intersection rule*. For example,

```
extern ff( char*, int );
extern ff( int, int );

// ff( int, int )
ff( 0, 'a' );
```

The instance of `ff()` taking two arguments of type `int` is invoked because of the following:

1. Its first argument is strictly better. `0` is an exact match of a formal argument of type `int`.

2. Its second argument is equally as good. `'a'` equally matches the second argument of both functions.

A call is considered ambiguous if no one function instance contains a better match. In the following example, both instances of `min()` require two standard conversions to achieve a match:

```
int i, j;
extern min( long, long );
extern min( double, double );

// error: ambiguous, no ``best'' match
min( i, j );
```

A call is also considered ambiguous if more than one function instance contains a better match. For example,

```
extern foo( int, int );
extern foo( double, double );

// error: ambiguous: two ``best'' matches
foo( 'a', 3.14F );
```

Both instances of `foo()` contain one best match through promotion.

Default Argument Initializers

An overloaded function instance with default argument initializers will match a call that provides all or some subset of its arguments. For example,

```
extern void ff( int );
extern void ff( long, int = 0 );

main() {
    ff( 2L );    // matches ff( long, 0 );
    ff( 0, 0 ); // matches ff( long, int );
    ff( 0 );     // matches ff( int );
    ff( 3.14 ); // error: ambiguous
}
```

The last call is ambiguous because both instances can match through application of a standard conversion. There is no precedence given to ff(int) because it has exactly one argument.

Overloading and Scope

The overloaded set of function instances associated with a particular name must all be declared within the same scope. A locally declared function, for example, hides rather than overloads a function instance declared at file scope. For example,

```
extern void print( char* );
extern void print( double ); // overloads print

void fooBar( int ival )
{
    // separate scope: hides both instances of print
    extern void print( int );

    // error: print(char*) is not visible in this scope
    print( "Value: " );
    print( ival );       // ok: print(int);
}
```

Since each user-defined class maintains its own scope, the member functions of two distinct classes can *never* overload one another.

Exercise 4-1. How should the following error() function be defined in order to handle the following calls:

```
error( "Array out of bounds: ", index, upperBound );
error( "Division by zero" );
error( "Invalid selection", selectVal );
```

□

Overloading Operator new

Operator new can be overloaded by the programmer. The predefined instance has the following prototype:

```
void *operator new( size_t size );
```

where size represents the storage requirements of the type in bytes. Every user-defined instance of operator new must return a void* and take a first argument of the system typedef size_t, defined in the stddef.h system header file. For example, a second overloaded instance of operator new is provided by the standard C++ library. Its prototype looks as follows:

```
#include <stddef.h>
void *operator new( size_t size, void *memAddress );
```

The size argument is provided automatically by the compiler. Additional arguments must be specified in a comma-separated argument list placed between the keyword new and the type specifier:

```
#include <new.h>
char buf[ sizeof(Array) ];

main() {
    // default instance of new
    Array *pa = new Array( 10 );

    // operator new( size_t, void* )
    Array *pbuf = new (buf) Array( 10 );
}
```


4.2 Template Functions

A strongly typed language can sometimes seem an obstacle to implementing what otherwise are straightforward functions. For example, although the algorithm for min() is trivial, strong-typing requires that we implement an instance for each type pair we wish to compare:

```
int min(int a, int b) {
    return a < b ? a : b;
}

double min(double a, double b) {
    return a < b ? a : b;
}
```

An attractive but subtly dangerous alternative to the explicit listing of
each instance of min() is that of the macro expansion facility of the preprocessor. For example,

```
#define min(a,b) ((a) < (b) ? (a) : (b))
```

Although this definition works correctly for simple calls of min() such as
the following,

```
min(10, 20);
min(10.0, 20.0);
```

it behaves unexpectedly under more complex calls because its mechanism
provides a simple text substitution of its arguments. This results in the minimum of its two arguments being evaluated *twice*: once during the the test of
a and b and a second time during the execution of the return statement. For
example,

```
#include <iostream.h>
#define min(a,b) ((a) < (b) ? (a) : (b))

const int size = 10;
int ia[size];

main() {
    int elem_cnt = 0;
    int *p = &ia[0];

    // count the number of array elements
    while ( min(p++,&ia[size]) != &ia[size] )
        ++elem_cnt;

    cout << "elem_cnt : " << elem_cnt
         << "\texpecting: " << size << endl;
    return 0;
}
```

This program provides an admittedly roundabout method of computing
the number of elements of the integer array ia. The macro expansion of
min() fails in this case because the postfix increment operation applied to its
pointer argument p is applied twice with each expansion. The outcome of

executing this program is the following incorrect calculation:

```
elem_cnt : 5     expecting: 10
```

Template functions provide a mechanism by which the programmer can take advantage of the compactness of the macro solution without forfeiting any of the benefits of a strongly-typed language. The programmer *parameterizes* all or a subset of the interface types (the arguments and return type) to a function whose body otherwise remains invariant. For example, here is a template definition of min():

```
template <class Type>
Type min( Type a, Type b ) {
    return a < b ? a : b;
}

main() {
    // ok: int min(int,int);
    min(10, 20);

    // ok: double min(double,double);
    min(10.0, 20.0);
    return 0;
}
```

By substituting the template instance of min() in the previous program, that program's output is now computed correctly:

```
elem_cnt : 10    expecting: 10
```

Template Function Definition

The template keyword always begins both a definition and a forward declaration of a template function. This is followed by a comma-separated list of formal type parameters bracketed by the less-than ('<') and greater-than ('>') tokens. This list is spoken of as the *formal parameter* list of the template. It cannot be empty.

Each formal parameter consists of the keyword class followed by an identifier. The keyword class indicates that the parameter represents a potential built-in or user-defined type. In our example, min() declares a single formal type parameter named Type. Each of the types int, double, char*, Array, or List* are valid actual parameter types that could be substituted for Type. The name of a formal parameter can occur only once within the template parameter list. The following, for example, is flagged at compile time as an error:

```
// error: illegal reuse of name
template <class Type, class Type>
Type min(Type, Type);
```

The name of a formal parameter can be reused across template function declarations:

```
// ok: reuse of name across templates
template <class Type>
    Type min(Type, Type);

template <class Type>
    Type max(Type, Type);
```

Each formal type parameter must be preceded by the `class` keyword. The following template declaration, for example, is illegal:

```
// error: must be <class T, class U>
template <class T, U>
  T sum(T*, U);
```

Once declared, the formal type parameter serves as a type specifier for the remainder of the template definition. It can be used in exactly the same way as a built-in or user-defined type specifier, such as for variable declarations and casts.

The function definition or declaration follows the formal template parameter list. Except for the presence of the formal parameters as type specifiers, the definition of a template function looks the same as that of a nontemplate instance. Let's look at an example.

```
template <class Type>
Type min(const Type* array, int size)
/* parameterized instance of finding
 * minimum value contained in array*/
{
    Type min_val = array[0];
    for (int i = 1; i < size; ++i)
        if (array[i] < min_val)
            min_val = array[i];

    return min_val;
}
```

In our example, `Type` is used to indicate the return type of `min()`, the type of its first formal argument, `array`, and the type of the local variable `min_val`. In the course of the program, `Type` will be substituted with various built-in and user-defined types determined by the actual uses of `min()`. (Recall, the two uses of a function are to invoke it and to take its address.)

This process of type substitution is referred to as *template instantiation*.

The only constraint on the use of the formal parameters is that each must appear at least once in the signature of the function. Of course, there is no constraint on how many times each can appear nor any restriction on the presence of non-parameterized argument types. For example,

```
// ok: Array is a template class
template <class Type>
    Type sum( Array<Type>, int size );

// error: T1 not in function signature
template <class T1, class T2, class T3>
    T1 min( T2, T3 );
```

The names of the formal parameters do not need to be the same across forward declarations and the definition of the template. The following three instances of min (), for example, all refer to the same template function:

```
// all three instances of min()
// resolve to the same template definition

// forward declarations of the template
template <class T> T min(T,T);
template <class U> U min(U,U);

// actual definition of the template
template <class Type>
    Type min( Type a, Type b ) { /* ... */ }
```

The name of the formal parameter remains in scope for the extent of the template definition. Other uses of the name at global scope are hidden; any reference to them within the template requires the use of the global scope operator.

A template function can be declared extern, inline, or static the same as a nontemplate function. The specifier is placed following the formal parameter list — not in front of the template keyword.

```
// ok: keyword follows formal parameter list
template <class Type>
    inline Type
    min(Type, Type);

// error: incorrect placement of specifier
extern
template <class Type>
    Type min(Array<Type>, int);
```

Function Template Instantiation

The function template specifies how individual functions can be constructed given a set of one or more actual types. This process of construction is referred to as instantiation. It occurs as a side-effect of either invoking or taking the address of a template function. For example, in the following program, min() is instantiated twice, once with type int and once with type double.

```
template <class Type>
Type min(Type* array, int size) {
    Type min_val = array[0];
    for (int i = 1; i < size; ++i)
        if (array[i] < min_val)
            min_val = array[i];

    return min_val;
}

int ia[] = { 10, 7, 14, 3, 25 };
double da[] = { 10.2, 7.1, 14.5, 3.2, 25.0 };

#include <iostream.h>
main() {
    int size = sizeof (ia) / sizeof (int);
    int i = min(ia, size);
    if (i != 3)
        cout << "??oops: integer min() failed\n";
    else cout << "!!ok: integer min() worked\n";

    size = sizeof (da) / sizeof (double);
    double d = min(da, size);
    if (d != 3.2)
        cout << "??oops: double min() failed\n";
    else cout << "!!ok: double min() worked\n";
    return 0;
}
```

The call

```
int i = min(ia, size);
```

is instantiated to the following integer instance of min():

```
int min(int* array, int size) {
    int min_val = array[0];
    for (int ix = 1; ix < size; ++ix)
        if (array[ix] < min_val) min_val=array[ix];
    return min_val;
}
```

Similarly, the call

```
double d = min(da, size);
```

is instantiated into a double instance.

The determination of the actual type to which to bind `Type` is made by an evaluation of the actual first argument — that is, `ia` in the integer invocation and `da` in that of the double. The return type is not considered. Had the call been

```
double d1 = min(ia, size);
```

the instantiation of `min()` still would be to that of type `int`. In this case, the integer return value is promoted to `double` before initializing `d1`. Similarly, the following call

```
char *string;
char ch = min(string, strlen(string)+1);
```

is instantiated into a character instance of `min()`:

```
char min(char *array, int size) {
    char min_val = array[0];
    // ...
}
```

The first formal argument of the template function is `Type*`. Therefore, the first actual argument of a use of `min()` must be of a pointer type. The following call is an error because `ival` is an object of type `int` and not of type `int*`.

```
int ival;

// error: Type* != int
int jval = min(ival, 1);
```

In the next example, the call of `min()` is an error because the type of the first argument is `const int*`. Type-checking is not suspending in the handling of a template function. A `const` pointer must never be bound to a pointer that is not a constant.

```
const int ci = 10;

// error: Type* != const int*
int i = min(&ci, 1);
```

The solution in this case is to change the signature of min() to define its first argument as a const pointer:

```
int nci = 10;
template <class Type>
    Type min( const Type*, int );

// ok: const Type* == const int*
int i = min(&ci, 1);

// ok: trivial conversion to const
int i = min(&nci, 1);
```

How is the binding of the type parameter actually accomplished? By a matching up of the formal and actual arguments of the template function. The general algorithm is as follows:

1. Each formal argument of the template function is examined in turn for the presence of a formal type parameter.

2. If a formal type parameter is found, the type of the corresponding actual argument is determined.

3. The types of the formal and actual argument are then matched by pruning away corresponding type modifiers.

   For example, if the formal parameter is declared as

```
Type *tpr // formal parameter type
```

and the actual argument is of type

```
int * // actual parameter type
```

then the formal parameter, Type, is bound to type int. Similarly, if the actual argument is of type

```
int ** // actual parameter type
```

then the formal parameter, Type, is bound to type int*. If the formal parameter is declared as

```
Type t // formal parameter type
```

then an actual argument of type

```
int * // actual parameter type
```

binds to type int*.

If a formal parameter occurs multiple times in the argument list of a template function, each subsequent type binding must match exactly the type first bound to the parameter. No nontrivial type conversions or promotions are performed. For example,

```
template <class T> T min(T,T);
unsigned int ui;

// error: min(unsigned int, int)
min(ui, 1024);
```

Both arguments to min() must be either int or unsigned int since the formal parameter T must be bound to a type common to both.

No nontrivial type conversions or promotions are performed on the non-parameter arguments of a template function either. This means, for example, that a formal argument of type int cannot be passed an actual argument of type unsigned int. To do so requires an explicit cast of the actual argument. For example,

```
template <class Type>
    Type sum(Type*, int size);

int ia[] = { ... };
unsigned int usize;

// no match to template instance:
// second argument requires conversion
long sum_val = sum(ia, ui); // no match

// ok: explicit cast
double svals = sum(ia, (int)ui);
```

An alternative solution to that of an explicit cast is to define a second instance of the template with an unsigned int second argument. Section 4.2 (page 198) provides a further discussion of this issue of applying type conversions to the actual arguments of a template function.

Overloading a Template Function

A template function can be overloaded provided that the signature of each instance can be distinguished either by argument type or number. The following program, for example, provides three instances of sum().

```
// class template definition of class Array

template <class Type>
   class Array{ /* ... */ };

// three function template instances of sum()

template <class Type>
    Type sum(Array<Type>, int); // #1

template <class Type>
    Type sum(Type*, int); // #2

template <class Type>
    Type sum(Type, Type); // #3
```

The template Array class definition was introduced in Chapter 1. It is included here to give a flavor of how template functions are actually used in programs. (Chapter 7 presents a full discussion of class templates.) The following definition of main() illustrates how these instances of sum() might be invoked.

```
#include <math.h>

main()
{
    Array<int> iA(1024); // class instantiation
    int ia[1024];

    // Type == int; sum(Array<int>,int)
    int ival0 = sum(iA,1024);

    // Type == int; sum(int*,int)
    int ival1 = sum(ia,1024);

    // Type == double; sum(double, double)
    double d = sum(sqrt(iA[0]),sqrt(ia[0]));

    return 0;
}
```

The resolution of the following call might surprise you. Can you see why the compiler complains that ival2 is initialized with an incompatible type?

```
main() {
    // ...
    Array<int> iA2[1024];

    // which instance of sum() invoked?
    // error: invalid initializer for ival2
    int ival2 = sum(iA2, 1024);
}
```

iA2 is an array of 1024 elements of the Array template class instantiated to an integer type. Its type when passed as an argument to sum() is that of Array<int>*. The resolution of the overloaded instance, therefore, matches sum(Type*,int) rather than sum(Array<Type>,int). Type, that is, is bound not to type int but to that of Array<int>. The return type of this instantiation of sum(), therefore, is Array<int>. The correct call and assignment look as follows:

```
main() {
    // ...
    Array<int> iA2[1024];

    // Type == Array<int>
    // Array<int> sum(Array<int>*,int);
    Array<int> iA3 = sum(iA2, 1024); // ok
}
```

The following declaration pair is an illegal overloading of max(). It declares the same signature but specifies two different return types.

```
// illegal overloading: same signature
//      but two different return types

// implicit return type of int
template <class T> max(T,T);

// return type determined by instantiation
template <class U> U max(U,U);
```

Successfully declaring a set of overloaded template instances does not guarantee that they can be successfully invoked. For example, earlier we saw that, given a template definition such as match(),

```
template <class T>
int match(T,T);
```

a call of match() with arguments of two different data types is *not* resolved to the template instance. The two arguments must be of the same type.

```
int i; unsigned int ui;

// ok: both arguments are same type
match( 1024, i );

// no match: argument types differ
match( i, ui );
```

A solution to the problem of the second call is to provide a second instance of match() allowing for two different argument types.

```
template <class T, class U>
    int match( T, U );
```

This instance is matched in the two argument call:

```
// ok: int match(int, unsigned int)
match( i, ui );
```

Unfortunately, the earlier call is now ambiguous!

```
// error: ambiguous: two possible:
// match(T,T) and match(T,U)
match( 1024, i );
```

The two parameter definitions of match() allows for two different argument types. However, it does not require that they be different. T and U can both be of type int in this case. Both template definitions exactly match each call with two arguments of the same type. There is no way to indicate that one or the other is to be preferred.

In this case, the solution is easy: the set of calls handled by the match() instance with two formal parameters is a superset of those handled by the one parameter instance. Therefore, the one parameter instance can be removed.

The two parameter solution to a function template can present problems of its own. For example, which of the two parameters should sum() declare to be its return type?

```
// T or U as the return type?
template <class T, class U>
??? sum( T, U );
```

The answer is neither. Using either parameter is bound to fail at some point:

```
char ch; unsigned int ui;

// neither T nor U works as return type
sum( ch, ui ); // ok: U sum(T,U);
sum( ui, ch ); // ok: T sum(T,U);
```

Nor can the template function definition introduce a third formal parameter simply to designate the return type:

```
// illegal: each formal type parameter must
// appear in the signature of the function
template <class T1, class T2, class RT>
   RT sum( T1, T2 );
```

The return type needs to be large enough to contain the sum of any two types passed in any order. A general solution might be to provide a dummy third argument indicating the type of the return value.

```
template <class T1, class T2, class RT>
   RT sum( T1, T2, RT dummy );

typedef unsigned int uint;
uint ui; char ch;

// uint sum( uint, char, uint );
sum( ui, ch, (uint)0 );

// uint sum( char, uint, uint );
sum( ch, ui, (uint)0 );
```

Specializing a Template Function

Cases do occur in which the general template expansion either is inappropriate or inefficient for a particular type. An expansion of min (T, T), for example, for two arguments of type char* will not provide the expected semantics if the programmer intends each argument to be interpreted not as a pointer to a character but as a character string. For this case, the programmer must provide a specialized instance of the function. For example,

```
// general template definition
template <class T>
   T min(T t1, T t2) {
      return (t1 < t2 ? t1 : t2);
}

#include <string.h>
// char* specialization: overrides template definition

char *min(char* s1, char* s2) {
      return (strcmp(s1,s2) < 0 ? s1 : s2);
}
```

For all calls of min () with two arguments of type char*, the specialized

instance is invoked; for all others, the general template definition is instantiated and then invoked. These definitions might be invoked as follows. For
example,

```
#include <iostream.h>
main() {
    // template: int min(int,int);
    int i = min(10,5);

    // specialized char* min(char*,char*);
    char *p = min("hello","world");

    cout << "i: " << i << " p: " << p << endl;
    return 0;
}
```

The steps in resolving a reference to a function are the following:

1. Examine all nontemplate instances of the function (possibly an empty
   set). How many exact matches are there?

(a) Exactly one. The reference is resolved. Stop.

(b) More than one. Stop. Issue an error message: *ambiguous call of foo(): choices
    are ....*

(c) None. Proceed.

2. Examine all template instances of the function (possibly an empty set).
   How many exact matches are there?

(a) Exactly one. Does an instantiation exist? Yes. Stop. The reference is
    resolved. No. Instantiate the instance, then stop.

(b) More than one. Stop. Issue an error message: *ambiguous call of template
    class foo().*

(c) None. Proceed.

3. Reexamine all nontemplate instances of the function, attempting to
   resolve the reference as an ordinary (possibly overloaded) function
   through coercions.

Let's step through an example. Here are two declarations, a general template
instance and a specialization taking two arguments of type char.

```
template <class Type>
Type min(Type,Type);

// specialization
char min(char,char);
```

The following are three calls of min(). Can you tell which instance is invoked for each call?

```
main() {
    char ch;
    int ival;
    unsigned int ui;

    min(0,ival);
    min('a',ch);
    min(0,ui);
}
```

Let's look at each call in turn:

- min(0,ival): The two arguments are both of type int. This matches the general template instance exactly. An int min(int,int) instance is generated and invoked. Step 2 determines the resolution.

- min('a',ch): The two arguments are both of type char. This matches the specialized instance of min(); this instance is invoked. Step 1 determines the resolution. The template instances are never examined.

- min(0,ui): The two arguments are of type int and unsigned int. No exact match is made with either the specialized or general template definition (steps 1 and 2). If the specialized instance was not present, the call would be flagged as an error. The template instance requires both arguments to be of the same type. However, since the specialized instance is present, the attempt is made to coerce the actual argument to match the specialized instance. This is successful and a call of min(char,char) is invoked. Step 3 determines the resolution.

What if we had defined a second specialized instance of min()? For example,

```
template <class T> T min( T, T );

// two specializations
char min( char, char );
double min( double, double );
```

Is the resolution of the call any different? Yes.

```
main() {
    unsigned int ui;

    // resolved to which instance?
    min(0,ui);
}
```

Rule 3 states that the call should be resolved as an ordinary (possibly overloaded) function through coercions. The actual arguments can now be converted to both specializations of min(). The call, therefore, is now ambiguous and flagged as an error at compile time.

A Template Function Example

This section provides a program example of how template functions might be defined and used. First, let us reimplement the quick sort function discussed in Section 3.9 (page 137) as a template function:

```
template <class Type>
void qsort( Type *ia, int low, int high )
{ // quick sort
    if (low < high) {
        int lo = low;
        int hi = high + 1;
        Type elem = ia[low];

        for (;;) {
            while (ia[++lo] < elem) ;
            while (ia[--hi] > elem) ;

            if (lo < hi)
                swap(ia,lo,hi);
            else break;
        }

        swap(ia,low,hi);
        qsort(ia,low,hi-1);
        qsort(ia,hi+1,high);
    }
}
```

Quicksort makes use of a helping function swap(). This, too, needs to be defined as a template function:

```
template <class Type>
static void swap (Type *ia, int i, int j)
{ // swap two elements of an array
    Type tmp = ia[i];
    ia[i] = ia[j];
    ia[j] = tmp;
}
```

In order to be sure the sorting function actually works, the programmer needs to display the contents of the array after the array has been sorted. This display function also needs to be defined as a template function:

```
#include <iostream.h>

template <class Type>
void display(Type *ia, int size)
{ // display format: < 0 1 2 3 4 5 >

    cout << "< ";
    for (int ix = 0; ix < size; ++ix)
        cout << ia[ix] << " ";
    cout << ">\n";
}
```

The next step is to write a function exercising these template functions. Quicksort is passed in turn an array of doubles and an array of ints. Here is the program:

```
#include <iostream.h>
#include "pt_sort.c"
#include "pt_display.c"

double da[] = {
    26.7, 5.7, 37.7, 1.7, 61.7, 11.7, 59.7,
    15.7, 48.7, 19.7, 14.9 };

int ia[] = {
    503, 87, 512, 61, 908, 170, 897, 275, 653,
    426, 154, 509, 612, 677, 765, 703 };
```

```
main() {
    int size = sizeof(da)/sizeof(double);
    cout << "Quicksort of double array (size == "
        << size << ")" << endl;
    qsort(da,0,size-1);
    display(da,size);

    size = sizeof(ia)/sizeof(int);
    cout << "\nQuicksort of int array (size == "
        << size << ")" << endl;
    qsort(ia,0,size-1);
    display(ia,size);
    return 0;
}
```

When compiled and executed, this program generates the following output
(The output of the array has been manually broken up in order that it fit on
the page):

```
Quicksort of double array (size == 11)
< 1.7 5.7 11.7 14.9 15.7 19.7 26.7
    37.7 48.7 59.7 61.7 >

Quicksort of int array (size == 16)
< 61 87 154 170 275 426 503 509 512
    612 653 677 703 765 897 908 >
```

Exercise 4-2. Identify which, if any, of the following template function definitions are illegal. Correct each one that you identify.

a.   ```
template <class T, U, class V>
void foo(T, U, V);
```

b.   ```
template <class T>
T foo( int *T );
```

c.   ```
static template <class T>
T foo(T, unsigned int*);
```

d.   ```
template <class T>
foo( T, T );
```

   ```
template <class U> U
foo( U, U );
```

Exercise 4-3. Given the following set of template instances, specializations, and variable declarations:

```
int i;              unsigned int ui;
char str[24];       int ia[24];

template <class T> T max(T*,int);
template <class T> T max(T,T);
char max( char*, int );
double max( double, double );
```

Identify which, if any, template instance is invoked for each of the following calls:

```
a. max( str, 24 );        d. max( i, ui );
b. max( ia, 24 );         e. max( ia, ui );
c. max( ia[0], i );       f. max( &i, i );
```

□

Exercise 4-4. Rewrite the binary search function defined in Section 3.10 (page 140) as a template function. Write a program to call it. Pass it in turn an array of doubles and an array of ints. □

Exercise 4-5. Define a function to count() the number of occurrences of some value in an array. Write a program to call it. Pass it in turn an array of doubles, ints, and chars. □

Exercise 4-6. Introduce a specialized template instance of the count() function defined in the previous exercise to handle character arrays. Rerun the program defined in the previous exercise. □

Some Words on Instantiation

No doubt you have noticed that our programs include the template program text files rather than their associated template header files. This is because the definition of a template serves only as a prescription for the definition of an infinite set of instances. In itself, a template does not define anything. For example, when the compiler sees

```
template <class Type>
Type min(Type t1, Type t2)
{
    return t1 < t2 ? t1 : t2;
}
```

it stores an internal representation of min() but does not otherwise cause anything to happen. Later, when the compiler sees an actual use of min(), such as

```
int i, j;
double d = min(i,j);
```

it then instantiates an integer instance of min():

```
int min(int t1, int t2)
{
    return t1 < t2 ? t1 : t2;
}
```

In order for the compiler to instantiate the template function, it must see the actual definition and not simply its prototype declared within the header file. This is why the program file is included rather than the header file.

This method of instantiation works quite well for single file programs such as those illustrated within this text. Once the application becomes larger, however, a more sophisticated instantiation mechanism is required. Why? If an integer use of min() occurs in two or more of the files making up the application, multiple definitions of the integer instance will be generated and the compile will fail at link-time.

For small applications, management of the instantiations can be done by hand. The idea is to create just one file in which all the instantiations are generated. This file alone includes the template program text files. All the other program files include the template header file. The proper calls are invoked but the instantiations are absent within these files.

Beyond the small application, management of the instantiations is best managed by programming environment tools. There is no current standard for these tools (but quite a bit of debate). Interested readers (and there is no reason why single programmers and small applications should not also make use of these tools) should refer to the User Guide of their C++ implementations for information on the availability and extent of such tools. Within this text, we'll restrict ourselves to the inclusion of the template program text files.

Function Templates: Extending the ARM

The discussion of template functions presented here reflects the AT&T Bell Laboratories Release 3.0 implementation. It conforms to Chapter 14 of the *Annotated C++ Reference Manual* — the formal definition of the template facility accepted as part of the C++ language by the ANSI C++ committee in the summer of 1990 — *except* for two small extensions in its treatment of exact matches.

In the current template facility definition, trivial conversions are not per-mitted when resolving a template function instance. In practice, this leads to typical code like the following being rejected:

```
template <class T> T min(const T*,int);
const int array_size = 12;
int ia[ array_size ] = { ... };

// no match under strict conformance
min( ia, array_size );
```

Under a strict interpretation of the current ANSI template definition, this call fails because of three necessary trivial conversions:

1. `array_size` is of type `const int`. The formal argument is of type `int`. The conversion of a constant to nonconstant object is a trivial conversion. Since objects are passed by value, the conversion is completely type-safe. To effect an exact match of this call without considering trivial conver-sions means that the programmer must redefine `min()`:

```
template <class T>
    T min(const T*, const int);
```

Unfortunately, under this definition, a call such as

```
min(ia, 10);
```

fails to match since the type of an integer constant is that of `int`, not `const int`. Without this extension, the programmer needs to define both instances.

2. The match of an integer pointer to an array of integers also requires a triv-ial conversion. `ia` does not exactly match the formal argument type of `int *` without application of a trivial conversion. Without this extension, the programmer needs to define the following two instances of `min()`:

```
template <class T> T min(const T*, int);
template <class T> T min(const T[], int);
```

3. Similarly, the specification of the formal argument as `const` means that each actual argument not explicitly defined as type `const int *` fails to match exactly without application of a trivial conversion. Once again, without this extension, the programmer needs to define two instances of `min()`, making a total of six altogether.

In the implementation under discussion in this text, trivial conversions are considered as effecting an exact match. Both the following

```
min( ia, array_size );
min( ia, 12 );
```

exactly match the single `min()` template function definition.

The second small extension has to do with permitting type and subtype classes to match one another — this is a central feature in support of object-oriented programming. Discussion of this, however, is deferred until the introduction of object-oriented programming in Chapter 9.

Possible ANSI C++ Extensions

There are two likely proposals to be submitted to the ANSI C++ committee to extend the current template function specification:

1. To provide full argument matching on template functions, rather than requiring a strict exact match. (Some version of this is very likely to be accepted.)

2. To permit template functions to accept both type and expression parameters. (It's not clear what the outcome of this proposal will be.) Currently, only template classes can accept expression parameters. The argument for this proposal is exemplified in the following example,

```
template <class T, int size> class Array;
template <class T, int size>
   T min( Array<T,size> );
```

Template classes and expression parameters are discussed at length in Chapter 7.

4.3 Pointers to Functions

We have been asked to provide a general sorting function. In most cases the quicksort algorithm is appropriate. Users need write only the following:

```
sort( array, lowBound, highBound );
```

Under some circumstances, however, quicksort is inappropriate. If the array is arranged in descending order, for example, a merge sort will perform better. If storage is at a premium, a heap sort is most appropriate. For a small set of elements, a bubble sort usually is good enough.

The `sort()` function must provide some facility for specifying an alternative sorting algorithm. The problem is how to provide the flexibility required in a few cases without overly complicating the general use of the function. Typically, the solution is a default value. In this case, the default value is the `quickSort()` function.

A second requirement is the ability to change sorting algorithms without requiring a change to user code, allowing the code to be fine-tuned after it is up and running. Typically, this can be accomplished by having the user code manipulate a function argument or pointer. In this case the argument would need to be a sorting function. Since a function, however, cannot be passed as an argument, a pointer to a function will need to be used.

This section considers how both these requirements can be met.

The Type of a Pointer to Function

What will a pointer to function look like? What will its type be? How will it be declared? Here is the declaration of `quickSort()`:

```
void quickSort( int*, int, int );
```

The function's name is not part of its type. A function's type is determined by its return value and the signature of its argument list. A pointer to `quickSort()` must specify the same signature and return type:

```
void *pf( int*, int, int );
```

This is almost correct. The problem is that the compiler interprets the statement as the definition of a function `pf()` taking three arguments and returning a pointer of type `void*`. The dereference operator is associated with the type specifier, not `pf`. Parentheses are necessary to associate the dereference operator with `pf`:

```
void (*pf)( int*, int, int );
```

This statement declares `pf` to be a pointer to a function taking three arguments and with a return type of void — that is, a pointer of the same type as `quickSort()`.

Other functions may or may not have the same function type. The following three sort functions share the same type:

```
void bubbleSort( int*, int, int );
void mergeSort( int*, int, int );
void heapSort( int*, int, int );
```

However, both `min()` and `max()` declare functions of a different type:

```
int min( int*, int sz );
int max( int*, int sz );
```

A pointer to these two functions will be defined like this:

```
int (*pfi)( int*, int );
```

There are as many distinct function types as there are distinct combinations of function signatures and return types.

Initialization and Assignment

Recall that an array identifier evaluates as a pointer to its first element when not modified by the subscript operator. A function name, when not modified by the call operator, evaluates as a pointer to a function of its type. For example,

```
quickSort;
```

evaluates as an unnamed pointer of the type

```
void (*)( int*, int, int );
```

Applying the address-of operator to the function name also yields a pointer to its function type. Thus, both quickSort and &quickSort evaluate to the same type. A pointer to a function is initialized as follows:

```
void (*pfv)( int*, int, int ) = quickSort;
void (*pfv2)(int*, int, int ) = pfv;
```

Assignment is similar:

```
pfv = quickSort;
pfv2 = pfv;
```

An initialization or assignment is legal only if the argument list and return type match exactly. Otherwise, a compile-time error message is issued. For example,

```
extern int min( int*, int );
extern void (*pfv)( int*, int, int ) = 0;
extern int (*pfi)( int*, int ) = 0;
main() {
    pfi = min; // ok
    pfv = min; // error
    pfv = pfi; // error
    return 0;
}
```

A function pointer can be initialized with and assigned zero.

Pointers can also address instances of an overloaded function. When a function is overloaded, the compiler resolves the instance by finding an exact match of the return type and the signature. If no instance matches exactly, the initialization or assignment results in a compile-time error. For example,

```
extern void ff( char );
extern void ff( unsigned );

// ok: void ff(char)
void ( *pf1 )(char) = ff;

// error: no match: invalid signature
void ( *pf2 )(int) = ff;

// error: no match: invalid return type
char ( *pf3 )(char) = ff;
```

Similarly, pointers can address instances of a function template. The signature and return type must match exactly. If a matched instance of the template has not yet been instantiated, the instantiation is done prior to the initialization or assignment of the pointer. For example,

```
template <class Type>
    Type min(Type,Type);

// exact match: int min(int,int);
int (*pfi)(int,int) = min;

// exact match: double min(double,double);
double (*pfd)(double,double) = min;

// error: no match of the signature
double (*pfdi)(double,int) = min;
```

Invocation

The dereference operator is not required in order to invoke a function through a pointer. Both the direct and indirect calls of a function are written the same. For example,

```
#include <iostream.h>

extern min( int*, int );
int (*pf)( int*, int ) = min;

const int iaSize = 5;
int ia[ iaSize ] = { 7, 4, 9, 2, 5 };
```

```
main() {
    cout << "Direct call: min: "
        << min( ia, iaSize ) << endl;

    cout << "Indirect call: min: "
        << pf( ia, iaSize ) << endl;
}

min( int* ia, int sz) {
    int minVal = ia[ 0 ];
    for ( int ix = 1; ix < sz; ++ix )
        if ( minVal > ia[ ix ] )
            minVal = ia[ ix ];
    return minVal;
}
```

The call

```
pf( ia, iaSize );
```

is a shorthand notation for the explicit pointer notation:

```
(*pf)( ia, iaSize );
```

The two forms are equivalent.

Arrays, Arguments, and Return Type

An array of pointers to functions can be declared. For example,

```
int (*testCases[10])();
```

declares testCases to be an array of ten elements. Each element is a pointer to a function taking no arguments and with a return type of int. Execution of the elements of testCases might look as follows:

```
extern const size = 10;
extern int (*testCases[size])();
extern int testResults[size];

void runtests() {
    for ( int i = 0; i < size; ++i )
        testResults[ i ] = testCases[ i ]();
}
```

An array of pointers to functions may be initialized as follows:

```
extern void quickSort( int*, int, int );
extern void mergeSort( int*, int, int );
extern void heapSort( int*, int, int );
extern void bubbleSort( int*, int, int );

void ( *sortFuncs[] )( int*, int, int ) =
{
    quickSort,
    mergeSort,
    heapSort,
    bubbleSort
};
```

A pointer to sortFuncs, which can also be declared, is of the type "pointer to an array of pointers to functions." The definition will look like this:

```
void ( **pfSort )( int*, int, int ) = sortFuncs;
```

The two dereference operators declare pfSort to be a pointer to a pointer.

```
*pfSort;
```

evaluates to the address of sortFuncs.

```
**pfSort;
```

evaluates to the address of quickSort(), the first element of sortFuncs — the equivalent of writing

```
*pfSort[ 0 ];
```

To execute quickSort() through pfSort, the programmer would write either of the following:

```
// equivalent invocations
pfSort[ 0 ]( ia, 0, iaSize-1 ); // shorthand
(*pfSort[ 0 ])( ia, 0, iaSize-1 ); // explicit
```

Pointers to functions can also be declared as arguments to functions and can be provided with default values.

```
extern void quickSort( int*, int, int );
void sort( int*, int, int,
           void (*)(int*,int,int)=quickSort );
```

A simple definition of sort() might look as follows:

```
#include <assert.h>

void sort( int *ia,
            int low, int high,
            void (*pf)(int*, int, int))
{
    assert( ia != 0 );
    assert( pf != 0 );

    pf( ia, low, high );
}
```

sort () might be called in any of the following ways:

```
// normally, these would be in a header file
extern int *ia;
extern const iaSize;

extern void quickSort( int*, int, int );
extern void bubbleSort( int*, int, int );

typedef void (*PFV)( int*, int, int );
extern void sort( int*, int, int, PFV=quickSort );
extern void setSortPointer( PFV& );

PFV mySort;
void ff()
{
    sort( ia, 0, iaSize );
    sort( ia, 0, iaSize, bubbleSort );

    setSortPointer( mySort );
    sort( ia, 0, iaSize, mySort );
}
```

A pointer to a function can also be declared as the return type of a function. For example,

```
int ( *ff( int ))( int*, int );
```

declares ff () to be a function taking one argument of type int. It returns a pointer to a function of type

```
int (*)( int*, int );
```

The use of a typedef name can make the use of a pointer to a function considerably easier to read. For example,

```
// typedefs make pointers to functions readable
typedef int (*PFI)( int*, int );

PFI ff( int );
```

is an equivalent declaration of `ff()`.

Exercise 4-7. Section 3.9 (page 136) defines the function `fibonacci()`. Define a pointer to a function that can point to `fibonacci()`. Invoke the function through this pointer to generate a Fibonacci series of eight elements.

☐

Exercise 4-8. Section 3.10 (page 140) defines the function `binSearch()`. Define a function `search()` that can be invoked as follows:

```
extern int size, val, ia[];
int index = search( ia, size, val, binSearch );
```

☐

_new_handler

`_new_handler`, a pointer to a function provided in the C++ standard library, is set to 0 by default. The declaration of `_new_handler` looks as follows:

```
void ( *_new_handler )();
```

`_new_handler` is a pointer to a function with a `void` return value and taking no arguments.

When new fails, it tests `_new_handler` to see whether it points to a function. If `_new_handler` is not set, new will return 0; if `_new_handler` is set, the function to which it points is invoked.

The function to which `_new_handler` points must be supplied by the user. In addition, `_new_handler` must be explicitly set by the user to point to this function. This can either be done directly, as follows,

```
// to be invoked if new fails
extern void freeStoreException();

// set _new_handler to freeStoreException
_new_handler = freeStoreException;
```

or through the `set_new_handler()` library function. The latter can be accomplished as follows:

```
// new.h contains a declaration of set_new_handler
#include <new.h>

// set _new_handler with library function
set_new_handler( freeStoreException );
```

The purpose of _new_handler, then, is to provide access to a function that is only to be called under the exception condition that the free store is exhausted. Providing _new_handler with a function frees the user from having to test each call of new for failure.

The simplest function with which to provide _new_handler reports the error and causes the program to exit under its own power:

```
#include <iostream.h>
#include <stdlib.h>

extern char *progName; // current file
enum Exceptions { FS_EXHAUST = 1, /* ... */ };

void freeStoreException() {
    cerr << progName
        << ": free store exhausted!\n";

    // do any clean-up here ...
    exit( FS_EXHAUST );
}
```

Exercise 4-9. Set _new_handler to freeStoreException and rerun the exhaustFreeStore() program defined in Section 3.11 (page 149) of the previous chapter. □

4.4 Type-Safe Linkage

Overloading gives the appearance of permitting multiple occurrences of the same nonstatic function identifier. This is a lexical convenience that holds at the program source level. The downstream components of most compilation systems, however, require that each nonstatic function identifier be uniquely named. Most link editors resolve external references lexically. If the link editor sees two or more instances of the identifier print, it cannot analyze the signature types to distinguish between instances (by this point in the compilation, that information is usually lost). Rather, the link editor flags print as multiply defined and quits.

To handle this problem, each function identifier is *encoded* with a unique internal name. The downstream components of the compilation system see only this encoded name. The exact details of the name transformation are unimportant; they are likely to vary across implementation. The general algorithm encodes the type information of the signature and appends it to the function name. In two special cases, the encoding will generate linkage errors and the program will fail to compile:

1. Inconsistent declarations of a function signature within separate files.

2. Calls of functions of other languages, notably C.

This section considers these two special cases.

InterFile Declarations

In the first case, a function is accidentally declared differently in two separate files; both declarations are meant to represent the same function. For example, in the file token.C, the function addToken() is defined as taking one argument of type unsigned char. In the file lex.C, where it is called, addToken() is declared as taking one argument of type char.

```
// in file token.C
addToken( unsigned char tok ) { /* ... */ }

// in file lex.C
extern addToken( char );
```

A call of addToken() in lex.C will cause the program to fail at the link edit phase. Arguments of type unsigned char and char are encoded differently. The addToken() function declared in lex.C will be flagged as an undefined function. Were the program were to compile successfully, the following scenario might occur.

The compiled program is tested on an AT&T 3B20. The program executes correctly and is sent out to a field location using a VAX 8550. The program compiles without a hitch. Unfortunately, the first time it is executed, it fails miserably. Not even the simplest test program works.

What happened? Here is part of the set of Token declarations:

```
enum Tokens { INLINE = 128; VIRTUAL = 129; };
```

The call of addToken() looks as follows:

```
curTok = INLINE;
// ...
addToken( curTok );
```

chars are implemented as a signed type on the 8550. On the 3B20 they are implemented as unsigned. The misdeclaration of addToken() does not show up on the 3B20; on the 8850, however, each token with a value greater than 127 causes an overflow.

Because the compiler processes one file at a time, it cannot ordinarily detect type violations across files. As we have seen, these type violations can be a source of serious program error. The internal encoding of function names with their signature provides some measure of interfile type checking of function calls. This error and others like it are caught at link time.

Erroneous inter-file declarations of external variables or of the return types of functions, however, are not caught during compilation. Errors such as the following reveal themselves only in run-time exceptions or in the incorrect output of the program.

```
// in token.C
unsigned char lastTok = 0;
unsigned char peekTok() { ... }

// in lex.C
extern char lastTok;      // one token history
extern char peekTok();    // one token lookahead
```

Some Words on Header Files

The disciplined use of header files is fundamental to the prevention of the sort of interfile error presented in the last section. A header file provides a centralized location for the declaration of all extern variables, function prototypes, class definitions, and inline functions. Files that must use or define a variable, function, or class *include* the header file(s).

This provides two safeguards. First, all files are guaranteed to contain the same declaration. Second, should a declaration require updating, only one change to the header file need be made. Failing to update a declaration in a particular file is no longer a possibility. Our addToken() example would provide a token.h header file.

```
// in token.h
enum Tokens { /* ... */ };
const max_tokens = 205;
typedef unsigned char uchar;

extern uchar lastTok;
extern addToken(uchar);
inline is_relational(uchar tok)
     { return (tok >= LT && tok <= GT); }
```

```
// in lex.C
#include "token.h"
// ...

// in token.C
#include "token.h"
// ...
```

Some care should be taken in designing header files. The declarations provided should logically belong together. A header file takes time to compile. If it is too large or filled with too many disparate elements, programmers may be reluctant to incur the compile-time cost of including them.

A second consideration is that a header file should never contain a nonstatic definition. Each of the following, for example, represents a definition and therefore should not appear in a header file:

```
extern int ival = 10;
double fica_rate;
extern void dummy() {}
```

Although ival is declared to be extern, its explicit initialization makes it an actual definition. Similarly, although dummy() is explicitly declared as extern, the empty brace pair stands as the definition of that function. fica_rate, although not explicitly initialized, is also considered an actual definition in C++ because the extern specifier is absent. The inclusion of any of these definitions in two or more files of the same executable will result in a multiple definition linkage error.

In the token.h example header file, above, both the constant max_tokens and the inline function is_relational() appear to violate this rule. However, they do not. The default linkage of both symbolic constants and inline functions, recall, is static. That said, can you see why the following declaration, when placed inside a header file, causes a linkage error when included in two separate modules of the executable?

```
// oops: shouldn't be in a header file
const char *msg = "?? oops: error: ";
```

The problem is that msg is not a constant; rather, it is a nonconstant pointer that addresses a constant value. The proper declaration looks as follows:

```
const char *const msg = "?? oops: error: ";
```

When possible, the value of a symbolic constant will replace the occurrence of its name during the compilation of the program. This process of substitution is referred to as *constant folding*. Ideally, then, although an initialized constant may be included in 14 separate files, constant folding will have made it unnecessary for even one static definition to occur in the executable. In some cases, however, constant folding is not possible, and it would be preferrable to move the initialization of the constant to a single program text file. This can be done by explicitly declaring the constant extern. For example,

```
// header file
const int buf_chunk = 1024;
extern char *const bufp;

// program text file
char *const bufp = new char[buf_chunk];
```

Although bufp is a symbolic constant, its value cannot be computed at compile time. Were it initialized within the header file, a static instance would be defined within each file that included it. Not only would this be wasteful of space, but it would likely be counterintuitive to the intentions of the programmer. Unfortunately, it would happen "under the covers," so to speak, and the programmer would likely not even be aware of how the code has been translated.

A similar problem can occur with inline functions. An inline function of interest to more than a single file must be placed within a header file. The inline specification, recall, is only a hint. Whether the compiler can actually inline the function — in general, or at any particular call within the program — will vary across implementations. Within each file that an inline function is used but cannot be expanded, a static definition of the function is generated. This can result in multiple static instances being defined within a single executable.

Most compilers will generate a warning if either of the following cases hold:

1. The definition of the function makes it inherently uninlineable. For example, the compiler may complain that the function is *too complex* to inline. In this case, if possible, rewrite it; otherwise, remove the inline declaration and place the function within a program text file.

2. A particular call of the function cannot be inlined. For example, in the Bell Laboratories implementation, a second call of an inline function within the same expression is not inlined. In this case, the expression can be rewritten to separate the two inline function calls.

Prior to making inline functions generally available, their program behavior needs to be analyzed. Under no circumstances should an inherently uninlineable function be declared as inline and placed in a header file.

Other Language Function Calls

If the programmer wishes to call a function written in another programming language — most notably, C — an escape mechanism is necessary to inhibit the encoding of the function name. The escape mechanism, referred to as a *linkage directive*, has a single line and compound syntactic form:

```
extern "C" void exit(int);

extern "C"  {
    printf( const char* ... );
    scanf( const char* ... );
}

extern "C" {
#include <string.h>
}
```

The linkage directive consists of the `extern` keyword followed by a string literal, followed by an "ordinary" function prototype. Although the function is written in another language, calls to it are still fully type checked. Multiple functions may be enclosed within braces. The braces serve as delimiters and do not introduce a new level of scope.

The linkage directive may be specified only at file scope. The following code fragment is illegal and will be flagged as an error at compile time:

```
char *copy( char *src, char *dst )
{
    // error: linkage directive must be at file scope
    extern "C" strlen( const char* );
    if ( !dst )
        dst = new char[ strlen(src)+1 ];
    // ...
    return dst;
}
```

By moving the linkage directive to file scope, the function will compile:

```
extern "C" strlen( const char* );
char *copy( char *src, char *dst )
{
    if ( !dst )
        dst = new char[ strlen(src)+1 ];
    // ...
    return dst;
}
```

The linkage directive is more appropriately placed, however, within a header file.

If a C++ function is intended to be invoked by routines written in other languages, the function must also be escaped.

The linkage directive may be specified only for one instance of an overloaded function. A program that includes the following two header files is illegal:

```
// in string.h
extern "C" strlen( const char* );

// in String.h
extern "C" strlen( const String& );
```

The overloading of `sqrt()`, which follows, illustrates a typical use of the linkage directive:

```
class Complex;
class BigNum;

extern Complex& sqrt( Complex& );
extern "C" double sqrt( double );
extern BigNum& sqrt( BigNum& );
```

The C language `sqrt()` instance is escaped; the additional C++ class instances are not. The order of declarations is not significant.

Exercise 4-10. `exit()`, `printf()`, `malloc()`, `strcpy()`, and `strlen()` are C language library routines. Modify the following C program so that it compiles and links under C++.

```
char *str = "hello";

main()
{   /* C language program */
    char *s, *malloc(), *strcpy();

    s = malloc( strlen(str)+1  );
    strcpy( s, str );
    printf( "%s, world\n", s );
    exit( 0 );
}
```

□

Exercise 4-11. Section 3.10 (page 140) defines the function `binSearch()`. We wish to make it available to programs written in C. How should it be declared? □

Chapter 5

The C++ Class

The C++ class mechanism allows users to define their own data types. These types may add functionality to an already existing type — such as the Array class introduced in Chapter 1. Classes can also be used to introduce altogether new types, such as a Complex number class or a BitVector class. Classes are typically used to define abstractions that do not map naturally into the predefined or derived data types — for example, a computer Task class, a terminal display Screen class, or an Employee or ZooAnimal class. The possible class types are unlimited. In the next four chapters we will implement a number of different classes.

A C++ class has four associated attributes:

1. A collection of *data members*, the representation of the class. There may be zero or more data members of any type in a class.

2. A collection of *member functions*, the set of operations that may be applied to objects of that class. There may be zero or more member functions for a class. They are referred to as the class *interface*.

3. Levels of program access. Members of a class may be specified as `private`, `protected`, or `public`. These levels control access to members from within the program. Typically, the representation of a class is private while the operations that may be performed on the representation are public. This sort of public/private specification is referred to as *information hiding*. A private internal representation is said to be *encapsulated*.

4. An associated class *tag name*, serving as a *type specifier* for the user-defined class. A class name may appear anywhere in a program the predefined type specifiers may appear. Given the class name `Screen`, for example, a user may write

```
Screen myScreen;
Screen *tmpScreen = &myScreen;
Screen& copy( const Screen[] );
```

A class with a private representation and a public set of operations is referred to as an *abstract data type*. In this chapter and Chapter 6 we examine the design, implementation, and use of abstract data types in C++. In Chapter 7, we extend that discussion to cover the definition and use of template classes.

5.1 The Class Definition

A class definition has two parts: the *class head*, composed of the keyword `class` followed by the class tag name, and the *class body*, enclosed by a pair of curly braces, which must be followed by either a semicolon or a declaration list. For example,

```
class Screen { /* ... */ };
class Screen { /* ... */ } myScreen, yourScreen;
```

Within the class body, the data members, member functions, and levels of information hiding are specified. The following subsections consider the various types of specification.

Data Members

The declaration of class data members is the same as for variable declarations with the exception that an explicit initializer is not allowed. For example, the Screen class may define its representation as follows:

```
class Screen {
    short height; // number of Screen rows
    short width;  // number of Screen columns
    char *cursor; // current Screen position
    char *screen; // screen array (height*width)
};
```

As with variable declarations, it is not necessary to declare the two `short` members, or the two `char*` members, separately. The following definition is equivalent:

```
class Screen {
/*
 * height and width refer to row and column
 * cursor points to current Screen position
 * screen addresses array height*width
 */
    short height, width;
    char *cursor, *screen;
};
```

In general, unless there is a reason to do otherwise, declare the members of a class in order of increasing size. This usually gives optimal alignment on all machines. The data members can be of any type. For example,

```
class StackScreen {
    int topStack;
    void (*handler)(); // handles exceptions
    Screen stack[ StackSize ];
};
```

A class object can be declared as a data member only if its class definition has already been seen. In cases where a class definition has not been seen, a forward declaration of the class can be supplied. A forward declaration permits pointers and references to objects of the class to be declared as data members. Pointers and references are permitted because both are a fixed size independent of the type they address. For example, here is a definition of StackScreen using a forward declaration:

```
class Screen; // forward declaration
class StackScreen {
    // pointer to StackSize Screen objects
    int topStack;
    Screen *stack;
    void (*handler)();
};
```

A class is not considered defined until the closing brace of the class body is seen — precluding a class from declaring a *nonstatic* member object of its own type. (The discussion of static members is deferred until later in this chapter.) The class is considered to be declared, however, and may define pointer and reference data members of its own class type. For example,

```
class LinkScreen {
    Screen window;
    LinkScreen *next;
    LinkScreen *prev;
};
```

Member Functions

Users of the Screen class must perform a wide range of operations on a Screen class object. A set of cursor movement operations will be required. The ability to test and set portions of the screen must also be provided. The user should be able to copy one Screen object to another and indicate at run time the actual dimensions of the screen. This set of operations to manipulate a Screen object is declared within the class body. These operations are spoken of as the *member functions* of the class.

The member functions of a class are declared inside the class body. A declaration consists of the function prototype. For example,

```
class Screen {
public:
    void home();
    void move( int, int );
    char get();
    char get( int, int );
    void checkRange( int, int );
    // ...
};
```

The definition of a member function can also be placed inside the class body. For example,

```
class Screen {
public:
    void home() { cursor = screen; }
    char get() { return *cursor; }
    // ...
};
```

home() positions the cursor at the top left-hand corner of the screen. get() returns the value of the current cursor position. Because they are defined inside the class body, they are *automatically* handled as inline functions.

Member functions larger than one or two lines are best defined outside the class body. This requires a special class syntax to identify the function as a member of its class. For example, here is the definition of checkRange():

```
#include "Screen.h"
#include <iostream.h>
#include <stdlib.h>

void Screen::checkRange( int row, int col )
{ // validate coordinates
    if ( row < 1 || row > height ||
         col < 1 || col > width ) {
        cerr << "Screen coordinates ( "
             << row << ", " << col
             << " ) out of bounds.\n";
        exit( -1 );
    }
}
```

A member function defined outside the class body must explicitly declare itself to be inline. For example, the following implementation defines move() to be an inline member function of Screen:

```
inline void
Screen::move( int r, int c )
{ // move cursor to absolute position
      checkRange( r, c ); // valid address?
      int row = (r-1)*width; // row location
      cursor = screen + row + c - 1;
}
```

Member functions are distinguished from ordinary functions by the following attributes:

- Member functions have full access privilege to both the public and private members of the class while, in general, ordinary functions have access only to the public members of the class. Of course, the member functions of one class, in general, have no access privileges to the members of another class.

- Member functions are defined within the scope of their class; ordinary functions are defined at file scope. This means that their names are not visible outside the scope of the class. Section 5.8 (page 257) considers class scope in detail.

A member function can overload only other member functions of its class. This is because overloaded functions must occur in the same scope. The following second instance of get(), for example, has no relationship with a nonmember, global get() or a member function get() of another class.

```
inline char
Screen::get( int r, int c )
{
     move( r, c );   // position cursor
     return get();   // other Screen get()
}
```

Information Hiding

It often happens that the internal representation of a class type is modified subsequent to its initial use. For example, imagine that a study is conducted of users of our Screen class, and that it is determined that all the Screen class objects defined are of the dimension 24 x 80. In this case, a less flexible but more efficient representation for the Screen class is the following:

```
        const Height = 24;
        const Width = 80;
        class Screen {
                char screen[ Height ][ Width ];
                short cursor[2];
        };
```

Each member function must be reimplemented, but the interface of each function (that is, its signature and return type) will remain unchanged. What is the effect of this change to the internal representation of Screen on users of the class?

- Every program that made direct access to the data members of the old Screen representation is broken. It is necessary to locate and rewrite all those portions of code before the program can be used again.

- Every program that limited its Screen object access to the Screen member functions requires no change to its working code. Recompilation, however, is necessary.

Information hiding is a formal mechanism for restricting user access to the internal representation of a class type. It is specified by labeled public, private, and protected sections within the class body. Members declared within a public section become public members; those declared within a private or protected section become private or protected members.

- A public member is accessible from anywhere within a program. A class enforcing information hiding limits its public members to the member functions meant to define the functional operations of the class.

- A protected member behaves as a public member to a *derived class*; it behaves as a private member to the rest of the program. (We saw an instance of how protected members are used in the ArrayRC class derivation in Chapter 1. A full discussion of protected members is deferred until Chapter 8, in which derived classes and the concept of *inheritance* are introduced.)

- A private member can be accessed only by the member functions and *friends* of its class. (See Section 5.5 (page 239) later in this chapter for a discussion of friends.) A class that enforces information hiding declares its data members as private.

The following definition of Screen specifies its public and private sections:

```
class Screen {
public:
    void home (){ move ( 1, 1 ); }
    char get () { return *cursor; }
    char get ( int, int );
    inline void move ( int, int );
    // ...
private:
    short height, width;
    char *cursor, *screen;
};
```

By convention, the public members of a class are presented first. The private members are listed at the bottom of the class body.

A class may contain multiple public, protected, or private labeled sections. Each section remains in effect until either another section label or the closing right brace of the class body is seen. If no label is specified, by default the section immediately following the opening left brace is private.

5.2 Class Objects

The definition of the Screen class did not cause any memory to be allocated. Memory is allocated for a class with the definition of each class object. The definition

```
Screen myScreen;
```

for example, allocates a chunk of storage sufficient to contain the four Screen class data members.

Objects of the same class can be initialized and assigned to one another. By default, copying a class object is equivalent to copying all its elements. For example,

```
// bufScreen.height = myScreen.height
// bufScreen.width  = myScreen.width
// bufScreen.cursor = myScreen.cursor
// bufScreen.screen = myScreen.screen
Screen bufScreen = myScreen;
```

By default, class objects are passed by value as the argument and return type of a function. A pointer to a class object can be initialized or assigned the result either of operator new or of the address-of operator ("&"). For example,

```
        Screen *ptr = new Screen;
        myScreen = *ptr;
        ptr = &bufScreen;
```

Outside the scope of the class, the member selection operators are required to access either the data members or member functions of a class. The class object selector (".") is used with a class object or reference; the class pointer selector ("->") is used with a pointer to a class object. For example,

```
        #include "Screen.h"

        int isEqual( Screen& s1, Screen *s2 )
        { // return 0 if not equal, 1 if equal

            if ( s1.getHeight() != s2->getHeight() ||
                 s1.getWidth() != s2->getWidth() )
                    return 0;

            for ( int ix = 0; ix < s1.getHeight(); ++ix )
                for ( int j = 0; j < s2->getWidth(); ++j )
                    if (s1.get( ix, j ) != s2->get( ix, j ))
                        return 0;

            return 1; // still here? equal.
        }
```

isEqual() is a nonmember function that compares two Screen objects for equality. isEqual() has no access privilege to the private data members of Screen; it must rely on the public member functions of the Screen class.

getHeight() and getWidth(), referred to as access functions, provide read-only access to the private data members of the class. Their implementation is straightforward. For efficiency, they are defined as inline:

```
        class Screen {
        public:
            int getHeight() { return height; }
            int getWidth() { return width; }
            // ...
        private:
            short height, width;
            // ...
        };
```

Members of a class may be accessed directly within the scope of the class. Each member function is contained within the scope of its class regardless of whether it is defined within or outside the class body. A member function can access the members of its class without using the member selection operators. For example,

```
#include "String.h"
#include <string.h>
#include <assert.h>

void Screen::copy( Screen& s )
{
    delete screen; // free up existing storage
    height = s.height;
    width = s.width;

    screen = cursor = new char[ height * width + 1 ];
    assert( screen != 0 );
    strcpy( screen, s.screen );
}
```

Exercise 5-1. copy() resizes the target Screen object to the size of the Screen object it is to duplicate. Reimplement copy() to allow the source and target Screen objects to be of different sizes.

☐

Exercise 5-2. What is the behavior of copy() given the following invocation?

```
Screen myScreen;
myScreen.copy( myScreen );
```

☐

Exercise 5-3. An interesting and possibly dangerous assumption is being made about the characters contained within screen. This assumption allows the screen members to be copied using the strcpy() library function. What is this assumption? Reimplement copy() so that it does not depend on this assumption. ☐

5.3 Class Member Functions

Member functions provide the set of operations a user may perform on the class type. This set is referred to as the *public interface* of the class. The success or failure of a class depends on the completeness and efficiency of this set of member functions. This section considers the member functions a Screen class requires. It is divided into the following four subsections: manager functions, implementor functions, helping functions, and access functions.

These categories of member functions are not part of the C++ language. Rather, they are a method of thinking about the kinds of member functions a class generally requires.

Manager Functions

One set of specialized member functions — manager functions — manage class objects, handling activities such as initialization, assignment, memory management, and type conversion. Manager functions are usually invoked implicitly by the compiler.

An initialization member function, called a *constructor*, is implicitly invoked each time a class object is defined or allocated by operator new. A constructor is specified by giving it the class name. Here is a Screen class constructor:

```
Screen::Screen( int high, int wid, char bkground )
{   // Screen initializer function: constructor

    int sz = high * wid;
    height = high; width = wid;
    cursor = screen = new char[sz+1];
    assert( cursor != 0 );

    char *ptr = screen;
    char *endptr = screen + sz;
    while ( ptr != endptr ) *ptr++ = bkground;
    *ptr = '\0'; // end of screen marked by null

}
```

The declaration of the Screen constructor within the class body provides a default high, wid, and bkground argument value.

```
class Screen {
public:
    Screen( int=8, int=40, char='#' );
    // ...
};
```

Each declared Screen object is automatically initialized by the Screen constructor. For example,

```
Screen s1;                          // Screen(8,40,'#')
Screen *ps = new Screen( 20 );      // Screen(20,40,'#')

main() {
    Screen s(24,80,'*');            // Screen(24,80,'*')
    // ...
}
```

Chapter 6 considers constructors and the other manager functions in detail.

Implementor Functions

A second set of member functions, referred to as *implementor* functions, provides the capabilities associated with the class abstraction. A Screen, for example, is expected to support cursor movement such as home() and move(). Additional required cursor movements include forward(), back(), up(), and down(). The member functions forward() and back() move the cursor one character at a time. On reaching the bottom or top of the screen, the cursor wraps around.

```
inline void Screen::forward()
{
    // advance cursor one screen element
    ++cursor;

    // check for bottom of screen; wraparound
    // bottom of screen is null element
    if ( *cursor == '\0' )
        home();
}


inline void Screen::back()
{ // move cursor backward one screen element

    // check for top of screen; wraparound
    if ( cursor == screen )
        bottom();
    else
        --cursor;
}
```

bottom() is an implementor function that sets the cursor to the last column of the screen.

```
inline void Screen::bottom ()
{
   int sz = width*height - 1;
      cursor = screen + sz;
}
```

up() and down() move the cursor up or down one row of the screen. On reaching the top or bottom row of the screen, the cursor does not wrap around, but rather sounds a bell, remaining where it is.

```
const char BELL = '\007';

inline void Screen::up()
{ // move cursor up one row of screen
   // do not wraparound; rather, ring bell

   if ( row() == 1 ) // at top?
      cout.put( BELL );
   else
      cursor -= width;
}


inline void Screen::down()
{
   if ( row() == height ) // at bottom?
      cout.put( BELL );
   else
      cursor += width;
}
```

Exercise 5-4. Additional cursor movements might include moving forward or backward one word, where a word is delimited by white space. Implement wordForward().

☐

Exercise 5-5. Another useful capability is to position the cursor at the occurrence of a string. For example,

```
myScreen.find( "this" );
```

Implement find(char*). ☐

Helping Functions

Another set of member functions carries out auxiliary tasks. Usually these helping functions are not intended to be invoked directly by the user. Rather, they provide support for the other class member functions. Generally, they are declared as private. checkRange(), defined earlier, is a helping function. Here are four additional helping functions. row() returns the current row of the cursor position:

```
inline int Screen::row()
{ // return current row
  int pos = cursor - screen + 1;
  return (pos+width-1)/width;
}
```

col() returns the current column of the cursor position:

```
inline int Screen::col()
{ // return current column
  int pos = cursor - screen + 1;
  return ((pos+width-1) % width)+1;
}
```

remainingSpace() returns the amount of space remaining on the screen, not counting the current position:

```
inline int Screen::remainingSpace()
{ // current position is no longer remaining
  int sz = width*height;
  return( screen + sz - cursor - 1 );
};
```

stats() displays the information returned by the three previous helping functions; it was useful in testing the code incorporated here.

```
inline void Screen::stats()
{
    cout << "row: " << row() << "\t";
    cout << "col: " << col() << "\t";
    cout << "rm: " << remainingSpace() << endl;
}
```

The following is a small program written to exercise a portion of the member functions implemented thus far.

```
#include "Screen.h"
#include <iostream.h>

main() {
  Screen x(3,3);
  int sz = x.getHeight() * x.getWidth();

      cout << "Screen Object ( "
           << x.getHeight() << ", " << x.getWidth()
           << " ) ( size: " << sz << " )\n\n";

      x.home();
      for ( int ix = 0; ix <= sz; ++ix )
      { // ``<='' in order to wraparound
             x.stats();
             x.forward(); }
      return 0;
}
```

When compiled and executed, the program generates the following output:

```
Screen Object ( 3, 3 ) ( size: 9 )

row: 1   col: 1   rm: 8
row: 1   col: 2   rm: 7
row: 1   col: 3   rm: 6
row: 2   col: 1   rm: 5
row: 2   col: 2   rm: 4
row: 2   col: 3   rm: 3
row: 3   col: 1   rm: 2
row: 3   col: 2   rm: 1
row: 3   col: 3   rm: 0
row: 1   col: 1   rm: 8
```

Access Functions

Information hiding encapsulates the internal representation of the class object, thereby protecting user code from changes to that representation. Equally important, the internal state of the class object is protected from random program modification. A specific small set of functions provides all write access to the object. If an error occurs, the search space for the mistake is limited to this function set, greatly easing the problems of maintenance and program correctness. Member functions supporting user access to otherwise private data are referred to as *access functions*. So far we have seen only read access functions. Here are two set() functions that allow a user to write to the screen:

```
void Screen::set( char *s )
{ // write string beginning at screen element

    int space = remainingSpace();
    int len = strlen( s );
    if ( space < len ) {
        cerr << "Screen: warning: truncation: "
             << "space: " << space
             << "string length: " << len << endl;
        len = space;
    }

    for ( int ix = 0; ix < len; ++ix )
        *cursor++ = *s++;
}



void Screen::set( char ch )
{
    if ( ch == '\0' )
        cerr << "Screen: warning: "
             << "null character (ignored).\n";
    else *cursor = ch;
}
```

A simplifying assumption of our Screen class implementation is that the screen does not contain embedded null characters. This is the reason that set() does not permit a null character to be written to the screen.

Access functions may also augment the class abstraction by providing a set of predicate operations. The Screen class, for example, might be augmented with a collection of isEqual() functions.

isEqual(char ch) returns true if ch is equal to the character contained at the current cursor location. Its implementation is straightforward:

```
class Screen {
public:
  isEqual( char ch ) {
        return (ch == *cursor ); }
  // ...
}
```

isEqual(char* s) returns true if the array of characters beginning with the current cursor location is equal to s.

```
#include <string.h>

int Screen::isEqual( char *s )
{ // yes? return 1; otherwise, 0

    int len = strlen( s );
    if ( remainingSpace() < len )
        return 0;

    char *p = cursor;
    while ( len-- > 0 )
        if ( *p++ != *s++ )
            return 0;

    return 1;
}
```

isEqual(Screen&) returns true if two screens are equal; that is, the height, width, and contents of the two screens must all be the same.

```
int Screen::isEqual( Screen& s )
{
    // first, are they physically unequal?
    if ( width != s.width || height != s.height )
        return 0;

    // do both share the same screen?
    char *p = screen;
    char *q = s.screen;
    if ( p == q ) return 1;

    // be careful not to walk off the Screens
    while ( *p && *p++ == *q++ );

    if ( *p ) // loop broke on not equal
        return 0;

    return 1;
}
```

There is one special case this implementation fails to consider: the case when a Screen object is compared to itself. For example,

```
// sanity check: must evaluate as true
myScreen.isEqual( myScreen );
```

In order for this case to be recognized, there needs to be a way for the programmer to access the class object through which the member function is invoked. How can we do this?

The language reserves a keyword named this. The this keyword, when referenced inside a member function, represents a pointer holding the address of the invoking class object. Thus, the first statement of isEqual() is now the following:

```
// test if both objects are the same
if (this == &s) return 1;
```

The this pointer is considered in detail later in this chapter.

Exercise 5-6. Compare the nonmember implementation in Section 5.2 (page 222) with this implementation. Why do the two look so different? Are they equivalent? □

const Member Functions

An attempt to modify a nonclass const object from within a program is flagged as a compile-time error. For example,

```
const char blank = ' ';
blank = '\0'; // error
```

A class object, however, ordinarily is not directly modified by the programmer. Rather, the public set of member functions are invoked. In order to enforce the *constness* of a class object, the compiler must distinguish between safe and unsafe member functions. For example,

```
const Screen blankScreen;
blankScreen.display();  // safe
blankScreen.set( '*' ); // unsafe
```

The class designer indicates which member functions are safe by specifying them as const. For example,

```
class Screen {
public:
    char get() const { return *cursor; }
    // ...
};
```

Only member functions specified as const can be invoked by a const class object.

The const keyword is placed between the argument list and body of the member function. A const member function defined outside the class body must specify the const keyword in both its declaration and definition. For example,

```
class Screen {
public:
    int isEqual( char ch ) const;
    // ...
private:
    char *cursor;
    // ...
};

int Screen::isEqual( char ch ) const
{
    return( ch == *cursor );
}
```

It is illegal to declare as const a member function that modifies a data member. In the following simplified Screen definition, for example,

```
class Screen {
public:
    void ok(char ch) const { *cursor = ch; }
    void error(char *pch) const { cursor = pch; }
    // ...
private:
    char *cursor;
    // ...
};
```

ok() is a legal const member function because it does not change the value of cursor — rather, it changes the value of the object cursor addresses. error(), however, does modify the actual value of cursor and therefore cannot be specified as a const member function. The declaration results in the following error message:

```
error: assignment to member Screen::cursor of
       const class Screen
```

A const member function can be overloaded with a nonconst instance that defines the same signature. For example,

```
class Screen {
public:
    char get(int x, int y);
    char get(int x, int y) const;
    // ...
};
```

In this case, the constness of the class object determines which of the functions is invoked:

```
main() {
    const Screen cs;
    Screen s;

    char ch = cs.get(0,0); // const member
    ch = s.get(0,0);        // nonconst member
}
```

Constructors and destructors are exceptions in that they are not required to be declared const in order to be applied to constant class objects. In general, any class that is expected to be used extensively should declare the permissible member functions for a const class object as const.

A member function can also be specified as volatile:

```
class Screen {
public:
    char poll() volatile;
    // ...
};
char Screen::poll() volatile { ... }
```

Only the destructor, constructors, and volatile member functions of a class can be invoked for a volatile class object.

5.4 The Implicit this Pointer

There is a certain inelegance in the current implementation of the Screen class member functions. Manipulations of a screen tend to occur as a sequence of actions: clear, move, set, display. The programmer is constrained, however, to code each action as a separate statement:

```
main() {
    Screen myScreen( 3, 3 ), bufScreen;

    myScreen.clear();
    myScreen.move(2,2);
    myScreen.set('*');
    myScreen.display();

    bufScreen.reSize(5,5)
    bufScreen.display();
}
```

The need to specify a new statement for each action applied to a Screen object is unnecessarily verbose. What we would prefer is to support the concatenation of member calls. For example,

```
main () {
    myScreen.clear().move(2,2).set('*').display();
    bufScreen.reSize(5,5).display();
}
```

This section illustrates how to implement this syntax. First, let us examine the class member function itself more closely.

What Is the this Pointer?

Each class object maintains its own copy of the class data members. myScreen has its width, height, cursor, and screen; bufScreen has its own separate set. Both myScreen and bufScreen, however, will call the same copy of any particular member function. There exists only one instance of each class member function. This presents two problems:

1. If only one instance of a member function exists, it cannot be stored inside the class object. That would proliferate function copies with each object defined.

2. If only one instance of a member function exists, how are the particular data members of a class object bound to the data members manipulated within the member function? How, for example, does the cursor manipulated by move() become bound in turn to the cursor belonging to myScreen and bufScreen?

The answer is the this pointer. Each class member function contains a pointer of its class type named this. Within a Screen member function, for example, the this pointer is of type Screen*; within an List member function, it is of type List*.

The this pointer contains the address of the class object through which the member function has been invoked. In this way, the cursor manipulated by home() becomes bound in turn to the cursor belonging to myScreen and bufScreen.

One way of understanding this is to take a brief look at how one compiler, the one developed within Bell Laboratories, implements the this pointer. It is accomplished in the following two steps:

1. Translate the class member functions. Each class member function is translated into a uniquely named nonmember function with one additional argument — the this pointer. For example,

```
home__Screen( Screen *this )
{
    this->cursor = this->screen;
}
```

2. Translate each class member invocation. For example,

```
myScreen.home()
```

is translated into

```
home__Screen( &myScreen );
```

The programmer can reference the `this` pointer explicitly. For example, it is legal, although silly, to write the following:

```
inline void Screen::home()
{
    this->cursor = this->screen;
}
```

There are circumstances, however, when the programmer does need to reference the `this` pointer explicitly, such as in the `IsEqual()` and `copy()` Screen operations.

Using the this Pointer

The `this` pointer is the key to implementing the Screen class concatenation syntax. The member selection operators ("." and "->") are left-associative binary operators. The order of execution is left to right. `myScreen.clear()` is invoked first. For `move()` to be invoked next, `clear()` must return a Screen class object. For `move()` to be invoked correctly, `clear()` must return the `myScreen` object. Each member function must be modified to return the class object that has invoked it. Access to the class object is through the `this` pointer. Here is an implementation of `clear()`:

```
Screen& Screen::clear( char bkground )
{ // reset the cursor and clear the screen

    char *p = cursor = screen;
    while ( *p ) *p++ = bkground;
    return *this;   // return invoking object
}
```

`move()`, `home()`, the `set()` functions, and the four cursor movement functions will all need to add a `return *this` to their definitions and revise their return types from `void` to `Screen&`.

Let's see how these functions can be used — first, from within a member function, then within a nonmember function.

```
Screen&
Screen::lineX( int row, int col, int len, char ch)
{ // draw a line of some length along row
    move( row, col );
    for ( int ix = 0; ix < len; ++ix )
        set( ch ).forward();
    return *this;
}
```

The following nonmember function provides the capability of drawing a line of some length down a particular column:

```
Screen&
lineY( Screen& s, int row, int col, int len, char ch )
{
    s.move( row, col );
    for ( int ix = 0; ix < len; ++ix )
        s.set(ch).down();
    return s;
}
```

The Screen member function display() might be implemented as follows:

```
Screen& Screen::display()
{
    for ( int ix = 0; ix < height; ++ix )
    {   // for each row
        cout << endl;
        int offset = width * ix; // row position
        for ( int j = 0; j < width; ++j )
        {   // for each column, write element
            char *p = screen + offset + j;
            cout.put( *p );
        }
    }
    return *this;
}
```

It is also possible to overwrite the class object addressed by the this pointer, as illustrated by the reSize() member function. reSize() generates a new Screen object. The following assignment replaces the invoking Screen object by this new object:

```
*this = *ps;
```

where ps points to the new Screen object. One implementation of reSize() is as follows:

```
Screen&
Screen::reSize( int h, int w, char bkground )
{ // reSize a screen to height h and width w

    Screen *ps = new Screen( h, w, bkground );
    assert( ps != 0 );
    char *pNew = ps->screen;

    // Is this screen currently allocated?
    // If so, copy old screen contents to new
    if ( screen )
    {
        char *pOld = screen;
        while ( *pOld && *pNew )
            *pNew++ = *pOld++;
        delete screen;
    }

    *this = *ps; // replace Screen object
    return *this;
}
```

Linked list management also often requires having access to the this pointer. For example,

```
class DList { // doubly-linked list
public:
    void append( DList* );
    // ...
private:
    DList *prior, *next;
};

void DList::append( DList *ptr )
{
    ptr->next = next;
    ptr->prior = this;
    next->prior = ptr;
    next = ptr;
}
```

Here is small program to exercise some of the Screen member functions defined in this and the previous section.

```
#include <iostream.h>
#include "Screen.h"

main() {
  Screen x(3,3);
  Screen y(3,3);
  cout << "isEqual( x, y ): (>1<) "
       << x.isEqual(y) << endl;

  y.reSize( 6, 6 ); // double it
  cout << "isEqual( x, y ): (>0<) "
       << x.isEqual(y) << endl;

  lineY( y,1,1,6,'*' ); lineY( y,1,6,6,'*' );
  y.lineX(1,2,4,'*').lineX(6,2,4,'*').move(3,3);
  y.set("hi").lineX(4,3,2,'^').display();

  x.reSize( 6, 6 );
  cout << "\n\nisEqual( x, y ): (>0<) "
       << x.isEqual(y) << endl;

  x.copy( y );
  cout << "isEqual( x, y ): (>1<) "
       << x.isEqual(y) << endl;
  return 0;
}
```

When executed, the program generates the following output:

```
isEqual( x, y ): (>1<) 1
isEqual( x, y ): (>0<) 0

******
*####*
*#hi#*
*#^^#*
*####*
******

isEqual( x, y ): (>0<) 0
isEqual( x, y ): (>1<) 1
```

where the values surrounded by brackets are the expected values and the values outside the parentheses are the actual values generated by calls of isEqual().

5.5 Friends to a Class

In some instances, the information-hiding access rules are too prohibitive. The friend mechanism gives nonmembers of the class access to the nonpublic members of a class. Before discussing the rules for declaring a friend, let's first illustrate an instance in which a friend is necessary.

The iostream input and output operators ("">>"", ""<<"") can be overloaded to handle class types. Once the operators are defined for a class type, objects of the class can be output in the same way as the built-in types. For example,

```
Screen myScreen;
cout << myScreen;
cout << "myScreen: " << myScreen << endl;
```

The input and output operators require, respectively, an istream and ostream object as their left operand; both return the object upon which they operate. This allows successive input or output operators to be concatenated. For example,

```
((( (cout << "myScreen: ") << myScreen) << endl)
```

Each parenthetical subexpression returns the ostream object cout, which becomes the left operand of the next outermost expression.

```
cout << myScreen
```

must be implemented as

```
ostream &operator<<( ostream&, Screen& );
```

This implementation, however, precludes defining the operator function as a member function of Screen.

Here is the declaration of the output operation as a member function of Screen:

```
class Screen {
public:
    ostream &operator<<( ostream& );
    // ...
};
```

The left operand of every member function is an object or pointer to an object of its class. This is why the member function instance of the output operator declares only the one ostream argument. A call of this instance takes the following form:

```
myScreen << cout;
```

It would be very confusing both to the programmer and the human readers of the program to provide this instance. Providing the nonmember

instance, however, means that our output operator has no access privilege to
the nonpublic members of the Screen class — the very members it is
intended to display. This is where the friend mechanism comes in.

A friend is a nonmember of a class that is given access to the nonpublic
members of a class. A friend may be a nonmember function, a member function of a previously defined class, or an entire class. In making one class
friend to another, the member functions of the friend class are given access to
the nonpublic members of the class.

A friend declaration begins with the keyword `friend`. It may appear
only within the class definition. Since friends are nonmembers of the class,
they are not affected by the public, private, or protected section in which
they are declared within the class body. A stylistic convention is to group all
friend declarations immediately following the class header:

```
class Screen {
    friend istream&
        operator>>( istream&, Screen& );
    friend ostream&
        operator<<( ostream&, Screen& );
public:
    // ... rest of the Screen class
};
```

How might the output Screen operator be written? The three necessary data
members are the Screen's `height` and `width`, and the actual character array
that `screen` addresses. For simplicity, the cursor position becomes reset to
"home" whenever a Screen object is read. The format of the Screen object
output is as follows:

```
<height,width>linearScreenDump
```

The output operator might be implemented as follows:

```
#include <iostream.h>
ostream& operator<<( ostream& os, Screen& s )
{
    os << "<" << s.height
       << "," << s.width << ">";

    char *p = s.screen;
    while ( *p ) os.put( *p++ );

    return os;
}
```

Here is a simple exercise of the output operator. `main()` is implemented as
follows:

```
#include <iostream.h>
#include "Screen.h"

main() {
   Screen x(4,4,'%');
   cout << x << endl;
   return 0;
}
```

When compiled and executed, it generates the following output:

```
<4,4>%%%%%%%%%%%%%%%%
```

The input operator will read as input the result of the Screen output operator. Let's store the output in a file named `output`. An implementation of the input operator is presented next; the verification of the input format is omitted to save space.

```
istream& operator>>( istream& is, Screen& s )
{ // read Screen object output by operator <<
    int wid, hi;
    char ch;

    // format verification not shown
    // <hi,wid>screenDump
    is >> ch;   // '<'
    is >> hi;   // get height
    is >> ch;   // ','
    is >> wid;  // get width
    is >> ch;   // '>'

    delete s.screen;

    int sz = hi * wid;
    s.height = hi; s.width = wid;
    s.cursor = s.screen = new char[ sz + 1 ];

    char *endptr = s.screen + sz;
    char *ptr = s.screen;
    while ( ptr != endptr ) is.get( *ptr++ );
    *ptr = '\0';

    return is;
}
```

The following small program exercises both the input and output operator instances for the Screen class.

```
#include <iostream.h>
#include "Screen.C"

main() {
   Screen x(5,5,'?');
   cout << "x(5,5,?) :\t" << x << endl;

   cin >> x;
   cout << "cin >> x :\t" << x << endl;
   return 0;
}
```

Its input is the output of the previous program. When compiled and executed, it generates the following output:

```
x(5,5,?) :        <5,5>??????????????????????????
cin >> x :        <4,4>%%%%%%%%%%%%%%%%%
```

Exercise 5-7. The input operator should verify the correctness of the format that it is reading. Modify it to do that.

☐

Exercise 5-8. Implementing the output operator so that it preserves the cursor position is not difficult. The member functions col() and row() can be of help. Reimplement the output operator to preserve the current cursor position.

☐

Exercise 5-9. Reimplement the input operator so that it can handle the format of the output operator reimplemented in the preceding exercise. ☐

A class must specify each instance of an overloaded function it wishes to make a friend to the class. For example,

```
extern ostream& storeOn( ostream&, Screen& );
extern BitMap& storeOn( BitMap&, Screen& );

class Screen
{
    friend ostream& storeOn( ostream&, Screen& );
    friend BitMap& storeOn( BitMap&, Screen& );
    // ...
};
```

If a function manipulates objects of two distinct classes, the function may either be made a friend to both classes or be made a member function of one class and a friend to the other. Let's look at how this might be done.

In one instance, a function should logically be made a member of both classes. Since this is impossible, the function instead is made a friend to both classes. For example,

```
class Window; // forward declaration
class Screen {
    friend Boolean is_equal(Screen&,Window&);
    // ...
};

class Window {
    friend Boolean is_equal(Screen&,Window&);
    // ...
};
```

In the second instance, a function logically belongs as a member of one class. It still, however, requires access to the second class. Therefore, it is made a friend to that second class:

```
class Window;
class Screen {
public:
    Screen& copy(Window&);
    // ...
};

class Window {
    friend Screen& Screen::copy(Window&)
    // ...
};
Screen& Screen::copy( Window& ) { /* ... */ }
```

A member function of a class cannot be declared a friend until its class definition has been seen. This is not always possible. For example, what if the Screen and Window classes need to be friends to one another? In a case such as this, the entire Window class can be declared as a friend to the Screen class. For example,

```
class Window;
class Screen {
    friend class Window;
    // ...
};
```

The nonpublic members of the Screen class may now be accessed within each of the Window member function. Additionally, all nonpublic nested types within the Screen class can now be accessed within Window. This is another reason for declaring an entire class friend to a class.

5.6 Static Class Members

It is sometimes necessary that all the objects of a particular class have access to the same variable. This may be some condition flag or counter related to the class that changes dynamically in the course of the program — perhaps a count is needed of how many objects of a class exist at any one point in the program. Sometimes it is simply more efficient to provide one variable for all the objects of one class rather than having each object maintain its own copy. This variable may be a pointer to an error-handling routine for that class or a pointer to the free store of the class. For these cases a static class member can provide a solution.

A static data member acts as a global variable for its class. Two advantages of a static data member over the use of a global variable are the following:

1. Information hiding can be enforced. A static member can be made non-public; a global variable cannot.

2. A static member is not entered into the program's global name space, thus removing the possibility of an accidental conflict of names.

There is only one instance of a static data member of a class. It is in scope whenever the class is in scope; that is, whenever the class definition is accessible. A static data member is a single shared object accessible to all objects of its class.

A data member is made static by prefixing its declaration with the keyword `static`. Static data members obey the public/private/protected access rules.

For example, in the CoOp class defined next, `costPerShare` is declared a private static member of type double.

```
class CoOp {
friend compareCost( CoOp&, CoOp* );
public:
    CoOp( int, char * );
    inline double monthlyMaint();
    void raiseCost(double incr) { costPerShare += incr; }
    double getCost() { return costPerShare; }
private:
    static double costPerShare;
    int shares;
    char *owner;
};
```

The decision to make `costPerShare` static has two purposes: to conserve storage and to limit the chance of error. Each CoOp object must be able to access `costPerShare`. Although its current value is the same for each object, the value changes over time. Therefore, it cannot be made a constant. But since it is inefficient to have every class object maintain a copy of the same value, we declare it static. By having `costPerShare` static, it need only be updated once and we are assured that each class object is accessing the same value. Were each class object to maintain its own copy, each copy would have to be updated, leading to inefficiency and error.

A static data member is initialized outside the class definition in the same manner as a nonmember variable. The only difference is that the class scope operator syntax must be used. For example, here is how we might initialize `costPerShare`:

```
// explicit initialization of a static class member

#include "CoOp.h"
double CoOp::costPerShare = 23.99;
```

As with nonmember variables, only one initialization of a static data member can occur within a program. This means that static member initializations should be placed in a file together with the definitions of the noninline member functions, and not in the class header file. The access level of a static data member pertains only to the read and write access of that member and not to its initialization. This is why `costPerShare` can be initialized at file scope.

Static data members can be a constant or a class object. For example,

```
#include "List.h"
typedef unsigned long u_long;

class CoOp {
    // ...
private:
    static List *share_distribution;
    static const u_long total_shares;
    static String str;
};

List *CoOp::share_distribution = new List;
const u_long CoOp::total_shares = getShares();
String CoOp::str( "CoOp" );
```

Access of a static class member is syntactically identical to access of a nonstatic member. For example,

```
inline double
CoOp::monthlyMaint()
{
    return( costPerShare * shares );
}

// Pointer and Reference arguments in order to
// illustrate object and pointer access
int compareCost( CoOp& unit1, CoOp* unit2 )
{
    double maint1, maint2;
    maint1 = unit1.costPerShare * unit1.shares;
    maint2 = unit2->costPerShare * unit2->shares;
    // ...
}
```

Both `unit1.costPerShare` and `unit2->costPerShare` reference the static member `CoOp::costPerShare`.

Because there is only one copy of a class static data member, it can also be accessed directly. This looks as follows:

```
if ( CoOp::costPerShare < 100.00 ))
```

The class scope operator ("`CoOp::`") must be specified because the static member occurs in the class scope and not the global scope of the program.

The following definition of the friend function `compareCost` is the equivalent of the one just presented:

```
int compareCost( CoOp& unit1, CoOp *unit2 )
{
    double maint1, maint2;
    maint1 = CoOp::costPerShare * unit1.shares;
    maint2 = CoOp::costPerShare * unit2->shares;
    // ...
}
```

The two member access functions, `raiseCost()` and `getCost()` access only the static class member `costPerShare`. The problem with this is that each must be called with a particular class object. It is irrelevant which object. The object is required only for the calling syntax since there is only one `costPerShare` instance shared by all class objects. This can result in misleading program code.

Alternatively, a member function which accesses only the static members of a class may also be declared as static. This can be done as follows:

```
class CoOp {
    friend compareCost( CoOp&, CoOp* );
public:
    CoOp( int, char* );
    inline double monthlyMaint();
    static void raiseCost(double incr);
    static double getCost() { return costPerShare; }
private:
    static double costPerShare;
    int shares;
    char *owner;
};

inline void CoOp::raiseCost(double incr)
{
    costPerShare += incr;
}
```

A static member function does not contain a `this` pointer; therefore, any implicit or explicit reference to the `this` pointer results in a compile-time error. Attempting to access a nonstatic class member is an implicit reference to the `this` pointer. For example, `monthlyMaint()` could not be declared as a static member function since it needs to access the data member `shares`. The definition of a static member function is the same as that of a nonstatic class member function except that it may not be declared as either `const` or `volatile`.

A static member function may be invoked through a class object or a pointer to a class object in the same way a nonstatic member function is invoked. However, both a static data member and static member function can be accessed or invoked directly even if no class objects are ever declared. Here is a small program to illustrate the use of static class members:

```
#include <iostream.h>
#include "CoOp.h"

canAfford( double affordShare ) {
    enum { FALSE, TRUE };

    // no CoOp class objects defined
    if ( affordShare >= CoOp::getCost() )
        return TRUE;
    else return FALSE;
}
```

```
main() {
    double affordShare = 29.95;

    if ( canAfford( affordShare ) )
    {
        // pointer to static class member is
        // declared as non-member pointer
        void (*psf)(double) = &CoOp::raiseCost;
        psf( affordShare );

        CoOp studio( 250, "danny" );
        if ( affordShare < studio.getCost() )
            cout << "oops, price must have risen since\
the if clause!\n";


    }
    return 0;
}
```

The unique nature of the static data member — that a single instance exists independently of any object of the class — allows it to be used in ways that are illegal for nonstatic data members:

- A static data member can appear as a default argument to a member function of the class — a nonstatic member cannot. For example,

```
extern int a;

class Foo {
private:
    int a;
    static int b;
public:
    // error: resolves to nonstatic Foo::a
    // there is no associated class object
    int mem1( int = a );

    // ok: resolves to static Foo::b
    // an associated class object unnecessary
    int mem2( int = b );

    // ok: global instance of int a
    int mem3( int = ::a );
};
```

Note that in the case of a default argument, name resolution occurs at the point of declaration. Had the member a, therefore, been defined following the definition of mem1(), the default argument would have referred to the global instance of a. Similarly, had the member b been defined following the definition of mem2(), the reference to b would have generated an "undefined variable" error.

- A static data member can be an object of the class of which it is a member. A nonstatic member is restricted to being declared as a pointer or reference to an object of its class. For example,

```
class Bar {
public:
    // ...
private:
    static Bar a; // ok
    Bar *b; // ok
    Bar c; // error
};
```

Exercise 5-10. Given the following class Y, with two static class members and two static member functions:

```
class X {
public:
    X( int i ) { val = i; }
    int getVal() { return val; }
private:
    int val;
};

class Y {
public:
    Y( int i );
    static X getXval();
    static int getCallsXval();
private:
    static X Xval;
    static int callsXval;
};
```

Initialize Xval to 20 and callsXval to 0.

□

Exercise 5-11. Implement the two static member access functions. callsXval simply keeps count of how many times getXval() is called. □

5.7 Class Member Pointer

Pointers, especially pointers to functions, provide a useful form of program generality. Users of the Screen class, for example, have been asking for a "repeat" function that performs some user-specified operation n times. A nongeneral implementation could be the following:

```
Screen &repeat( char op, int times )
{
    switch( op ) {
        case DOWN: // ... invoke Screen::down()
            break;
        case UP: // ... invoke Screen::up()
            break;
        // ...
    }
}
```

Although this works, it has a number of drawbacks. One problem is that it is too explicitly reliant on the member functions of Screen. Each time a member function is added or removed, repeat() must be updated. A second problem is its size. By having to test for each possible member function, the full listing of repeat() is large and seems very complex.

An alternative, more general implementation replaces op with a pointer to Screen member function argument type. repeat() no longer needs to determine the intended operation. The entire switch statement can be removed. The definition and use of pointers to class members is the topic of the following subsections.

The Type of a Class Member

A pointer to a function may not legally be assigned the address of a member function even when the return type and signature of the two match exactly. For example, pfi, which follows, is a pointer to a function taking no arguments and with a return type of int:

```
int (*pfi)();
```

Screen defines two access functions, getHeight() and getWidth(), which also take no arguments and define a return type of int:

```
inline Screen::getHeight() { return height; }
inline Screen::getWidth()  { return width; }
```

Two nonmember functions, HeightIs() and WidthIs(), are also defined for purposes of illustration:

```
HeightIs()  { return HEIGHT; }
WidthIs()   { return WIDTH; }
```

Assignment of either or both of `HeightIs()` and `WidthIs()` to `pfi` is legal and correct,

```
pfi = HeightIs;
pfi = WidthIs;
```

The assignment of either the `getHeight()` or `getWidth()` member function, however, is a type violation and will generate a compile-time error:

```
// illegal assignment: type violation
pfi = Screen::getHeight;
```

Why is there a type violation? A member function has an additional type attribute absent from a nonmember function — *its class*. A pointer to a member function must match exactly not in two but in three areas:

1. The data type and number of formal arguments; that is, its signature.

2. The return data type.

3. The class type of which it is a member.

The declaration of a pointer to a member function requires an expanded syntax that takes the class type into account. The same also holds true for pointers to class data members. Consider the type of the Screen class member `height`. The complete type of `Screen::height` is "short member of class Screen." Consequently, the complete type of a pointer to `Screen::height` is "pointer to short member of class Screen." This is written as follows:

```
short Screen::*
```

A definition of a pointer to a member of class Screen of type `short` looks like this:

```
short Screen::*ps_Screen;
```

`ps_Screen` can be initialized with the address of `height` as follows:

```
short Screen::*ps_Screen = &Screen::height;
```

Similarly, it can be assigned the address of `width` like this:

```
ps_Screen = &Screen::width;
```

`ps_Screen` may be set to either `width` or `height` since both are Screen class data members of type `short`. An attempt to take the address of a non-public class member in a portion of the program without access privilege to the class results in a compile-time error.

Exercise 5-12. What is the type of the Screen class members `screen` and `cursor`?

□

Exercise 5-13. Define, initialize and assign a pointer to class member for `Screen::screen` and `Screen::cursor`. □

A pointer to member function is defined by specifying its return type, signature, and class. For example, a pointer to the Screen members `getHeight()` and `getWidth()` is defined as follows:

```
int (Screen::*)()
```

this defines a pointer to a member function of Screen taking no arguments and returning a value of type `int`. A pointer to a member function can be initialized and assigned to as follows:

```
// all pointers to class member may be assigned 0
int (Screen::*pmf1)() = 0;
int (Screen::*pmf2)() = Screen::getHeight;

pmf1 = pmf2;
pmf2 = Screen::getWidth;
```

Use of a typedef can make the pointer to member syntax easier to read. For example, the following typedef defines `Action` to be an alternative type name for

```
Screen& (Screen::*)()
```

that is, a pointer to a member function of Screen taking no arguments and returning a reference to a Screen class object.

```
typedef Screen& (Screen::*Action)();

Action deFault = Screen::home;
Action next = Screen::forward;
```

Exercise 5-14. Define a typedef for each distinct type of Screen member function. □

Pointers to members may be declared as arguments to functions; a default argument initializer may also be specified. For example,

```
action( Screen&, Screen& (Screen::*)() );
```

`action()` is declared as taking two arguments:

1. A reference to a Screen class object.

2. A pointer to a member function of Screen taking no arguments and
   returning a reference to a Screen class object.

   `action()` can be invoked in any of the following ways:

```
Screen myScreen;
typedef Screen& (Screen::*Action)();
Action deFault = Screen::home;

extern Screen&
action( Screen&, Action = Screen::display );

void ff()
{
    action( myScreen );
    action( myScreen, deFault );
    action( myScreen, Screen::bottom );
}
```

A pointer to member behaves differently from a nonmember pointer to
function in two important ways:

- There is no implicit conversion of a pointer to member to a pointer of
  type `void*`. For example,

```
int (*pfi) ();
void (X::*pmf)();

void *pfv1 = pmi; // ok: implicit conversion
void *pfv2 = pmf; // error: no implicit conversion
```

- A pointer to class member can be invoked only when bound to an object
  or pointer of that class (or of a class derived from it — see Section 8.6,
  page 421, for a discussion of using a pointer to class member under inheritance). The invocation and use of a pointer to class member is covered in
  the next section.

Exercise 5-15. Pointers to members may also be declared as class data members. Modify the Screen class definition to contain a pointer to Screen member function of the same type as `home()` and `bottom()`.

□

Exercise 5-16. Modify the existing Screen constructor (or introduce a new
constructor) to take a pointer to Screen member argument of the type specified in the previous exercise. Provide a default argument. Provide an access
function to allow the user to set this member. □

Using a Pointer to Class Member

Pointers to class members must always be accessed through a specific object of the class. We do this by using the two pointer to member selection operators (".*" for class objects and references and "->*" for pointers to class objects.) For example, pointers to member functions are invoked as follows:

```
int (Screen::*pmfi)() = Screen::getHeight;
Screen& (Screen::*pmfS)(Screen&) = Screen::copy;

Screen myScreen, *bufScreen;

// direct invocation of member function
if (myScreen.getHeight() == bufScreen->getHeight())
    bufScreen->copy( myScreen );

// equivalent invocation through pointers to members
if ((myScreen.*pmfi)() == (bufScreen->*pmfi)())
    (bufScreen->*pmfS)(myScreen);
```

The calls

```
(myScreen.*pmfi)()
(bufScreen->*pmfi)()
```

require the parentheses because the precedence of the call operator ("()") is higher than the precedence of the pointer to member selection operators. Without the parentheses,

```
myScreen.*pmfi()
```

would be interpreted to mean

```
myScreen.*(pmfi())
```

That is, invoke the function pmfi() and bind its return value to the pointer to member object selection operator (".*").

Similarly, pointers to data members are accessed in the following manner:

```
typedef short Screen::*ps_Screen;
Screen myScreen, *tmpScreen = new Screen(10,10);

void ff()
{
    ps_Screen pH = &Screen::height;
    ps_Screen pW = &Screen::width;

    tmpScreen->*pH = myScreen.*pH;
    tmpScreen->*pW = myScreen.*pW;
}
```

Since height and width are private members of the Screen class, the initialization of pH and pW within ff() is legal only if ff() is declared a friend to Screen. Otherwise, ff()'s attempt to take the address of these private class members will be flagged as an error at compile time.

Here is an implementation of the repeat() member function we discussed at the beginning of this section:

```
typedef Screen& (Screen::*Action)();

Screen& Screen::repeat( Action op, int times )
{
    for ( int i = 0; i < times; ++i )
            (this->*op)();
    return *this;
}
```

A declaration wishing to provide default arguments for repeat() might look as follows:

```
class Screen {
public:
    Screen &repeat(Action=Screen::forward,int=1);
    // ...
};
```

Invocation of repeat() might look as follows:

```
Screen myScreen;
myScreen.repeat(); // repeat( Screen::forward, 1 );
myScreen.repeat( Screen::down, 20 );
```

A table of pointers to class members can also be defined. In the following example, Menu is a table of pointers to Screen member functions that provide for cursor movement. CursorMovements is an enumeration providing a set of indices into Menu.

```
Action Menu[] = {
    Screen::home,
    Screen::forward,
    Screen::back,
    Screen::up,
    Screen::down,
    Screen::bottom
};

enum CursorMovements {
    HOME, FORWARD, BACK, UP, DOWN, BOTTOM
};
```

Next, we provide an overloaded instance of move() that accepts a
CursorMovements argument. Here is its implementation:

```
Screen& Screen::move( CursorMovements cm )
{
    (this->*Menu[ cm ])();
    return *this;
}
```

This instance of move() might be utilized in an interactive program in
which the user selects a cursor movement from a menu displayed on the
screen.

Exercise 5-17. Define an overloaded instance of repeat() that takes a cur-
sorMovement as an argument. □

Pointers to Static Class Members

Static class members fall outside the pointer to class member syntax. Static
class members belong to the class and not to any instance of a class object.
The declaration of a pointer to a static class member looks the same as that of
a pointer to a nonclass member. Dereferencing the pointer does not require a
class object. For example, let's look at the CoOp class again:

```
class CoOp {
    friend compareCost( CoOp&, CoOp* );
public:
    CoOp( int, char* );
    inline double monthlyMaint();
    static void raiseCost(double incr);
    static double getCost() { return costPerShare; }
private:
    static double costPerShare;
    int shares;
    char *owner;
};

inline void CoOp::raiseCost(double incr)
{
    costPerShare += incr;
}
```

The type of &costPerShare is double*; it is not double CoOp::*. The
definition of a pointer to costPerShare looks as follows:

```
    // not double CoOp::*pd
    double *pd = &CoOp::costPerShare;
```

It is dereferenced in the same way as an ordinary pointer is dereferenced. It does not require an associated CoOp class object. For example,

```
    Coop unit;
    double maint = *pd * unit1.shares;
```

Similarly, the type of getCost() is that of an ordinary pointer to function: double (*)(). It is not a pointer to member of class CoOp: double (CoOp::*)(). The pointer definition and indirect call to getCost() are also handled in the same way as those of nonclass pointers:

```
    // not double (CoOp::*pf)()

    double (*pf)() = CoOp::getCost;
    double maint = pf() * unit1.shares;
```

5.8 Class Scope

Every class maintains its own associated scope. The names of class members are said to be local to the scope of their class. If a variable at file scope has its name reused by a class member, that variable is hidden within the scope of the class. For example,

```
    int height;

    class FooBar {
    public:
        // FooBar::height <== 0
        FooBar() { height = 0; }
    private:
        short height;
    };
```

Although height is not declared until the bottom portion of the Screen definition, height is in scope within the entire class body. Name resolution within a member function defined within the class body is the same *as if* the function had been defined immediately following the definition of the class. Name resolution within FooBar(), for example, occurs as if it had been defined as follows:

```
class FooBar {
public:
    FooBar();
private:
    short height;
};


FooBar::FooBar() { height = 0; }
```

As a general principle, an inline member definition can be moved outside the class body without any change in meaning.

How, then, might the global instance of height be accessed? Through the use of the scope operator. For example,

```
int height;

class FooBar {
public:
    FooBar() { height = ::height; }
private:
    short height;
};
```

In contrast, a variable defined within a function is not visible until its declaration is seen. In the following example, localFunc() references two different instances of height.

```
int height = 66;

localFunc() {
    int hi = height; // ::height
    int height = 24; // hides ::height
    hi = height;     // hi <== 24
}
```

The following example is even more confusing. Which instance of height do you think is referenced?

```
int height = 66;

badPractice() {
    int height = height; // which height?
}
```

A variable is considered defined once its identifier is specified in the declaration statement. In this case, the reference to height in the initializer accesses the just-defined local instance. This means that height is being initialized to an undefined value. Here is one solution:

```
int height = 66;

bdPrac() {
    int height = ::height;
}
```

The compiler is not likely to confuse the two instances of the variable; the human readers of the program, however, might. The preferred solution in this case is to rename the local instance to something other than `height`.

A member function occurs within the scope of its class. It also maintains its own local scope, the same as does a nonmember function. If a class member name is reused within the member function's local scope, the class member name becomes hidden at the point the local instance is defined. For example,

```
Screen::badPractice() {
    int hi = height; // Screen::height
    int height = height; // height local instance
}
```

The hidden class member can be accessed through the class scope operator. For example,

```
Screen::bdPrac() {
    int height = Screen::height;
}
```

It is also possible to access a hidden global variable through the scope operator. For example,

```
Screen::badPractice() {
    int height =
        (Screen::height > ::height)
        ? ::height : Screen::height;
}
```

Members defined outside the class definition still occur within the scope of their class. For example, given the following set of declarations:

```
int ix;
class Foo {
private:
    static int si;
    static int ix;
public:
    void bar(int);
};
```

the members `bar` and `si` both access `Foo::ix` and not the global instance:

```
int Foo::si = ix; // Foo::ix
void Foo::bar(int i = ix) // Foo::ix
    { ... }
```

In order to access the global instance of ix, the definitions need to use the scope resolution operator. For example,

```
int Foo::ix = ::ix;
```

The Scope of a Class

A class can occur either at global, class, or local scope. A class occurring at class scope is referred to as a *nested* class; its definition occurs within a public, protected, or private section of an enclosing class. A class occurring at local scope is defined within either a member or nonmember function. In the following example, class Tree occurs at global scope; its name is visible within the entire program. Class TreeNode occurs within the class scope of Tree; its name is visible only within the scope of Tree. The attempt, below, to declare a TreeNode pointer at global scope results in a compile-time error. Class Bar occurs within the local scope of Tree::foo(); its name is visible only within the scope of the member function. The attempt, below, to declare a Bar object within Tree also results in a compile-time error.

```
class Tree {
public:
    class TreeNode {...}; // nested class
    foo() {
        class Bar {...};  // local class
        Bar foo_bar;
        // ...
    }
private:
    // Bar not visible outside Tree::foo()
    Bar bar; // error: Bar not in scope
    TreeNode *left, *right;
};

// TreeNode not visible outside Tree
TreeNode *root; // error: TreeNode not in scope
```

When should a class be made global, nested, or local? The answer depends on how the class is used. If the class is of interest only to a single function or block within a function, then it should be defined locally within that block or function. Similarly, if the class is of interest only to a single other class, such as TreeNode or the ListItem class used to support the implementation of a

SECTION 5.8 CLASS SCOPE 261

List class in Chapter 3, then it should be defined within that class. Otherwise, it's probably best to define a class at global scope.

Scope Resolution

When an identifier appears within a member function of a class, the algorithm to resolve the identifier is as follows:

1. The immediate block containing the identifier is searched for a declaration of the identifier. If a declaration is found, the identifier is resolved; otherwise, the enclosing scope is searched.

2. If the immediate block in which the identifier occurs is a local block nested within a member function, then the enclosing block is that of the member function itself. The scope of the member function is searched. If a declaration is found, the identifier is resolved; otherwise, the enclosing scope is searched. These two steps are exactly analogous to the resolution of a name occurring in a nonmember function.

3. If the immediate block in which the identifier occurs is the member function itself, then the enclosing scope is that of the class. If a class member has been declared with a member of the same name as the identifier, the identifier is resolved to refer to that member; otherwise, the enclosing scope is searched.

4. The enclosing scope of a class is one of the following:

(a) for a non-derived class, such as Tree, defined at global scope, the enclosing scope is the global scope. If the declaration is found, the identifier is resolved; otherwise, the reference is flagged as an illegal reference to an undeclared variable.

(b) for a non-derived class, such as TreeNode, defined at class scope, the enclosing scope is the class in which the nested class is defined — Tree, in this case. The Section below entitled *Nested Classes* discusses the resolution of a member of an enclosing class.

(c) for a non-derived class, such as Bar, defined at local scope, the enclosing scope is the enclosing block or function in which the local class is defined. The Section below entitled *Local Classes* discusses the resolution of a local variable of an enclosing class.

(d) for a derived class, such as the range-checking array class of Chapter 1, the enclosing scope is the set of its immediate base classes. Chapters 8 and 9 discuss derivation in great detail. Further consideration of class derivation is deferred until then.

When an identifier is prefixed with either the file or class scope operator, the resolution of that identifier is limited to a search of the explicitly named scope. Let's consider an example. First, we define a set of identifiers.

```
extern int f( int ), ff(), f3();
int i = 1024;

class Example {
public:
    int f(); // hides ::f( int )
    Example( int ii = 0 ) { i = ii; }
private:
    int i; // hides ::i
    int ff; // hides ::ff()
};
```

An identifier is hidden when its name is reused within an inner scope even if the type of the local instance is different. The global identifiers i, ff(), and f(int) are hidden within the class scope of Example. Within Example::f(), references to these hidden identifiers must be prefixed with the file scope operator.

```
#include "Example.h"

int Example::f()
{
    int j;

    // error: file scope f() is hidden
    // Example::f() takes no argument
    j = f( 1 );

    // ok: explicit reference to ::f( int );
    // i is resolved to Example::i;
    j = ::f( i );

    // ok: explicit references
    ::i = ::f( ::ff() );

    // ok: explicit reference is unnecessary
    // file scope f3() is visible within Example
    return( f3() );
}
```

Example::f() can also define local instances of i and f. These local instances will hide the class member instances. To reference the class members, the class scope operator must be used.

```
#include "Example.h"
int Example::f() {
    // hides Example::i
    int i = ff ? Example::i : ( ::ff() ? ::i : 0 );

    // hides Example::f
    float f = (float) Example::f();
    return( i + Example::i + ::i );
}
```

Use of the scope resolution operator limits the lookup of an identifier to the specified scope. The class scope operator cannot be used to reference a file scope identifier. For example, `Example::f3()` will result in an error message declaring `Example::f3()` to be undefined.

```
#include "Example.h"
int Example::f() {
    int i = f3(); // ok: ::f3() invoked

    // error: Example::f3() undefined
    return( Example::f3() );
}
```

Nested Classes

The visibility of a nested class is limited to the scope of its enclosing class. This means that its name can be reused multiple times without collisions within the global name space.

```
class Node { ... };

class Tree {
public:
    // Node is encapsulated within the scope of Tree
    // hides ::Node within scope of Tree
    class Node {...};

    // ok: resolves to nested instance within Tree
    Node *tree;
};

// ok: Tree::Node is not visible at global scope
// Node *pnode resolves to global instance of Node
Node *pnode;
```

```
class List {
public:
    // Node is encapsulated within the scope of List
    // hides ::Node within scope of List
    class Node {...};

    // ok: resolves to nested instance within List
    Node *list;
};
```

When should a class be defined within an enclosing class? When the enclosing class (and possibly those classes derived from the enclosing class) is the only anticipated client of the class.

The definition of a nested class is no different from that of a non-nested class:

```
class List {
public:

    class ListItem {
        friend class List;
        ListItem(int val = 0);
        ListItem *next;
        int value;
    };

    // ...
private:
    ListItem *list;
    ListItem *at_end;
};
```

The enclosing class has no special access privileges with regard to the classes nested within it. This is why ListItem declares List to be a friend. Nor does the nested class have any special access privileges to the members of its enclosing class(es). An alternative implementation would be the following:

- Make the entire ListItem class public.

- However, move the ListItem class definition into a nonpublic section of List.

This makes the friend declaration unnecessary while still disallowing the general program access to ListItem. For example,

```
class List {
public:
    // ...
private:
    class ListItem {
    public:
        ListItem(int val = 0);
        ListItem *next;
        int value;
    };
    ListItem *list;
    ListItem *at_end;
};
```

The ListItem constructor is not defined within the ListItem class definition. Where can it be placed, then? At the same scope as its enclosing class definition. The following, however, does not work:

```
class List {
public:
    // ...
private:
    class ListItem {
    public:
        ListItem(int val = 0);
        // ...
    };
};

// error: ListItem not in scope
ListItem::ListItem(int val) { ... }
```

The definition needs to indicate that ListItem is a nested class within the scope of List. This is indicated by using an extended class scope operator. Note that the public or nonpublic nature of the nested class does not constrain the definition of any of its members.

```
// extended class scope operator
List::ListItem::ListItem( int val ) {
    value = val; next = 0;
}
```

If ListItem had defined a static member, its definition would also be defined as global scope:

```
int List::ListItem::static_mem = 1024;
```

The extended class scope operator also permits the use of the nested class as a type specifier outside the scope of the enclosing class. For example,

```
// error: ListItem not in scope
ListItem *headptr; // error: ListItem not in scope

// ok: if ListItem is public
List::ListItem *headptr;
```

Similarly, members of the nested class can be accessed using the extended class scope operator:

```
// ok: if ListItem and static_mem public
int i = List::ListItem::static_mem;
```

A nested class may not directly access the nonstatic members of the enclosing class. For example,

```
List::ListItem::ListItem(int val)
    : value( val )
{
    // List::list is a nonstatic member
    // of the class enclosing ListItem
    next = list; // error: illegal reference
}
```

Any access of a nonstatic member of the enclosing class requires that it be done through a pointer, reference, or object of the enclosing class:

```
void List::ListItem::mf(List &il) {
    next = il.list; // ok
}
```

In the following code fragment, is it the global or member instance of list accessed within the ListItem member function mf()?

```
int list = 0;

class List { public: // ...
private:
    class ListItem {
        public:
                void mf();
                int value;
                // ...
    };
    ListItem *list;
};

void List::ListItem::mf() {
    value = list;  // which list?
}
```

It is very likely that the programmer intended the reference to list within mf() to refer to the global instance:

- value and the global list are both of type int. The List::list member is a pointer type and cannot be assigned to value without an explicit cast.

- ListItem is not permitted to access a nonstatic (and private) data member, such as list, of its enclosing class

However, given all that, the reference to list *is* resolved to the list data member. An error message is then generated.

A reference to an identifier is always resolved lexically — that is, to the first occurrence of the name in the look-up algorithm. Access permission and type compatibility are checked only after the name is resolved. In the case of a nested class, if the name is not found within its scope, the scope of its enclosing class is searched next. list is a member of the enclosing List class, and so the reference is resolved. Subsequent checking discovers the reference to be illegal. To access the global list instance, the global scope operator needs to be used:

```
void List::ListItem::mf() {
    value = ::list; // ok
}
```

The nested class may legally access the static members, type names, and enumerators of the enclosing class. A type name is either a typedef name, the name of an enumeration, or the name of a class. For example,

```
class List {
public:
    typedef int (List::*pmList)();
    enum ListStatus { Good, Empty, Corrupted };
    // ...
private:
    class ListItem {
    public:
        void check_status();
        ListStatus status; // ok
        pmList action; // ok
        ListItem *next;
        // ...
    };
    // ...
};
```

pmList, ListStatus, and ListItem each are nested type names within the scope of the enclosing List class. Within ListItem, all three names and the

enumerators of ListStatus can be referenced without qualification. This is
also true within ListItem member functions:

```
void List::ListItem::check_status()
{
    ListStatus s = status;
    switch (s) {
        case Empty: ...
        case Corrupt: ...
        case Good: ...
    }
}
```

Outside the scope of the enclosing List class, a reference to a nested type
name requires the extended class scope operator. For example,

```
List::pmList myAction; // ok
List::ListStatus stat = List::Empty; // ok
```

We don't write

```
List::ListStatus::Empty
```

because the enumerators are entered directly into the enclosing scope of the
enumeration. Why? An enumeration does not, as a class does, maintain its
own associated scope.

Local Classes

The visibility of a local class is limited to the scope of its enclosing local block
or function. Unlike a nested class, the member functions of a local class must
be defined within the class definition. In practice, this limits the complexity
of the member functions of a locally defined class to a few lines of code each.
Beyond that, the code becomes difficult for the human reader to understand.
There is no class scope syntax to allow a local class to be referenced outside
its enclosing scope. A local class is not permitted to declare static data members.

The enclosing function has no special access privileges to the nonpublic
members of the local class. This can be granted, of course, by making the
enclosing function a friend to the local class. However, this would hardly
ever seem necessary. A local class is encapsulated within its enclosing scope;
further encapsulation through information hiding is likely overkill. There is
hardly ever a reason in practice not to make all the members of a local class
public.

As with a nested class, a local class is limited by which names within its
enclosing scope it may reference. A local class can legally access only type

names, static variables, and enumerators defined within the enclosing local
scopes. For example,

```
int a, val;

void foo( int val )
{
    static int si;
    enum Loc { a = 1024, b };
    class Bar {
    public:
        Loc locVal; // ok;
        int barVal;
        void fooBar( Loc l = a ) { // ok: Loc::a
            barVal = val;          // error: nonstatic local
            barVal = ::val;        // ok
            barVal = si;           // ok
            locVal = b;            // ok
        }
    };
}
```

A reference to a name within the local class is resolved lexically by a search
of its enclosing scopes. Only after resolution of the name is the legality of the
reference verified. This is why a reference to the global val requires it be
prefixed with the global scope operator.

5.9   Unions: A Space-Saving Class

A union is a special instance of a class. The amount of storage allocated for a
union is the amount necessary to contain its largest data member. Each member begins at the same memory address. Only one member at a time may be
assigned a value. For example, in a compiler, the lexical analyzer separates
the user's program into a sequence of tokens. The statement

```
int i = 0;
```

is converted into a sequence of five tokens:

1. The type keyword int

2. The identifier i

3. The operator =

4. The integer constant 0

5. The separator ;

These tokens are passed from the lexical analyzer to the parser. The first step of the parser is to identify the token sequence. Information must be present so that the parser can recognize the token stream as a declaration — for example, as the sequence

```
Type ID Assign Constant Semicolon
```

Once the parser identifies the general token sequence, it then requires the particular information of each token. In this case, it must know that

```
Type <==> int
ID <==> i
Constant <==> 0
```

It does not need any further information about Assign and Semicolon.

A representation of a token, therefore, requires two members, `token` and `value`. `token` will hold a unique number that is assigned to each possible token. For example, an identifier may be represented by 85, a semicolon by 72. `value` will hold the particular information about that token instance. For example, for ID, `value` will contain the string "i"; for Type, `value` will contain a code representing the type `int`.

The representation of `value` is problematic. Although it will contain only one value for any given token, `value` can hold multiple data types. One representation of multiple data types, of course, is a class. The compiler writer can declare `value` to be of class type TokenValue and can then define TokenValue to contain a member for each possible data type of `value`.

This representation solves the problem. `value`, however, can be only one of multiple possible data types for each particular token object. TokenValue, however, carries around the storage necessary for all the possible data types. Preferably, TokenValue would maintain storage sufficient only to hold any one of the multiple possible data types, not storage to hold them all. A union permits just that. Here is a definition of a TokenValue union:

```
union TokenValue {
        char cval;
        char *sval;
        int  ival;
        double dval;
};
```

Since the largest data type among the members of TokenValue is `double`, the size of TokenValue is also of type `double`. The members of a union by default are public. The tag name of a union serves as a type specifier. For example,

```
    TokenValue last_token;
    TokenValue *pt = new TokenValue;
```

Members are accessed through a union object using the member selection operators the same as for a class:

```
    last_token.ival = 97;
    char ch = pt->cval;
```

Union members can be declared as either public, protected, or private:

```
    union TokenValue {
    public:
        char cval;
        // ...
    private:
        int priv;
    };

    main() {
        TokenValue tp;
        tp.cval = '\n'; // ok

        /*
         * error:  main() cannot access
         *             TokenValue::priv: private member
         */
        tp.priv = 1024;
    }
```

A union cannot declare a static data member. Nor can it declare as a member an object of a class that defines either a constructor or destructor. For example,

```
    union illegal_members {
        Screen s; // error: has constructor
        Screen *ps; // ok
        static int is; // error: static
    };
```

Member functions, including constructors and destructors, can be defined for a union.

```
union TokenValue {
public:
    TokenValue(int ix) { ival = ix; }
    TokenValue(char ch) { cval = ch; }
    // ...
    int get_ival() { return ival; }
    char get_cval() { return cval; }
private:
    int ival;
    char cval;
    // ...
};

main() {
    TokenValue tp = 10;
    int ix = tp.get_ival();
    // ...
}
```

Here is an example of how TokenValue might be used:

```
class Token {
public:
        int tok;
        TokenValue val;
};
```

A Token object might be used as follows:

```
lex() {
    Token curToken;
    char *curString;
    int curIval;

    // ...
    case ID: // identifier
        curToken.tok = ID;
        curToken.val.sval = curString;
        break;

    case ICON: // integer constant
        curToken.tok = ICON;
        curToken.val.ival = curIval;
        break;

    // ... etc.
}
```

The danger of using a union is the possibility of accidentally retrieving the current union value through an inappropriate data member. For example, if the last union assignment is an integer value to ival, the programmer does not want to retrieve that value through the character pointer sval. Doing so will certainly lead to a program error.

To help safeguard against this kind of error, an additional variable is defined whose purpose is to keep track of the type of the value currently stored in the union. This additional variable is referred to as the *discriminant* of the union. This is the role the tok member of Token serves. For example,

```
char *idVal;
if ( curToken.tok == ID )
     idVal = curToken.val.sval;
```

A good practice when handling a union object as part of a class is to provide a set of access functions for each union data type. For example,

```
#include <assert.h>
char *Token::get_sval() {
    assert( tok==ID );
    return val.sval;
}
```

The tag name of a union is optional. There is no reason to provide a tag name if the union is going to be used only in one instance. For example, the following definition of Token is *equivalent* to its previous definition. The only difference is that the union is without a tag name:

```
class Token {
public:
    int tok;
    union {
        char cval;
        char *sval;
        int ival;
        double dval;
    } val;
}
```

There is a special instance of a union referred to as an *anonymous union*. An anonymous union is a union without a tag name that is *not* followed by an object definition. For example, here is a Token class definition containing an anonymous union:

```
class Token {
public:
    int tok;
    // anonymous union
    union {
        char cval;
        char *sval;
        int  ival;
        double dval;
    };
};
```

The data members of an anonymous union can be accessed directly. For example, here is the lex() fragment recoded to use the Token class definition containing an anonymous union:

```
lex() {
    Token curToken;
    char *curString;
    int curIval;

    // ... figure out what the token is
    // ... now set curToken
    case ID:
        curToken.tok = ID;
        curToken.sval = curString;
        break;
    case ICON: // integer constant
        curToken.tok = ICON;
        curToken.ival = curIval;
        break;
    // ... etc.
}
```

An anonymous union removes one level of member selection because the member names of the union enter the enclosing scope. An anonymous union cannot have private or protected members, nor can it define member functions. An anonymous union defined at file scope must be declared static.

5.10 Bit Field: A Space-Saving Member

A special class data member, referred to as a *bit field*, consists of a specified number of bits. A bit field must have an integral data type. It can be either signed or unsigned. For example,

```
class File {
    // ...
    unsigned modified : 1; // bit field
};
```

The bit field identifier is followed by a colon (":") followed by a constant expression specifying the number of bits. modified, for example, is a bit field consisting of a single bit.

Bit fields defined in consecutive order within the class body will, if possible, be packed within adjacent bits of the same integer, thereby providing for storage compaction. For example, in the following declaration, the five bit fields are to be stored in the single unsigned int first associated with the bit field mode.

```
typedef unsigned int Bit;

class File {
public:
    // ...
private:
    Bit mode: 2;
    Bit modified: 1;
    Bit prot_owner: 3;
    Bit prot_group: 3;
    Bit prot_world: 3;
    // ...
};
```

A bit field is accessed in the same manner as the other data members of a class. For example,

```
File::write()
{
    modified = 1;
    // ...
}

File::close()
{
    if ( modified )
        // ... save contents
}
```

Here is a simple example of how a bit field larger than one bit might be used (Section 2.9 (page 79) discusses the bitwise operators utilized in the example):

```
enum { READ = 01, WRITE = 02 }; // File modes

main() {
    File myFile;

    myFile.mode |= READ;
    if (myFile.mode & READ )
        cout << "myFile.mode is set to READ\n";
}
```

Typically, a set of inline member functions are defined to test the value of a member bit field. For example, File might define the members isRead() and isWrite().

```
inline File::isRead() { return mode & READ; }
inline File::isWrite() { return mode & WRITE; }

if (myFile.isRead()) /* ... */
```

The address-of operator ("&") cannot be applied to a bit field, and so there can be no pointers to class bit fields. Nor can a bit field be declared to be static.

Chapter 6:   **Member Functions**

This chapter considers the following three special categories of member functions that aid in managing classes:

1. Constructors and destructors for the automatic initialization and destruction of class objects.

2. Overloaded operator functions that can be applied to class objects using operator notation rather than member function names. For example, rather than the following explicit invocation of the Screen member function isEqual():

```
        if ( myScreen.isEqual(yourScreen) )
```

operator overloading allows users of the Screen class to write the following equivalent invocation:

```
        if ( myScreen == yourScreen )
```

In addition, a class can take over its own memory management by providing member instances of operators new and delete.

3. Conversion operators that define a set of permissible type conversions for a class. These conversions can be applied implicitly by the compiler in much the same manner as the standard conversions are applied.

The invocation of these special member functions is generally transparent to users of the class. Together, these functions serve to make the syntax and use of a class as "natural" for the programmer as that of a built-in type.

6.1 Class Initialization

A class object is initialized by the initialization of its data members. Provided all the members are public, the object may be initialized using a comma-separated list of values enclosed in braces. For example,

```
class Word {
public:
        int occurs;
        char *string;
};


// explicit member initialization
Word search = { 0, "rosebud" };
```

More generally, C++ supports a mechanism for the automatic initialization of class objects. A special class member function, called a *constructor*, is invoked implicitly by the compiler whenever a class object is defined or allocated through operator new. The constructor is a user-supplied initialization function that is named with the tag name of its class. For example, here is a constructor for Word:

```
class Word {
public:
    // Word class constructor
    Word( const char*, int=0 );
private:
    int occurs;
    char *string;
};

#include <string.h>
#include <assert.h>

inline Word::Word( const char *str, int cnt )
{
    string = new char [ strlen(str) + 1 ];
    assert( string != 0 );

    strcpy( string, str );
    occurs = cnt;
}
```

The constructor must not specify a return type or explicitly return a value. Otherwise, the definition of a constructor is the same as that of an ordinary member function. In this case, the constructor for Word requires one argument of type const char*. An optional second argument of type int may also be supplied. Several examples follow of how a Word object might be defined in the presence of this constructor.

```
#include "Word.h"

// Word::Word( "rosebud", 0 )
Word search = Word( "rosebud" );

// Word::Word( "sled", 1 )
Word *ptrAns = new Word( "sled", 1 );


main()
{ // shorthand constructor notations

    // Word::Word( "CitizenKane", 0 )
    Word film( "CitizenKane" );

    // Word::Word( "OrsonWelles", 0 )
    Word director = "OrsonWelles";
}
```

The definition of a const object, recall, must include the specification of an initial first value.

```
const int buf_size = 1024;  // ok
extern const double pi;     // ok: forward declaration
const int max_users;        // error: no initializer
```

Since the same holds true for const class objects, is the following definition an error?

```
// ok? or an error?
const Buffer sink;
```

It depends on whether the Buffer class defines a default constructor — that is, a constructor that requires no arguments. If it does, then the definition of sink is correct; if it does not, the definition of sink is an error. The initialization of a constant class object can either be by an explicit initialization list or by a constructor of its class.

Constructor Definition

One of the most heavily used data types is that of a string. In C++, however, strings are a derived type (an array of char) without built-in operator support. (There are no assignment or relational operators, for example.) A string type is an inevitable candidate for implementation as an abstract data type. We will use the design of a String class to illustrate the syntax and semantics of constructors, destructors, and overloaded operators. We begin by looking more closely at constructors.

A constructor is identified by assigning it the tag name of a class. It may be overloaded to provide a set of alternative initializations. Our String class, for example, contains two data members:

1. `str`, of type `char*`, that addresses the character array of the string.

2. `len`, of type `int`, that contains the length of the character array pointed to by `str`.

Let's declare two String constructors, one to initialize `str` and a second to initialize `len`.

```
class String {
public:
    String( const char* );
    String( int );
private:
    int len;
    char *str;
};
```

The definition of a class object allocates the storage necessary to contain the nonstatic data members defined for the class. The constructor provides for the initialization of this storage. Here is the definition of our first String constructor:

```
#include <string.h>
#include <assert.h>

String::String( const char *s )
{
    len = strlen( s );
    str = new char[ len + 1 ];
    assert( str != 0 );
    strcpy( str, s );
}
```

There is nothing complicated about the definition of this constructor. Its power lies in the class mechanism that invokes it implicitly for each class object the user defines that takes an initial character string. `strlen()` and `strcpy()` are string functions of the standard C library. We will provide similar support for our String class. It is worth taking a moment to understand why `str` is not simply assigned the address of s:

```
str = s;
```

but rather is allocated its own dynamic storage into which s is copied. The primary reason is that we cannot know for certain the *extent* of the storage in which s is contained:

- If it is of *local extent* — that is, allocated on the run-time stack — then its storage will disappear when the block it is defined in terminates. Any subsequent use of str will be in error. For example,

```
String *readString()
{ // example of a string with local extent
    char inBuf[ maxLen ];
    cin >> inBuf;
    String *ps = new String( inBuf );
    assert( ps != 0 );
    return ps;
}

String *ps = readString();
```

- If it is of *dynamic extent* — that is, has been allocated from the free store — then it is important that it be deleted before the class object goes out of scope. However, application of the delete operator on memory not allocated by operator new can cause serious run-time program error.

The moral is that pointer assignment across scopes is potentially dangerous and requires careful management from the programmer. The problem of pointer assignment will come up again when we consider the initialization and assignment of one class object with another object of its class.

Here is a definition of the second String constructor:

```
String::String( int ln )
{
    len = ln;
    str = new char[ len + 1 ];
    assert( str != 0 );
    str[0] = '\0';
}
```

The decision to maintain the string length as a separate field might reasonably be questioned. The trade-off is between the required storage and the run-time cost of computing the length. The choice of an explicit length field is based on two factors: First, the length is needed often enough that the savings in time will offset the storage cost (this must be borne out in practice). Second, a String object will be used not only to store an explicit string but also to provide a fixed-length buffer.

Because the definition of a class object results in an implicit call of a constructor, full type checking of the definition is applied. The following three String object definitions are invalid. In the first case, no argument is supplied. In the second, the argument is of the wrong type. In the third, there is one too many arguments.

```
int len = 1024;

String myString; // error: no argument
String inBuf( &len ); // error: bad type: int*
String search( "rosebud", 7 ); // error: two arguments
```

There are both explicit and shorthand forms for passing arguments to a constructor. The following are all legal forms of defining a String class object:

```
// explicit form: reflects actual invocation
String searchWord = String( "rosebud" );

// shorthand forms
String commonWord( "the" ); // preferred
String inBuf = 1024;

// use of new requires explicit form:
String *ptrBuf = new String( 1024 );
```

Although these three forms of constructor invocation all successfully initialize their respective String class object, the shorthand form `String s(args)` is preferred. Only this form is guaranteed across compiler implementations not to introduce a temporary String class object.

An invocation of operator new invokes the constructor for the class after the necessary storage is allocated. If new fails to allocate the required storage, the constructor is *not* executed. The class pointer is set to 0. For example,

```
// constructor not executed if new fails
String *ptrBuf = new String( 1024 );
if ( ptrBuf == 0 )
    cerr << "free store exhausted\n";
```

It is useful to allow the definition of a String object without requiring that an argument be supplied. For example,

```
String tmpStr;
```

This can be done either by providing a default argument to either of the already-defined constructors, or by providing a constructor that takes no arguments. A constructor taking no arguments is referred to as a *default constructor*. The implementation of a default constructor for the String class might look as follows:

```
class String {
public:
    String() { len = 0; str = 0; }
    // ...
}
```

A common programmer mistake is the following:

```
String st();
```

This does *not* define a String class object st initialized with the default String constructor. Rather, it declares a function st that takes no arguments and returns a String class object. The following are both correct definitions of st as a class object of String:

```
String st;
String st = String();
```

Exercise 6-1. Define a single String constructor that accepts all the following declarations:

```
String s1( "rosebud", 7 );
String s1( "rosebud", 8 );
String s2( "", 1024 );
String s3( "The Raw and the Cooked" );
String s4;
```

□

Constructors and Information Hiding

A constructor assumes the level of accessibility of the public, private, or protected section in which it is declared. For example, to restrict use of the String class as a buffer, String::String(int) can be declared private:

```
class String {
    friend class Buf;
public:
    String( const char* );
    String();
private:
    String( int );
    // ... rest of String class
};
```

Within the program, only the String member functions and the friend class Buf may declare String objects that take an argument of type int. There is no restriction on the declaration of String objects that take either no argument or an argument of type const char*.

```
void f()
{
    // ok: String::String( char* ) is public
    String search( "rosebud" );

    // error: String::String( int ) is private
    String inBuf( 1024 );
    ...
}

Buf::in()
{
    // ok: String::String( char* ) is public
    String search( "rosebud" );

    // ok: String::String( int ) is private
    // Buf is a friend to String
    String inBuf( 4096 );
    ...
}
```

A private class is one with no public constructors. Only the member functions and friends may declare objects of the class. The Item class defined in Section 3.12 (page 155) is an example of a private class. Item class objects can be defined only by the List class, which is declared a friend of Item.

Destructors

C++ supports a mechanism complementary to constructors for the automatic "deinitialization" of class objects. A special, user-defined member function, referred to as a *destructor*, is invoked whenever an object of its class goes out of scope or operator delete is applied to a class pointer. When a reference to a class object goes out of scope, however, no destructor is invoked. This is because a reference serves as an alias for an already defined object; it is not itself the class object. The destructor for String is declared as follows:

```
class String {
public:
    ~String(); // destructor
    // ...
};
```

A member function is designated the class destructor by giving it the tag name of the class prefixed with a tilde (``"~"``). A destructor cannot take an argument (and therefore may not be overloaded). It must not specify a return type or return a value. The String class destructor is defined as follows:

```
String::~String() { delete str; }
```

A constructor, recall, does not actually allocate storage. Rather, a constructor serves to initialize the newly allocated storage associated with a class object. Similarly, a destructor does not actually deallocate storage. Rather, it "deinitializes" the class object prior to the normal deallocation of storage that occurs when an object goes out of scope. In this case, because `str` addresses memory allocated through operator `new`, the String destructor explicitly deletes it. The storage associated with the class member `len`, however, does not require any special handling.

There is no constraint on what can be done within the destructor. A common program debugging technique, for example, is to place print statements within both the constructors and destructor of a class:

```
String::~String()
{
#ifdef DEBUG
    cout << "~String() "
         << len << " " << str << endl;
#endif
    delete str;
}
```

Destructors, in short, can perform any operations that the programmer wishes to have executed subsequent to a last use of the object.

A destructor is not invoked automatically for a pointer to a class object that exits scope. Rather, the programmer must explicitly apply the `delete` operator. The destructor for the class object addressed will then be invoked. For example,

```
#include "String.h"
String search( "rosebud" );

void f()
{
    // would not want destructor applied to p
    String *p = &search;

    // must have destructor applied to pp
    String *pp = new String( "sleigh" );

    // ...

    // String::~String() invoked for pp
    delete pp;
}
```

If the pointer to which `delete` is applied does not address a class object
(that is, the pointer is set to 0), the destructor is not invoked. It is unnecessary to write

```
if ( pp != 0 ) delete pp;
```

There is one case in which the programmer may need to invoke a
destructor explicitly. This is the case where the programmer wishes to delete
an object of the class but does not wish to delete the storage associated with
the object. This occurs in cases where a class object is allocated at a specific
address using operator new. For example,

```
#include <string.h>
#include <iostream.h>
#include <new.h>
#include <assert.h>

class inBuf {
public:
    inBuf( const char* );
    ~inBuf();
private:
    char *st;
    int sz;
};

inBuf::inBuf( const char *s ) {
    st = new char [ sz = strlen(s)+1 ];
    assert( st != 0 );
    strcpy( st, s );
}

inBuf::~inBuf() {
        cout<<"inBuf::~inBuf(): " << st << endl;
        delete st;
}

char *pBuf = new char[ sizeof( inBuf ) ];
main() {
  inBuf *pb = new (pBuf) inBuf("free store inBuf #1");
  pb->inBuf::~inBuf();  // explicit destructor call

  pb = new (pBuf) inBuf("free store inBuf #2");
  pb->inBuf::~inBuf();  // explicit destructor call

  return 0;
}
```

When compiled and executed, this program generates the following output:

```
inBuf::~inBuf(): free store inBuf #1
inBuf::~inBuf(): free store inBuf #2
```

The explicit destructor call does not require the use of the class scope operator. Both of the following invocations are legal:

```
pb->inBuf::~inBuf(); // ok
pb->~inBuf(); // ok
```

Class Arrays

An array of class objects is defined in the same way as an array of a built-in data type. For example, tbl and tbl2 each define a String class array of 16 class objects:

```
const int size = 16;
String tbl[ size ];
String *tbl2 = new String[size];
```

The individual elements are accessed using the subscript operator in the same way as that used for an array of a built-in data type. To access the class members of a particular array element, the class member selector operators are applied to the array element after the subscript operator is specified. Here is an example:

```
while ( cin >> tbl[ i ] )
        tbl[i].display();
```

The class objects of the array are initialized using the defined class constructors in the same way that individual class objects are used. The arguments to the constructor are specified in a brace-enclosed array initialization list. In the case of multiple arguments, the full constructor syntax must be used; otherwise, either the full or shorthand constructor notation is acceptable.

```
String ar1[] = { "phoenix", "crane" };
String ar2[3] = {String(),String(1024),String("string")};
String ar3[2] = { 1024, String( 512 ) };

Screen as[] = { Screen(24,80,'#') };
```

A class that defines a default constructor (that is, a constructor requiring no arguments) will have that constructor applied in the case of a partial initialization list. If the class does not define a default constructor, the initialization list must supply a value for each element of the array.

Before an array allocated on the free store, such as tbl2, above, goes out of scope, an explicit delete is required to reclaim the free store. However, simply writing

```
delete tbl2;
```

is insufficient because it causes the String destructor to be applied to only the initial element of tbl2. delete does not know that tbl2 points not to one String object but to an array of String objects. The programmer must indicate to delete that the pointer addresses an array. This is done by writing

```
delete [] tbl2;
```

(Providing the explicit size of the array is not required.) Now, the String destructor is invoked for each of the elements of tbl2.

An array allocated from the free store cannot be explicitly initialized. For example, each of the ten elements addressed by ps

```
String *ps = new String[10];
```

is initialized by the default String constructor. The following is one possible strategy for individually initializing a class array allocated on the free store.

```
#include "String.h"
#include <new.h>

const int count = 5;
String* init_String_array() {
    static char *tbl[count] = {
        "do", "for", "while", "if", "switch" };

    // grab a chunk of memory
    char *p = new char[sizeof(String)*count];

    // individually initialize each String
    for (int ix = 0; ix < count; ix++) {
        int offset = sizeof( String );
        new( p+offset*ix ) String( tbl[ix] );
    }
    return (String*)p;
}
```

```
void dealloc_String_array(String *ps, int count) {
    for (int ix = 0; ix < count; ++ix)
            ps[ix].String::~String();
    delete (char*)ps;
}

main() {
    String *ps = init_String_array();
    for (int ix = 0; ix < count; ++ix)
        cout<< "[" << ix << "] " << ps[ix] << endl;
    dealloc_String_array(ps, count);
    return 0;
}
```

The trick here is to "preallocate" a chunk of memory sufficient to hold the desired class array. This is what the following statement does:

```
char *p = new char[sizeof(String)*count];
```

Next, the program walks through the chunk, setting p to the address of the next String element.

```
for (int ix = 0; ix < count; ix++) {
    int offset = sizeof( String );
    new( p+offset*ix ) String( tbl[ix] );
}
```

The strange-looking call of new is the predefined overloaded instance. See Section 4.1 (page 179) for a discussion. Its effect is to apply the String constructor to the pre-allocated memory addressed by p.

Since we've overridden the ordinary allocation mechanism in generating our initialized array class, we must also take care to deallocate it. That is the purpose of dealloc_String_array(). When this program is compiled and executed, its output looks as follows:

```
[0] do
[1] for
[2] while
[3] if
[4] switch
```

Member Class Objects

Having introduced the String class, let's now redefine the Word class to replace its char* member with a member of type String, while remaining compatible with our previous public interface.

```
class Word {
public:
    // Word class constructors
    Word( const char*, int=0 );
    Word( const String&, int=0 );
private:
    int occurs;
    String name;
};
```

Two constructors must now be invoked for each Word object — its own and the constructor for its String class member. Two questions must be considered:

1. Is there a defined order of constructor invocation? If so, what is it?

2. How can the programmer pass arguments to the member class constructor?

There is a defined order of constructor invocation. The member class constructors are always executed before the constructor for the containing class. In the case where there are multiple member class objects, the order of constructor invocation follows the member class order of declaration. (The destructor order is the reverse.)

```
// first String::String( const char* )
// then Word::Word( const char*, int=0 )
Word flower( "iris" );
```

Arguments are passed to member class constructors through the *member initialization list*, a comma-separated list of member name/argument pairs. For example,

```
Word::Word(const char *s, int cnt) : name( s )
{
    occurs = cnt;
}
```

The member initialization list follows the signature of the constructor and is set off by a colon. Each member may be named once in the list. The member initialization list can appear only in the definition of a constructor; it cannot be specified in the declaration of a constructor. In the preceding example name is passed the character pointer s, which in turn is passed as the argument to the String constructor. Data members of built-in types of the class may also be specified in the member initialization list. occurs, for example, is initialized to the value of cnt:

```
Word::Word( const char *s, int cnt )
    : name( s ), occurs( cnt ) {}
```

The execution of a constructor consists of two phases — those of initialization and assignment. When the body of the constructor is null, there is no assignment phase. For example,

```
class Simple {
public:
    Simple( int, float );
private:
    int i;
    float f;
};

Simple::Simple( int ii, float ff )
      : i(ii), f(ff)   // initialization
      {}               // assignment
```

The assignment phase begins with execution of the body of the constructor. Implicit initialization occurs in the presence of a member class that defines a constructor that requires no argument. The member initialization list makes the initialization phase explicit. There is no initialization phase in the following redefined Simple class constructor:

```
Simple::Simple( int ii, float ff ) {
    i = ii; f = ff; // assignment phase
}
```

Under most circumstances, the distinction between the initialization and assignment phase of a constructor's execution is transparent to the programmer. The handling of const and reference class data members, however, is one instance in which the distinction is *not* transparent. The member initialization list is the only mechanism by which const and reference class data members can be initialized. The following constructor implementation, for example, is illegal:

```
class ConstRef {
public:
    ConstRef( int ii );
private:
    int i;
    const int ci;
    int &ri;
};
```

```
ConstRef::ConstRef( int ii )
{ // assignment
      i = ii;    // ok
      ci = ii;   // error: cannot assign to a const
      ri = i;    // error: ri is uninitialized
}
```

By the time the body of the constructor begins execution, the initialization of all const and reference class data members must already have taken place. This can be done only by specifying them in the member initialization list. For example,

```
ConstRef::ConstRef( int ii )
        : ci( ii ), ri( i ) // initialization
{ // assignment
        i = ii;
}
```

The initialization argument is not limited to a simple identifier or constant value. It may be any complex expression. For example,

```
class Random {
public:
    Random( int i ) : val( seed( i ) ) {}
    int seed( int );
private:
    int val;
}
```

The initialization argument to a class member object may be another object of its class.

```
Word::Word( const String &str, int cnt )
         : name( str ), occurs( cnt )
         {}

String msg( "hello" );
Word greetings( msg );
```

A class member object must appear in a member initialization list if its constructor requires an argument list. Failure to provide a required argument list results in a compile-time error. The class SynAntonym, for example, contains three class member objects: wd, a Word class object, and synonym and antonym, both String class objects. All Word class objects require at least one argument of type char* or type String&. The member initialization list must provide an argument list for wd.

```
class SynAntonym {
public:
    SynAntonym(const char* s) : wd(s) {}
    SynAntonym(const char* s1,
               const char* s2, const char* s3)
              : wd(s1), synonym(s2), antonym(s3) {}
    ~SynAntonym();
private:
    String synonym;
    Word wd;
    String antonym;
};


SynAntonym sa1( "repine" );
SynAntonym sa2( "cause", "origin", "effect" );
```

The order of constructor invocation for sa1 and sa2 is the following:

1. In order of declaration within the class body, the constructor of each class member (the initialization order within the member initialization list is not considered):

```
/* SynAntonym( const char* );
 *
 * String();            // synonym String member
 * String( "repine" );  // String member of wd
 * Word( "repine" );    // wd Word member
 * String();            // antonym String member
 */

sa1( "repine" );

/* SynAntonym(const char*,const char*,const char*);
 *
 * String( "origin" );  // synonym String member
 * String( "cause" );   // String member of wd
 * Word( "cause" );     // wd Word member
 * String( "effect" );  // antonym String member
 */

sa2( "cause", "origin", "effect" );
```

2. The constructor of the containing class is invoked.

A class member object itself containing a class member object will recursively apply these constructor-ordering rules. The order of destructor calls is the reverse of the constructor call order. That is, the destructor for the containing class is called before that of a member class object. If there are

multiple class objects, the order of destructor calls is the reverse of the declaration order of the member class objects.

Exercise 6-2. Here is a skeleton definition of a Buffer class:

```
#include "String.h"
class Buf {
public: // ...
private: String buf;
};
```

Declarations can take any of the following forms:

```
String s1;

Buf();
Buf( 1024 );
Buf( s1 );
```

Implement the constructor and destructor set. □

An important abstract data type is the binary tree. A skeleton for one
implementation of a binary tree class for integer values is presented below.
The implementation of this class will evolve from the exercises at the end of
this subsection and in the other sections of this chapter.

```
class BinTree;
class INode { // private class
    friend class BinTree;
    int val;
    BinTree *left;
    BinTree *right;
};

class BinTree {
public:
    // ... public interface
private:
    INode *node;
};
```

A binary tree can either be empty (node is set to 0) or point to an INode. An
INode consists of three members: an integer value, a left child, and a right
child. Each child is either empty or points to a binary tree.

Exercise 6-3. Discuss the benefits and/or drawbacks of defining the INode
class as a private class.

□

Exercise 6-4. Define the constructor(s) and destructor for the INode class.

□

Exercise 6-5. Define the constructor(s) and destructor for the BinTree class.

□

Exercise 6-6. Discuss the design choices you made in exercises 6–4 and 6–5.
□

6.2 Memberwise Initialization

There is one instance in which the constructors provided by the class designer are not invoked to initialize a newly defined class object — this is, when a class object is initialized with another object of its class. For example,

```
String vowel( "a" );
String article = vowel;
```

The initialization of `article` is accomplished by copying in turn each member of `vowel` into the corresponding member of `article`. This is referred to as *memberwise initialization*.

The compiler accomplishes memberwise initialization by internally defining a special constructor of the following general form:

```
X::X( const X& );
```

In the case of the String class, the constructor is defined something like the following:

```
String::String( const String& s )
{
    len = s.len;
    str = s.str;
}
```

The initialization of a class object with another object of its class occurs in three program situations:

1. The explicit initialization of one class object with another. For example,

```
// String::String( char* );
String color( "blue" );

// memberwise initialization generated
String mood = color;
```

2. The passing of a class object as an argument to a function. For example,

```
extern int count ( String s, char ch );

// local instance of s <== mood
int occurs = count ( mood, 'e' );
```

3. The return of a class object as the return value of a function. For example,

```
extern String sub ( String&, char, char );

main ()
{
    String river ( "mississippi" );
    cout << river << " "
         << sub ( river, 'i', 'I' ) << endl;
}
```

Neither the passing of a reference argument nor the return of a reference, however, results in object initialization, unless a temporary class object needs to be created. This is because pass-by-reference, unlike pass-by-value, does not result in the creation of a local copy of the class object. (Section 3.6 (page 126) discusses pass-by-reference.)

Memberwise initialization copies each built-in or derived data member from one class object to another. The member classes, however, are not copied; rather, memberwise initialization is recursively applied. For example, the Word class defines an integer member, occurs, and a String class member, name. Here are two Word object definitions:

```
Word noun ( "book" );
Word verb = noun;
```

verb is initialized in the following two steps:

1. The occurs member is initialized with the value of noun.occurs.

2. The name member is memberwise initialized with the internally generated constructor for the String class.

Default memberwise initialization is sometimes insufficient. Figure 6.1 illustrates the resulting storage allocation of noun and verb.

There are two problems:

1. The occurrence count of noun must not be copied to the occurrence count of verb. In fact, the two values are disjoint. The default memberwise mechanism violates the semantics of the Word class.

2. The str members of both noun and verb address the same memory. This will cause a serious problem if the two class objects do not exit scope at the same time.

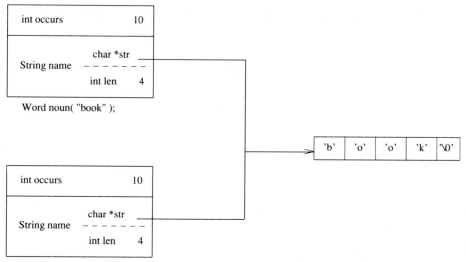

Figure 6.1 Memberwise Initialization

In general, default memberwise initialization is insufficient for classes that contain pointer members and also define a destructor. This is because the destructor is invoked for every class object, even those that are memberwise initialized rather than "constructed."

As Figure 6.1 illustrates, this means that the storage addressed by two or more class objects is "destructed" two or more times. In one case, a dangling reference may result. In another case, the result may be the destruction of storage subsequently reallocated for another purpose entirely. In either case, the program is likely to be in error. The solution is for the class designer to provide an explicit memberwise initialization constructor instance. This is the topic of the following subsections.

A Special Constructor: X(const X&)

As we have seen, under some circumstances, a class requires more control of initialization of one class object with another than is provided by default memberwise initialization. A class can assume this additional control by defining an explicit instance of the X(const X&) constructor. If explicitly defined within a class, it is invoked for each initialization of one class object with another. For example,

```
#include <assert.h>

String::String( const String& s )
{
    len = s.len;
    str = new char[ len + 1 ];

    assert( str != 0 );
    strcpy( str, s.str );
}
```

`String(const String&)` is now invoked whenever one String object is initialized with another. Each `str` member will address a distinct area of memory.

Exercise 6-7. Implement a `Screen(const Screen&)` constructor for the Screen class defined in Chapter 5. Illustrate three different situations in which the constructor is invoked.

□

Exercise 6-8. Implement a `List(const List&)` constructor for the List class defined in Chapter 3. Illustrate three different situations in which the constructor is invoked. □

X(const X&) and Class Member Objects

In this subsection, we examine two cases of `X(const X&)` for classes containing class member objects:

1. The containing class does not define an `X(const X&)` instance, but the member class does.

2. Both the containing and the member class define an `X(const X&)` instance.

In the first case, illustrated by the Word class definition, Word is without a `Word(const Word&)` instance. The member class, String, however, has been expanded to define `String(const String&)`

```
class Word {
public:
    Word( char *s, int cnt = 0 )
         : name(s), occurs(cnt) {}
    Word( String& s, int cnt = 0 )
         : name(s), occurs(cnt) {}
private:
        int occurs;
        String name;
};
```

The initialization of one Word object with another defaults to memberwise initialization. The String class member, however, is initialized through an invocation of String(const String&) For example,

```
String mystery( "rosebud" );
Word resolve( mystery );

extern search( Word wd );
search( resolve );
```

String(const String&) is invoked to initialize the name member of resolve and the name member of the local copy of wd. In general, memberwise initialization is applied recursively to each class member object. For each member class that defines an X(const X&) instance, however, that instance — rather than memberwise initialization — is invoked.

The default memberwise initialization behavior is no longer applied with the introduction of an explicit Word(const Word&) instance. The String memberwise instance is no longer invoked automatically. The Word instance has assumed responsibility for the initialization of its members. Before we illustrate the correct implementation of the Word instance, let's look at the following incorrect implementation:

```
// this implementation is incorrect
Word::Word( const Word& w )
{
        occurs = 0;
        name = w.name;
}
```

This instance fails to correctly initialize the name String class member. Let's consider the following example step by step:

```
Word weather( "warm" );
Word feeling = weather;
```

The initialization steps occur as follows:

1. feeling is recognized as being initialized with a Word class object. Is

there a Word(const Word&) instance defined? If yes, invoke it; otherwise, apply memberwise initialization. Word(const Word&) is found.

2. Is there a member initialization list? No.

3. Are there any class member objects? Yes. There is a String class object, name.

4. Does this String member class define a constructor that does not require arguments? If no, issue a compile-time error; otherwise, invoke it.

5. String() is invoked to initialize feeling.name.

6. Word(const Word&) is invoked. The assignment name=w.name is executed. By default, as with initialization, class object assignment is accomplished by memberwise assignment. See Section 6.3 (page 318) for a discussion. String(const String&) is never invoked.

This is the second instance in which the distinction between the initialization and assignment phases in the execution of a constructor becomes important. (Section 6.1 (page 291) describes the first — that of initializing const and reference class members.) In order for the String object constructor to be invoked, name must be initialized with w.name. This means that name must be placed in the member initialization list. The correct definition of the Word object initialization constructor is as follows:

```
Word::Word( const Word& w )
     : name( w.name ) // initialization
{ // assignment
     occurs = w.occurs;
}
```

In summary, if a containing class does not define an X(const X&) instance, each member class object is memberwise initialized. If the member class defines an X(const X&) instance, that instance will be invoked. If a containing class does define an X(const X&) instance, however, it becomes the responsibility of that class, through its member initialization list, to explicitly initialize its member class objects.

Exercise 6-9. Implement Buf(const Buf&) (Exercise 6.2).

☐

Exercise 6-10. Implement an instance of both the INode(const INode&) and BinTree(const BinTree&) constructor. ☐

Summary of Constructors and Destructors

The special constructor and destructor mechanism allows for the automatic initialization and deallocation of class objects. Constructors can be overloaded to provide a set of initialization options; for efficiency, they can be defined as inline.

Member class objects have their constructors invoked before the constructor for the containing class. The order of member class object constructor invocation is the order of declaration of the member class objects. Destructor calls are invoked in the reverse order.

A constructor may specify a member initialization list which provides a mechanism for passing arguments to member object constructors. It may also be used to initialize data members that are not class objects, allowing const and reference class members to be initialized.

In one instance, a constructor is not invoked for a new class object: when the new class object is initialized with an existing class object. In this case, referred to as *memberwise initialization*, the value of each class member is copied in turn. If a class contains a member class object, memberwise initialization is recursively applied to that object.

Memberwise initialization may become a problem for classes with pointer members. Multiple class objects can end up pointing to the same area of memory, each believing itself to be the sole possessor of that memory. A special object initialization constructor,

```
class X {
public:
    // explicit memberwise initialization constructor
    X( const X& );
};
```

can be explicitly defined to handle these cases. The initialization of one class object with another object of its class invokes this special constructor, if defined, rather than applying default memberwise copy.

6.3 Operator Overloading

In the previous section we defined the data members and member functions necessary to initialize and deallocate the String class. What additional functionality must a String class provide?

Users must perform tests on Strings: Is a String empty? Is one String equal to another? Is one String a substring of another? Users must also input and output a String object, assign one String to another, concatenate two Strings, determine the length of a String, index into a String, and iterate over a String. Code utilizing a String class might look as follows:

```
String inBuf;
while ( readString( cin, inBuf ))
{
    if ( inBuf.isEmpty()) return;
    if ( inBuf.isEqual( "done" )) return;

    switch ( inBuf.index(0) ) { /* ... */ }
    cout << "String is ";
    writeString( cout, inBuf );
}
```

Use of the String class is not quite as easy as is the use of the built-in data types. For example, the names chosen for the String operations, although both logical and mnemonic, are not easy to remember. In contrast, here is the same code fragment with overloaded operator instances replacing the named String operations.

```
String inBuf;

while ( cin >> inBuf )
{
    if ( !inBuf ) return;
    if ( inBuf == "done" ) return;

    switch ( inBuf[ 0 ] ) { /* ... */ }
    cout << "String is " << inBuf;
}
```

In the remainder of this section, we implement the set of operators necessary to support this style of String class programming.

Overview of Operator Overloading

A class designer can provide a set of operators to work with objects of the class. An operator function need not be a member function, but it must take at least one class argument. This prevents the programmer from overriding the behavior of operators for the built-in data types. An operator function is defined in the same way as an ordinary function except that its name consists of the keyword operator followed by one of a large subset of the predefined C++ operators (see Table 6.1). A concatenation operator for the String class, for example, might be implemented as follows:

```
#include <assert.h>
#include <string.h>

String&
String::operator+=( const String &s )
{
    len += s.len;
    char *p = new char[len+1];
    assert( p != 0 );
    strcpy(p,str);
    strcat(p,s.str);
    delete str;
    str=p;
    return *this;
}
```

strcat() is a standard library function. It concatenates its second argument to the end of its first. To use it, one must include the <string.h> standard header file.

The String operator is used in the same way ordinary operators are used. For example,

```
#include <iostream.h>
#include "String.h"

main() {
    String s1("gobbledy");
    String s2("gook");
    s1 += s2; // s1 <== gobbledygook
    cout << s1 << endl;
    return 0;
}
```

Operator functions within the same class can be overloaded provided that their argument lists can be distinguished. For example, users of our String class should be able to concatenate a String object with a value of type char*:

```
class String {
public:
    String(const char*);
    String& operator+=(const String&);
    String& operator+=(const char*);
    // ...
}
```

Are the two instances of the concatenation operator necessary? No. Without the char* instance, expressions of the form

```
s1 += "mumble";
```

would be resolved into calls of

```
String::operator+=(const String&)
```

because of the presence of the String constructor taking a single argument of
type const char*. This constructor serves as a conversion operator, turning character pointers into Strings. It is applied implicitly by the compiler
whenever necessary. The const char*. version, if present, avoids the
expense of the conversion and a statement such as

```
s1 += "mumble"
```

will execute more efficiently. Section 6.5 (page 334) discusses user-defined
conversions in detail.

What if users of the String class wish to concatenate two Strings, leaving
both unchanged and creating a third? This will require a separate concatenation operator. For example,

```
#include <iostream.h>
#include "String.h"

main() {
    String s1("cobble");
    String s2("stone");
    String s3 = s1 + s2;
    cout << s3 << endl;
    return 0;
}
```

Here is an implementation of this general concatenation operator that makes
use of the previous operator+=():

```
String
String::operator+( const String &s ) const
{
    String result = *this;
    result += s;
    return result;
}
```

Operator Function Definition

Only the predefined set of C++ operators can be overloaded. The designer of
a class may not introduce a new operator ("**", for example, for exponentia-
tion). Table 6.1 lists the operators that may be overloaded. The following
four operators cannot be overloaded:

```
// non-overloadable operators
::          .*          .                ?:
```

Overloadable Operators							
+	−	*	/	%	^	&	|
~	!	,	=	<	>	<=	>=
++	--	<<	>>	==	!=	&&	||
+=	-=	/=	%=	^=	&=	|=	*=
<<=	>>=	[ ]	( )	->	->*	new	delete

Table 6.1 Overloadable Operators

The predefined meaning of an operator for the built-in types may not be overridden. For example, the built-in integer addition operation cannot be replaced with an operation that checked for overflow. Nor may additional operators be defined for the built-in data types. Integer array addition, for example, cannot be added to the set of operations. The programmer may define operators only for class types. This is enforced by the requirement that an operator function take at least one class argument.

The predefined precedence of the operators (Section 2.10 (page 84) discusses operator precedence) cannot be overridden. Regardless of the class type and operator implementation,

```
x == y + z;
```

will always perform operator+ before operator==. As with the predefined operators, precedence can be overridden with the use of parentheses.

The predefined *arity* of the operator must be preserved. The unary logical NOT operator ("!"), for example, cannot be defined as the binary inequality operator for two String class objects. The following implementation is illegal:

```
// illegal: ! is a unary operator
operator!( String st1, String st2 )
{
    return( strcmp(st1.str, st2.str) != 0 );
}
```

Additionally, default arguments for an operator function are illegal.

Four predefined operators ("+", "−", "*", and "&") serve as both unary and binary instances. Either or both arities of these operators can be defined.

Member or Nonmember

An operator function can be defined as either a member or nonmember function. The member instance will always take one fewer arguments because of the implicit `this` pointer . For example, here are the member and nonmember definitions of a String class unary NOT operator ("!") that returns true if the String is empty:

```
int operator!(const String &s) {
    return s.length() == 0;
}

int String::operator!() const {
    return len == 0;
}
```

`length()` is an inline read-access function. It is implemented as follows:

```
class String {
public:
    int length() const { return len; }
    // ...
};
```

The expression syntax for invoking both the member and nonmember instances of an operator function are the same. For example,

```
#include <iostream.h>
#include "String.h"

main() {
    String s1;
    cout << s1 << endl;
    cout << "result of !s1: "
        << (!s1 == 1 ? "true" : "false") << endl;
    return 0;
}
```

How does one decide, then, between making an operator a member or nonmember function? In some cases, the programmer has no choice.

- A member function requires that its left operand be an object of its class. If the operator requires a left operand of another type, then it *must* be made a nonmember function. If it requires access to nonpublic members of the class, then it must also be made a friend. For example,

```
String s1("Anna Rachel");
cout << s1 << endl;
```

requires that the output operator take a first argument of class `ostream`.

Therefore, it must be declared as a nonmember operator function. Because it requires access to the nonpublic `str` member, it is declared to be a friend to String.

```
#include <iostream.h>
class String {
    friend ostream&
    operator <<( ostream& os, String& s );
    // ...
};


ostream& operator<<(ostream& os, String& s)
{
    if ( !s ) // String::operator!()
        return os << "<empty>";
    return os << s.str;
}
```

One could argue, successfully, I think, that a better output strategy for a general String class is to allow an empty String object to print a null string — that is, to print nothing. The generation of `<empty>` in this instance is provided simply as an aid in illustrating the use of the String class with template functions in Chapter 7.

• The assignment ("="), subscript ("[]"), call ("()"), and member selection ("->"), operators are required by the language to be defined as class member functions. A global instance of any of these, including a global template function instance, is flagged at compile time as an error. For example,

```
// error: must be a member function
template <class Type>
Type operator[](Array<Type>&,int ix);
```

Otherwise, it is the choice of the class designer whether to declare the operator as either a member or nonmember. Let's look at an example of when it makes sense to make an operator a nonmember.

Our String class needs to support the following three forms of concatenation:

```
String + String
"cobble" + String
String + "stone"
```

Do we, then, require three separate operators?

```
String::operator+(const String&);
String::operator+(const char*);
operator+(const char*, const String&);
```

No. As we saw earlier with `operator+=()`, the String constructor

```
String::String(const char*);
```

serves as a conversion operator on the right hand character pointer.

```
String + String
String + "stone"
```

are both handled by

```
String::operator+(const String&);
```

The second operator member function, therefore, is unnecessary. However, the same is not true of the nonmember instance. The String constructor does not convert the left operand of

```
"cobble" + String
```

into a String object. Why? A member function is only invoked if the left operand is an explicit class object. Therefore, we cannot discard the non-member instance. Or at least not yet.

What if we turned our member instance into a nonmember?

```
operator+(const String&, const String&);
```

Now, either the left or right operand may be implicitly converted by the compiler into a String. This instance of the operator handles all three forms of String concatenation. Now we can discard the other nonmember instance.

Symmetric operators such as binary + are best defined as nonmembers if the left operand can either be or not be a class object, as is the case with our String class. The run-time costs of an implicit type conversion, however, may mandate providing multiple explicit instances of an operator.

Exercise 6-11. Why does the following *not* invoke `operator+(const String&, const String&)`?

```
"cobble" + "stone"
```

□

Exercise 6-12. Given our definition of the String class, why is the following definition of the equality operator not the most efficient implementation?

```
String::operator==(String &st) {
    return(strcmp(str,st.str)==0);
}
```

□

Exercise 6-13. Provide an equality operator that can handle the following three cases:

```
String == String
"cobble" == String
String == "stone"
```

Why isn't this operator invoked for the following statement?

```
"cobble" == "stone";
```

□

Operator [ ]

Users of our String class need to have both read and write access of the individual characters of the `str` class member. We must support the following coding style using String class objects:

```
String sentence( "Ash on an old man's sleeve" );
String tempBuf( sentence.length() );

for ( int ix = 0; ix < sentence.length(); ++ix )
    tempBuf[ ix ] = sentence[ ix ];
```

The subscript operator must be able to appear on both the right- and the left-hand side of an expression. In order to appear on the left-hand side, its return value must be an lvalue. This is achieved by specifying the return value as a reference type:

```
inline char&
String::operator[]( int elem ) {
    assert( elem >= 0 && elem < len );
    return str[ elem ];
}
```

The return value of the subscript operator is the lvalue of the indexed element. This is why it can appear as the target of an assignment. For example,

```
String st( "mauve" );
st[0] = 'M';
```

assigns the character constant to the zeroth element of st.str.

Operator ()

An important facility for a data abstraction that encompasses a collection of elements, such as a list, array, or string, is that of an iterator. An iterator returns a *next* element each time it is invoked, or 0 if there is no next element (or whatever would represent a 0 for a particular data abstraction). The function call operator (" () ") provides a convenient syntax for implementing an iterator. Let's see how we might implement one for our String class.

First, what is the behavior we wish for the iterator? Here is a sketch of the sort of code we need to support:

```
String myString;
while (cin >> myString)
{
    char ch;

    // iterate over myString,
    // returning next element each time
    while (ch = myString()) // ...
```

The call operator applied to myString invokes the iterator. One possible implementation is the following:

```
char String::operator()
{
    char ch = str[ index ];
    index = (index == len) ? 0 : index+1;
    return ch;
}
```

where index is an additional String data member holding the position of the next element to be returned.

While this implementation supports the code fragment above, there are two significant drawbacks to its design:

1. Every String object has to haul around the additional memory required of index. This may or may not be a reasonable tradeoff depending on the average String length and frequency of iterator use. The likelihood, however, is that a String class for general use cannot justify this additional per object memory.

2. There can be only one iterator per object operating at a time. One can easily imagine numerous iterators operating on an object at the same time, perhaps a current, previous, and next.

An alternative design resolving both problems is to define a special String iterator class. One member of this class would be index, another, a pointer to a String object over which to iterate. The iterator class will require a constructor to initialize its members and, of course, the call operator to actually implement the iterator. Here is one possible implementation:

```
class StringIterator {
public:
    StringIterator(String& s)
        : ps(&s), index(0) {}
    char operator()();
private:
    String *ps;
    int index;
};

char StringIterator::operator()()
{ // must be friend to String
    if (index < ps->len)
        return ps->str[index++];
    return index=0;
}
```

To create an iterator for a particular String object, we might write the following:

```
String myString;
StringIterator next( myString );
StringIterator prev( myString );
```

These can be used as follows:

```
// examples of using StringIterator
char pch = '\0';
char ch = next();
while (ch) {
    // do something
    ch = next();
    pch = prev();
}
```

Before we can write a program to illustrate how a StringIterator might be used, we need to provide a String input operator:

```
#include <iostream.h>

istream& operator>>( istream &io, String &s ) {
    char inBuf[ String_size ];
    io >> inBuf; // operator>>(ostream&,char*);
    s = inBuf;   // String::operator=(const char*);
    return io;
}
```

and a copy operator that turns a `char*` operand into a String object:

```
String& String::operator=( const char *s ) {
    len = strlen( s );
    delete str;
    str = new char[ len + 1 ];
    assert( str != 0 );
    strcpy( str, s );
    return *this;
}
```

Figure 6.2 contains a small program to illustrate how a StringIterator might be used. The program strips out punctuation and changes all uppercase letters to lowercase. The routines `isalpha()`, `isupper()`, and `tolower()` are provided in the `ctype.h` system header file.

The program's input is the following:

```
We were her pride of ten; she named us: benjamin,
phoenix, the prodigal, and perspicacious, pacific
Suzanne.  Benjamin, hush now.  Be still, child.
People are never just.
```

When compiled and executed, the program generates the following output:

```
we were her pride of ten   she named us
benjamin  phoenix  the prodigal  and perspicacious
pacific suzanne  benjamin  hush now  be still  child
people are never just
```

The use of the function call operator is not, of course, limited only to the implementation of iterators. Here, for example, is how the call operator might be used to generate substrings of a String object:

```
String str = "Mississippi";
String girl = str(0,4);
String sister = str(3,3);
String cautious_drink = str(6,3);
String a_difficult_calculation = str(9,2);
```

where the first argument is the position within the String at which to begin (starting at 0) and the second argument is the count of characters to include. Here is one possible implementation:

```
#include <iostream.h>
#include "String.h"
#include <ctype.h>

const LINESIZE = 40;
enum {BLANK=' ',PERIOD='.',COMMA = ',',SEMI=';',COLON=':'};

main() {
    String inBuf;
    int lineSize = 0;

    // operator>>( istream&, String& )
    while ( cin >> inBuf )
    {
        char ch;
        int index = 0;
        StringIterator next(inBuf);

        while (ch = next())
        {
            switch (ch) {
                default:
                {
                    if (isalpha(ch) && isupper(ch))
                        inBuf[index] = tolower(ch);
                    break;
                }
                case PERIOD:
                case COMMA:
                case SEMI:
                case COLON:
                    inBuf[index] = BLANK;
                    break;
            }
            ++index; ++lineSize;
        }
        if ( lineSize >= LINESIZE )
        {
            cout << endl;
            lineSize = 0;
        }
        cout << inBuf << " ";
    }
    cout << endl;
    return 0;
}
```

Figure 6.2 Program Example Using StringIterator

```
String& String::operator()( int pos, int cnt )
{// return a substring of ''this'' string

    assert( pos >= 0 && pos <= len-1 && cnt > 0 );
    if ( cnt + pos - 1 > len ) {
        cerr << "warning: String::operator( " << pos
                << ", " << cnt << " ) substring truncation "
                << str << endl;
        cnt = len - pos + 1;
    }

    String *ps = new String(cnt+1);
    assert( ps != 0 );
    for ( int ix = pos, j = 0; j < cnt; ++ix, ++j )
        ps->str[ j ] = str[ ix ];
    ps->str[ cnt ] = '\0';

    return *ps;

}
```

Another common use of the call operator is to provide multidimensional array indices, such as for a matrix class.

Exercise 6-14. Provide an iterator class for the list class implemented in Chapter 3. Illustrate its use. □

Operators new and delete

By default, the free store allocation of a class object is provided by the predefined, global instance of operator new (discussed in Section 3.11 (page 144)). A class may assume its own memory management by providing member class new and delete operators. If defined, these member class operators new and delete are invoked in place of the default instances. User programs need not change. As an example, let's define a class member new and delete operator for the Screen class defined in Chapter 5.

Our memory allocation strategy is to manage a linked list of available Screen class objects addressed by a single freeStore pointer. Each call of the Screen instance of operator new returns the next class object pointed to by freeStore. Each call of the operator delete member returns the class object to the list addressed by freeStore. If the linked list of class objects freeStore points to is empty, a call is made to the global operator new to allocate a screenChunk of class objects that are linked together and addressed by freeStore.

Both screenChunk and freeStore contain values that are of interest only to the Screen class; therefore, we want to encapsulate them as nonpublic members of Screen. Additionally, there must be only a single instance of each; therefore, they are declared to be static members. A third data member, next, is defined in order to maintain the linked list.

```
class Screen {
public:
    // ...
private:
    Screen *next;
    static Screen *freeStore;
    static const int screenChunk;
};
```

A class member instance of operator new must specify a return type of void* and take a first argument of the system typedef size_t, defined in the stddef.h system header file. This argument is automatically initialized by the compiler with the size in bytes of the class type. Here is the Screen class declaration of operator new:

```
class Screen {
public:
        void *operator new(size_t);
        // ...
};
```

Additional instances of operator new can also be defined, provided that each has a unique signature. When new is applied to a class name, the compiler looks to see if the class has provided its own instance. If it has, that instance is selected; otherwise, the predefined global instance is applied. Adding or backing out a class instance of operator new does not require a change to user code.

Here is a possible implementation of the Screen member instance of operator new.

```
#include "Screen.h"
#include <stddef.h>

// static members are initialized within
// program text files, not header files
Screen *Screen::freeStore = 0;
const int Screen::screenChunk = 24;
```

```
void *Screen::operator new(size_t size) {
    register Screen *p;
    if (!freeStore) {
        // linked list empty: grab a chunk
        // this call is to the global new
        size_t chunk = screenChunk*size;
        freeStore = p =
            (Screen*) new char[chunk];

        // now thread the screenChunk
        for ( ;
                p != &freeStore[screenChunk-1];
                p->next = p+1, p++)
                    ;  // null for body
        p->next = 0;
    }

    p = freeStore;
    freeStore = freeStore->next;
    return p;
}
```

The member operator `delete` returns the Screen object to `freeStore`'s linked list. Here is its implementation:

```
void
Screen::operator delete(void *p, size_t) {
    // insert the ``deleted'' object back
    //      into the free list

    ((Screen*)p)->next = freeStore;
    freeStore = (Screen*)p;
}
```

The `delete` operator must have a first argument of type `void*`. A second argument of the predefined type `size_t` may be specified (remember to include `stddef.h`). If present, it is initialized by the compiler with the size in bytes of the object addressed by the first argument. (This argument is essential in an object-oriented class hierarchy in which the `delete` operator may be inherited by a derived class. See Section 8.11 (page 442) for a discussion of the inheritance of operators `new` and `delete`.) The `delete` operator must have a return type of `void`.

A class instance of operator `new` is invoked only for the allocation of individual class objects, not for the allocation of an array of class objects. For example,

```
    // invokes Screen::operator new()
    Screen *ps = new Screen(24,80);
```

invokes the Screen instance of new, while

```
    // invokes ::operator new
    Screen *psa = new Screen[10];
```

invokes the predefined instance that handles the allocation of an array of
objects from the free store.

The programmer can selectively invoke a nonclass instance of operator
new through use of the scope operator. For example,

```
    Screen *ps = ::new Screen;
```

invokes the default operator new. Similarly,

```
    ::delete ps;
```

invokes the default instance of operator delete.

The new and delete operator functions are static members of their class,
and they obey the usual constraints for static member functions. In particular, recall that a static member function is without a this pointer and can
therefore only directly access static data members of its class. (See Section
5.6 (page 246) for a discussion of static member functions.) These operators
are made static member functions because they are invoked either before the
class object is constructed (operator new) or after it has been destroyed (operator delete). An allocation using operator new, such as

```
    Screen *ptr = new Screen(10,20);
```

is equivalent to the following two-statement sequence:

```
    ptr = Screen::operator new(sizeof(Screen));
    Screen::Screen(ptr,10,20);
```

while a deallocation using operator delete, such as

```
    delete ptr;
```

is equivalent to the following two statement sequence:

```
    Screen::~Screen(ptr);
    Screen::operator delete(ptr, sizeof(*ptr));
```

X::Operator=(const X&)

The assignment of one class object with another object of its class is performed as the memberwise assignment of the nonstatic data members; the mechanics are the same as those of memberwise initialization, described in Section 6.2 (page 295) of this chapter.

The compiler generates a class instance of the assignment operator which has the form

```
X& X::operator=( const X& );
```

to handle the default memberwise assignment of class objects. For example, given the two String objects

```
String article( "the" );
String common( "For example" );
```

the assignment

```
common = article;
```

is handled by the implicit memberwise assignment operator:

```
String& String::operator=( const String& s )
{
    len = s.len;
    str = s.str;
    index = s.index;
}
```

There are a number of problems with this assignment.

1. As with memberwise initialization, article and common both now address the same area of free store. The destructors for both String objects will be applied to that single area.

2. The free store allocated to contain *For example* is never reclaimed. It is lost in the memberwise assignment.

3. The semantics of the String class design prohibit a simple-minded copy of each data member. In Section 6.3 (page 310) we defined an index data member of the String class that allows a user to iterate through the String's character array. The value of index after a memberwise copy must be 0 for the target String class object — not the value of the source object's index. Default memberwise copy violates the String iterator semantics.

The designer of the class can resolve these problems by providing an explicit instance of the memberwise assignment operator. The String class instance might be defined as follows:

```
String& String::operator=( const String& s )
{
    index = 0;
    len = s.len;
    delete str;

    str = new char[ len + 1 ];
    strcpy( str, s.str );
    return *this;
}
```

This definition, however, fails in the following special case:

```
String s1( "it can happen" );
s1 = s1; // oops: s1.str has been deleted!
```

A correct implementation needs to test whether the two Strings are, in fact, the same. This is accomplished with use of the `this` pointer. For example,

```
if (this == &s) // the same class object
    return *this;
```

The Word class, defined earlier during the discussion of memberwise initialization (see Section 6.2 (page 299) for the code) contains a String class member called name. Word does not define a memberwise assignment operator. When a Word object is assigned to another object of the Word class, the string memberwise assignment operator is implicitly invoked to handle the memberwise copy of name. For example,

```
#include "Word.h"

main() {
Word wd1( "horseless_carriage" );
Word wd2( "automobile" );

    // wd1.occurs = wd2.occurs
    // wd.name.String::operator=(wd2.name)
    wd1 = wd2;
}
```

If Word defines its own memberwise assignment operator, the String instance is invoked only if, within the body of the operator, an explicit String assignment takes place. For example,

```
Word&
Word::operator=(const Word& wd) {
    // String::operator=(const String&);
    name = wd.name;
    occurs = 0;
    return *this;
}
```

If the assignment

```
name = wd.name;
```

is not specified, the String memberwise operator will not be invoked — name
will not be changed.

Initialization and assignment are often not adequately distinguished by
programmers implementing class types. This can sometimes result in an inefficient class implementation. For example, given the two class definitions

```
class X {
public:
    X();
    X( int );
    X( const X& );
    X& operator=( const X& );
    // ...
};

class Y {
public:
    Y();
private:
    X x;
};
```

the following simple implementation of the Y class constructor

```
Y::Y() { x = 0; }
```

causes the implicit invocation of two X class constructors plus the invocation
of the assignment operator for X:

1. The default constructor

```
X::X()
```

is invoked before Y's constructor to initialize the member class object x.

The assignment of x with 0 cannot be carried out directly since the class X
does not define an assignment operator accepting an argument of type
int. The assignment is carried out in two steps,

2. The constructor

```
X::X( int )
```

is invoked to convert the integer 0 into an object of type X. The use of
constructors in type conversion is discussed in Section 6.5 (page 340) later
in this chapter.

3. This newly created class X object is assigned to x by invoking

```
X::operator=( const X& )
```

The second and third invocations are unnecessary, and they are not
invoked when the constructor for Y properly initializes its class member x, as
follows:

```
Y::Y()  :  x( 0 )  {}
```

Now, only

```
X::X( int )
```

is invoked with each invocation of the constructor for the Y class.

Operator ->

The member selection operator ("->") may be overloaded as a unary operator. It must be defined as a member function. It must return either a pointer
to a class object or an object of a class for which the member selection operator is overloaded. For example, given the statement

```
x->mem();
```

x is examined to determine its type. If x is a pointer of some class type, the
statement invokes the ordinary member selection semantics. If x is an object
or reference of some class type, the class is then examined for an overloaded
instance of the member selection operator. If an instance is not defined, the
statement, of course, is in error since a class object or reference must ordinarily use the "." selection operator. If an instance is defined, it is bound to x
and invoked. If the return value is a pointer of some class type, the ordinary
member selection semantics are then applied. If the return value is another
class object or reference, the process is applied recursively until either a
pointer type is returned or the statement is in error. The behavior of the
member selection operator is often referred to as that of a *smart pointer*.

For example, imagine that we wish to implement an interactive children's
story in which the narrative flow of the story varies with each terminal ses-
sion. Our story begins with the hero, an orange and gray tabby named
Phoenix, attempting to reach an August full moon by climbing a very old

oak tree overhanging the family's garage. Her eyes fix on the moon. Her body tenses. Phoenix is about to leap! Stop. Present the child with a set of alternative actions. Allow his or her choice to determine how the story will proceed.

We'd like our code to look something like the following:

```
// constructor displays first text segment
Story story;

main() {
    while (story.continue()) {
        // overloaded operator->()
        // returning a Text* object
        story->display();
        story.get_choice();
        // ...
    }
}
```

where the overloaded `operator->()` returns a pointer to the selected Text object to be displayed next on the terminal.

One might define a Text class to store and `display()` each discrete story text segment and accompanying picture.

```
class Text {
public:
    void display();
    // ...
private:
    String *text;
    Picture *pic;
};
```

The expression

```
story->display();
```

is resolved in two steps. First, the overloaded instance of the operator is invoked. Second, its return value — the Text pointer — is bound to the actual pointer operator and the `Text::display()` member function is invoked. The member selection operator is always bound to its left operand.

The declaration of the operator within Story might look as follows:

```
class Story {
public:
    Text *operator->();
    int get_choice();
    void get_text_segment();
    // ...
private:
    // holds array of possible
    // next story text segments
    Text *text_array;
};
```

One possible definition is the following:

```
Text*
Story::operator->() {
    if (text_array == 0)
        get_text_segment();
    return text_array[ get_choice() ];
}
```

Operators ++ and −−

Both a prefix and postfix instance of the increment ("++") and decrement
("−−") operators can be defined. The prefix operator looks as one might
expect:

```
class Screen {
public:
    char operator++() { return *++cursor; }
    char operator--(} { return *--cursor; }
    // ...
};
```

That is, it defines a unary operator function. It can be used as follows:

```
Screen myScreen;
// ...

if (++myScreen == '\n' ||
    myScreen == '\0')
        --myScreen;
```

Prior to Release 3.0, there was no way to overload either operator within
a class to provide both a prefix and postfix instance. The problem is that
each overloaded function must have a unique signature. The post- and prefix operators, however, share the exact same signature. The ability to be able

to specify both instances was vigorously petitioned for by users, and so the following design compromise was reached: A postfix instance of either operand is defined by specifying a second argument of type int. In the following example, a pre- and postfix pair of operators for the Screen class are declared. The decrement operator is declared as a friend only to illustrate a nonmember declaration.

```
class Screen {
    // nonmember definitions
    friend char operator--(Screen&); //prefix
    friend char operator--(Screen&,int); //postfix
public:
    // member definitions
    char operator++(); // prefix
    char operator++(int); // postfix
    // ...
};
```

The postfix increment operator might be implemented as follows:

```
char Screen::operator++(int) {
    char ch = *cursor++;
    return ch;
}
```

Similarly, here is a definition of the postfix decrement operator:

```
char operator--( Screen &s, int ) {
    char ch = *s.cursor--;
    return ch;
}
```

Note that an argument need not be given a name if it is not accessed within the function. The additional integer argument is transparent to users of the postfix operator. The compiler provides a default value for it, which can be ignored. This is why the argument is left unnamed. Here is an example of the use of the postfix operator:

```
Screen myScreen, yourScreen;

// apply postfix operator to each Screen
while ( myScreen++ == yourScreen++ ) ;
```

An explicit call of the postfix operator allows you to provide an actual value to the integer second argument. For example,

```
myScreen.operator++(1024);
```

Overloaded Operator Function Design

The only predefined but overloadable operators for a class are the assignment ("=") and address of operators ("&"). For any other operator to have
meaning when applied to a class object, the designer of the class must explicitly define it. The choice of which operators to provide is determined by the
expected uses of the class.

Always begin by defining the public interface of the class. Which operations must the class provide for its users? These will be the minimum set of
public member functions. Once this set is defined, it is possible to consider
which operators the class type should provide.

Each operator has an associated meaning from its predefined use. Binary
+, for example, is strongly identified with addition. Mapping binary + to an
analogous operation within a class type can provide a convenient notational
shorthand. For example, String concatenation, which adds one String to
another, is an appropriate extension of binary +.

Notice that in the previous section, I did not provide an increment or
decrement operator for the String class. This is because I could not think of
an operation performed on a String that logically maps onto either operator.
I somewhat fancifully thought of providing a lowercase to uppercase ("++")
and uppercase to lowercase ("--") ability but then dismissed it.

The worst abuse of operator overloading is not the obvious abuse of
defining subtraction for `operator + ()`. No responsible programmer would
do that. The worst abuse is an operator whose operation is ambiguous to its
users.

An ambiguous operator, in this sense, is one that supports equally well a
number of different interpretations. My perfectly clear and well-reasoned
explanation of `operator++()` is of very little comfort to the user of my
String class who believed it to serve as an iteration operator advancing
through the internal character array. When the meaning of a class operator
is not obvious, it is probably a good idea not to provide it.

Once the public interface of the class is defined, look for a logical mapping between the operation and an operator:

* `isEmpty()` becomes the logical NOT operator, `operator! ()`.

* `isEqual()` becomes the equality operator, `operator==()`.

* `copy()` becomes the assignment operator, `operator=()`.

Operator equivalence of compound operators, such as +=, for example,
must also be explicitly defined for a class. String operators, for example,
support concatenation and memberwise copy:

```
String s1( "C" );
String s2( "++" );

s1 = s1 + s2; // s1 <== "C++"
```

These operators, however, do *not* support the equivalent compound assignment operator:

```
s1 += s2;
```

That operator must also be explicitly defined and provided with an equivalent semantics.

Exercise 6-15. Identify which member functions of the Screen class implemented in Chapter 5 are candidates for operator overloading.

☐

Exercise 6-16. Implement the Screen class overloaded operator functions identified in the previous exercise.

☐

Exercise 6-17. Section 3.12 (page 150) presents an integer List class. Identify and implement the overloaded operator functions for this class.

☐

A binary tree class must provide the following general functionality: `isEmpty()`, `isEqual()`, `print()`, `addNode()`, `build()`, `copy()`, and `deleteNode()`,

Exercise 6-18. Which of these member functions are candidates for overloading? Which of these member functions are candidates for operator overloading? ☐

Exercise 6-19. Implement the binary tree member functions listed in the above paragraph. ☐

Exercise 6-20. INodes are generated quite frequently while managing a Bin-Tree. Using operators `new` and `delete`, take over the memory management of INodes. ☐

6.4   A BitVector Class Example

In Section 2.9 (page 82) bit vectors were shown to be a useful method of encoding yes/no information. In the previous sections, the String class is used to introduce the concepts of operator overloading. In this section, we consider the implementation of a bit vector class, with particular emphasis on the design choices of overloaded operator functions. We shall name our class BitVector.

The internal representation of the BitVector class is defined as follows:

```
typedef unsigned int BitVecType;
typedef BitVecType *BitVec;

class BitVector {
private:
    BitVec bv;
    unsigned short size;
    short wordWidth;
};
```

`size` contains the number of bits the BitVector class object represents. `bv` points to the actual bit vector, stored as a contiguous sequence of one or more unsigned integers. `wordWidth` holds the number of unsigned integers pointed to by `bv`. For example, if an unsigned integer is 32 bits, a BitVector of 16 bits initializes its members with the following values:

```
// number of bits in bit vector
size = 16;

// number of unsigned ints to hold bit vector
wordWidth = 1;
```

A BitVector of 107 bits, however, cannot represent its bit vector with less than four unsigned integers. Its members are initialized with the following values:

```
size = 107;
wordWidth = 4;
```

In both cases, `bv` is initialized to an array of BitVecType of size `wordWidth`. For example,

```
bv = new BitVecType[ wordWidth ];
```

The bit and byte sizes of data types are guaranteed to vary among different machines, and so we want to localize the explicit references to these machine-dependent values in our code:

```
#ifdef vax
const BITSPERBYTE = 8;
const BYTESPERWORD = 4;
#endif

#ifdef sun
const BITSPERBYTE = 8;
const BYTESPERWORD = 2;
#endif

// The size of a machine integer
const WORDSIZE = BITSPERBYTE * BYTESPERWORD;
```

A user should have the option of selecting the bit vector's size but should not be required to indicate a size. The most logical default value for a bit vector is the size in bits of a single unsigned integer, the smallest unit that can be pointed to by bv. Here is the constructor for our BitVector class:

```
#include <assert.h>
enum { OFF, ON };

// default values: sz => WORDSIZE, init => OFF
BitVector::BitVector( int sz, int init )
{
    assert( sz > 0 );
    size = sz;
    wordWidth = (size + WORDSIZE - 1)/WORDSIZE;
    bv = new BitVecType[ wordWidth ];
    assert( bv != 0 );

    // now initialize bv to either all 0's or 1's
    if ( init != OFF ) init = ~0;

    // assign 0 or -1 to each word of bv
    for ( int i = 0; i < wordWidth; i++ )
        *(bv + i) = init;
}
```

Users must be able to set() and unset() individual bits. These are binary operations, requiring a BitVector class object and an integer value representing the bit to be modified. A number of possible operators come to mind. For example, to set a single bit, the user might specify one of the following:

```
BitVector bvec;

// possible operators for set()
bvec | 12;
bvec |= 12;
bvec + 12;
bvec += 12;
```

Setting a bit to one is more similar to an addition operation than a bitwise OR operation. How do we choose, however, between the operators "+" and "+="? Or should we implement both? Let's consider what the operation actually does.

As a nonoperator set() function, the invocation looks as follows:

```
bvec.set(12);
```

bvec, that is, is modified by having its 12th bit set to 1. This means that the left operand of the expression stores the result of the expression. This is not the normal behavior of the "+" operator, but it does reflect the behavior of the "+=" operator. This is our choice of an operator. Here is our implementation:

```
void BitVector::operator+=( int pos )
{// turn on bit at position pos
    assert( pos >= 0 && pos < size );

    int index = getIndex( pos );
    int offset = getOffset( pos );

    // turn on bit offset at word index
    *(bv + index) |= (ON << offset);
}
```

getIndex() and getOffSet() are both private helping functions. getIndex() returns an index indicating which unsigned integer contains the bit. For example, on a machine in which an integer is represented as 32 bits, bit 16 returns an index of 0; bit 33 returns an index of 1; and bit 107 returns an index of 3. Here is the implementation:

```
inline BitVector::getIndex( int pos ) const {
    // return word bit is positioned in
    return( pos / WORDSIZE );
}
```

getOffSet() returns the position of the bit in the unsigned integer which contains it. For example, on a machine in which an integer is represented as 32 bits, bit 16 returns an offset of 16; bit 33 returns an offset of 1; and bit 107 returns an offset of 11. Here is the implementation:

```
inline BitVector::getOffset( int pos ) const {
    // return position of bit in word
    return( pos % WORDSIZE );
}
```

The implementation of `BitVector::operator-=(int)` is the same as that of the addition operator except for the bitwise operation to turn off the bit:

```
// turn off bit in word index at position offset
*(bv + index) &= (~(ON << offset));
```

Users of a BitVector need to be able to test an individual bit. `isOn()` and `isOff()` are each binary operations with a left operand of a BitVector class object and an integer right operand representing an individual bit. We have chosen to represent these functions with the equality ("`==`") and inequality ("`!=`") operators.

For example, the user code to test whether bit 17 is set might look as follows:

```
BitVector bvec;
if (bvec == 17 ) // ...
```

Here are the implementations:

```
BitVector::operator==( int pos ) const
{// true if bit at position pos is 1
    assert( pos >= 0 && pos < size );

    int index = getIndex( pos );
    int offset = getOffset( pos );
    return( *(bv + index) & (ON << offset) );
}

BitVector::operator!=( int pos ) const {
    return ( !(*this == pos) );
}
```

The user of a BitVector must be able to display class objects as well as to intermix the display of a BitVector object freely with the display of built-in data types. This is done by overloading the output operator ("`<<`") and making its return value of type `ostream&`. The BitVector user will then be able to write the following:

```
cout << "my BitVector: " << bv << endl;
```

Were bits 7, 12, 19, 27, and 34 set, the output of bv would look as follows:

```
< 7 12 19 27 34 >
```

Were none of bv's bits set, it would look as follows:

```
< >
```

The operator function can be defined like this:

```
ostream&
operator<<(ostream& os, BitVector& bv)
{
    os << "< ";
    for ( int cnt = 0, i = 0; i < bv.size; ++i )
        // BitVector::operator==(int)
        if ( bv == i ) os << i << " ";
    return os << ">";
}
```

An operation should sometimes not be translated into an operator function. For example, in order to reuse a BitVector object, the programmer must be able to reset() all its elements to 0. reset() could be implemented as a unary operation applied to a BitVector class object. It is represented by the logical NOT operator ("!"):

```
// Example of a inappropriate operator

BitVector& BitVector::operator!()
{ // reinitialize all elements to 0
    for ( int i = 0; i < wordWidth; ++i )
        *( bv + i ) = 0;
    return *this;
}
```

This implementation of the logical NOT operator is counterintuitive to its predefined meaning.

- In its predefined role, it returns a true value if its operand evaluates to 0. It does not modify its operand.

- In its BitVector implementation, it returns a reference to its operand. It resets all the bit elements of its operand to 0.

In our implementation, reset() is left as a named member function.

BitVectors are commonly used in compiler optimizers to aid in what is referred to as program data flow analysis. Two operations frequently performed are the bitwise ANDing and ORing of two bit vectors; both are essential to a BitVector class.

The operators & and | are used to represent these operations. For simplicity, the implementations presented assume that both BitVector objects are the same size.

```
BitVector
BitVector::operator|( const BitVector& b ) const
{// simplifying assumption: both have same size
    BitVector result( size, OFF );
    BitVec tmp = result.bv;
    for ( int i = 0; i < wordWidth; ++i )
        *(tmp + i) = *(bv + i) | *(b.bv + i);
    return result;
}
```

Notice that the operator & implementation is the same as that of the operator | except for the bit operation to perform the ANDing:

```
*(tmp + i ) = *( bv + i ) & *(b.bv + i );
```

Figure 6.3 presents a small interactive program that uses a BitVector object to keep track of type attributes. For example, entering

```
unsigned const char * ;
```

will set four bits of the BitVector object typeFlag. To simplify the presentation of the program, strings rather than individual characters are read, requiring the user to enter each attribute and terminating semicolon separated by a space.

When compiled and executed, the program of Figure 6.3 generates the following output:

```
Type in a declaration -- end with ';'
preceded by white space.  For example, try
        'unsigned const char * ;'
Hit ctrl-d to exit program

unsigned const char * ;

flags set for declaration are:
        unsigned
        const
        *
        char
```

Figure 6.4 presents the BitVector.h header file for the BitVector class as implemented in this section.

Exercise 6-21. Modify the program listed in Figure 6.3 to handle input of the following form:

```
const char * const ;
```

□

```cpp
#include <iostream.h>
#include <string.h>
#include "BitVector.h"

const int maxBits = 8;
enum {
    ERROR, CHAR, SHORT, INT, PTR,
    REFERENCE, CONST, UNSIGNED };

static char *typeTbl[] = {
    "OOPS, no type at slot 0",
    "char", "short", "int",
    "*", "&", "const", "unsigned" };

static char *msg =
"Type in a declaration -- end with ';' \
\npreceded by white space.  For example, \
try\n\t'unsigned const char * ;' \
\nHit ctrl-d to exit program\n";

main() {
    BitVector typeFlags( maxBits );
    char buf[ 1024 ];

    cout << msg;
    while ( cin >> buf ) {
        for ( int i = 0; i < maxBits; i++ )
            if (strcmp( typeTbl[i], buf ) == 0)
            { // a keyword?  BitVector::operator+=()
                typeFlags += i; break;
            }

        if ( buf[0] == ';' ) { // end of entry
            cout << "\nflags set for declaration are:\n\t";

            for ( i = maxBits-1; i > 0; i -- )
                // BitVector::operator==()
                if ( typeFlags == i )
                    cout << typeTbl[i] << "\n\t";
            cout << endl;

        // reinitialize: BitVector::reset()
        typeFlags.reset();
        }
    }
}
```

Figure 6.3 Program Example Using BitVectors

Exercise 6-22. Add the X(const X&) and operator=(const X&) instances for the BitVector class.

☐

Exercise 6-23. Define an equality operator for two BitVector objects.

☐

Exercise 6-24. Modify the AND operator function to handle BitVectors of different sizes.

☐

Exercise 6-25. Modify the OR operator function to handle BitVectors of different sizes.

☐

Exercise 6-26. Modify the BitVector output operator instance to condense multiple consecutive bits. For example, it currently prints out

```
< 0, 1, 2, 3, 4, 5, 6, 7 >
< 0, 2, 3, 4, 7, 8, 9, 12 >
```

Reimplement the output operator to group consecutive values as a hyphen-separated pair. For example,

```
< 0 - 7 >
< 0, 2 - 4, 7 - 9, 12 >
```

☐

6.5 User-Defined Conversions

The predefined standard conversions for the built-in data types prevent a combinatorial explosion of operators and overloaded functions. For example, without arithmetic conversions, the following six addition operations each require a unique implementation:

```
#ifndef BITVECTOR_H
#define BITVECTOR_H

#ifdef vax
const BITSPERBYTE = 8;
const BYTESPERWORD = 4;
#endif

#ifdef sun
const BITSPERBYTE = 8;
const BYTESPERWORD = 2;
#endif

const WORDSIZE = BITSPERBYTE * BYTESPERWORD;
enum { OFF, ON };
typedef unsigned int BitVecType;
typedef BitVecType *BitVec;

#include <iostream.h>
class BitVector {
    friend ostream&
        operator<<(ostream&, BitVector&);
public:
    BitVector( int = WORDSIZE, int = OFF );
    ~BitVector() { delete [] bv; }
    void operator+=( int pos ); // turn on pos
    void operator-=( int pos ); // turn off pos
    BitVector operator &( BitVector& ) const;
    BitVector operator |( BitVector& ) const;
    operator == ( int pos ) const;
    operator != ( int pos ) const;
    void reset(); // reinit to 0
private: // helping functions
    inline getOffset( int ) const;
    inline getIndex( int ) const;
private: // internal representation
    short wordWidth;
    short size;
    BitVec bv;
};
#endif
```

Figure 6.4 BitVector.h

```
char ch; short sh; int ival;

/* without type conversion, each addition
 * would require a unique operation */

ch + ival;      ival + ch;
ch + sh;        sh + ch;
ival + sh;      sh + ival;
```

With arithmetic conversions, each operand is promoted to type int. Only one operation is necessary — the addition of two integer values. These conversions are handled implicitly by the compiler and are therefore transparent to the user.

In this section, we consider how the designer of a class can provide a set of user-defined conversions for that class. These conversions are implicitly invoked by the compiler when necessary. To illustrate our discussion, a SmallInt class is implemented.

A SmallInt class can hold the same range of values as an 8-bit unsigned char — that is, 0 – 255. Its additional functionality is that it catches under- and overflow errors. Other than that, we wish for it to behave in the same way as an unsigned char

For example, we would like to add and subtract SmallInt objects both with other SmallInt objects and from the built-in arithmetic types. To support these operations, we must implement *six* SmallInt operator functions:

```
class SmallInt {
    friend operator+( SmallInt&, int );
    friend operator-( SmallInt&, int );
    friend operator-( int, SmallInt& );
    friend operator+( int, SmallInt& );
public:
    operator+( SmallInt& );
    operator-( SmallInt& );
    // ...
};
```

Only six operators are required because any built-in arithmetic type will be converted to match the operand of type int. For example, the expression

```
SmallInt si( 3 );

si + 3.14159
```

is resolved in two steps:

1. The double literal constant 3.14159 is converted to the integer value 3.

2. operator+(si,3) is invoked and returns a value of 6.

If we should wish to support the bitwise, logical, relational and compound assignment operators as well, the number of required operators becomes — well, daunting. What we would prefer instead is a way to convert a SmallInt class object into an `int`.

C++ provides a mechanism by which each class can define a set of conversions that can be applied to objects of its class. For SmallInt, we shall define a conversion of a SmallInt object to that of type `int`. Here is the implementation:

```
class SmallInt {
public:
    // conversion operator:
    // SmallInt ==> int
    operator int() { return value; }

private:
    int value;
};
```

User-defined conversions for a class type provide a set of conversion rules for a class. They define the allowable conversions that can be performed on individual class objects. In addition, they define for the compiler what the conversion means.

A SmallInt class object can now be used anywhere an `int` object can be used. For example, the expression

```
SmallInt si( 3 );
si + 3.14159;
```

is now resolved in the following two steps:

1. The SmallInt conversion operator is invoked, yielding the integer value 3.

2. The integer value 3 is promoted to `3.0` and added to the double literal constant `3.14159`, yielding the double value `6.14159`.

The following program illustrates the use of the SmallInt class:

```
#include <iostream.h>
#include "SmallInt.h"
SmallInt si1, si2;
```

```
main() {
    cout << "enter a SmallInt, please:   ";
    while ( cin >> si1 ) {
        cout << "\n\nThank you.\n";
        cout << "The value read is "
             << si1 << "\nIt is ";

        // SmallInt::operator int() invoked twice
        cout << (( si1 > 127 )
            ? "greater than "
            : (( si1 < 127 )
                ? "less than "
                : "equal to ")) << "127\n";

        cout << "\nenter a SmallInt, please \
(ctrl-d to exit):   ";
    }
    cout << "bye now\n";
}
```

When compiled and executed, the program generates the following results:

```
enter a SmallInt, please:   127

Thank you.
The value read is 127
It is equal to 127


enter a SmallInt, please (ctrl-d to exit):   126

Thank you.
The value read is 126
It is less than 127


enter a SmallInt, please (ctrl-d to exit):   128

Thank you.
The value read is 128
It is greater than 127


enter a SmallInt, please (ctrl-d to exit):   256
***SmallInt range error: 256 ***
```

The code implementing the SmallInt class looks as follows:

```
#include <iostream.h>

class SmallInt {
    friend istream&
        operator>>(istream& is, SmallInt& s);
    friend ostream&
        operator<<(ostream& os, SmallInt& s)
        { return ( os << s.value ); }
public:
    SmallInt(int i=0) : value( rangeCheck(i) ){}
    int operator=(int i)
        { return( value = rangeCheck(i) ); }
    operator int() { return value; }
private:
    int rangeCheck( int );
    int value;
};
```

The member functions defined outside the class body look as follows:

```
istream& operator>>( istream& is, SmallInt& si ) {
    int ix;
    is >> ix;
    si = ix; // SmallInt::operator=(int)
    return is;
}

SmallInt::rangeCheck( int i )
{
/* if any bits are set other than the first 8
 * the value is too large: report, then exit */

    if ( i & ~0377 )
        cerr << "\n***SmallInt range error: "
            << i << " ***" << endl;
        exit( -1 ); // stdlib.h
    return i;
}
```

Exercise 6-27. Why is the overloaded input operator not implemented in the following manner?

```
istream& operator>>( istream& is, SmallInt& si )
{
    return ( is >> si.value );
}
```

□

A Constructor as a Conversion Operator

The collection of single-argument constructors for a class, such as SmallInt, defines the set of implicit conversions of non-SmallInt types into objects of type SmallInt. Standard conversions, if necessary, are applied to the types before the invocation of the constructor.

A constructor that takes a single argument, such as `SmallInt(int)`, serves as a conversion operator between that argument type and the class. `SmallInt(int)`, for example, converts integer values into SmallInt objects.

```
extern void f( SmallInt );
int i;

// need to convert i into a SmallInt
// SmallInt(int) accomplishes this
f( i );
```

In the call `f(i)`, i is converted into a SmallInt object by invoking `SmallInt(int)`. A temporary SmallInt object is constructed by the compiler and passed to `f()`.

```
// a temporary SmallInt Object is created
{
    SmallInt temp = SmallInt(i);
    f(temp);
}
```

The braces in the example indicate the lifetime of the generated SmallInt temporary.

If necessary, a standard conversion is applied before the invocation of `SmallInt(int)`. For example,

```
double d;
f( d );
```

becomes

```
{
    // warning: narrowing conversion
    SmallInt temp = SmallInt( (int)d );
    f(temp);
}
```

The invocation of a conversion operator is applied only if no other conversion is possible. Were `f()` overloaded as follows, for example, `SmallInt(int)` would *not* be invoked.

```
extern void f( SmallInt );
extern void f( double );
int ival;

// matches f(double) by standard conversion
f( ival );
```

The argument may also be another user-defined class type. For example,

```
class Token {
public:
    // ... public members
private:
    SmallInt tok;
    // ... rest of Token members
};


// create a SmallInt object from a Token
SmallInt::SmallInt( Token& t ) { /* ... */ }

extern void f( SmallInt& );
Token curTok;

main()
{ // invoke SmallInt( Token& )
    f( curTok );
}
```

Conversion Operators

A conversion operator, a special instance of a class member function, specifies an implicit conversion of a class object into some other type. SmallInt,
for example, might define the conversion of a SmallInt object into a value of
type unsigned int:

```
SmallInt::operator unsigned int()
{
    return( (unsigned)value );
}
```

A Token class, defined next, may choose to define multiple conversion
operators:

```
#include "SmallInt.h"

typedef const char *cchar;
class Token {
public:
    Token( char*, int );
    operator SmallInt() { return val; }
    operator cchar()    { return name; }
    operator int()      { return val; }
    // ... rest of public members
private:
    SmallInt val;
    char *name;
};
```

Notice that the Token conversion operators for SmallInt and int are the same. SmallInt::operator int() is implicitly applied to the SmallInt object val in Token::operator int(). For example,

```
#include "Token.h"

void f( int i )
{
    cout << "f(int) : " << i << endl;
}

Token t1( "integer constant", 127 );

main() {
    Token t2( "friend", 255 );

    f( t1 ); // t1.operator int()
    f( t2 ); // t2.operator int()
    return 0;
}
```

When compiled and executed, this small program generates the following output:

```
f(int) : 127
f(int) : 255
```

A conversion operator takes the general form

```
operator <type> ();
```

where <type> is replaced by a specific built-in, derived, or user-defined data type. (Conversion operators for either an array or a function are not allowed.) The conversion operator must be a member function. It must not specify a return type nor can an argument list be specified. Each of the following declarations, for example, are illegal:

```
operator int( SmallInt& ); // error: nonmember

class SmallInt {
public:
    int operator int();  // error: return type
    operator int(int=0); // error: argument list
    // ...
};
```

The programmer may explicitly invoke a conversion operator by using either form of cast notation. For example,

```
#include "Token.h"
Token tok( "function", 78 );

// function cast notation: operator SmallInt()
SmallInt tokVal = SmallInt( tok );

// type cast notation: operator char*()
char *tokString = (char *)tok;
```

If a class object is present and is not of the appropriate type, a conversion operator, if defined, will be applied implicitly by the compiler. For example,

```
#include "Token.h"
extern void f( char * );
Token tok( "enumeration", 8 );
enum { ENUM }; // token constant

main() {
    f( tok ); // tok.operator char*();

    // explicit functional cast notation
    switch ( int(tok) ) // tok.operator int()
    {
        case ENUM:
        {   // tok.operator SmallInt();
            SmallInt si = tok;
            // ...
        }
    }
}
```

Suppose that the required type does not match any of the conversion operator types exactly. Will a conversion operator still be invoked?

- Yes, if the required type can be reached through a standard conversion. For example,

```
extern void f( double );
Token tok( "constant", 44 );

// tok.operator int() invoked
// int ==> double by standard conversion
f( tok );
```

- No, if to reach the required type a second user-defined conversion operator must be applied to the result of the first user-defined conversion operator. (This is why Token defines both operator SmallInt() and operator int().)

For example, if Token did *not* provide an operator int() instance, the following call would be illegal:

```
extern void f(int);
Token tok( "pointer", 37 );

// without Token::operator int() defined,
// this call will generate a compile-time error
f( tok );
```

Without Token::operator int() defined, the conversion of tok to type int would require the invocation of two user-defined conversion operators.

```
Token::operator SmallInt();
```

would convert tok into a SmallInt object.

```
SmallInt::operator int();
```

would complete the conversion to type int.

The rule, however, is that only one level of user-defined conversions can be applied. If Token::operator int() is not defined, the call f(tok), requiring an argument of type int, is flagged at compile time as a type violation.

The most useful String conversion operator is that which substitutes a char* for a String class object. This is easily coded:

```
inline String::operator char*() { return str; }
```

but presents something of a problem. Can you see what it is?

For example, given the following String object:

```
String lottery_winner( "Rick" );
```

the following attempt to directly access the character array member is detected and flagged as an error:

```
// error: String::str is nonpublic
char *ps = lottery_winner.str;
```

However, our conversion operator provides the very access we sought to protect:

```
ps = lottery_winner; // ok: implicit conversion
*ps = 'N'; // oops: Nick's now the winner!
```

Our intention is to permit read-only access on our converted String class object. To enforce this, our conversion operator needs to return a type const char*:

```
typedef const char *cchar;
inline String::operator cchar() { return str; }

// error: char* <== const char*
char *ps = lottery_winner;
const char *ps2 = lotter_winner; // ok
```

The introduction of this conversion operator actually may break some existing code making use of the String class. For example,

```
String dudette( "cowabunga" );
void foo( char *str ) {
    // equality test no longer compiles!
    if (dudette == str)
        cout << str << " dudette!\n";
    // ...
}
```

Previously, the comparison

```
dudette == str
```

resolved itself into a call of the String equality operator

```
String::operator==(const String&);
```

by applying the String conversion constructor to the right operand, str:

```
String::String( const char* );
```

Now, however, an equally valid conversion is that of applying the const char* String conversion operator to the left operand, dudette. This will resolve the comparison into a call of the built-in equality operator for pointers. Since both conversions are equally possible, the call is now flagged as ambiguous and the compilation fails.

The constructor and operator conversion instances have equal priority in
their application. The solution, in this case, is to define an additional String
equality operator taking a right operand of type const char*:

```
inline String::operator==(const char *s) {
    return strcmp(str,s)==0;
}
```

Because they are applied implicitly, conversion operators can cause programs to behave in unanticipated ways. Conversion operators should, in
general, therefore, be used judiciously. In the next section, the issue of ambiguity between conversion operators is examined in more detail.

Ambiguity

Ambiguity may arise in connection with the implicit invocation of conversion operators. For example,

```
extern void f( int );
extern void f( SmallInt );
Token tok( "string constant", 3 );

f( tok ); // error: ambiguous
```

Token defines a conversion operator for both SmallInt and int: both conversions are equally possible. The call f(tok) is ambiguous since there is no
way for the compiler to choose between the two conversions, and the call is
flagged at compile time as an error. The programmer can resolve the ambiguity by making the conversion explicit:

```
// explicit conversion resolves ambiguity
f( int(tok) );
```

Were Token::operator int() not defined, the call would not be
ambiguous. It would resolve to Token::operator SmallInt(). The fact
that SmallInt defines an int conversion operator is not considered. In determining the permissible conversions of an object, only the first level of user-
defined conversion operators is examined.

If two conversion operators are possible, but one is an exact match while
the other also requires a standard conversion, there is no ambiguity — the
conversion operator that effects an exact match is chosen. For example,

```
class Token {
public:
    operator float();
    operator int();
    // ...
};
Token tok;
float ff = tok; // ok: operator float()
```

However, if both conversion operators are equally applicable, the statement is flagged as ambiguous:

```
// error: both operators float() and int()
long lval = tok;
```

Ambiguity can also occur when two classes define conversions between themselves. For example,

```
SmallInt::SmallInt( Token& ){}
Token::operator SmallInt(){}
extern void f( SmallInt );
Token tok( "pointer to class member", 197 );

f( tok ); // error: two conversion possible
```

In this case, there are two equally possible ways to convert tok into a Small-Int object. The call is ambiguous since there is no way for the compiler to choose between the two; the call is flagged at compile time as an error. The programmer can resolve the ambiguity by making the conversion explicit. For example,

```
// explicit conversion resolves ambiguity
f( (SmallInt)tok ); // Token::operator SmallInt()
```

The programmer can also resolve the ambiguity by explicitly invoking the Token class conversion operator:

```
// ok: explicit conversion resolves ambiguity
f( tok.operator SmallInt() );
```

Notice that the explicit cast in functional notation is still ambiguous.

```
f( SmallInt(tok) ); // error: still ambiguous
```

SmallInt(Token&) and Token::operator SmallInt() are equally possible interpretations of the call.

A second form of ambiguity relates to the human reader of a program making use of conversion operators. When a SmallInt object is converted to an int value, the meaning of that conversion is clear. When a String object is converted to a type char*, the meaning of that conversion is also clear. In both cases, there is a one-to-one mapping between a built-in data type and the internal representation of a class type. When there is no logical mapping between a conversion operator and the class type, however, the use of objects of that class may become ambiguous to the reader of the program. For example,

```
class Date {
public:
    // guess which member is returned!
    operator int();
private:
    int month, day, year;
};
```

What value should be returned by the int conversion operator of Date? Whatever choice is made for whatever good reason, the use of Date objects will be ambiguous to a reader of the program because there is no logical one-to-one mapping. In this case, it would be better *not* to define a conversion operator.

Exercise 6-28. What are the conversion operators necessary to support the following uses of a String class object?

```
extern int strlen( const char* );
const maxLen = 32;

String st = "a string";
int len = strlen( st );
if ( st >= maxLen ) ...
String st2 = maxLen;
```

☐

Exercise 6-29. Discuss the benefits and drawbacks of supporting the conversion operation represented by

```
if ( st >= maxLen ) ...
```

☐

Exercise 6-30. An interesting conversion operator for BinTree would return an IntArray class object of the Inode values. (Section 1.8 (page 49) contains the definition of the IntArray class). Implement the following two conversion operations:

```
BinTree::BinTree( IntArray& );
BinTree::operator IntArray();
```

☐

Note that the order of tree traversal must be the same in both operations. A preorder traversal of the following general form might be used:

```
BinTree::preOrder( /* ??? */ )
{
    if ( !node ) return;
    node->visit( /* ??? */ ); // do work
    if ( left ) left->preOrder( /* ??? */ );
    if ( right ) right->preOrder( /* ??? */ );
```

Exercise 6-31. The previous exercise provides for the handling of an expression involving objects of both the IntArray and BinTree classes. For example,

```
extern BinTree bt;
extern IntArray ia;

if ( ia == bt ) ...
```

The order of operations is as follows: The BinTree conversion operator is first invoked to convert bt into an IntArray class object. Then the IntArray equality operator is invoked to compare two IntArray class objects. What would happen, however, if the IntArray class defines the following two conversion operations?

```
IntArray::IntArray( BinTree& );
IntArray::operator BinTree();
```

☐

Template Functions and Class Types

The difficulty of designing and implementing template function instances is that of coding in a general enough fashion to accommodate multiple data types noninvasively — that is, in not requiring a modification of the data type's implementation in order to instantiate the template. One extension to the language to help support type generality is the legality of constructor and destructor syntax both for built-in types and class types that have not defined these members. For example,

```
class Dummy {};

Dummy d = Dummy();      // ok
int i = int();          // ok
p->int::~int();         // ok
p->Dummy::~Dummy();     // ok
```

Certainly, the programmer is unlikely to write such code explicitly. The following template instance, however, is not quite as unlikely:

```
// call of foo_bar with built-in type
// such as int or double is ok

template <class Type>
void foo_bar(Type t, void *buf)
{
    Type tt = Type();
    Type *p = new (buf) Type;
    // ...
    p->Type::~Type();
}
```

Another helpful language extension is the ability to initialize a built-in type using the constructor syntax of a class:

```
int ix(10); // ok
int iy(ix); // ok

template <class Type>
Type foo_bar( Type t )
{
    Type xyz( t );
    // ...
}
```

It is not always possible to determine the legality of a template function until it is instantiated. For example,

```
template <class classType>
void operator++( classType );
```

is legal only if the actual parameter is a class type. (Recall, operator functions must take at least one argument of a class type.)

```
String str( "Pinnochio" );
int ival = 1024;

main() {
    // ok: instantiate operator++(String)
    operator++( str );

    ++str; // ok: same instance
    ++ival; // ok: built-in operator

    // error: instantiate operator++(int)
    operator++(ival);
}
```

Here is another pair of function templates whose legality can be determined only at the time of their instantiation:

```
template <class classType> classType
foo(classType, classType (classType::*)());

template <class classType> classType
bar( classType ct )
{
    classType (classType::*pmf)() = 0;
    return foo( ct, pmf );
}
```

There is no language support for constraining an actual parameter to be of certain category of type. A call such as the following, however,

```
int ix = bar(10);
```

is caught at compile time and the following error message is generated:

```
illegal parameterized pointer to member  int ::*
```

Even a template function as simple as the following can be legally instantiated only for those types that can be initialized with an arithmetic value:

```
template <class Type>
void cannot_tell( Type t )
{
    // ok for all types except classes that
    // define a nonpublic memberwise constructor
    Type local_t = t;

    // ok only for those types can support
    // initialization with an arithmetic value
    Type local_too = 1;

    // ...
}
```

The following instantiation of the quicksort template function defined earlier (see Section 4.2 (page 194) for the actual code) works for an array of Strings. Here is our program:

```
#include <iostream.h>
#include "String.h"
#include "pt_sort.c"
#include "pt_display.c"
```

```
String Sa[] = { "I", "do", "not", "know", "Crane",
        "what", "is", "worse", "this", "job", "or",
        "this", "job", "of", "writing", "you"
};


main() {
  int size = sizeof(Sa)/sizeof(String);
  cout << "Quicksort of String array (size == "
      << size << ")" << endl;
  qsort(Sa,0,size-1);
  display(Sa,size);

  return 0;
}
```

The program, when executed, generates the following output:

```
Quicksort of String array (size == 16)
( 16 )< Crane, I, do, is, job, job, know, not
        of, or, this, this, what, worse, writing, you >
```

The instantiation succeeds because the String class happens to define both less-than and greater-than operators. A quicksort instantiation would not succeed with an array of Screen classes, for example, or an array of BitVectors. Template functions are more easily instantiated when they implement the more general operators. Had quicksort used a greater-than-or-equal operator rather than a less-than, for example, the String class instantiation, too, would have failed.

A container class is one that operates on a collection of 0 or more objects of a particular type. A linked list is a container class. So is an array. In Chapter 1, an Array class is implemented to handle collections of integers. Were the programmer to assign an element of the Array an object of another type, the object is either converted to an integer or, if no conversion exists, the assignment is flagged at compile time as an error. For example,

```
String str( "Plurabelle" );
Complex c( 2.0, 1.732 );
Array ia[3];

ia[0] = 3.14159; // ok: ia[0] = 3
ia[1] = c;    // ok: ia[1] = 2
ia[2] = str; // error: no conversion
```

The C++ type system guarantees that each element in the Array class in fact is an integer. This is good when the programmer wishes to use integers, of course. This is less good, however, when the programmer wishes to use an Array class of doubles, characters, Complex numbers, BitVectors, or Strings.

One method of coping is simple brute force. The programmer copies the entire integer Array class implementation, modifying it to work with doubles, then with the Complex number class, then with Strings, etc. And, since class names cannot be overloaded, each implementation must be given a unique name: intArray, doubleArray, ComplexArray, StringArray. As each new type of Array class is needed, the code is copied, changed, and renamed.

What are the problems with this method of class propagation? There is the lexical complexity of each uniquely named Array class. Then, too, there is the administrative complexity — imagine having to propagate a modification in the general implementation of the Array class to each specific instance. In general, providing manually generated copies for individual types is never-ending and endlessly complicated to maintain.

An alternative method is that of the preprocessor macro facility. The idea here is to automatically generate a new instance of the Array class for each unique type. For example, here is a macro implementation of a simplified Array class. First, a macro is defined to concatenate two names together:

```
#ifdef sun
#      define name2(a,b)   a/**/b
#else
#ifdef  BSD
#      define name2(a,b) a\
b
#else /* System V */
#      define name2(a,b)   a/**/b
#endif
#endif
```

Given the macro call

```
name2(int,Array);
```

the macro expansion generates the concatenated name `intArray`. The conditional test is necessary because the concatenation facility differs across systems.

Next, a facility is defined for explicitly declaring an Array of a particular type (this is placed in a file named `array.h`.

```
#define declare(a,t)  name2(a,declare)(t)

#define Array(type)  name2(type,Array)
#define Arraydeclare(type)                  \
class Array(type) {                         \
public:                                     \
        Array(type)(int sz) :               \
            ia(new type[sz]),size(sz) {} \
        ~Array(type)() { delete ia; }    \
private:                                     \
        type *ia;                            \
        int size;                            \
};
```

The programmer uses this facility as follows:

```
#include "array.h"

declare(Array,int);

main() {
    Array(int) ia(24);
    // ...
}
```

The statement

```
declare(Array,int);
```

expands to

```
name2(Array,declare)(int);
```

This, in turn, expands to

```
Arraydeclare(int)
```

which, in turn, expands to

```
// note: expands to a single line
// separated manually to fit on this page!

class intArray { public: intArray(int sz) : ia(new
int[sz]),size(sz) {} ~intArray() { delete ia; }
private: int *ia; int size; };;

main() {
    intArray ia(24);
    // ...
}
```

One drawback to this method is that the macro expansion is done as a single line of text (that's the meaning of the backslash in the macro definition). Often, this line is too large for text editors and other facilities (such as mailers) to handle. Certainly, the line is extremely difficult for people to read. (Unfortunately, at times one does have to edit it, mail it, read it — usually when the program is not working correctly.)

Another drawback to this method is that it is simply a lexical substitution separate from the C++ language. If I write

```
declare (Array,int*);
```

the preprocessor on my system goes into an infinite loop, printing out the message

```
Array: argument mismatch
```

at the rate of about 10 per second. To correct that, I can write

```
typedef int *pi;
declare (Array,pi);
```

However, if I write

```
typedef int[] pi;
declare (Array,pi);
```

then the expansion of the Array macro generates illegal C++ code.

The C++ template facility also provides for the automatic generation of class instances bound to a particular type. Unlike the macro facility, it is an integral part of the C++ language. The analogous template definition of the macro Array class looks as follows:

```
template <class type>
class Array {
    Array(int sz = 12)
        : ia(new type[sz]), size(sz) {}
    ~Array(type)() { delete ia; }
private:
    type *ia;
    int size;
};
```

The programmer writes

```
Array<int> ia;
Array<Complex> ic;
Array<String> is;
```

to generate, in turn, an Array class of integers, Complex numbers, and Strings. The definition and use of template classes are looked at in detail in the following sections.

A Template Queue Class

A queue is a data structure in which items are entered at one end, the back, and removed at the other end, the front. Its behavior is spoken of as first in, first out, or *FIFO*. A line of people waiting to buy tickets for the latest Woody Allen movie exhibits the behavior of a queue. This is likely the reason the English refer to getting in line as "queuing up."

The operations upon a queue consist of the following:

- Add an item to the back of the queue:

```
void add( item );
```

- Remove an item from the front of the queue:

```
item remove();
```

- Determine if the queue is empty:

```
Boolean is_empty();
```

- Determine if the queue is full:

```
Boolean is_full();
```

The implementation of a Queue is presented in the following sections to illustrate the definition and use of template classes. The Queue is implemented as a pair of class abstractions:

1. The Queue itself, providing the public interface and a pair of data members: `front` and `back`. The Queue is implemented as a linked list.

2. A QueueItem. Each item entered into the Queue is represented by a QueueItem. A QueueItem contains a `value` and a link to the `next` QueueItem. The actual type of `value` varies with each instantiation of a Queue.

7.1 Template Class Definition

Template and nontemplate classes behave essentially the same. The template class syntax at first can seem intimidating. Beneath the unfamiliar syntax, however, is often rather familiar-looking code. For example, here is the forward declaration of the template QueueItem class:

```
template <class T>
    class QueueItem;
```

The `template` keyword begins every forward declaration and definition of a template class. It is followed by a formal template parameter list surrounded by angle brackets. The formal parameter list cannot be empty. Multiple parameters are separated by a comma:

```
template <class T1, class T2, class T3>
```

The use of the `class` keyword in this context indicates that the identifier that follows represents a *type* parameter. A class may also declare *expression* parameters. For example, a Buffer template class may define a type parameter to indicate the type of elements it holds and an expression parameter to indicate its size. For example,

```
template <class Type, int size>
    class Buffer;
```

Once the template class has been made known to the program, it can be used as a type specifier the same as a nontemplate class name. One difference, however, is that the use of a template class name must always include its parameter list enclosed by angle brackets — everywhere, that is, except within its own class definition. For example, here is the definition of the QueueItem template class. Notice how similar it is to a nontemplate class definition — apart from the template keyword and parameter list:

```
template <class Type>
class QueueItem {
public:
    QueueItem( const Type& );
private:
    Type item;
    QueueItem *next;
}
```

Each occurrence of the QueueItem class name within the class definition is a shorthand notation for

```
QueueItem<Type>
```

Outside the class definition, the programmer must make the parameter list explicit:

```
template <class Type>
inline
QueueItem<Type>::
    QueueItem( const Type &t ) : item( t )
    { next = 0; }
```

The second occurrence of QueueItem in the constructor definition is *not* modified with the formal parameter list of the class. It serves as the member name within the scope of the template class and not as a type specifier.

The class definition of QueueItem serves as a template for the automatic generation of type-specific instances of a QueueItem class: integer, String, BitVector, pointer to char, etc. To create a QueueItem class of integers, for example, the programmer writes

```
QueueItem<int> qi( 1024 );
```

substituting the formal parameter list with a set of actual types and/or expressions. Similarly, to create a QueueItem class of Strings, the programmer writes

```
String str( "Beth" );
QueueItem<String> qs( str );
```

qi and qs can now be used the same as nontemplate class objects.

Whenever the template class name is used as a type specifier in the context of a template definition, the full parameter list must be specified:

```
template <class Type>
void
display( QueueItem<Type> &qi )
{
    QueueItem<Type> *pqi = &qi;
    // ...
}
```

The generation of an integer or String QueueItem class is spoken of as an *instantiation*. Each occurrence of the formal parameter is replaced by the actual type of the instantiation. The String QueueItem class literally becomes

```
class QueueItem {
public:
    QueueItem( const String& );
private:
    String item;
    QueueItem *next;
};
```

Can you see why the following definition of the QueueItem constructor is likely to be unacceptable for a wide range of type instantiations?

```
template <class Type>
class QueueItem {
public:
    QueueItem(Type); // bad design choice
    // ...
```

This definition of the QueueItem constructor implements the default pass-by-value argument semantics. This performs adequately when QueueItem is instantiated to a built-in type. However, when QueueItem is instantiated to a large class type, the run-time impact of the implementation is no longer acceptable. This is why the argument to the constructor is declared as a constant reference:

```
QueueItem(const Type&);
```

A similar efficiency consideration underlies the implementation of the QueueItem constructor. The following definition is acceptable if the instantiated type does not have an associated constructor:

```
// potentially very inefficient
QueueItem( const Type &t ) {
    item = t; next = 0;
}
```

For a class type with a constructor, however, this implementation is too inefficient. It results in item being initialized twice! The default class constructor is invoked prior to the execution of the body of the QueueItem constructor. `item`, newly constructed, is then memberwise assigned. Explicitly initializing `item` to the constructor's argument resolves this potential problem:

```
QueueItem( const Type &t )
    : item(t) { next = 0; }
```

Outside the context of a template definition, only the instantiations of a template class can be used. For example, a nontemplate function must always specify a particular instance of the QueueItem class:

```
void
foo( QueueItem<int> &qi )
{
    QueueItem<int> *pqi = &qi;
    // ...
```

A template function, however, can specify either a particular instance of a template class or the general, parameterized instance:

```
template <class Type>
void
bar( QueueItem<Type>&,
     QueueItem<Complex>&);
```

7.2 Queue and QueueItem Class Definition

QueueItem is intended as an auxiliary class to help in the implementation of a Queue. It is not intended to be used by the general program. To enforce this, the declaration of its constructor is moved into a private section of the class. Queue must now be declared a friend to QueueItem in order that it can create and manipulate QueueItem class objects. There are two methods of declaring a template class to be a friend. The first declaration declares all possible Queue instances to be friends to each QueueItem instantiation:

```
template <class Type>
class QueueItem {
    // all Queue instantiations are friend
    // to each QueueItem instantiation
    template <class T> friend class Queue;
};
```

This is not really the design intention, however. It makes no sense, for example, having a Queue of Strings be friend to a BitVector QueueItem. A String instance of a Queue should be a friend only to the String QueueItem instantiation. That is, we want a one-to-one mapping between a Queue and

QueueItem instance for every type instantiated. This is achieved by the following friend declaration

```
template <class Type>
class QueueItem {
    // each QueueItem instantiation has as its
    // friend the associated Queue instantiation
    friend class Queue<Type>;

    // ...
};
```

This declaration specifies that for every instantiation of QueueItem to a particular type, the corresponding Queue instantiation is its friend. That is, an integer Queue is friend to an integer QueueItem; it is not a friend to a Complex or String QueueItem instance.

When might the first form of the template class declaration be appropriate? It is appropriate, in general, when declaring a template class to be a friend to a nontemplate class. For example,

```
class Foo {
    // each class instantiations of Bar
    // is a friend to the nontemplate Foo class
    template <class T> friend class Bar;

    // ...
};
```

Each instantiation of Bar is a friend to the nontemplate Foo class.

Here is our definition of the Queue template class. It is placed in a header file named Queue.h together with the QueueItem class definition.

```
#ifndef QUEUE_H
#define QUEUE_H

enum Boolean { false=0, true };

// forward declaration of QueueItem
template <class T> class QueueItem;
```

```
template <class Type>
class Queue {
public:
    Queue() { front = back = 0; }
    ~Queue();

    Type remove();
    void add( const Type& );
    Boolean is_empty() {
        return front==0 ? true : false; }
private:
    QueueItem<Type> *front;
    QueueItem<Type> *back;
};
#endif
```

Within the template Queue class definition, the use of QueueItem must be qualified with its parameter list. The following declaration of front, for example, is wrong:

```
template <class Type>
class Queue {
public:
    // ...
private:
    // error: which QueueItem instance?
    QueueItem *front;
};
```

Each instantiation of a Queue results in the instantiation of the associated QueueItem.

The destructor empties the Queue of items:

```
template <class Type>
Queue<Type>::~Queue()
{
    while (is_empty() != true)
        (void) remove();
}
```

add() places a new item at the back of the Queue. Here is its implementation:

```
template <class Type>
void
Queue<Type>::add(const Type &val)
{
    // allocate a new QueueItem object
    QueueItem<Type> *pt =
        new QueueItem<Type>( val );

    if ( is_empty() )
        front = back = pt;
    else {
        back->next = pt;
        back = pt;
    }
}
```

`remove()` returns the value of the item at the front of the Queue. The associated QueueItem is deleted.

```
#include <iostream.h>
#include <stdlib.h>

template <class Type>
Type
Queue<Type>::remove()
{
    if (is_empty() == true) {
        cerr << "remove() on empty queue\n";
        exit( -1 );
    }

    QueueItem<Type> *pt = front;
    front = front->next;
    Type retval = pt->item;
    delete pt;
    return retval;
}
```

At any given point in the operation of a Queue, a user may need the ability to display the Queue's content. One method of allowing this is to provide an overloaded instance of the output operator. What should its signature look like?

```
// what form of Queue argument?
ostream& operator<<( ostream&, ??? );
```

Since Queue is a template class, its type specifier must be qualified with its full parameter list. For example,

```
ostream& operator<<(ostream&, Queue<int>&);
```

That defines an output operator for a Queue of integer items. However,
what about a Queue of Strings?

```
ostream& operator<<(ostream&, Queue<String>&);
```

Rather than explicitly define each particular output operator as it is needed,
let's define a general output operator that can handle all Queue instantiations. For example,

```
ostream& operator<<(ostream&,Queue<Type>&);
```

For this to work, however, we must in turn make our overloaded output
operator a template function:

```
template <class Type> ostream&
operator<<(ostream&, Queue<Type>&);
```

That done, each time a Queue instantiation is passed to an ostream, an
instance of the template definition is invoked. Here is one possible implementation of the output operator for a Queue:

```
template <class Type>
ostream&
operator<<(ostream &os, Queue<Type> &q)
{
    os << "< ";
    QueueItem<Type> *p;
    for (p=q.front; p; p=p->next)
        os << *p << " ";
    os << " >";
    return os;
}
```

If a Queue of integers contains the values 3, 5, 8, and 13, the output of this
Queue displays as follows:

```
< 3 5 8 13 >
```

The next thing we need to do is to declare the operator as a friend to
Queue. One way to do this is the following:

```
template <class Type>
class Queue {
    template <class T>
        friend ostream&
        operator<<(ostream&,Queue<T>&);
    // ...
};
```

As happened with the friend declaration of Queue earlier in this section, this friend declaration is not quite what we intend. This declaration makes all instances of the output operator a friend to each Queue instantiation. Rather, we'd like a one-to-one mapping of friendship between a Queue and operator instance for each instantiated type. This is achieved with the following declaration:

```
template <class Type>
class Queue {
    friend ostream&
        operator<<(ostream&,Queue<Type>&);
    // ...
};
```

The actual display of the Queue elements is pushed back onto the QueueItem output operator.

```
os << *p;
```

The QueueItem output operator also needs to be implemented as a template function.

```
template <class Type>
ostream&
operator<<(ostream &os,  QueueItem<Type> &qi)
{
    os << qi.item;
    return os;
}
```

Because it accesses the nonpublic QueueItem members, it also needs to be declared a friend.

```
template <class Type>
class QueueItem {
    friend class Queue<Type>;
    friend ostream&
        operator<<(ostream&,QueueItem<Type>&);
    // ...
};
```

The actual display of the item is not handled by the QueueItem output operator. Rather, it is pushed back on the item itself:

```
os << qi.item;
```

This introduces a subtle type dependency on the instantiation of a Queue. In effect, each user-defined class type bound to a Queue that intends to display itself is obligated to provide an output operator. There is no language supported mechanism either to specify or enforce that dependency. If the output operator is not defined for a Queue instantiation and an attempt is made to display it, a compile-time type violation at the call of the invalid output operator results. A Queue can be instantiated with a type that does not define an output operator — provided there is no attempt to output the Queue.

7.3 Template Class Instantiation

A template class is instantiated by appending the full list of actual parameters enclosed by angle brackets to the template class name. For example,

```
Queue<int> qi;
```

instantiates both an integer Queue and an integer QueueItem class.

The template class type specifier can be used everywhere that an ordinary type specifier can be used:

```
// the return type and two arguments are of
// a Queue class instantiation of type Complex.

extern Queue<Complex>
    foo(Queue<Complex>&, Queue<Complex>&);

// pointer to member function of a Queue
// class instantiation of type double

int (Queue<double>::*pmf)() = 0;

// explicit cast of 0 to a pointer to a
// Queue class instantiation of type char*

((Queue<char*>*) 0);
```

Objects of an instantiated template class are declared exactly the same as objects of a nontemplate class.

```
extern Queue<double> aqd;
Queue<int> *pqi = new Queue<int>;
Queue<int> aqi[1024];
```

Objects of an instantiated template class are used exactly the same as objects of a nontemplate class.

```
main() {
    int ix;
    if (pqi->is_empty() == false)
        ix = pqi->remove();
    // ...
    for (ix=0; ix < 1024; ++ix)
        aqi[ix].add(ix);
    // ...
}
```

The following program illustrates how a Queue class might be instantiated and used.

```
#include <iostream.h>
#include "Queue.c"

main() {
    Queue<int> *p_qi = new Queue<int>;
    cout << *p_qi << endl;

    int ival;
    for (ival = 0; ival < 10; ++ival)
        p_qi->add(ival);
    cout << *p_qi << endl;

    int err_cnt = 0;
    for (ival = 0; ival < 10; ++ival) {
        int qval = p_qi->remove();
        if ( ival != qval ) err_cnt++;
    }

    cout << *p_qi << endl;
    if ( !err_cnt )
        cout << "!! queue executed ok\n";
    else cout << "?? queue errors: " << err_cnt << endl;
    return 0;
}
```

When compiled and executed, it generates the following output:

```
<   >
< 0  1  2  3  4  5  6  7  8  9   >
<   >
!! queue executed ok
```

7.4 Template Class Specialization

There are particular types for which a default template member function is
not sufficient. In these cases, the programmer can provide an explicit implementation to handle a particular type. The specialized instance, when present, is invoked in place of the default instantiation. For example, here is a
use of a character pointer to represent a string:

```
q_pc.add( "Phoenix" );
q_pc.add( "Crane" );
```

The default QueueItem constructor initializes item as follows:

```
template <class Type>
inline
QueueItem<Type>::
    QueueItem( const Type &t ) : item( t )
                { next = 0; }
```

For this particular instantiation, the semantics of the default constructor
are inappropriate. To resolve this, the programmer overrides the template
constructor for the QueueItem instantiation of type char*:

```
#include <string.h.
#include <assert.h>
#include "Queue.h"

QueueItem<char*>::QueueItem( char *str )
{
    item = new char[ strlen( str )+1 ];
    assert( item != 0 );

    strcpy( item, str );
    next = 0;
}
```

Each character array QueueItem is constructed using this specialized
instance.

Similarly, the programmer can provide a specialized class definition for a
particular type. When present, this definition is used in place of the default
instantiation. For example, the programmer may choose to provide a complete definition of a QueueItem of type char*:

```
class QueueItem<char*> {
    friend class Queue<char*>;
    friend ostream&
        operator<<(ostream&,QueueItem<char*>&);
private:
    QueueItem(char*);
    ~QueueItem() // additional member
        { delete item; }
    char *item;
    QueueItem *next; // not QueueItem<char*>
};
```

A specialized template class instance can be defined only after the general template class definition has been seen. If a specialized template class instance is defined, each of the member functions that are used must also be provided explicitly. The general template class member functions are not automatically instantiated since there is no necessary correlation between the general and specialized template class definitions.

Specialization is primarily used as a method of improving the efficiency of a template for a particular type.

7.5 Template Class Static Members

A template class can declare static data members. Each type instantiation of the template class has an associated set of the static data members. To illustrate this, let's introduce new and delete operators for QueueItem. We will need two static data members:

```
static QueueItem<Type> *free_list;
static const unsigned chunk_QueueItem;
```

The modifications to the QueueItem class definition look as follows:

```
#include <stddef.h>

template <class Type>
class QueueItem {
private:
    void *operator new(size_t);
    void operator delete(void*,size_t);
    // ...
    static QueueItem *free_list;
    static const unsigned chunk_QueueItem;
};
```

Operator new might be implemented as follows:

```
template <class Type> void*
QueueItem<Type>::operator new(size_t size)
{
    register QueueItem<Type> *p;
    if (!free_list) {
        size_t chunk = chunk_QueueItem*size;
        free_list = p =
            (QueueItem<Type>*) new char[chunk];

        for (; p!=&free_list[chunk_QueueItem-1];
                p->next = p+1, p++)   ;
        p->next = 0;
    }

    p = free_list;
    free_list = free_list->next;
    return p;
}
```

The template class syntax can at first seem somewhat bewildering. Beneath the unfamiliar syntax, however, is often rather familiar-looking code. Compare, for example, this instance of operator new with the nontemplate Screen instance (see 6.3 (page 315) for the actual code). Here is the template implementation of the delete operator:

```
template <class Type>
void QueueItem<Type>::
    operator delete(void *p, size_t)
{
    ((QueueItem<Type>*)p)->next = free_list;
    free_list = (QueueItem<Type>*)p;
}
```

All that remains to be done now is to initialize the static members free_list and chunk_QueueItem. The template form of initializing a static data member is the following:

```
/* for each QueueItem instantiation, generate the
 * associated free_list, initialize it to 0. */

template <class T>
    QueueItem<T> *QueueItem<T>::free_list = 0;
```

```
/* for each QueueItem instantiation, generate the
 * associated chunk_QueueItem, initialize it to 24. */

template <class T>
    const unsigned int
    QueueItem<T>::chunk_QueueItem = 24;
```

With each instantiation of a QueueItem, an instantiation of both static members also occurs. Specialized instances for particular types can also be specified. For example,

```
const unsigned int
    QueueItem<char*>::chunk_QueueItem = 1024;
```

When present, the specialized instance takes precedence over the generation of the general template instance. In the case of a character array, for example, chunk_QueueItem is always initialized to 1024. If the programmer has specialized a template class containing static data members, then those members also need to be specialized.

For a nontemplate class static data member, memory is allocated immediately following the class definition. The member can be accessed using the fully qualified name independent of an object of the class. For example,

```
class Foo {
public:
    static int bar;
    // ...
};

int ival = Foo::bar; // ok
```

For a static template class data member, memory is allocated upon each instantiation of the class. The general template definition itself serves only as a prescription for the generation of a potentially infinite set of template class instantiations. Access of a static member of a template class, then, is always through a particular instantiation. For example,

```
// error: QueueItem is not an actual type
int ival0 = QueueItem::chunk_QueueItem;

int ival1 = QueueItem<String>::chunk_QueueItem; // ok
int ival2 = QueueItem<int>::chunk_QueueItem; // ok
```

7.6 Template Constant Expression Parameters

The formal parameter of a template class can either be a type parameter (the only parameter we've looked at so far) or a constant expression. For example, the following definition parameterizes the Screen class of Chapter 5 by its height and width:

```
template <int hi, int wid>
class Screen {
public:
    Screen();
private:
    char screen[hi][wid];
    int height, width;
};

template <int hi, int wid>
Screen<hi,wid>::Screen()
{
    height = hi;
    width = wid;
}

typedef Screen<24,80> termScreen;
termScreen hp2621;

Screen<8,24> ancientScreen;
```

The actual expression the parameter is bound to must be able to be evaluated at compile time. For example, the following instantiation is illegal since operator new invokes an associated library allocation routine at run time:

```
template <int *p> class BufPtr { ... };

// error: cannot be evaluated at compile time
BufPtr<new int[24]> bp;
```

Similarly, an attempt to evaluate a non-const identifier is illegal, although taking its address or returning its sizeof value is fine:

```
template <int size> Buf{ ... };

int size_val = 1024;
const int c_size_val = 1024;

Buf<1024> buf0; // ok
Buf<c_size_val> buf1; // ok
Buf<sizeof(size_val)> buf2; // ok: sizeof(int)
BufPtr<&size_val> bp0; // ok

// error: cannot be evaluated at compile time
Buf<size_val> buf3;

// error: cannot pass a const int* to int*
BufPtr<&c_size_val> bp1;
```

Expressions that evaluate to the same value are considered equivalent. The following three Screen instances, for example, are all handled as being of type Screen<24,80>:

```
const int width = 24;
const int height = 80;

// all: type Screen<24,80>
Screen< 2*12, 40*2> scr0;
Screen< 6+6+6+6, 20*2+40> scr1;
Screen< width, height> scr2;
```

The type of an actual expression must match the type of the formal expression parameter exactly. For example, given the following set of declarations,

```
extern void foo(char*);
extern void bar(void*);
typedef void (*PFV)(void*);

const unsigned int x = 1024;

template <class Type,
          unsigned int size,
          PFV handler> class Array{ ... };
```

only the Array class objects a1 and a5 are correctly defined:

```
Array<int, 1024U, bar> a1; // ok
Array<int, 1024U, foo> a2; // error: foo != PFV

Array<int, 1024, bar> a3; // error: 1024 != unsigned
Array<int, 1024, foo> a4; // error: both 1024, foo

Array<int, x, bar> a5; // ok
Array<int, x, foo> a6; // error: foo != PFV
```

Each of the erroneous instantiations can be turned legal by providing an explicit cast. Here is another example:

```
template <int *ptr>
class BufPtr { ... };

// error: no match; 0 is of type int.
BufPtr<0> nil;

// ok: explicit cast
BufPtr<(int*) 0> nil;
```

The following is an example of how constant expression parameters might be used:

```
template <class Type, int size>
class Fixed_Array {
public:
    Fixed_Array(Type*);
private:
    Type array[ size ];
    int count;
};

template <class Type, int size>
Fixed_Array<Type,size>::
Fixed_Array(Type *ar) : count(size)
{
    for ( int ix = 0; ix < size; ++ix )
        array[ ix ] = ar[ ix ];
}

int ia[4] = { 0, 1, 2, 3 };
Fixed_Array<int,4> iA( ia );
```

7.7 Template Class Nested Types

QueueItem is designed to serve only in the implementation of Queue. To enforce this, QueueItem is implemented as a private class with Queue as its only friend. Although QueueItem is visible to the program, the program is unable either to create QueueItem objects or to access any of QueueItem's members.

. An alternative implementation strategy is to nest the definition of QueueItem within a private section of Queue. This removes QueueItem's visibility from the general program. Only Queue and the friends of Queue — the output operator — now have access to QueueItem. There's no longer a need, in fact, to declare QueueItem a private class. If we make the members of QueueItem public, it no longer becomes necessary to declare Queue a friend to QueueItem.

This implementation preserves the semantics of our original implementation and more elegantly models the relationship between the QueueItem and Queue classes. There is only one problem — a seemingly insurmountable one at that. Template definitions can only occur at global scope; they cannot be nested within a class or defined within a function. For example,

```
template <class Type>
class Queue {
    // ...
private:
    // error: nested template class
    template <class T>
    class QueueItem {
    public:
            // ...
    };

    QueueItem<Type> *front, *back;
    // ...
};
```

A moment's reflection, however, reveals that this constraint is not actually a problem. A Queue requires an associated QueueItem class for each type instantiation. The mapping of the association is one-to-one. A nested template, however, provides a one-to-many mapping. The problem is analogous to the one we twice faced trying to determine the form of the QueueItem friend declarations of Queue and the ostream output operator. What we need, then, is the analogous one-to-one nested class definition of QueueItem. For example,

```
template <class Type>
class Queue {
    // ...
private:
    class QueueItem {
    public:
        QueueItem(Type val)
            : item(val), next(0) {}

        Type item;
        QueueItem *next;
    };
    QueueItem *front, *back;
    // ...
};
```

QueueItem can be thought of as a bound nested class. Each instantiation of Queue needs to generate its own QueueItem class with the appropriate type replacement for Type. The mapping between QueueItem and the enclosing Queue template class is one-to-one.

Enumerations and typedefs can also be bound to an enclosing template class. For example,

```
template <class Type, int size>
class Buffer {
public:
    enum Buf_vals {last=size-1, Buf_size};
    typedef Type BufType;
    BufType array[ size ];
    // ...
};
```

Rather than providing an explicit Buf_size data member, the Buffer class initializes a pair of nested enumerator constants using the value passed to the template. For example, the declaration

```
Buffer<int, 512> small_buf;
```

sets its Buf_size to a value of 512 and last to a value of 511. Similarly, the declaration

```
Buffer<int, 1024> medium_buf;
```

sets its Buf_size to a value of 1024 and last to a value of 1023.

Whenever a nested type (or an enumerator of a nested enum) is referenced outside the scope of the enclosing template class, the template type name must be qualified with the full parameter list. For example,

```
    // error: which instantiation of Buffer?
    Buffer::Buf_vals bfv0;

    Buffer<int,512>::Buf_vals bfv1; // ok
```

This rule holds even in the case of an invariant nested type — that is, where the values remain constant across instantiations. For example,

```
    template <class T> class Q {
    public:
        enum QA { empty, full }; // invariant
        QA status;
        // ...
    };

    #include <iostream.h>

    main() {
        Q<double> qd;
        Q<int> qi;

        qd.status = Q::empty; // error
        qd.status = Q<double>::empty; // ok

        if (Q<double>::empty != Q<int>::empty)
            cerr << "implementation error!" << endl;
        return 0;
    }
```

Although `empty` is the same value in each instantiation of Q, each reference must still be made through a particular Q instance. This program generates the following compile-time error message:

```
    error: template class member
           Q::empty requires Q<instance>::empty
```

There is no special relationship between the instantiations of a template class. Rather, each instantiation of a template constitutes an independent class type. An integer QueueItem has no access permission, for example, to the nonpublic members of a String QueueItem instantiation. Access permission can only be conferred by friendship.

7.8 Template Class Friend Declarations

There are three kinds of friend declarations within a template class:

1. A nontemplate friend class or function. In the following example, `foo ()` and `bar` are friends to all instantiations of QueueItem.

```
template <class T>
class QueueItem {
    friend class foobar;
    friend void foo();
    friend void Foo::bar();

    // ...
};
```

2. A *bound* template friend class or function. In the following example, a one-to-one mapping is defined. For each type instantiation of QueueItem, a single associated instantiation of foobar, foo(), and Queue::bar() is friend.

```
template <class Type>
class QueueItem {
    friend class foobar<Type>;
    friend void foo( QueueItem<Type> );
    friend void Queue<Type>::bar();

    // ...
};
```

3. An unbound template friend class or function. In the following example, a one-to-many mapping is defined. For each type instantiation of QueueItem, all instantiations of foobar, foo(), and Queue<T>::bar() are friend.

```
template <class Type>
class QueueItem {
    template <class T>
        friend class foobar;

    template <class T>
        friend void foo(QueueItem<T>);

    template <class T>
        friend void Queue<T>::bar();

    // ...
};
```

Exercise 7-1. Identify which, if any, of the following template class declarations (or declaration pairs) are illegal. Correct any that you identify as illegal.

```
(a) template <char **ppc,
              void (*pfc)(char*&)> class Array0;

(b) template <class Type,
              int Type::*bkptr> class Array1;

(c) template <class Type>
        class Array2;

    template <class Type, int size>
        class Array2;

(d) template <class Type>
        class Array3 {};

    class Array3<char **pt> {};

(e) template <class Type>
        class Array4 {};

    class Array4 {};
```

☐

Exercise 7-2. Given the two template class declarations

```
template <int w, int h> class Screen {};
template <int*> class BufPtr{};
```

and the variable declarations

```
int i = 24;
int *pi = &i;
const ci1 = i;
const ci2 = 24;
```

which, if any, of the following declarations result in compile-time errors?

```
(a) Screen<i,80> s1;       (e) Screen<ci1,80> s2;
(b) Screen<ci2,80> s3;     (f) Screen<*pi,80> s4;
(c) BufPtr<&i> bp1;        (g) BufPtr<&ci2> bp2;
(d) BufPtr<pi> bp3;        (h) BufPtr<new int> bp4;
```

☐

Exercise 7-3. Reimplement the List class of Chapter 3 into a template class. Rewrite the programs that exercise the List class within that chapter to work with your template version.

☐

Exercise 7-4. Reimplement the Screen class of Chapter 5 into a template class taking two integer parameters. Rewrite the programs that exercise the Screen class within that chapter to work with your template Screen version.
□

7.9   A Template Array Class

In this section, the Array class introduced in Chapter 1 is reimplemented as a template class (in Chapter 9, this class will be extended using both single and multiple inheritance). Figure 7.1 presents the complete template class Array header file.

The member function `print()` handles the actual output of an Array class object. Its output is perhaps more elaborate than necessary, but displays nicely on a page. Given an integer Array instantiation containing the elements 3, 5, 8, 13, and 21, the output of the Array looks as follows:

```
(5) < 3, 5, 8, 13, 21 >
```

The ostream output operator simply invokes `print()`. Here is an implementation of both operations:

```
template <class Type> ostream&
operator<<( ostream& os, Array<Type>& ar)
{
    ar.print(os);
    return os;
}

template <class Type>
void Array<Type>::print(ostream& os)
{
    const lineLength = 12;

    os << "( " << size << " )< ";
    for (int ix = 0; ix < size; ++ix) {
        if (ix % lineLength == 0 && ix) os << "\n\t";
        os << ia[ ix ];

        // don't generate comma for last item on line
        // nor for the last element of the array
        if (ix % lineLength != lineLength-1 &&
                ix != size-1)   os << ", ";
    }
    os << " >\n";
}
```

The implementation of the memberwise copy operator is straightforward.

```
#ifndef ARRAY_H
#define ARRAY_H

#include <iostream.h>

template <class Type> class Array;
template <class Type> ostream&
    operator<<(ostream&,Array<Type>&);

const int ArraySize = 12;

template <class Type>
class Array {
public:
    Array(int sz=ArraySize) { init(0,sz); }
    Array(const Type *ar, int sz) { init(ar,sz); }
    Array(const Array &iA) { init(iA.ia,iA.size); }
    ~Array() { delete [] ia; }

    Array& operator=(const Array&);
    int getSize() { return size; }
    void grow();
    void print(ostream& = cout);

    Type& operator[](int ix) { return ia[ix]; }
    void sort(int,int);
    int find(Type);
    Type min();
    Type max();
private:
    void swap(int,int);
    void init(const Type*, int);

    int size;
    Type *ia;
};

#endif
```

Figure 7.1 Array.h

One special case that needs to be recognized is that of an Array object being
copied to itself. In this implementation, a copy of an object to itself leaves the
object unchanged.

```
template <class Type> Array<Type>&
Array<Type>::operator=(const Array<Type> &iA)
{
    if (this == &iA) return *this;
    delete ia;
    init( iA.ia, iA.size );
    return *this;
}
```

init() contains the code common to the three Array class constructors
and the memberwise copy operator. Since it is not intended to be invoked by
users of the Array class, it is made a private member.

```
#include <assert.h>

template <class Type> void
Array<Type>::init(const Type *array, int sz)
{
    ia = new Type[size = sz];
    assert( ia != 0 );

    for (int ix = 0; ix < size; ++ix)
            ia[ix] = (array!=0) ? array[ix] : (Type)0;
}
```

The grow() member function increases the size of the Array object's
actual array. For our example, it simply grows the array an additional half
of the current size.

```
template <class Type> void
Array<Type>::grow()
{
  Type *oldia = ia;
  int oldSize = size;
  int newSize = oldSize + oldSize/2 + 1;

  ia = new Type[size=newSize];
  assert( ia != 0 );

  for (int i=0; i<oldSize; ++i) ia[i] = oldia[i];
  for (; i<size; ++i) ia[i] = (Type)0;

  delete oldia;
}
```

The find(), min(), and max() member functions implement an iterative search of the internal array. These functions could be implemented
much more efficiently, of course, were the array guaranteed to be sorted.

```
template <class Type>
Type Array<Type>::min()
{
    assert( ia != 0 );
    Type min_val = ia[0];
    for (int ix=1; ix<size; ++ix)
        if (min_val > ia[ix]) min_val = ia[ix];
    return min_val;
}


template <class Type>
Type Array<Type>::max()
{
    assert( ia != 0 );
    Type max_val = ia[0];
    for (int ix=1; ix<size; ++ix)
        if (max_val < ia[ix]) max_val = ia[ix];
    return max_val;
}



template <class Type>
int Array<Type>::find(Type val)
{
    for (int ix=0; ix<size; ++ix)
        if (val == ia[ix]) return ix;
    return -1;
}
```

Finally, the Array class provides a sort() member function. The implementation is that of the quicksort algorithm and mirrors the earlier nonmember implementation. swap() is intended simply as a helping function to sort(); it is not part of the Array class public interface, and is therefore made a private member.

```
template <class Type>
void Array<Type>::swap(int i, int j)
{
    Type tmp = ia[i];
    ia[i] = ia[j];
    ia[j] = tmp;
}
```

```
template <class Type>
void Array<Type>::sort(int low, int high)
{
    if (low >= high) return;
    int lo = low;
    int hi = high + 1;
    Type elem = ia[low];

    for (;;) {
        while (ia[++lo] < elem) ;
        while (ia[--hi] > elem) ;

        if (lo < hi)
            swap(lo,hi);
        else break;
    }

    swap(low,hi);
    sort(low,hi-1);
    sort(hi+1,high);
}
```

Implementing the code, of course, is no guarantee that the code actually works. try_array() is a template function intended to test our Array class implementation. It is pictured in Figure 7.2.

Let's take a look at try_array(). The first step is to print out the intial array. This confirms the instantiation of the template output operator and provides us with a snapshot of the initial Array against which to compare the success (or failure) of our subsequent modifications of the Array. find_val holds a value to later pass to find(). Were this a nontemplate function, the value would have been hardcoded. try_array(), however, cannot hard-code a value to pass to find(), since no one value will serve every possible type instantiation. The elements of the Array are randomly assigned to the Array, exercising min(), max(), getSize(), and, of course, the subscript operator. iA2 is memberwise initialized with iA, invoking the Array class copy constructor. iA2 then exercises its subscript operator with an assignment to element mid/2. (These two lines are of more interest when iA is actually a derived subtype of Array and the subscript operator is declared a virtual function — we'll look at this again in Chapter 9 in our discussion of inheritance.) iA is subsequently memberwise copied with the modified iA2, invoking the Array class assignment operator. Following that, the grow() and find() member functions are exercised. The function deliberately fails to test the return type of find(); recall, find() returns a value of −1 if the element it searches for is not found. A −1 index into an Array will result in an underflow error. (In Chapter 9, a bounds-checking Array class is derived

```
#include "Array.h"

template <class Type>
void try_array( Array<Type> &iA )
{
    cout << "try_array: initial array values:\n";
    cout << iA << endl;

    Type find_val = iA[iA.getSize()-1];
    iA[iA.getSize()-1] = iA.min();

    int mid = iA.getSize()/2;
    iA[0] = iA.max(); iA[mid] = iA[0];
    cout << "try_array: after assignments:\n";
    cout << iA << endl;

    Array<Type> iA2 = iA;
    iA2[mid/2] = iA2[mid];
    cout << "try_array: memberwise initialization\n";
    cout << iA << endl;

    iA = iA2;
    cout << "try_array: after memberwise copy\n";
    cout << iA << endl;

    iA.grow();
    cout << "try_array: after grow\n";
    cout << iA << endl;

    int index = iA.find(find_val);
    cout << "value to find: " << find_val;
    cout << "\tindex returned: " << index << endl;

    Type value = iA[index];
    cout << "value found at index: ";
    cout << value << endl;
}
```

Figure 7.2 try_array.c

from Array in order to catch this error.)

We'd like to confirm that our template implementation works over a variety of data types — for example, integers, floating point values, and Strings. Here is a version of main() to exercise try_array() with each of these three data types:

```
#include "Array.c"
#include "try_array.c"
#include "String.h"

main()
{
    static int ia[] = { 12,7,14,9,128,17,6,3,27,5 };
    static double da[] = {12.3,7.9,14.6,9.8,128.0 };
    static String sa[] = { "Eeyore", "Pooh", "Tigger",
        "Piglet", "Owl", "Gopher", "Heffalump" };

    Array<int> iA(ia,sizeof(ia)/sizeof(int));
    Array<double> dA(da,sizeof(da)/sizeof(double));
    Array<String> SA(sa,sizeof(sa)/sizeof(String));

    cout << "template Array<int> class\n" << endl;
    try_array(iA);

    cout << "template Array<double> class\n" << endl;
    try_array(dA);

    cout << "template Array<String> class\n" << endl;
    try_array(SA);

    return 0;
}
```

Here is the output of the type double instantiation of the template Array class.

```
try_array: initial array values:
( 5 )< 12.3, 7.9, 14.6, 9.8, 128 >

try_array: after assignments:
( 5 )< 14.6, 7.9, 14.6, 9.8, 7.9 >

try_array: memberwise initialization
( 5 )< 14.6, 7.9, 14.6, 9.8, 7.9 >

try_array: after memberwise copy
( 5 )< 14.6, 14.6, 14.6, 9.8, 7.9 >
```

```
try_array: after grow
( 8 )< 14.6, 14.6, 14.6, 9.8, 7.9, 0
          0, 0 >

value to find: 128        index returned: -1
value found at index: 3.35965e-322
```

The out-of-bounds index causes the last value returned by the program to be invalid. The same out-of-bounds index causes the String instantiation of the template Array class to crash during execution. Here is that output:

```
template Array<String> class

try_array: initial array values:
( 7 )< Eeyore, Pooh, Tigger, Piglet, Owl, Gopher
          Heffalump >

try_array: after assignments:
( 7 )< Tigger, Pooh, Tigger, Tigger, Owl, Gopher
          Eeyore >

try_array: memberwise initialization
( 7 )< Tigger, Pooh, Tigger, Tigger, Owl, Gopher
          Eeyore >

try_array: after memberwise copy
( 7 )< Tigger, Tigger, Tigger, Tigger, Owl, Gopher
          Eeyore >

try_array: after grow
( 11 )< Tigger, Tigger, Tigger, Tigger, Owl, Gopher
          Eeyore, <empty>, <empty>, <empty>, <empty> >

value to find: Heffalump          index returned: -1
Memory fault(coredump)
```

Exercise 7-5. Rewrite the Stack class implementation of Chapter 2 as a template class containing an Array member class object.

☐

Exercise 7-6. In Chapter 6, the implementation of a binary tree class was presented as an exercise to the reader (see Section 6.1 (page 294) for the discussion). Reimplement the binary tree as a template class.

☐

Exercise 7-7. Try the following Screen class instantiation of the Array class. Provide the necessary operations to have this program execute.

```
#include "Array.c"
#include "try_array.c"
#include "Screen.h"

main()
{
    Screen sa[5];
    Array<Screen> SA(sa,5);
    try_array(SA);
    return 0;
}
```

□

Chapter 8: **Derivation and Inheritance**

Object-oriented programming extends abstract data types to allow for type/subtype relationships. This is achieved through a mechanism referred to as *inheritance*. Rather than reimplementing shared characteristics, a class can inherit selected data members and member functions of other classes. In C++, inheritance is implemented through the mechanism of *class derivation*, the topic of this chapter and the next.

In this section we answer the following questions: Why are type/subtype relationships important? What kinds of design problems led programmers to extend abstract data types? What is really meant by the terms inheritance and object-oriented programming? By way of illustration, let's return to the Screen class defined in Chapter 5.

Our Screen class represents an old technology. The newer generation of workstations and terminals supports the concept of windowing. A window serves as a screen, but with additional capabilities:

- A window can be made larger or smaller.

- A window can be moved from one position to another.

- Multiple windows can be defined on a single screen.

The author's terminal, for example, supports up to seven windows. In one, this chapter of the book can be written. In a second window, program examples can be implemented and edited. These programs can be compiled and executed in a third window. In a fourth window, electronic mail can be read. In short, each window can be used simultaneously in the same manner that a single screen was used on an older terminal.

A window must know not only its size, but also its position on the workstation screen. The window requires coordinates to locate itself, as well as member functions to resize and move itself. It will also need the same data members as defined for the Screen class. Some of the Screen member functions can be reused directly; others require reimplementation.

A window is a kind of specialized Screen. It is more an extended subtype of Screen than it is an independent abstract data type. On a conceptual level, Window and Screen represent two elements of a terminal display class. On an implementation level, they share both data members and member functions.

Abstract data types cannot model this kind of type/subtype relationship. The closest representation would be to make Screen a member class of Window:

```
class Window {
public:
        // ... member functions go here
private:
        Screen base;
        // ... data members go here
};
```

One problem with this representation is that the Screen data members are private and therefore not directly accessible to Window. If the source for Screen is available, Window can be made a friend to Screen.

For programmers to use the Screen members directly, base must be a public member of Window:

```
Window w;
w.base.clear();
```

This violates information hiding. The programmer must know of the implementation of Window as well as which of the Screen member functions are active within the Window class and which have been redefined (since the calling syntax in the two cases is different). home(), for example, would be redefined in the Window class. The following two calls invoke different functions:

```
w.home();
w.base.home();
```

This design is too prone to programmer error.

To enforce information hiding and to maintain a uniform syntax, Window must define an interface function for each active Screen member function. For example, for the programmer to write

```
w.clear();
```

the class designer must define

```
inline void Window::clear() { base.clear(); }
```

This is tedious but feasible.

If a Window is extended further, however, the complexity of the implementation becomes a serious constraint on the design. For example, a Menu is a kind of Window. It will have its own data members and member functions. A menu will also share a subset of Window's members, and possibly a different subset of Screen's members than those used by Window. A better solution is needed — that of inheritance.

8.1 Object-Oriented Programming

Class inheritance allows the members of one class to be used as if they were members of a second class. Were Window to inherit the members from Screen, for example, all the operations a user could perform on a Screen class object could also be performed on a Window class object. No additional programming is required to implement Window except for those operations that either extend or replace the members inherited from the Screen class.

Inheritance is the primary characteristic of object-oriented programming. In C++, it is supported by the mechanism of *class derivation*. The derivation of Window from the Screen class allows Window to inherit the Screen class members. Window can access the nonprivate members of Screen as if they had been declared members of Window. For example,

```
Window w;
w.clear().home();
```

In order to derive a class, the following two extensions to the class syntax are necessary:

1. The class head is modified to allow a *derivation list* of classes from which to inherit members. The class head of the Window class looks as follows:

   ```
   class Window : public Screen { ... }
   ```

   The colon following Window indicates that Window is being derived from one or more previously defined classes. The keyword `public` indicates that Window is to be a publicly derived class. Derivations can be either public or private — the specification affects the visibility of the inherited members within the derived class. The class name Screen indicates the object of the derivation, referred to as a *base* class. We say that Screen is a public base class of Window.

2. An additional access level, that of `protected`, is provided. A `protected` class member behaves as a public class member to a derived class; to the rest of the program, the protected class member is private. The members of Screen must be changed from private to protected in order to allow the member functions and friends of Window to access them.

A derived class can itself be an object of derivation. Menu, for example, can be derived from Window:

```
class Menu : public Window { ... };
```

Menu, in turn, inherits members from both Window *and* Screen. The additional programming required is only for those operations that either extend or replace the inherited members. The syntax remains uniform:

```
Menu m;
m.display();
```

The special relationship between base and derived classes is recognized by a set of predefined standard conversions. A derived class can be assigned to any of its public base classes without requiring an explicit cast. For example,

```
Menu m;
Window &w = m;    // ok
Screen *ps = &w;  // ok
```

This special relationship between inherited class types promotes a "generic" style of programming in which the actual type of a class is unknown. The following declaration of dumpImage() is an example:

```
extern void dumpImage( Screen *s );
```

dumpImage() can be invoked with an argument of any class type for which Screen serves as a public base class, however far removed it occurs in the chain of class derivations. An attempt to pass it an argument of an unrelated class type, however, results in a compile-time error. For example,

```
Screen s;
Window w;
Menu m;
BitVector bv;

// ok: Window is a kind of Screen
dumpImage( &w );

// ok: Menu is a kind of Screen
dumpImage( &m );

// ok: argument types match exactly
dumpImage( &s );

// error:  BitVector has no relationship with Screen
dumpImage( &bv );
```

Screen, Window, and Menu each provide an instance of the dumpImage() member function. The purpose of the nonmember dumpImage() function is to take an argument of any of these three class types and invoke the appropriate function. In a nonobject-oriented implementation, the main effort of this general dumpImage() function is to determine the actual data type of its argument. For example,

```
#include "Screen.h"
extern void error( const char*, ... );

enum { SCREEN, WINDOW, MENU };
// nonobject-oriented code
void dumpImage( Screen *s )
{
    // figure out the actual type of s
    switch( s->typeOf() )
    {
        case SCREEN:
            s->dumpImage();
            break;

        case WINDOW:
            ((Window*)s)->dumpImage();
            break;

        case MENU:
            ((Menu*)s)->dumpImage();
            break;

        default:
            error( "unknown type", s->typeOf() );
            break;
    }
}
```

The burden of type resolution, in this case, rests with the programmer. The second primary characteristic of object-oriented programming shifts the burden of type resolution from the programmer to the compiler. This characteristic is referred to as *dynamic binding*. Under dynamic binding, the implementation of dumpImage() is considerably simplified:

```
void dumpImage( Screen *s )
{
    s->dumpImage();
}
```

With each invocation of dumpImage(), the correct dumpImage() member function is invoked automatically. Not only does this reduce the complexity and size of the code; it also makes for *extensible* code: A subsequent derivation — Border, for example — can be added to a program without the need to change any existing code. A call of dumpImage() with a Border class type is handled without problem once the code has been recompiled. In C++, dynamic binding is supported by the mechanism of *virtual member functions*. A member function is made virtual by preceding its declaration in the class body with the keyword `virtual`. For example,

```
class Screen {
public:
    virtual void dumpImage();
    // ...
};
```

A function is declared to be virtual under the following two conditions:

1. A class expects to be an object of derivation.

2. The implementation of the function is type-dependent.

Each member instance of `dumpImage()`, for example, is dependent on the representation of its class type — its implementation differing for a Screen, Window, and Menu. The designer of the Screen class indicates this type implementation dependency by declaring `dumpImage()` to be a virtual member function.

The type/subtype relationship between a base and derived class is referred to as a *derivation* or *inheritance hierarchy*. A derivation from multiple base classes is referred to as a *derivation* or *inheritance graph*.

Object-oriented programming is built on the extended concept of an abstract data type that supports the definition of an inheritance hierarchy. `Simula` was the first programming language to recognize the need for and to provide the class mechanism for this extended abstract data type. The `Smalltalk` language originated the term "object-oriented," which is used to emphasize the encapsulated nature of the user-defined class type. In Smalltalk, object-oriented programming transforms information hiding from a design methodology into a model of the program world.

8.2 The Zoo Animal Representation

To help organize the discussion of class derivation in C++, an extended example is presented that centers around the representation of animals maintained by a zoo.

Ling-ling, a giant panda from China, is to be on loan to a local zoo for six months. The zoo anticipates a four-fold increase in visitor attendance during these months. Fearing a shortage of staff, the zoo proposes installing display terminals in its information center that will answer questions posed by visitors about the animals.

The zoo animals exist at different levels of abstraction. There are individual animals, such as Ling-ling. Each animal belongs to a species; Ling-ling, for example, is a giant panda. Species in turn are members of families. A giant panda is a member of the bear family. Each family in turn is a member of the animal kingdom — in this case, the more limited kingdom of a particular zoo.

The taxonomy of the zoo animals maps nicely into an inheritance hierarchy. Figure 8.1 illustrates a subportion of the Bear family derivation. This inheritance hierarchy is referred to as *single inheritance*. In such a hierarchy, each derived class has only one immediate base class.

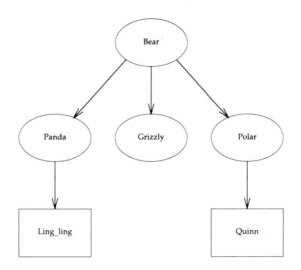

Figure 8.1 Single Inheritance

The taxonomy of the zoo animals does not provide a complete representation. For example, Panda is a species of Bear. However, it is also an endangered species, although the Polar and Grizzly Bear species are not. The Leopard species of the Cat family is also endangered.

"Endangered" is an independent abstraction that randomly cuts across the taxonomy. A single inheritance hierarchy cannot represent the endangered nature of both a Leopard and a Panda, but multiple inheritance can. Figure 8.2 illustrates a subportion of a multiply derived inheritance graph.

Multiple inheritance defines a relationship between independent class types. The derived class can be thought of as a composite of its multiple base classes. C++ supports both single and multiple inheritance.

Figure 8.3 illustrates three levels of a zoo animal derivation. The ZooAnimal class, referred to as an *abstract base class*, is designed specifically as a class from which other classes can be derived. It can be thought of as an incomplete class that is more or less finished with each subsequent derivation.

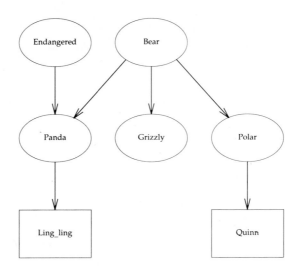

Figure 8.2 Multiple Inheritance

ZooAnimal attempts to define the set of data and function members that are common to all zoo animals; derivations from ZooAnimal attempt to define what is unique to a particular class of animal. Subsequent derivations attempt to refine this even more. A Bear, for example, is a particular instance of ZooAnimal. A Panda is an even more particular instance.

In the course of building up the derivation hierarchy, the design of an abstract base class such as ZooAnimal will almost certainly be modified and extended many times. Although the design process originates with an abstraction and culminates with an implementation, the path connecting the two points is not a straight line, but rather a feedback loop. The process of object-oriented design is looked at informally in Chapter 10.

A class that serves as the root class of a derivation hierarchy is sometimes referred to as an *abstract superclass*. ZooAnimal plays the role of an abstract superclass, serving as the root base class of all the animal class types.

The abstract superclass is central to the design of a derivation hierarchy. Regardless of how deeply nested and complex the hierarchy becomes, the relationship between classes is maintained by the common set of class members inherited from the abstract superclass. It provides a common public interface for the entire class hierarchy.

"Endangered" is not currently a characteristic of all zoo animals, and thus it does not make sense to derive ZooAnimal from Endangered. Endangered serves as an auxiliary abstract base class because Endangered is an

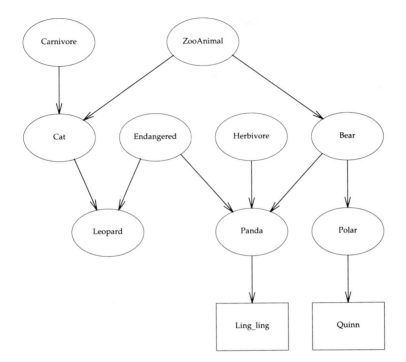

Figure 8.3　Zoo Animal Inheritance Graph

independent class type rather than a subtype of ZooAnimal. ZooAnimal serves as the abstract superclass of the animal taxonomy. Multiple inheritance allows for the composition of particular class types, such as Panda, with auxiliary abstract base classes that fall outside the taxonomy.

Could Endangered alternatively be made a member of Panda? No. Endangered is an abstract base class. Like ZooAnimal, it is an incomplete specification that is more or less finished with each of its derivations. Actual class objects of either ZooAnimal or Endangered do not actually exit — only their derived class instances are created in an actual application. Moreover, Panda must override virtual functions both as a kind of ZooAnimal *and* as a kind of Endangered species. Only by inheriting from both classes can it behave as a full subtype to each.

The remainder of this chapter and the next consider how the ZooAnimal class hierarchy representation might be implemented in C++ and the different design issues that need to be resolved.

Exercise 8-1. Geometric shapes are commonly used to illustrate class derivation. Such shapes minimally include a triangle, box, and circle. Draw an
inheritance hierarchy for these shapes.

☐

Exercise 8-2. How do a square and a rectangle fit into your shapes hierarchy? What about the different kinds of triangles such as the right triangle
and the equilateral triangle? ☐

8.3 Derivation Specification

A skeletal implementation of a portion of the relationship pictured in Figure
8.3 looks as follows.

```
class ZooAnimal  {};
class Endangered {};
class Carnivore  {};
class Herbivore  {};

// Bear: single inheritance
class Bear : public ZooAnimal {};

// Cat, Panda: multiple inheritance
class Cat : public ZooAnimal, Carnivore {};
class Panda : private Endangered, public Bear,
              private Herbivore {};
```

Bear, Panda, and Cat are referred to as *derived* classes. Bear is an example of
single inheritance. ZooAnimal is referred to as the *public base class* of Bear.
Both Cat and Panda are examples of multiple inheritance. Panda is composed of one public base class (Bear) and two private base classes (Herbivore
and Endangered). Cat is composed of one public base class (ZooAnimal) and
one private base class (Carnivore). Without an explicit public, private, or
protected attribute, a base class by default is handled as private. Thus,

```
class Cat : public ZooAnimal, Carnivore { ... };
```

declares Carnivore as a private base class of Cat.

Ling_ling is a Panda class object. A derived class object is declared in
the same way as a nonderived class object:

```
Panda Ling_ling; // derived class object
```

A derived class may itself serve as a base class in a subsequent derivation.
Bear, for example, derived from ZooAnimal, serves as a public base class of
Panda.

The syntax for defining a base class is the same as that of an "ordinary" class with two exceptions:

1. Members intended to be inherited but not intended to be public are declared as protected members. These members would be declared as private in an abstract data type such as BitVector.

2. Member functions whose implementation depends on representational details of subsequent derivations that are unknown at the time of the base class design are declared as virtual functions.

Here is a simple, preliminary definition of ZooAnimal:

```
class ZooAnimal {
public:
    ZooAnimal( char*, char*, short );
    virtual ~ZooAnimal();

    virtual void draw();
    void locate();
    void inform();

protected:
    char *name;
    char *infoFile;
    short location;
    short count;
};
```

Exercise 8-3. The members of an abstract class represent the attributes common to the entire hierarchy. Outline what you think are the common data members and member functions of the Shape hierarchy. Identify which functions you believe should be declared as virtual. □

Exercise 8-4. Provide a definition of the Shape class outlined in the previous exercise. □

Definition of a Derived Class

In this section let's examine the actual syntax of class derivation. Here is a simple, preliminary derivation of Bear from ZooAnimal:

```
#include "ZooAnimal.h"
class Bear : public ZooAnimal  {
public:
    Bear( char*, char*, short, char, char );
    ~Bear();
    void locate( int );
    int isOnDisplay();
protected:
    char beingFed;
    char isDanger;
    char onDisplay;
    char epoch;
};
```

The only necessary syntactic difference between a simple and a derived class definition lies in the class-head specification:

```
class Bear : public ZooAnimal
```

The colon following the class tag name indicates the presence of a *class derivation list*, a (possibly) comma-separated list of one or more base classes. There is no language-imposed limit on the number of base classes that may appear in the class derivation list; no class name, however, may appear more than once. Each listed base class must already have been defined.

A base class can be either a public, protected, or private base class. If no access keyword is specified, *the base class by default becomes private*. For example, the following two class heads both declare a private derivation of Bear:

```
// equivalent declarations of a private base class
class Bear : ZooAnimal
class Bear : private ZooAnimal
```

The preferred method of declaring a private base class is through explicit use of the keyword `private`. This coding style has proven less prone to misinterpretation, especially in the case of multiple base classes. (Most compilers issue a warning message when no access keyword is specified.)

In a multiple derivation, each base class must specify its own public, protected, or private attribute. A base class does not assume the attribute of the preceding base class. In the following class head, it is common to misinterpret Endangered as a public base class of Panda. In fact, Endangered is private by default.

```
// Endangered by default is private
class Panda : public Bear, Endangered
```

The access level of a base class is specific to the declaration list in which it appears. There is no constraint on declaring a class a public base class in one instance and a private base class in another. For example, although

ZooAnimal is a public base class of Bear and Cat, there is no reason it cannot be declared a private or protected base class of Rodent.

The meaning of public, protected, and private base classes and the reasons why one might choose one or the other are discussed in Section 8.5 (page 409) later in this chapter. The next subsection examines the syntax of accessing the inherited class members within the derived class.

Exercise 8-5. Provide a definition of a Circle class. ☐

Exercise 8-6. Provide a definition of a Box class. ☐

Exercise 8-7. Provide a definition of a Rectangle class derived from Box. ☐

Inherited Member Access

Bear inherits the following ZooAnimal class members: name, location, count, infoFile, locate(), and inform(). (Handling the virtual functions draw() and ˜ZooAnimal() is discussed in Chapter 9.) These inherited ZooAnimal members can be accessed as if they were members of Bear. For example,

```
void objectExample( Bear& ursus ) {
    if ( ursus.isOnDisplay() ) {
        ursus.locate(low_intensity); // enum constant
        if ( ursus.beingFed )
            cout << ursus.name << " is now being fed\n";
        ursus.inform();
    }
}
```

Although they may be accessed as if they were members of the derived class, the inherited members maintain their base class membership. Each can be accessed using the class scope operator. For example,

```
if ( ursus.beingFed )
        cout << ursus.ZooAnimal::name;
ursus.ZooAnimal::inform();
```

In most cases, use of the class scope operator is redundant. The compiler can find the intended member without the additional lexical aid. In two cases, however, this additional aid is necessary:

1. When an inherited member's name is reused in the derived class.

2. When two or more base classes define an inherited member with the same name.

Reuse of an inherited member's name within the derived class hides the inherited member. This is similar to a local identifier reusing the name of a variable defined at file scope. In both cases a reference to the name is resolved to mean the identifier defined in the most immediate scope. `Bear::locate(int)`, for example, hides the inherited ZooAnimal member. The statement

```
ursus.locate();
```

will always refer to `Bear::locate(int)` (and cause the error message *missing first argument* to be generated). To invoke the hidden inherited member function, the statement *must* read:

```
ursus.ZooAnimal::locate();
```

When a name is reused by the inherited members of two or more base classes, use of the unmodified name within the derived class is ambiguous and results in a compile-time error. The class scope operator must be used to disambiguate between the multiple instances of the inherited members. For example,

```
class Endangered { public: virtual highlight(short); };
class Herbivore  { public: virtual highlight(short); };

class Panda : public Bear, public Endangered,
              public Herbivore { public: locate(); };

Panda::locate() {
    if ( isOnDisplay() ) {
        // enum display_intensity { low_intensity ... }
        Bear::locate( low_intensity );
        highlight( location ); // error: ambiguous
        Endangered::highlight( location ); // ok
    }
}
```

This method of explicitly resolving the ambiguity has two significant drawbacks.

1. A virtual function explicitly invoked is resolved as a nonvirtual function. (Section 9.1 (page 461) considers this in detail.) In choosing this method of disambiguation, we have effectively disallowed `highlight()` to be specified as a virtual function.

2. The ambiguity is inherited by subsequent derivations. A rule of thumb about the design of a class hierarchy is that the derived class should not have to exhibit any implementation knowledge of classes in the hierarchy beyond that of its immediate base classes. This violates that rule.

When the inherited members that share the same name are all member functions, it is therefore a good design strategy to define a derived class member function of the same name. For example,

```
void Panda::highlight()
{
    // encapsulate the ambiguous inherited members
    Endangered::highlight( location );
    Herbivore::highlight( location );
}
```

The Panda instance of `highlight()` hides both inherited members at the same time that it provides the functionality of both. The ambiguity is resolved in a manner transparent to the user.

Exercise 8-8. A `debug()` member function is useful to the class designer. It displays the current values of the class data members. Implement a `debug()` member function for each class in the hierarchy of Shapes. □

Base Class Initialization

The member initialization list is used to pass arguments to a base class constructor. The tag name of a base class is specified, followed by its argument list enclosed in parentheses. (The member initialization list can appear only in the definition, not in the declaration, of the constructor.) For example, here is a member initialization list for Bear:

```
Bear::Bear(
        char *nm, char *fil, short loc,
        char danger, char age )

        /* member initialization list must be used
         * to initialize a base class requiring
         * arguments to it constructor --
         *    : base-class-name( arg-list ) */

        : ZooAnimal( nm, fil, loc )
{
    epoch = age;
    isDanger = danger;
}
```

In the case of multiple base classes, each base class may be listed in turn. Here is a member initialization list for Panda:

```
/* CHINA, BAMBOO, PANDA, MIOCENE :
 * enumeration constants defined elsewhere
 *
 * each base class constructor requiring arguments
 * is placed within member initialization list --
 * placement order is not significant */

Panda::Panda( char *nm, short loc, char sex )
        : Endangered( CHINA ),
          Herbivore( BAMBOO ),
          Bear( "Ailuropoda melaoleuca",
                "Panda", PANDA, MIOCENE )
{
    name = new char[ strlen(nm)+1 ];
    strcpy( name, nm );
    cell = loc;
    gender = sex;
}
```

A base class that either does not define a constructor or that defines a constructor that does not require an explicit argument need not be specified on the member initialization list. A base class may be initialized with the argument list expected by a constructor. Alternatively, it may be initialized with another class object. This class object can be of the same base class type. For example,

```
Bear::Bear( ZooAnimal& z )
        : ZooAnimal( z ) { ... };
```

The class object can also be of a publicly derived class type. For example,

```
Bear::Bear( const Bear& b )
        : ZooAnimal( b ) { ... };
```

Here is an example of where the class object has no relationship to the base class, but defines a conversion operator that does:

```
class GiantSloth : public Extinct {
public:
    GiantSloth();
    operator Bear() { return b; }
protected:
    Bear b;
};

// invokes GiantSloth::operator Bear()
Panda::Panda(GiantSloth& gs)
        : Bear(gs) { ... };
```

The base class constructors are invoked prior to the constructor of the derived class. Because of this, the member initialization list of a derived class may not explicitly initialize an inherited base class member; the base class members at this point have already been initialized. The following, for example, is illegal:

```
// illegal:  explicit initialization of the
// inherited base class member ZooAnimal::name
Bear ( char *nm ) : name ( nm ) /* ... */
```

Exercise 8-9. Define the Shapes class constructor(s). □

Exercise 8-10. Define the Circle class constructor(s). □

Exercise 8-11. Define the Box and Rectangle class constructors. □

8.4 Information Hiding Under Derivation

Inheritance introduces a second client group for a class — a design group intent on type extension. The public/private member division that serves the class user group is inadequate for derivation. Protected class members serve the needs of the design group while preserving the ability of the base class to declare private members.

A protected class member is public to the member functions and friends of a derived class; it is private to the rest of the program. For example,

```
class ZooAnimal {
public:
    int isNowFeeding () { return beingFed; }
protected:
    int beingFed;
    // ...
};
```

Ordinarily, the ZooAnimal data member beingFed would be declared private. However, the design intention is for this member to be set and reset by each subsequent derivation as the class of animal is being fed. It is "factored back" into the abstract base class in order that it need be declared only once. A protected member, in effect, serves as a kind of global member of the class hierarchy, except, of course, that each derived class object maintains its own instance.

```
class Bear : public ZooAnimal {
public:
    void activities();
    // ...

protected:
    void checkFeeding(); // sets beingFed

    // ...
};

main() {
    Bear yogi;

    // both compile-time errors:
    // illegal access of nonpublic members

    while (yogi.beingFed == 0)
        yogi.checkFeeding();

    // ...
}
```

Within main(), the protected members of ZooAnimal and Bear are in effect private. Any attempt to access either of them in the general program is flagged as a compile-time error. Within the scope of Bear, of course, there are no constraints on their access.

```
void Bear::activities() {
    // ...
    checkFeeding();
}

void Bear::checkFeeding() {
    // determine if Bear is now being fed
    beingFed = 1;
}
```

By making the constructors of a class protected, the class designer can restrict the creation of class instances to the inheritance hierarchy (and friends) of the class. An alternative method of defining a class that can be used only by an inheritance hierarchy is to nest the definition of the class within the protected section of the abstract base class of the hierarchy. This latter method is described below in the discussion of class scope under inheritance.

A derived class has *no* access privilege to the private members of a base class. For example, here is a simplified ZooAnimal derivation:

```
class ZooAnimal {
    friend void setPrice( ZooAnimal& );
public:
    isOnDisplay();
protected:
    char *name;
    char onDisplay;
private:
    char forSale;
};

class Primate : public ZooAnimal {
    friend void canCommunicate( Primate* );
public:
    locate();
protected:
    short zooArea;
private:
    char languageSkills;
};
```

A derived class inherits all the members of a base class; however, the derived class has access privilege only to the nonprivate members of the base class. Primate, for example, cannot access the private ZooAnimal data member forSale. As a friend to ZooAnimal, setPrice() has access to all the members of ZooAnimal. What, however, is its relationship to Primate or any other ZooAnimal derivation? For example,

```
void setPrice( ZooAnimal &z ) {
    Primate *pr;
    if ( pr->forSale              // legal? yes.
         && pr->languageSkills ) // legal? no.
    // ...
}
```

Primate is a kind of ZooAnimal. setPrice() has the same access privilege to the ZooAnimal members inherited by a Primate class object that it has with a ZooAnimal class object. forSale can therefore legally be accessed within setPrice().

The member functions and friends of ZooAnimal have access privilege only to the members of Primate inherited from ZooAnimal. The access of languageSkills within setPrice() is therefore illegal.

Specifying ZooAnimal as a friend to Primate extends access privilege to the nonpublic members of Primate to all the member functions of ZooAnimal. It does not, however, extend access privilege to setPrice(). The only way setPrice() can access the nonpublic Primate members is to be explicitly made a friend to Primate. In this way, the member functions and friends of a class behave differently.

`canCommunicate()` is a friend of Primate and has full access to its members. Were Orangutan derived from Primate, `canCommunicate()` would have full access right to those Primate members inherited by an Orangutan class object. But what access privilege, if any, does `canCommunicate()` have with the members of ZooAnimal? For example,

```
void canCommunicate( Primate *pr ) {
    ZooAnimal za;
    if ( pr->onDisplay              // legal? yes.
         && za.onDisplay            // legal? no.
         && pr->forSale )           // legal? no.
    // ...
}
```

In general, a friend function has the same access privilege as the member functions of that class. The member functions of Primate can access the inherited nonprivate members of ZooAnimal but not the inherited private members. The access of `onDisplay` is therefore legal while the access of `forSale` is not.

The derived class has no special access privilege to *objects* of its base class. Rather, the derived class has access privilege to the nonprivate *inherited* members of a derived class object. For example,

```
Primate::locate() {
    ZooAnimal za;
    Primate pr;

    if ( onDisplay          // ok
         && pr.onDisplay // ok
         && za.onDisplay // error: no access
    // ...
}
```

Derivation is not friendship. Primate has no access privilege to the non-public members of a ZooAnimal class object. The same holds true for friends of Primate. The expression

```
za.onDisplay
```

within `canCommunicate()` is also illegal.

Derivation provides for type extension. Primate is a specialized instance of a ZooAnimal. It shares the characteristics of a ZooAnimal, but adds a set of attributes that apply only to itself. Friendship provides for data access of otherwise nonpublic members. It does not define a type relationship. Derivation is not a special form of friendship — one that provides access to the protected but not private members of individual base class objects. Only the friends and member functions of ZooAnimal, for example, can access the nonpublic members of a ZooAnimal class object.

Exercise 8-12. Should the debug() member function implemented in Section 8.3 (page 403) for the Shape hierarchy be made a private, protected, or public member of its class? Why? □

8.5 Public, Protected, and Private Base Classes

The inherited members of a public base class maintain their access level within the derived class. name and isOnDisplay(), protected ZooAnimal members, are treated as protected members of Primate; a derivation of Baboon from Primate will inherit these members. In general, in a public derivation hierarchy, each subsequently derived class has access to the combined set of protected and public members of the previous base classes along the particular branch of the hierarchy. A public derivation from Panda, for example, can access the collection of Bear, ZooAnimal, Endangered and Herbivore public and protected members.

The inherited public and protected members of a protected base class become protected members of the derived class. Similarly, the inherited public and protected members of a private derivation become private members of the derived class. This has two significant effects:

1. The inherited public interface of the hierarchy cannot be accessed by the general program through instances of a class with a nonpublic derivation. For example,

```
class ZooAnimal {
public:
    void locate();
    void inform();
    // ...
};

class Bear : public ZooAnimal {};
class ToyAnimal : private ZooAnimal {
protected:
    // ok: ZooAnimal::locate() within ToyAnimal
    void where_is_it() { locate(); }
};
```

```
main() {
    Bear yogi;
    ToyAnimal pooh;

    yogi.inform(); // ok
    pooh.inform(); // error: private member
    // ...
}
```

2. There is no implicit conversion within the general program of a derived class to its nonpublic base class. An explicit cast by the programmer is necessary. For example,

```
extern void
draw( ZooAnimal* pz ) { px->draw(); }

main() {
    Bear fozzie;
    ToyAnimal eeyore;

    draw( &fozzie ); // ok
    draw( &eeyore ); // error: no standard conversion
    draw( (ZooAnimal*) &eeyore ); // ok

    ZooAnimal *pz = &eeyore; // again, error
    pz = (ZooAnimal*) &eeyore; // ok
    // ...
}
```

Before considering under what circumstances the class designer might wish to make use either of a protected or private class derivation, let's first consider a question: *When is a base class private?* For example, given the following private derivation:

```
class Base {
public:
    int set_val(int);
    // ...
};

class Derived : private Base {
public:
    void mem1(Base&);
    void mem2();
    // ...
};
```

when is the Base class private? The following, for example, is legal anywhere within the program:

```
main() {
    Base *bp = new Base; // ok
    int ival = bp->set_val(1024); // ok
    // ...
}
```

However, the attempt to call set_val() through a Derived class object is illegal and flagged as an error:

```
main() {
    Derived d;
    int ival = d.set_val(1024); // error: private
    // ...
}
```

Within the general program, Base is private whenever its members are accessed through a Derived class object. That is, the privacy of the Base class is an attribute of its derivation. Additionally, however, it is also an attribute of scope. For example,

```
void Derived::mem2()
{
    Derived d;
    int ival = d.set_val(1024); // ok
    // ...
}
```

The public members of Base are considered private when they are accessed through a Derived class object *outside* the scope of the Derived class. Within the scope of the Derived class, their access is not prohibited. The same holds true for the assignment of a derived class object to its private base class; it is only illegal outside the scope of the derived class.

For example, although the following two initializations are illegal and flagged as errors,

```
main() {
    // no standard conversion of Derived
    // class to private Base class
    Base *bp = new Derived; // error
    Derived d;
    d.mem1(d); // error
    // ...
}
```

the same two initializations are legal within the Derived class scope:

```
void Derived::mem2() {
    Base *bp = new Derived; // ok
    Derived d;
    d.mem1(d); // ok
    // ...
}
```

The following sections look at nonpublic derivation in more detail.

Protected Base Class

The zoo administration wishes to keep track of its rodent population. It does not, however, wish that information to be generally available. Moreover, the Rodent class itself serves as an abstract class to be subsequently derived from. The public interface of the hierarchy has to remain available to each class derived from Rodent; however, it must not be available to the general program through instances of either Rodent or those classes derived from Rodent. This is the purpose of a protected base class. For example,

```
// all public members of ZooAnimal
// become protected members of Rodent
class Rodent : protected ZooAnimal {
public:
    virtual void assuringMessage();
protected:
    virtual void reportSightings(ZooLoc);
    unsigned long howMany;
    // ...
};
```

The entire set of nonprivate inherited ZooAnimal members are protected members of Rodent. This permits them to be accessed by all subsequent class derivations while prohibiting the general program from having access to them. For example,

```
class Rat : public Rodent {
public:
    // ...
protected:
    void log() {
        inform(); // ok: ZooAnimal::inform()
    }
};
```

```
main() {
    Bear anyBear;
    Rat anyRat;

    anyBear.inform(); // ok
    anyRat.inform(); // error: nonpublic

    anyRat.assuringMessage(); // ok
    // ...
}
```

There is no standard conversion between a derived class and its nonpublic base class except within the scope of the derived class. For example,

```
extern void draw(ZooAnimal*);

Rat::loc() {
    Rat ratso;
    draw( &ratso );   // ok
}

main() {
    Rat ratso;
    draw( &ratso ); // error: no standard conversion
}
```

Private Base Class

A Stack class is designed in Chapter 2 to illustrate the use of the built-in increment and decrement operators. The internal stack representation chosen is that of an array. The definition and management of the array is implemented as part of the implementation of the Stack class. There are two likely areas of error in the implementation of the Stack class:

- The implementation of the Stack class abstraction; that is, does it behave correctly as a stack?

- The implementation of the array representation. Have we managed the memory allocation correctly? Is it deleted at the right time, etc?

What we'd really like is a fully guaranteed (that is, tested and *supported*) implementation of an array that we can plug into our Stack class. This frees us to concentrate on getting the stack representation correct. (It will also make any change to the stack implementation, such as moving from an array representation to that of a linked list, much easier, especially if there is a "plug in" List class available.)

As it happens, an Array class has already been implemented and tested (see Section 7.9 (page 380) for its definition). The question is how it might best be reused within the stack implementation. Our first thought, of course, is inheritance. (Note that we will need to modify the Array class to change its state members from private to protected.)

```
#include "Array.h"
const int BOS = -1; // Bottom Of Stack
const int StackSize = ArraySize; // in Array.h

template <class Type>
class Stack : public Array<Type> {
public:
    Stack(int sz=StackSize) :
        Array<Type>(sz), top(BOS) {}
    int is_empty() { return top == BOS; }
    int is_full() { return top == size-1; }
    void push( Type value ) {
        if (is_full()) /* error handling */ ;
        ia[++top] = value; }
    Type pop() {
        if (is_empty()) /* error handling */ ;
        return ia[top--]; }
private:
    int top;
};
```

This achieves exactly what we wanted — only more so. Program code using the new Stack class — accidentally or otherwise — is beginning to also inappropriately make use of its Array base class public interface:

```
template <class Type>
extern void swap(Array<Type>&,int,int);
Stack<int> is;

// oops: unexpected misuses of a Stack
swap(is,i,j);
is.sort();
is[0] = is[1];
```

The Stack class abstraction guarantees a "last in, first out" behavior with regard to the access of the elements it contains. However, the availability of the additional Array interface seriously compromises any guarantee of that behavior.

The problem is that a public derivation defines an *is-a* relationship. The derived class is a kind of base class. A Bear is a kind of ZooAnimal. A Window is a kind of Screen. These subtype relationships share a common interface. A Stack, however, is not a kind of Array. Rather, a Stack has an Array as part of its implementation. The public interface of an Array is not part of the Stack class public interface. The Stack class wishes to reuse the implementation of the Array class; however, a Stack is not an Array subtype.

A private base class reflects a form of inheritance not based on subtype relationships. The entire public interface of the base class becomes private in the derived class. Each of the following misuses of a Stack class instance is now illegal except within the friends and member functions of the derived class:

```
template <class Type>
extern void swap(Array<Type>&,int,int);
Stack<int> is;

// illegal under private derivation
swap(is,i,j);   // error
is.sort();      // error
is[0] = is[1]; // error
```

The only change required of our earlier Stack defintion is to replace the public keyword with that of private:

```
template <class Type>
class Stack : private Array<Type> { ... };
```

Inheritance Versus Composition

The implementation of the Stack class as a private derivation of the Array class works — but is it necessary? Is anything gained in this case by inheritance? In this case, no.

Inheritance is a powerful mechanism in support of an *is-a* subtype relationship. The Stack implementation, however, represents a *has-a* relationship with regard to the Array class. The Stack class has an Array as part of its implementation. A has-a relationship is in general best supported by *composition* rather than by inheritance. Composition is implemented by making one class a member of the other class. In this case, an Array object is made a member of Stack. Here is our *has-a* Array instance implementation of Stack.

```
#include "Array.h"

const int BOS = -1;
const int StackSize = ArraySize;
```

```
template <class Type>
class Stack {
public:
    Stack(int sz=StackSize)
        : stack(sz), top(BOS) {}
    int is_empty() { return top == BOS; }
    int is_full() {
        return top == stack.getSize()-1;
    }
    void push( Type value ) {
        if (is_full()) /* error handling */ ;
        stack[++top] = value; }
    Type pop() {
        if (is_empty()) /* error handling */ ;
        return stack[top--]; }
private:
    int top;
    Array<Type> stack;
};
```

Exempting Individual Members

In the private Stack derivation of Array, all the protected and public members of the Array class are inherited as private members of the Stack class. However, it would still be useful if clients of this Stack implementation were able to query a Stack instance as to its size:

```
is.getSize();
```

The class designer can exempt individual members of a base class from the effects of the nonpublic derivation. The following, for example, exempts the getSize() member function of Array:

```
template <class Type>
class Stack : private Array<Type> {
public:
    // maintain public access level
    // do not specify return type or signature
    Array<Type>::getSize;
    // ...
};
```

Recall, a derived class can access only the nonprivate members of its base class. This means that any class derived from Stack is unable to access the protected Array class members. One possible Stack class derivation is that of an unbounded stack — one that grows itself whenever its current memory allocation is exhausted. An unbounded stack needs access to the ia and `size` members of the private Array base class:

```
template <class Type>
class Stack : private Array<Type> {
protected:
    Array<Type>::size;
    Array<Type>::ia;
    // ...
};
```

The specification of `Array<Type>::size` and `Array<Type>::ia` within a `protected` section of Stack causes both members to be inherited at their original access level for each instantiation of the template Stack class. A subsequent derivation, such as an unbounded stack, also inherits these two members as protected. Were Array a nontemplate class, the programmer would write

```
// were Array a nontemplate class
Array::size;
Array::ia;
```

The derived class can only maintain the inherited member's access level. The access level cannot be made either more or less restrictive than the level originally specified within the base class. It is illegal, for example, to declare the protected Array class member `size` within a `public` section of Stack or to declare the public member `getSize()` within a `protected` section.

8.6 Standard Conversions Under Derivation

Four predefined standard conversions are applied between a derived class and its *public* base classes.

1. A derived class object will be implicitly converted into a public base class object.

2. A derived class reference will be implicitly converted into a public base class reference.

3. A derived class pointer will be implicitly converted into a public base class pointer.

4. A pointer to a class member of a base class will be implicitly converted into a pointer to a class member of a publicly derived class.

In addition, a pointer to any class object will be implicitly converted into a pointer of type `void*`. (A pointer of type `void*` requires an explicit cast in order to assign it to a pointer to any other type.)

For example, here is a simplified set of class definitions. In addition, a function f() is declared that takes as its argument a reference to an object of class ZooAnimal.

```
class Endangered {} endang;
class ZooAnimal {} zooanim;
class Bear : public ZooAnimal {} bear;
class Panda : public Bear {} panda;
class ForSale: private ZooAnimal {} forsale;

// all classes publically derived from ZooAnimal
// can be passed to f() without an explicit cast

extern void f( ZooAnimal& );
```

f() may legally be called with a ZooAnimal, Bear, or Panda class object. In the latter two calls, an implicit standard conversion takes place:

```
f( zooanim );    // ok: exact match
f( bear );       // ok: Bear ==> ZooAnimal
f( panda );      // ok: Panda ==> ZooAnimal
```

The following two invocations of f() are both illegal. Each is flagged as a type mismatch at compile time.

```
f( forsale ); // error: ZooAnimal private
f( endang );  // error: ZooAnimal not a base class
```

Figure 8.4 models the object layout of a derived class, using the following simplified ZooAnimal and Bear class definitions:

```
class ZooAnimal {
public:
    isA();
    // ...

protected:
    char *name;
    int typeOf;
    int someVal;
};
```

```
class Bear : public ZooAnimal {
public:
    locate();
    // ...
protected:
    short ZooArea;
    int someVal;
};

Bear b, *pb = &b;
ZooAnimal *pz = pb;
```

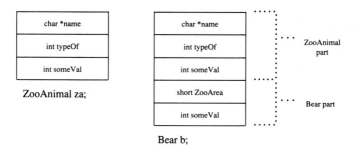

ZooAnimal za;

Bear b;

Figure 8.4 Class Object under Derivation

A derived class is pictured in Figure 8.4 as consisting of one (or more) base class "parts" plus the members unique to the derived class. Both a derived and base class object contain a "base part" — only a derived class object is guaranteed to contain a "derived part."

The conversion of a derived class object into an object of a base class is considered safe because every derived class object contains a base class object. The reverse conversion, however, is not safe. This is why an explicit cast is required. For example,

```
// pb and pz both address the Bear object ``b''
// ok: Bear::locate()
pb->locate(); // ok: Bear::locate()


// error: locate() not a ZooAnimal member
pz->locate();
```

```
pb->someVal; // ok: Bear::someVal
pz->someVal; // ok: ZooAnimal::someVal
```

Except when virtual functions are being invoked, an explicit cast is necessary in order to access a derived class member through a base class object, reference, or pointer. For example,

```
// nonobject-oriented implementation
void locate( ZooAnimal* pZ ) {
    switch ( pZ->isA() ) {
        case Bear:
            ((Bear *)pZ)->locate();
            // ...
        case Panda:
            ((Panda *)pZ)->locate();
            // ...
    }
```

Note that the additional set of parentheses around the cast of pZ is necessary. The statement

```
// invoke the Zoo_Animal member locate(),
// cast its return value to Bear*
(Bear *)pZ->locate();
```

invokes the ZooAnimal instance of locate() and cast its return value to Bear*.

The assignment or initialization of a derived class to one of its base classes always require an explicit cast by the programmer. For example,

```
Bear *pb = new Panda; // ok: implicit conversion
Panda *pp = new Bear; // error: no implicit conversion
Panda *pp = (Panda *) new Bear; // ok.
```

The explicit cast is necessary because the action is potentially quite dangerous. Why? A derived class is guaranteed always to contain a base class part — for example, a Panda object always contains a Bear part. However, a base class may or may not actually have its derived class part "under it" — that depends on what it was initialized with or last assigned. An explicit cast forces a kind of programmer intervention; it is an assertion of the programmer's apparent meta-knowledge about his or her code. Of course, sometimes, things go wrong. For example, the following sequence assigns 24 to an undefined location in memory:

```
Bear b;
// ok: derived class to public base
Bear *pb = new Panda;

// ok: public base to derived:
//      but it really is a Panda
Panda *pp = (Panda *) pb;

// ok: programmer knew best in this case
pp->cell = 24;

// ok: pb now addresses just a Bear object
pb = &b;

// oops: pp addresses a Bear object
//        this time no Panda part
*pp = (Panda*) pb;

// disaster! no Panda::cell
// run-time program arena has been corrupted
// this is a difficult bug to track down
pp->cell = 24;
```

Pointers to class members behave in a kind of reverse mirror image to that of class objects and pointers. It is always safe to assign a member of a public base class to a derived class pointer to class member. For example,

```
int (Panda::*pm_Panda)() = 0;
Panda yinYang;

// ok: implicit conversion
pm_Panda = Bear::member;

// ok: safe execution
(yinYang.*pm_Panda)();
```

This is safe because any member addressed by the base class member function is guaranteed to be present in the derived class. The opposite assignment, however — that of a derived class member to a pointer to class member of the base class — is not safe. For example,

```
int (Bear::*pm_Bear)() = 0;
Bear buddy;

// error: requires explicit cast
pm_Bear = Panda::member;
```

This is unsafe because the derived class member function may address members contained only within a derived class object. If the pointer is bound to an actual base class object, each attempt to access those members will be invalid. For this reason, an explicit cast is necessary when initializing or assigning a derived class member to a pointer to class member of a base class. pm_Zoo, for example, is a ZooAnimal pointer to class member initialized to isA():

```
int (ZooAnimal::*pm_Zoo)() = ZooAnimal::isA;
```

It is invoked by binding it to a class object of its type:

```
ZooAnimal z;
(z.*pm_Zoo)();
```

isA() accesses members of ZooAnimal. Since a Bear class object is guaranteed to contain a ZooAnimal part, it is safe to assign the address of isA() to a Bear pointer to class member:

```
int (Bear::*pm_Bear)() = ZooAnimal::isA;
Bear b;
(b.*pm_Bear)(); // ok
```

Let's assign pm_Zoo the address of the Bear member function locate(). The assignment, because it is unsafe, requires an explicit cast:

```
pm_Zoo = (int (ZooAnimal::*)()) Bear::locate;
```

pm_Zoo must be invoked by binding it to a ZooAnimal class object. locate(), however, accesses members of Bear not contained in a ZooAnimal class object. Whether the invocation of pm_Zoo "crashes" the program depends on the actual type of the base class object. For example,

```
ZooAnimal *pz = &b; // pz addresses a Bear
(pz->*pm_Zoo)();    // ok

pz = &z;            // pz address a ZooAnimal
(pz->*pm_Zoo)();    // disaster
```

Exercise 8-13. Given the following class hierarchy:

```
class Node {};
class Type : public Node {};

class Statement : public Type {};
class Expression : public Type {};

class Identifier : public Expression {};
class Function : public Expression {};
```

Which of the following initializations are illegal? Explain why.

```
(a) Node *pn = new Identifier( "i" );
(b) Identifier *pi = pn;
(c) Expression e = *pi;
(d) Statement s = e;
(e) Type *pt = &e;
(f) Identifier &ri = e;
(g) Function &rf = ri;
(h) Node n = rf;
```

☐

Exercise 8-14. Define a nonmember function debug() which can accept any shape class derivation. It should invoke the correct debug() member function. (In Chapter 9, debug() is rewritten as a virtual class member function.)

☐

Exercise 8-15. Define a set of pointers to class members for Shape, Circle, Box, and Rectangle. Illustrate which assignments are permitted and which require an explicit conversion. ☐

8.7 Class Scope Under Derivation

Inheritance provides for class scope nesting. As illustrated in Figure 8.5, a derived class can be thought of as enclosed by the scope of its base classes.

Each class and external function is visible within file scope; their scopes are represented in the figure by boxes drawn with a dashed line. Each member function is visible within the scope of its class; its local scope is represented by boxes drawn with a dotted line. The arrows link each scope with its enclosing scopes. In the case of multiple inheritance, there are multiple enclosing scopes. All of these multiple enclosing scopes must be searched within the same look-up step. Panda, for example, must search the Bear, Endangered, and Herbivore class scopes in the same look-up step. Figure 8.5 is a representation of the following set of class definitions:

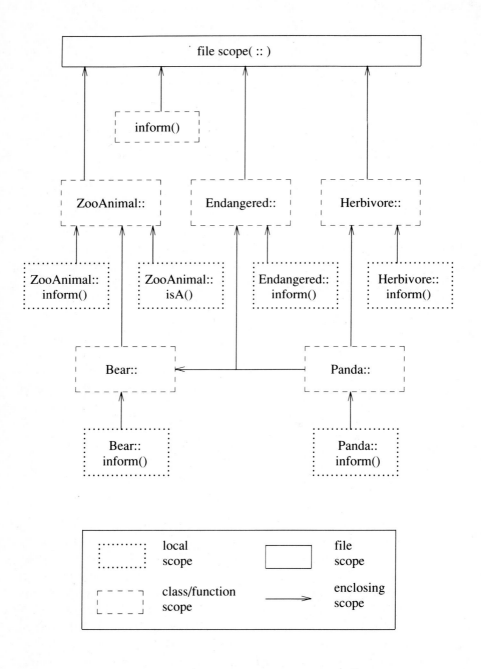

Figure 8.5 Class Scope Under Derivation

```
    extern inform();

    class ZooAnimal {
    public:
        int inform();
        int isA();
    };

    class Endangered { public: int inform(ZooAnimal*); };
    class Herbivore { public: int inform(ZooAnimal*); };

    class Bear : public ZooAnimal
        { public: int inform( short ); };

    class Panda : public Bear, public Endangered,
                  public Herbivore
        { public: int inform( char * ); };

    int Panda::inform( char *str ) {
        // ...
        int kval = isA();
        // ...
    }
```

The occurrence of isA() within Panda::inform() initiates the following look-up search:

1. Is isA() declared within Panda::inform()? If yes, stop; otherwise, follow the scope arrow. It is not.

2. Is isA() declared as a class member of Panda? If yes, stop; otherwise, follow the scope arrows of the multiple base classes. It is not.

3. Is isA() an inherited member from one and only one of the Bear, Endangered or Herbivore base classes? If yes, stop. If it is inherited from two or more base classes, the reference is ambiguous. Issue an error message and stop. Otherwise, are any of these base classes also derived? If yes, follow the scope arrow to their base classes; otherwise, follow the scope arrow to file scope. Repeat until either the reference is resolved or file scope has been searched. If the reference is unresolved following the search of file scope, issue an error message and stop.

The reference to isA() within Panda::inform() is resolved to the inherited member ZooAnimal::isA().

Derivation Is Not Overloading

The inherited `ZooAnimal::locate()` member has a signature distinct from that of the renamed `Bear::locate(int)`. Users new to C++ often assume that the signature is sufficient to distinguish the two instances — that, in effect, inherited member functions with the same name are handled as an overloaded function set to be resolved at the point of call. For example,

```
// derivation is not overloading
Bear ursus;
ursus.locate( 1 ); // ok: Bear::locate(int)
ursus.locate(); // error: ZooAnimal::locate() is hidden
```

Derivation, however, is *not* a form of overloading. The ZooAnimal instance of `locate()` is hidden. The call `ursus.locate()` resolves to `Bear::locate(int)`. The call is flagged as an error. The instance of `locate()` that is found requires one argument.

Derivation preserves the scope of the base classes. Overloading requires that the entire function set be defined at the same scope. To overload `locate()`, a second Bear instance must be defined:

```
inline void Bear::locate() { ZooAnimal::locate(); }
```

Nested Types Under Inheritance

A zoo often will sell its surplus animals, usually at auction set up by an independent agent. Many zoos try to keep track of these sales. A class to maintain this information might be named AuctionSales. Because AuctionSales represents a *has-a* relationship, it is made a member class rather than inherited from as a base class. Because it can apply to any and all zoo animals, it is factored up into the abstract ZooAnimal base class. For example,

```
class ZooAnimal {
public:
    int has_been_auctioned() {
            return sold != 0; }
    // ...
protected:
    AuctionSales *sold;
    // ...
};
```

At issue, then, is how the AuctionSales class should be defined.

```
class AuctionSales {
public:
    AuctionSales();
    // ...
};
```

This definition allows instances of AuctionSales to appear anywhere in the program. However, the intention is that AuctionSales should only be used within the ZooAnimal hierarchy. One strategy for restricting instances of AuctionSales to the ZooAnimal hierarchy is to make its constructors nonpublic. For example,

```
class AuctionSales {
    friend class ZooAnimal;
public:
    // ...
protected:
    AuctionSales();
    AuctionSales(const AuctionSales&);
    // ...
};
```

What would happen if these members were made private and if a class were subsequently derived from AuctionSales?

```
class CircusSales : public AuctionSales {};
```

A derived class instance first invokes the constructors of its base classes. However, a derived class has no access privilege to the private members of its base class. An attempt to create a CircusSales instance would be flagged as an error — AuctionSales::AuctionSales() is private. These members, therefore, are made protected so that any class derived from AuctionSales is able to create an AuctionSales instance.

ZooAnimal is made a friend of AuctionSales in order to be able to create its AuctionSales member class instance. This strategy is imperfect, however, since friendship is not inherited. A Panda has no access privilege to AuctionSales, for example, unless it is also made a friend. This holds true for each ZooAnimal derivation.

Another drawback to this strategy is that, although the general program is now prohibited from creating AuctionSale instances, the AuctionSales type specifier is visible to the entire program and therefore cannot be reused in another context.

An alternative strategy without either of these drawbacks is to make AuctionSales a nested class within the protected section of ZooAnimal. The class name, then, is encapsulated within the ZooAnimal hierarchy. All ZooAnimal derivations have access to the class; the general program, however, is still denied access. For example,

```
class ZooAnimal {
    int has_been_auctioned() {
            return sold != 0; }
    // ...
protected:
    class AuctionSales {...} *sold;
    // ...
};



class Grizzly : public Bear
    // ...
protected:
    void sales() {
        if (!sold) {
            sold = new AuctionSales; // ok
            // ...
};

// error: AuctionSales not visible
AuctionSales *p;

// error: AuctionSales not accessible
AuctionSales *pas = new AuctionSales;
```

A nested type can also be exempted from the effects of a nonpublic derivation. For example,

```
class Rodent : private ZooAnimal {
    // ...
protected:
    // maintains its protected access
    ZooAnimal::AuctionSales;
    // ...
};
```

When should a type definition be nested within a class? When the type serves as an auxiliary or helping type of interest only to a single class or class hierarchy. The actual behavior of a nested type is no different from that of its nonnested counterpart. Its visibility, however, becomes encapsulated, removed from the global name space of the application. For example, a possible redesign of the ZooAnimal hierarchy might nest the definition of the class Endangered:

```
class ZooAnimal {
public:
    // ...
protected:
    class Endangered { ... };
    // ...
};
```

Its member functions could still be defined outside its class definition; the class scope syntax is simply extended:

```
ZooAnimal::Endangered::Endangered() {}
ZooAnimal::Endangered::~Endangered() {}
ZooAnimal::Endangered::highlight() {}
ZooAnimal::Endangered::inform(){}
```

Moreover, it can still define virtual functions and serve as an object of derivation:

```
class Panda : public Bear,
              public ZooAnimal::Endangered {};
```

The extended class scope syntax can be used only to reference nested class names. For example, given the following inheritance hierarchy,

```
class ZooAnimal {
protected: int i; };

class Bear : public ZooAnimal {
protected: int i; };

class Panda : public Bear {
public: int foo(); };
```

the following use of the extended class scope syntax to reference the hidden ZooAnimal instance of i is illegal.

```
int Panda::foo() {
    // error: ZooAnimal is not a nested class
    return Bear::ZooAnimal::i;
};
```

8.8   Initialization and Assignment Under Derivation

A class object initialized with another object of its class by default is member-wise initialized (see Section 6.2 (page 295) for a discussion). The same default behavior holds for a derived class object. First, in the order they appear within the class derivation list, memberwise initialization is applied to each base class. That complete, memberwise initialization is then applied to each derived class member in order of its declaration.

Default memberwise initialization can be a source of problems in handling individual class objects that contain pointer members. This is particularly true if the class also defines a destructor to free the memory addressed by those members. The problem is that, by default, all nonclass members are simply copied — resulting in multiple pointers to the same object in memory.

Pointer members, however, are not the only indication that default memberwise initialization is a problem for a particular class. The semantics of the class abstraction may require that a copy of the class not propagate its current state — an iterator class, for example, needs to have its index member reset not copied.

To address these problems, the class designer provides an explicit memberwise initialization constructor, X(const X&). The class in effect provides its own memberwise initialization algorithm. The initialization of one class object with another is now handled with the invocation of the explicit X(const X&) constructor.

This section considers the handling of X(const X&) under class derivation. Three cases are discussed:

1. The derived class does not define an X(const X&) instance; one or more base classes do define an instance.

2. The derived class does define an instance; the base classes do not.

3. Both the derived and the base classes define an instance.

If the derived class does not define an X(const X&) instance, default memberwise initialization is applied whenever one object of the derived class is initialized with another. The base classes are memberwise initialized first; the order of initialization follows the declaration order of the base classes. X(const X&) is invoked for each base class for which it is defined. For example, given the following simplified set of class definitions,

```
class Carnivore { public: Carnivore(); };
class ZooAnimal {
public:
        ZooAnimal();
        ZooAnimal( const ZooAnimal& );
};

class Cat : public ZooAnimal,
            public Carnivore { public: Cat(); };
```

```
Cat Felix;
Cat Fritz = Felix;
```

The initialization of the Cat object `Fritz` with that of `Felix` will first invoke
`ZooAnimal(const ZooAnimal&)`. The Carnivore base class and members
of Cat are then memberwise initialized.

If the derived class defines an `X(const X&)` instance, it is invoked for all
initialization of a derived class object with another object of its class. The
base class parts are not memberwise initialized. Handling of the base class
parts becomes the responsibility of the derived `X(const X&)` instance. For
example,

```
class Bear : public ZooAnimal {
public:
        Bear();
        Bear( const Bear& );
};

Bear Yogi;
Bear Smokey = Yogi;
```

Initialization of the Bear object `Smokey` with that of `Yogi` results in the following pair of constructor invocations:

```
ZooAnimal();
Bear (const Bear&);
```

A base class constructor is always invoked before execution of a constructor for the derived class. The handling of `X(const X&)` is no exception. If the
base class constructor requires an argument, it must be provided in a member initialization list.

Since ZooAnimal defines its own instance of `X(const X&)`, it is preferable that it be invoked. This can be done as follows:

```
Bear::Bear( const Bear& b )
        // ZooAnimal(const ZooAnimal&) invoked
        : ZooAnimal( b )
        { /* ... */ }
```

Initialization of `Smokey` with `Yogi` now results in the following pair of
constructor invocations:

```
ZooAnimal( const ZooAnimal& );
Bear( const Bear& );
```

If the base class does not define an `X(const X&)` instance, default memberwise initialization is recursively applied to the base class.

In a similar manner, memberwise assignment (see Section 6.3 (page 318)
for a discussion) can be overridden by explicitly providing a memberwise

instance of operator=(const X&). Its handling parallels that of the X(const X&) constructor.

If a derived class does not define operator=(const X&), then each of its base class and member class objects that defines an object assignment operator will have that operator invoked whenever one object of the derived class is assigned to another. Each base class or member class object without an operator=(const X&) defined is memberwise assigned.

If a derived class defines an instance of operator=(const X&), it will be invoked to handle the initialization of a class object with another object of its class. Base class and member class object assignment becomes the responsibility of the derived class object assignment operator.

Given the following assignment of a derived class Bear object to a public base class object of ZooAnimal, which instance of the object assignment operator is invoked? Both ZooAnimal and Bear define operator=(const X&).

```
Bear ursus;
ZooAnimal onLoan;

onLoan = ursus; // which copy operator?
```

The class type of the assignment's left operand determines the class type of the assignment. The ZooAnimal part of the Bear object ursus is assigned to onLoan. Therefore, it is as though two ZooAnimal objects are being assigned, and the ZooAnimal object assignment operator is invoked. The same holds true for object initialization. The declaration

```
Bear Fozzie;
ZooAnimal On_Loan = Fozzie;
```

also invokes the object initialization constructor of ZooAnimal, rather than that of Bear.

In general, if a class provides an explicit instance of either the initialization or assignment member, it should also provide the other. Explicit instances are usually necessary when either of the following conditions hold:

1. The semantics of the class representation invalidates value copying of one or more members. The StringIterator class index member, for example, must be reset to 0 with each copy.

2. The class contains pointer members and a destructor. Copying requires either the handling of a reference count or additional allocation and copying of memory.

Exercise 8-16. Define an X(const X&) and operator=(const X&) instance for the Shape class but not for the Circle class. What are the constructors invoked for the following two objects of type Circle?

```
Circle c1;
Circle c2 = c1;
```

☐

Exercise 8-17. Define an `X(const X&)` and `operator=(const X&)` instance for the Box class but not for the Rectangle class. What are the constructors invoked for the following class objects?

```
Rectangle r1;
Box b1 = r1;
Rectangle r2 = r1;
```

☐

8.9　Initialization Order Under Derivation

Given the following simplified definition of Panda,

```
class Panda : public Bear,
    public Endangered, public Herbivore {
public:
    Panda();
    // ... rest of public members
protected:
    BitVector status;
    String name;
    // ... rest of Panda members
};
```

```
Panda yinYang;
```

The constructors for `yinYang` are invoked in the following order:

1. Each base class constructor in the order of base classes are declared within the derivation list:

```
ZooAnimal(); // base class of Bear
Bear();
Endangered();
Herbivore();
```

2. Each member class object constructor in the order of member class declarations:

```
BitVector();
String();
```

3. The derived class constructor: `Panda();`

The destructors for `yinYang` are invoked in the reverse order of the invocation of the constructors.

Although the fixed order of base and member class object constructor invocation is ordinarily of no concern to the user, the integrity of certain applications depends on this order. For example, a library that allows for arbitrarily complex user-defined class types to be written out and read from disk must be assured that objects will be constructed in the same order regardless of machines and regardless of compilers. The language guarantees uniformity across implementations by defining a fixed order of constructor (and destructor) invocation.

8.10   Overloaded Functions with Class Arguments

Often, a function is overloaded in order to introduce an instance of an existing function to handle objects of a class type. For example, having defined a Complex number class, the designer might next define an instance of the square root library function that handles a Complex class object:

```
extern Complex& sqrt( Complex& );
```

The original discussion of resolving a call of an overloaded function presented in Section 4.1 (page 170) did not consider argument-matching in the presence of class arguments. This is the subject of this section.

We will consider, in turn, the exact matching of a class argument, matching achieved by application of a standard conversion, and matching achieved by invoking a user-defined conversion operator.

Exact Match

A class object matches exactly only a formal argument of its own class type. Through a trivial conversion, a class object and a reference to a class object match. For example,

```
extern void ff( const Bear& );
extern void ff( const Panda& );

Panda yinYang;

// ok: ff( const Panda& )
ff( yinYang );
```

Similarly, a pointer to a class object matches exactly only a formal argument of a pointer to its own class type. Through a trivial conversion, an array of objects and a pointer to a class object match.

The argument-matching algorithm cannot distinguish between an object and a reference of a class type. Although the following two instances declare two distinct functions, the overload mechanism cannot distinguish between them. An error is therefore issued at compile time.

```
/* error: the overloading mechanism cannot tell an
 *            int ff(Panda) from an int ff(const Panda &) */

extern int ff( Panda );
extern int ff( const Panda& );
```

Standard Conversions

If the class argument is not an exact match and a match cannot be achieved through a trivial conversion, a match is attempted through the application of a predefined standard conversion.

- A derived class object, reference, or pointer is implicitly converted into a corresponding public base class type. For example,

```
extern void ff( const ZooAnimal& );
extern void ff( const Screen& );

// ok: ff( const ZooAnimal& )
ff( yinYang );
```

- A pointer of any class type is implicitly converted into a pointer of type void*.

```
extern void ff( const Screen* );
extern void ff( const void* );

// ok: ff( const void* )
ff( &yinYang );
```

A conversion of a base class object, reference, or pointer into its corresponding derived class type is *not* applied. The following call, for example, fails to achieve a match:

```
extern void ff( const Bear& );
extern void ff( const Panda& );

ZooAnimal za;

// error: no match
ff( za );
```

The presence of two or more immediate base classes results in the call being flagged as ambiguous. Panda, for example, is derived from both Bear and Endangered. Both conversions of a Panda class object require equal work. Since both conversions are possible, the call is an error.

```
extern void ff( const Bear& );
extern void ff( const Endangered& );

/* actual compiler error message:
 * error: ambiguous call: ff ( struct Panda )
 * choice of ff()s:
 *      void (const Bear &);
 *      void (const Endangered &);
 */
ff( yinYang );
```

To resolve the call, the programmer must supply an explicit cast:

```
ff( Bear(yinYang) ); // ok
```

A derived class is considered more nearly the type of its immediate base class than of a base class further removed. The following call is not ambiguous although a standard conversion is required in both instances. A Panda is treated as being more nearly a kind of Bear than a kind of ZooAnimal by the argument-matching algorithm.

```
extern void ff( const ZooAnimal& );
extern void ff( const Bear& );

// ok: ff( const Bear& );
ff( yinYang );
```

This rule extends to the handling of void*. For example, given the following pair of overloaded functions:

```
ff( void* );
ff( ZooAnimal* );
```

an argument of type Panda* matches ZooAnimal*.

User-Defined Conversions

A user-defined conversion can be either a constructor that takes one argument or an explicit conversion operator. User-defined conversions are applied only if no exact match, match by a trivial conversion, or match by a standard conversion has been found. For this subsection, let's provide ZooAnimal with two user-defined conversions:

```
class ZooAnimal {
public:
    // conversion: long ==> ZooAnimal
    ZooAnimal( long );

    // conversion: ZooAnimal ==> char*
    operator char*();

    // ...
};
```

Given the following pair of overloaded functions

```
extern void ff( const ZooAnimal& );
extern void ff( const Screen& );
```

a call with an actual argument of type long will be resolved to the ZooAnimal instance by invoking the user-defined conversion

```
long lval;

// ok: ff( const ZooAnimal& )
ff( lval );
```

What if the call is made with an argument of type int? For example,

```
ff( 1024 ); // ???
```

There is still no match either by an exact match or through a standard conversion. There is one applicable user-defined conversion — almost. The problem is that the conversion constructor for ZooAnimal expects a value of type long, not of type int.

The argument-matching algorithm will apply a standard conversion to help it find an applicable user-defined conversion. In this case, 1024 is converted to type long and passed to the ZooAnimal constructor. The call is resolved to the ZooAnimal instance.

A user-defined conversion is applied only when no match is otherwise possible. Were an instance of ff() declared which accepted a predefined type, the ZooAnimal conversion operator would not be invoked. For example,

```
extern void ff( const ZooAnimal& );
extern void ff( char );

long lval;

// ok: ff( char );
ff( lval );
```

In this case, an explicit cast is necessary to resolve the call to the ZooAnimal instance:

```
// ok: ff( const ZooAnimal& )
ff( ZooAnimal( lval ));
```

In the following example, the ZooAnimal `char*` conversion operator is applied since there is no standard conversion from a base class object to a derived class object.

```
extern void ff( const char* );
extern void ff( const Bear& );

ZooAnimal za;

// za ==> char*
// ok: ff( char* )
ff( za );
```

The argument-matching algorithm will apply a standard conversion to the result of a user-defined conversion, if doing so achieves a match. For example,

```
extern void ff( const Panda* );
extern void ff( const void* );

// za ==> char* ==> void*
// ok: ff( const void* )
ff( za );
```

Conversion operators (but not constructors) are inherited in the same way as other class members. Both Bear and Panda inherit the `char*` conversion operator of ZooAnimal. For example,

```
extern void ff( const char* );
extern void ff( const Bear* );

Bear yogi;
Bear *pBear = &yogi;

// yogi ==> char*
// ok: ff( const char* )
ff( yogi );

// ok: ff( const Bear* )
ff( pBear );
```

If two or more user-defined conversions can achieve a match, the call is ambiguous and results in a compile-time error. Conversion constructors and operator conversions share the same precedence. If one instance of each type can be applied, the call is ambiguous.

For example, let Endangered define a conversion operator of type int:

```
class Endangered {
public:
    // conversion: Endangered ==> int
    operator int();

    // ...
};
```

Then if Extinct defines a conversion constructor that accepts a reference to an Endangered class object such as the following

```
class Extinct {
public:
    // conversion: Endangered ==> Extinct
    Extinct( Endangered& );

    // ...
};
```

the following call is ambiguous. Both the conversion operator of Endangered and the conversion constructor of Extinct achieve a match.

```
extern void ff( const Extinct& );
extern void ff( int );

Endangered e;

ff( e ); // error: ambiguous
```

Here is a second example of ambiguity involving user-defined conversions. In this case, the conversion constructors of SmallInt and BitVector are equally applicable. The call is flagged as an error.

```
class SmallInt {
public:
    // conversion: int ==> SmallInt
    SmallInt( int );

    // ...
};
```

```
class BitVector {
    // conversion: unsigned long ==> BitVector
    BitVector( unsigned long );

    // ...
};

extern void ff( const SmallInt& );
extern void ff( const BitVector& );

ff( 1 ); // error: ambiguous
```

8.11 Inheriting Operator Functions

A derived class inherits all the member functions of each of its base classes
except the constructors, destructor, and assignment operators of each of its
base classes. Let's look at a number of situations in turn.

In the first situation, a base class defines an equality operator comparing a
base class object to an array of characters:

```
class Base {
public:
    int operator==(const char*);
    // ...
};
```

In the derived class, an equality operator is defined comparing a derived
class object to an integer:

```
class Derived : public Base {
public:
    int operator==(int);
    // ...
};
```

Since the Base class equality operator is inherited and public, the programmer is often surprised when the following code fails to compile:

```
main() {
    Derived d1;
    if ( d1 == 1024 && // ok
         d1 == "Anna Rachel" ) // error
         // ...
}
```

Operators in general behave the same as named member functions. The
Derived class equality operator lexically hides the name of the Base class
instance. The two are not considered overloaded because they are defined in

separate scopes. In order for this code to compile, the derived class must define a second instance:

```
class Derived: public Base {
public:
    int operator==(int);
    int operator==(const char *ch) {
        // call the Base instance explicitly
        return Base::operator==(ch);
    }
    // ...
};
```

In the second situation, the Base class defines an assignment operator taking as its argument an integer:

```
class Base {
public:
    const Base &operator=(int);
    // ...
};
```

The derived class does not define an assignment operator. It does, however, define a default constructor:

```
class Derived: public Base {
public:
    Derived();
    // ...
};
```

Because assignment operators are not inherited, of course, we expect the following code to fail:

```
main() {
    Derived d1;
    d1 = 1;
    // ...
}
```

What puzzles us is the error message:

```
``unexpected first argument for Derived::Derived()''
```

Do you see what is going on here?

There is a predefined meaning to the assignment operator, recall, when a class object appears as its left operand — that of default memberwise copy. Since the Derived class does not define an explicit instance of the assignment operator (and it does not inherit the Base class instance), the only interpretation of the assignment

```
d1 = 1;
```

is that of a default memberwise copy of one Derived class object with
another. Since the right operand is not a Derived class object, the compiler
attempts to convert it into one. The right operand is an integer. To make a
Derived class object from an integer, a conversion constructor of the form

```
Derived::Derived(int ival) { ... }
```

needs to be defined. Had it been, it would be applied to the right operand.
The resulting Derived class object would then be memberwise copied into
d1. Had the Derived class not defined any constructor, an error message of
the following general form would have been generated:

```
''error: cannot create a Derived class object''
```

Since a Derived constructor is defined, albeit the wrong instance in this case,
an attempt is made to apply it — perhaps it defines a default value for a single argument of an arithmetic type. The attempt fails, however; the default
instance does not accept an integer first argument. At this point the seemingly inexplicable error message is generated.

The third situation has to do with the inheritance of operators new and
delete. A class intended as a candidate for derivation should always, if it
provides a delete operator, supply the optional second argument of type
size_t. This second argument, if present, is initialized with the size in
bytes of the object to be deleted. If this argument is not present and the
derived class defines memory additional to that of the base class, there is no
way for the delete operator to act upon that additional memory.

The inheritance of a base class operator new too strictly tied to the size of
the base class can be a source of run-time problems. For example, in Section
6.3 (page 315) a Screen class operator new is defined. Let's derive a Screen-
Buf class from that:

```
class ScreenBuf: public Screen {
public:
    // ...
protected:
    long some_val;
};
```

The Screen class operator new, recall, allocates a contiguous chunk of
memory from the free store of size

```
new char[ screenChunk*size ]
```

where size is the size_t argument to operator new containing the size of
the object for which the operator has been invoked. This chunk of memory is
maintained as a linked list of screenChunk elements of available Screen

objects. Each call of

```
new Screen;
```

returns the next Screen object on the list. Each time the list of available objects is emptied, a new chunk of memory is allocated.

The Screen class operator `delete` returns the Screen object to the list of available objects. In an ideal implementation, after a program's initial start-up, this list is always just shy of being empty.

Unfortunately, the inherited Screen operator `new` only works correctly when either the derived class is the same size as Screen, or the program uses either all Screen or ScreenBuf objects. If the chunk is allocated by a call of

```
new Screen;
```

then each new object subsequently passed from the list for a call of

```
new ScreenBuf;
```

has insufficient memory to contain `ScreenBuf::some_val`. Each read operation reads the arbitrary bit pattern of the next contiguous Screen object. Each write operation corrupts that memory. There is no telling what actually will happen during execution of the program.

Before the designer of a derived class chooses to reuse the `new` and `delete` operators of the base class, these operators *must* be examined for type-dependent size assumptions.

Chapter 9: **Object-Oriented Programming**

Object-oriented programming is characterized by inheritance and dynamic binding. C++ supports inheritance through class derivation — the subject of the previous chapter. Dynamic binding is provided by virtual class functions.

An inheritance hierarchy defines a type/subtype relationship between class types. A Panda is a type of Bear, for example, which in turn is a type of ZooAnimal. Similarly, both a sorted array and an array with range checking are types of Array. Virtual functions define *type dependent operations* within an inheritance hierarchy — the ZooAnimal draw() function, for example, or the subscript operator of the array classes. Virtual functions provide a method of encapsulating the implementation details of an inheritance hierarchy from programs that make use of it. In this chapter, we look at virtual functions in detail. We also look at a special case of class inheritance — that of a virtual, or shared, base class. The chapter concludes with a discussion of template classes and inheritance.

9.1 Virtual Functions

A virtual function is a special member function invoked through a public base class reference or pointer; it is bound dynamically at run time. The instance invoked is determined by the class type of the actual object addressed by the pointer or reference. Resolution of a virtual function is transparent to the user.

draw(), for example, is a virtual function with an instance defined by ZooAnimal, Bear, Panda, Cat, and Leopard. A function invoking draw() might be defined as follows:

```
inline void draw( ZooAnimal &z ) {
        z.draw();
}
```

If an argument to this nonmember instance of draw() addresses a Panda class object, the statement z.draw() will invoke Panda::draw(). A subsequent argument addressing a Cat class object will result in the call of Cat::draw(). The compiler resolves which class member function to call based on the class type of the actual object.

Before examining how virtual functions are declared and used, let's look briefly at why we would want to use virtual functions.

Dynamic Binding Is a Form of Encapsulation

The final screen of the zoo animal application paints a collage of the animals about which the visitor has requested information. This screen, a special favorite of children, has made the display terminal an attraction in its own right.

In order to produce the collage, a linked list of pointers to the animals about which the visitor has inquired is maintained. When the QUIT button is pressed, the head of the linked list of ZooAnimals is passed to finalCollage(), which displays the animals in an appropriate size and layout to fill the screen.

Maintaining the linked list is simple since a ZooAnimal pointer can address any publicly derived class. With dynamic binding, it is also simple to determine the derived class type addressed by the ZooAnimal pointer. finalCollage() might be implemented like this:

```
void finalCollage( ZooAnimal *pz )
{
    for ( ZooAnimal *p = pz; p; p = p->next )
        p->draw();
}
```

In a language without run-time type resolution, it becomes the programmer's responsibility to determine the derived class type addressed by the ZooAnimal pointer. Typically, this involves an identifying isA() class member and an if-else or switch statement that tests and branches on the value of isA(). Without dynamic binding, finalCollage might be implemented like this:

```
/* nonobject-oriented implementation:

 * burden of type resolution is on programmer
 * code requires knowledge of type representation
 * it must be changed with each change to that
 * type representation */

void finalCollage( ZooAnimal *pz ) {
    for ( ZooAnimal *p = pz; p; p = p->next )
```

```
switch ( p->isA() ) {
    case BEAR:
        ((Bear *)p)->draw();
        break;
    case PANDA:
        ((Panda *)p)->draw();
        break;
    // ... every other derived class
}
```

Programs written in this style are bound to the implementation details of the derivation hierarchy. If those details change, the program may cease to work, and it may become necessary to rewrite source code extensively.

After the pandas leave the zoo to return to China, the Panda class type must be removed. When the koalas arrive from Australia, the Koala class type must be added. For each modification of the hierarchy, every if-else and switch statement that tests on the class type must be identified and modified. The source code is subject to change with each change to the hierarchy.

Even moderately sized switch statements increase the size of program code dramatically. Conceptually simple actions become obscured under the conditional tests necessary to determine the class type of an object. Programs become more difficult to read (and to get *and keep* right).

Users of the hierarchy and its applications who wish either to extend the hierarchy or to customize the applications must have access to the source code. This makes distribution and support much more difficult and expensive for both the originator and the client of the system.

Run-time type resolution encapsulates the implementation details of the derivation hierarchy from the user. Conditional tests on the class type are no longer necessary. This simplifies user code and makes it less volatile. User code, no longer subject to change with each change to the hierarchy, is simpler to program and maintain.

In turn, this simplifies extension of the hierarchy. Adding a new ZooAnimal derivation does not require modification of existing code. The general draw() function need not know about future ZooAnimal derivations. Its code remains functional regardless of how the hierarchy is altered, which means that the application, except for header files, can be distributed in binary form.

Customization is also simplified. Since both the implementation of the class types *and* the implementation of the class hierarchy are encapsulated, either can be altered with minimum impact on client code, provided that both public interfaces remain unchanged.

Virtual Function Definition

A virtual function is specified by prefacing a function declaration with the
keyword `virtual`. Only class member functions may be declared as virtual.
The virtual keyword can occur only within the class body. For example,

```
class Foo {
public:
    virtual int bar(); // virtual declaration
};


int Foo::bar() { ... }
```

The following simplified declaration of ZooAnimal declares four virtual
functions: `debug()`, `locate()`, `draw()`, and `isOnDisplay()`.

```
#include <iostream.h>
class ZooAnimal {
public:
    ZooAnimal( char *whatIs = "ZooAnimal" )
          : isa( whatIs ) {}
    void isA() { cout<< "\n\t" << isa << "\n"; }
    void setOpen(int status) { isOpen=status; }
    virtual int isOnDisplay() { return isOpen; }
    virtual void debug();
    virtual void draw() = 0;
protected:
    virtual void locate() = 0;
    char *isa;
    char isOpen;
};


void ZooAnimal::debug() {
    isA();
    cout << "\tisOpen: "
         << ((isOnDisplay()) ? "yes" : "no") << endl;
}
```

`debug()`, `locate()`, `draw()`, and `isOnDisplay()` are declared as
member functions of ZooAnimal because they provide a set of routines common
to the entire hierarchy of class types. They are declared as virtual functions
because the actual implementation details are dependent on the class
type and are not known at this time. The base class virtual function serves as
a kind of placeholder for as-yet-undetermined derived class types.

Virtual functions defined in the base class of the hierarchy are often never
intended to be invoked, as is the case with `locate()` and `draw()`. Neither
function makes sense in an abstract class such as ZooAnimal. The class
designer can indicate that a virtual function is undefined for an abstract class

by initializing its declaration to 0.

```
virtual void draw() = 0;
virtual void locate() = 0;
```

   `draw()` and `locate()` are spoken of as *pure virtual functions*. A class with one or more pure virtual functions can be used only as a base class for subsequent derivations. It is illegal to create objects of a class containing pure virtual functions. For example, the following two ZooAnimal definitions result in compile-time errors:

```
ZooAnimal *pz = new ZooAnimal; // error
ZooAnimal za; // error
```

Only an abstract class for which no class instances are intended can declare a pure virtual function.

   The class that first declares a function as virtual must either declare it as a pure virtual function or provide a definition.

- If a definition is provided, it serves as a default instance for a subsequent class derivation should the derived class choose not to provide its own instance of the virtual function.

- If a pure virtual function is declared, the derived class can either define an instance of the function or by default inherit the pure virtual function of its base class. If the class inherits a pure virtual function, it is treated as an abstract class; no objects of the class may exist within the program.

For example, Bear may either provide definitions for `draw()` and `locate()` or else inherit them as pure virtual functions. If we expect class objects of type Bear to be defined, then it cannot inherit the pure virtual instances. However, what if we still wish to defer implementation of `draw()` until a particular species, such as Panda or Grizzly, is derived? Here are three alternative solutions:

1. Define a null instance of the virtual function:

```
class Bear : public ZooAnimal {
public:
    void draw() {}
    // ...
};
```

2. Define an instance whose invocation results in an internal error:

```
void Bear::draw() {
    error( INTERNAL, isa, "draw()" );
}
```

3. Define an instance to log the unexpected behavior, while drawing a generic image of a Bear. That is, keep the system running, but also keep a record of run-time exceptions that need to be handled sometime in the future.

A derived class may provide its own instance of a virtual function or by default inherit the base class instance. In turn, it may introduce virtual functions of its own. Bear, for example, redefines debug(), locate(), and draw(); it inherits the ZooAnimal instance of isOnDisplay(). In addition, Bear defines two new virtual functions, hibernates() and feedingHours().

The Bear definition is simplified to highlight the declaration of virtual functions.

```
class Bear : public ZooAnimal {
public:
    Bear( char *whatIs = "Bear" )
        : ZooAnimal( whatIs ), feedTime( "2:30" )
        {} // intentionally null
    void draw(); // replaces ZooAnimal::draw
    void locate(); // replaces ZooAnimal::locate
    virtual char *feedingHours()
        { return feedTime; }
protected:
    void debug(); // replaces ZooAnimal::debug
    virtual int hibernates() { return 1; }
    char *feedTime;
};
```

The redefinition of a virtual function in a derived class *must match exactly* the name, signature, and return type of the base class instance. The keyword virtual need not be specified (although it may be if the user wishes). The definition is that of an ordinary member function.

```
void Bear::debug()
{
    isA();
    cout << "\tfeedTime: "
        << feedingHours() << endl;
}

void Bear::draw() {/*...code goes here */}
void Bear::locate() {/*...code goes here */}
```

The entire virtual mechanism is handled implicitly by the compiler. The class designer need only specify the keyword virtual for the first definition of each instance.

If the redeclaration in the derived class does not match exactly, the function is not handled as virtual for the derived class. If Bear, for example, declared debug() in either of the following ways,

```
// different return type
void *Bear::debug() {...}

// different signature
void Bear::debug( int ) {...}
```

debug() would not be a virtual function for the Bear class. For example,

```
Bear b;
ZooAnimal &za = b;
za.debug(); // invoke ZooAnimal::debug()
```

A class subsequently derived from Bear, however, can still provide a virtual instance of debug(), even if Bear does not. For example,

```
class Panda : public Bear {
public:
    void debug(); // virtual instance
    // ...
};
```

By exactly matching the virtual declaration of debug(), the Panda instance is also virtual:

```
Panda p;
ZooAnimal &za = p;
za.debug(); // Panda::debug()
```

Notice that the protection levels of two of the virtual functions differ between the base class and the derived class instance. The ZooAnimal instance of locate() is protected, while the Bear instance is public. Similarly, the ZooAnimal instance of debug() is public while the Bear instance is protected.

What, in general, are the protection levels of locate() and debug()? For example, our goal is to write general functions such as

```
void debug( ZooAnimal& z )
{
    // compiler resolves intended instance
    z.debug();
}
```

Since Bear::debug() is protected, does that make the following invocation illegal?

```
main()
{
    // outputs: Bear
    //          feedTime: 2.30
    Bear ursus;
    debug( ursus );
}
```

The answer is no: debug(ursus) is not illegal. The access level of a virtual function is determined by the class type of the pointer or reference through which the member function is invoked. Because debug() is a public member of ZooAnimal, each virtual invocation is treated as public. Note that both this example and the next presume ZooAnimal does not declare any pure virtual functions.

```
main ()
{
    ZooAnimal *pz = new Bear;
    pz->debug(); // invokes Bear::debug()

    pz = new ZooAnimal;
    pz->setOpen(1); // open the zoo
    pz->debug(); // invokes ZooAnimal::debug()
}
```

when compiled, outputs

```
Bear
feedTime: 2:30

ZooAnimal
isOpen: yes
```

Invocations of debug() virtual instances through a Bear class type, however, would all be treated as having protected access. The following invocation would be flagged as an illegal access of a protected class member:

```
main ()
{
    ZooAnimal *pz = new Bear;
    pz->debug(); // invokes Bear::debug()

    Bear *pb = (Bear *) new ZooAnimal; // dangerous

    // illegal: main has no access privilege
    // to the protected members of Bear!
    pb->debug();
}
```

Similarly, `locate()` is a protected member of ZooAnimal while a public member of Bear. Virtual invocations through a Bear pointer or reference would all be treated as having public access. Virtual invocations through a ZooAnimal pointer or reference, however, would all be treated as having protected access. The following invocation is flagged as an illegal access of a protected member unless the nonmember `locate()` is made a friend to ZooAnimal.

```
void locate( ZooAnimal *pz )
{
    // locate() has no access privilege;
    // unless made friend to ZooAnimal
    pz->locate(); // error
}
```

These two examples are chosen to illustrate that although virtual functions are resolved at run time, they still obey the access rules of information hiding. The only anomaly is that the access level of a virtual function is the level specified by the class type through which the call is being invoked.

Bear provides its own instances of three of the four virtual functions ZooAnimal defines; it also defines two additional virtual functions. A Panda class derivation inherits the six virtual functions visible within its base Bear class.

What of the three ZooAnimal virtual functions redefined within Bear? They remain inherited ZooAnimal members and can be invoked explicitly. For example, `debug()` can be reimplemented in the following way:

```
void Bear::debug()
{
    ZooAnimal::debug();
    cout << "Feed time: "
         << feedTime << endl;
}
```

Panda is derived from three base classes, those of Bear, Endangered, and Herbivore. Endangered and Herbivore each define two virtual functions:

```
class Endangered {
public:
    virtual void adjustPopulation( int );
    virtual void highlight( short );
    // ...
};
```

```
class Herbivore {
public:
    virtual void inform( ZooAnimal& );
    virtual void highlight( short );
    // ...
};
```

Panda inherits the ten virtual functions defined within its three base classes. It can provide its own instances of any of its virtual functions. In addition, it can introduce virtual functions of its own.

Panda inherits two virtual functions named highlight() — one from its Endangered derivation and one from its Herbivore derivation. This is a problem only if highlight() is invoked from a Panda class type or if Panda is subsequently an object of derivation. In both cases, a reference to highlight() is ambiguous. For example,

```
Endangered *pe = new Panda;
pe->highlight(); // ok: Endangered::highlight()

Herbivore *ph = new Panda;
ph->highlight(); // ok: Herbivore::highlight()

Panda *pp = new Panda;
pp->highlight(); // error: ambiguous: which instance?

RedPanda : public Panda { ... };
pp = new RedPanda;
pp->highlight(); // error: still ambiguous
```

To prevent the potential ambiguity, Panda defines its own instance of highlight(). See Section 8.3 (page 402) for a discussion of the problem. The following Panda class definition is simplified to highlight the declaration of virtual functions under multiple inheritance.

```
class Panda : public Bear,
              public Endangered,
              public Herbivore
{
public:
    Panda( char *whatIs = "Panda" )
        : Bear( whatIs ) {}
```

```
// class Panda
// continuation of class definition

    virtual int onLoan();
    void inform( ZooAnimal& );
    void draw();
    int debug();
    void locate();
    int hibernates() { return 0; }

protected:
    void highlight( short );
    short cell;
    short onLoan;
};
```

A base class knows of the redefinitions of its virtual functions in subsequent class derivations. The virtual instance invoked is determined by the actual class type of the base class reference or pointer. A base class does not, however, know about virtual functions introduced in subsequent derivations. It is not possible, for example, to invoke hibernate(), introduced by Bear, through a ZooAnimal reference or pointer. The following, for example, is illegal:

```
/* error: hibernate not a member of ZooAnimal
 * argument to hibernate needs to be Bear& */

int hibernate( ZooAnimal &za )
{
    return za.hibernate();
}
```

Bear is the "base class" of the hibernate() virtual function. Only the classes on its branch of the inheritance hierarchy can access it. If hibernate() is an activity common to a wider set of classes in the inheritance hierarchy, then its definition does not belong in Bear. hibernate() must either be moved further up in the hierarchy (in this case becoming a member of ZooAnimal) or else the branches of the hierarchy must be redesigned. In either case, hibernate() needs to be accessible to all the classes within the hierarchy for which hibernation is a common activity.

Table 9.1 lists the active virtual functions within Panda. The second column lists the class in which the active function is defined; the third column, the class in which the virtual function is first defined.

Virtual Function	Active Definition	First Definition
isOnDisplay()	ZooAnimal	ZooAnimal
locate()	Panda	ZooAnimal
draw()	Panda	ZooAnimal
debug()	Panda	ZooAnimal
feedingHours()	Bear	Bear
hibernates()	Bear	Bear
adjustPopulation(int)	Endangered	Endangered
highlight(short)	Panda	Endangered/Herbivore
inform(ZooAnimal&)	Panda	Herbivore
onLoan()	Panda	Panda

Table 9.1 Panda Virtual Functions

The good design of an inheritance hierarchy is difficult. The designer can expect to go through many iterations. Hierarchy design is an area of active research (and some controversy) and as yet is without an agreed upon set of rules.

Exercise 9-1. There is a clearly misplaced virtual function introduced in the definition of Bear. Which virtual function is it? Where should it be placed? Why?

☐

Exercise 9-2. Section 8.3 (page 399) presents first definitions of ZooAnimal, Bear, and Panda. These definitions are used to illustrate the derivation mechanism and do not necessarily represent the best design of a ZooAnimal hierarchy. Redefine these class definitions, including a set of virtual functions, and instances of X(const X&) and operator=(const X&).

☐

Exercise 9-3. Redesign the debug() member function of the Shapes hierarchy described in Section 8.3 (page 403) to be a virtual member function.

☐

Exercise 9-4. Reimplement the nonmember debug() function described in Section 8.6 (page 423) to handle the virtual implementation debug() member function of the Shapes hierarchy.

☐

Exercise 9-5. Implement the `draw()` virtual function for the Shapes hierarchy.

☐

Exercise 9-6. Implement a `reSize()` virtual function for the Shapes hierarchy. ☐

Virtual Destructors

The linked list of ZooAnimals passed to `finalCollage()` is no longer needed once that function is completed. Typically, a `for-loop` of the following sort is added to the end of `finalCollage` to free up storage:

```
for ( ZooAnimal *p = pz->next; p;
                pz = p, p = p->next )
    delete pz;
```

Unfortunately, this strategy does not work. The explicit deletion of `pz` causes the ZooAnimal destructor to be applied to the object to which `pz` points. Each object, however, is not a ZooAnimal but some subsequently derived class type such as Bear; the destructor for the actual class type of the ZooAnimal pointer must somehow be invoked. Any explicit invocation, however, reintroduces all the drawbacks that come with using the representational details of the derivation hierarchy.

```
for ( ZooAnimal *p = pz->next; p;
                pz = p, p = p->next )
    switch ( pz->isA() ) {
        case BEAR:
            // direct invocation of destructor
            ((Bear*)pz)->Bear::~Bear();
            break;

        case PANDA:
            // indirect invocation through delete
            delete (Panda *) pz;
            break;

        // ... more cases go here
    }
```

Although destructors do not share a common name, they can be declared as virtual. The destructor of a class derived from a class that declares its destructor virtual is also virtual. If ZooAnimal declares its destructor to be virtual, then every destructor in the derivation hierarchy will be virtual. For example,

```
class ZooAnimal {
public:
    virtual ~ZooAnimal();
    // ...
};
```

```
/* ok: this now correctly invokes the destructor
 * for the actual derived class type pz addresses
 * -- the actual type's base class destructors
 * are then invoked in turn */

for ( ZooAnimal *p = pz->next; p;
                 pz = p, p = p->next )
        delete pz;
```

Specifying the destructors in a derivation hierarchy as virtual guarantees that the appropriate destructors are invoked whenever delete is applied to a base class pointer. After the destructor of the actual derived type is invoked, the destructors for each of its base classes are invoked in turn in the normal fashion. For example, were pz to address a Panda object, the application of the delete operator invokes the Panda destructor through the virtual mechanism. Following that, the Bear then ZooAnimal destructors, statically resolved, are executed in turn. As a general rule of thumb, therefore, the destructor of an abstract class should always be specified as virtual.

Exercise 9-7. Define the destructors for the Shapes hierarchy as virtual. □

Virtual Function Invocation

A virtual function is invoked through a pointer or reference of a particular class type. The set of potential virtual functions that may be invoked at each call consists of the following:

• The instance defined by the invoking class type.

• Those instances *redefined* by subsequent derivations.

The virtual function instance executed at any particular call is determined by the actual class type addressed by the pointer or reference.

The most inclusive class type through which to invoke a virtual function is the abstract superclass of the derivation hierarchy — in our example, a pointer or reference of type ZooAnimal. ZooAnimal has access to the entire inheritance chain. That is the purpose of defining an abstract superclass.

For the purposes of illustrating the invocation of virtual functions, let us

provide a simplified set of class definitions. ZooAnimal will define two virtual functions, print() and isA(), and a virtual destructor instance.

```
#include <iostream.h>
enum ZooLocs { ZOOANIMAL, BEAR, PANDA };

class ZooAnimal {
public:
    ZooAnimal( char *s = "ZooAnimal" );
    virtual ~ZooAnimal() { delete name; }
    void link( ZooAnimal* );
    virtual void print( ostream& );
    virtual void isA( ostream& );
protected:
    char *name;
    ZooAnimal *next;
};
```

```
#include <string.h>
ZooAnimal::ZooAnimal( char *s ) : next( 0 )
{
    name = new char[ strlen(s) + 1 ];
    strcpy( name, s );
}
```

The idea is to build up a heterogeneous list of ZooAnimal derivations
linked by the member next. The actual class types of the list need not be of
concern to the programmer; the virtual function mechanism will determine
the class type of each element.

The ZooAnimal link() function accepts an argument of type
ZooAnimal* and assigns it to next. It is implemented as follows:

```
void ZooAnimal::link( ZooAnimal *za )
{
    za->next = next;
    next = za;
}
```

isA() and print() are each implemented as virtual functions. Each
subsequent derivation will define its own instances of these two functions.
isA() announces its class type; print() elaborates on the class type representation. Each takes an ostream reference as an argument. Here are the
implementations:

```
void ZooAnimal::isA( ostream& os )
{
    os << "ZooAnimal name: "
       << name << endl;
}


void ZooAnimal::print( ostream& os )
{
    isA( os ); // virtual invocation
}
```

One goal of our design is to support iostream output of any class type that is a member of the ZooAnimal inheritance hierarchy. To achieve that, we must overload the output operator to accept a ZooAnimal reference. This function is implemented as follows:

```
#include <iostream.h>

ostream&
operator <<( ostream& os, ZooAnimal& za )
{
    za.print( os );
    return os;
}
```

The programmer can now direct any member of the ZooAnimal inheritance hierarchy to an output operator and have the correct virtual print() function invoked. We will see an example of this after we define the Bear and Panda class types. Note that the operator function has not been made a friend to ZooAnimal. It does not need to be a friend since its access is limited to the ZooAnimal public interface.

The Bear class definition looks as follows:

```
class Bear : public ZooAnimal {
public:
    Bear( char *s = "Bear", ZooLocs loc = BEAR,
          char *sci = "Ursidae" );
    ~Bear() { delete sciName; }
    void print( ostream& );
    void isA( ostream& );
protected:
    char *sciName; // scientific name
    ZooLocs zooArea;
};
```

```
#include <string.h>
Bear::Bear( char *s, ZooLocs loc, char *sci )
    : ZooAnimal( s ), zooArea( loc ) {
    sciName = new char[ strlen(sci) + 1 ];
    strcpy( sciName, sci );
}
```

Bear introduces two additional data members:

- `sciName`, the scientific name associated with the animal.

- `zooArea`, the general area in the zoo where the animal is housed.

The `isA()` and `print()` virtual instances that Bear provides reflect its representation. They are implemented as follows:

```
void Bear::isA( ostream& os )
{
    // static invocation of ZooAnimal::isA()
    ZooAnimal::isA( os );

    os << "\tscientific name:\t";
    os << sciName << endl;
}


// for simplicity of the example, these are hardcoded */

static char *locTable[] = {
    "The entire animal display area",   // ZOOANIMAL
    "NorthWest: B1: area Brown",          // BEAR
    "NorthWest: B1.P: area BrownSpots"  // PANDA

    // ... and so on
};


void Bear::print( ostream& os )
{
    // static invocation of ZooAnimal::print()
    ZooAnimal::print( os );

    os << "\tZoo Area Location:\n\t";
    os << locTable[ zooArea ] << endl;
}
```

There are three cases in which an invocation of a virtual function is resolved statically at compile time:

1. When a virtual function is invoked through an object of the class type. In the following code fragment, for example, the `isA()` function invoked

through the ZooAnimal class object za is *always* resolved statically. The isA() function invoked through the dereferenced pointer pz, however, is still resolved as a virtual call.

```
#include "ZooAnimal.h"

main() {
     ZooAnimal za;
     ZooAnimal *pz;

     // ...

     za.isA( cout );      // nonvirtual invocation
     (*pz).isA( cout ); // virtual invocation
}
```

2. When a virtual function is explicitly invoked through a pointer or reference using the class scope operator. For example,

```
#include <iostream.h>
#include "Bear.h"
#include "ZooAnimal.h"

main() {
     Bear yogi ( "cartoon Bear", BEAR,
                 "ursus cartoonus" );
     ZooAnimal circus( "circusZooAnimal" );
     ZooAnimal *pz;

     pz = &circus;
     cout << "virtual: ZooAnimal::print()\n";
     pz->print( cout );

     pz = &yogi;
     cout << "\nvirtual: Bear::print()\n";
     pz->print( cout );

     cout << "\nnonvirtual: ZooAnimal::print()\n";
     cout << "note: isA() is invoked virtually\n";
     pz->ZooAnimal::print( cout );
}
```

When compiled and executed, this program generates the following output:

```
virtual: ZooAnimal::print()
ZooAnimal name: circusZooAnimal

virtual: Bear::print()
ZooAnimal name: cartoon Bear
        scientific name:        ursus cartoonus
        Zoo Area Location:
        NorthWest: B1: area Brown

nonvirtual: ZooAnimal::print()
note: isA() is invoked virtually
ZooAnimal name: cartoon Bear
        scientific name:        ursus cartoonus
```

3. When a virtual function is invoked within either the constructor or the
    destructor of a base class. In both cases, the base class instance of the vir-
    tual function is called since the derived class object is either not yet con-
    structed or already destructed.

Panda introduces two additional data members: indName, the name of
the individual animal, and cell, the cage location in which the animal is
housed. Here is the Panda class definition:

```
#include <iostream.h>

class Panda : public Bear {
public:
    Panda( char *nm, int room, char *s = "Panda",
           char *sci = "Ailuropoda Melaoleuca",
           ZooLocs loc = PANDA );
    ~Panda() { delete indName; }
    void print( ostream& );
    void isA( ostream& );
protected:
    char *indName; // name of individual animal
    int cell;
};

#include <string.h>
Panda::Panda ( char *nm, int room, char *s,
              char *sci, ZooLocs loc )
    : Bear( s, loc, sci ), cell( room ) {
    indName = new char[ strlen(nm) + 1 ];
    strcpy( indName, nm );
}
```

The isA() and print() virtual instances that Panda provides reflect its
representation. They are implemented as follows:

```
void Panda::isA( ostream& os )
{
    Bear::isA( os );
    os << "\twe call our friend:\t";
    os << indName << endl;
}


void Panda::print( ostream& os )
{
    Bear::print( os );
    os << "\tRoom Location:\t";
    os << cell << endl;
}
```

Let's step through a number of examples to get a feel for how things work. Our first example illustrates the virtual invocation of print() through a ZooAnimal reference. Each class object is passed to the overloaded instance of the output operator ("<<"). Each call of

```
za.print( os );
```

within the output operator instance invokes the virtual instance defined by the actual class type of za.

```
#include <iostream.h>
#include "ZooAnimal.h"
#include "Bear.h"
#include "Panda.h"

ZooAnimal circus( "circusZooAnimal" );
Bear yogi("cartoon Bear",BEAR,"ursus cartoonus");
Panda yinYang("Yin Yang",1001,"Giant Panda");

main() {
    cout << "Invocation by a ZooAnimal object:\n"
         << circus << endl;

    cout << "\nInvocation by a Bear object:\n"
         << yogi << endl;

    cout << "\nInvocation by a Panda object:\n"
         << yinYang << endl;
};
```

When compiled and executed, the program generates the following output:

```
Invocation by a ZooAnimal object:
ZooAnimal name: circusZooAnimal


Invocation by a Bear object:
ZooAnimal name: cartoon Bear
        scientific name:        ursus cartoonus
        Zoo Area Location:
        NorthWest: B1: area Brown


Invocation by a Panda object:
ZooAnimal name: Giant Panda
        scientific name:        Ailuropoda Melaoleuca
        we call our friend:     Yin Yang
        Zoo Area Location:
        NorthWest: B1.P: area BrownSpots
        Room Location:  1001
```

This next example illustrates the direct manipulation of pointers to class objects. It invokes the `isA()` virtual function.

```cpp
#include <iostream.h>
#include "ZooAnimal.h"
#include "Bear.h"
#include "Panda.h"

ZooAnimal circus( "circusZooAnimal" );
Bear yogi("cartoon Bear",BEAR,"ursus cartoonus");
Panda yinYang("Yin Yang",1001,"Giant Panda");

main() {
    ZooAnimal *pz;

    pz = &circus;
    cout << "virtual: ZooAnimal::isA():\n";
    pz->isA( cout );

    pz = &yogi;
    cout << "\nvirtual: Bear::isA():\n";
    pz->isA( cout );

    pz = &yinYang;
    cout << "\nvirtual: Panda::isA():\n";
    pz->isA( cout );
}
```

When compiled and executed, the program generates the following output:

```
virtual: ZooAnimal::isA():
ZooAnimal name: circusZooAnimal

virtual: Bear::isA():
ZooAnimal name: cartoon Bear
        scientific name:         ursus cartoonus

virtual: Panda::isA():
ZooAnimal name: Giant Panda
        scientific name:         Ailuropoda Melaoleuca
        we call our friend:      Yin Yang
```

In the next example, the actual class type addressed by pz is known at compile time. Let's override the virtual mechanism and invoke each function statically:

```
#include <iostream.h>
#include "ZooAnimal.h"
#include "Bear.h"
#include "Panda.h"

ZooAnimal circus( "circusZooAnimal" );
Bear yogi("cartoon Bear",BEAR,"ursus cartoonus");
Panda yinYang("Yin Yang",1001,"Giant Panda");

main() {
    ZooAnimal *pz = &yinYang;
    cout << "Nonvirtual invocation of Panda::isA():\n";
    ((Panda*)pz) ->Panda::isA( cout );

    pz = &yogi;
    cout << "\nNonvirtual invocation of Bear::isA():\n";
    ((Bear*)pz) ->Bear::isA( cout );
}
```

The nonvirtual invocation of Panda::isA() through a ZooAnimal pointer requires an explicit cast. ZooAnimal has no knowledge of its subsequent Panda class derivation; such knowledge is part of the virtual mechanism, not part of the base class itself. When compiled and executed, the program generates the following output:

```
Nonvirtual invocation of Panda::isA():
ZooAnimal name: Giant Panda
        scientific name:        Ailuropoda Melaoleuca
        we call our friend:     Yin Yang

Nonvirtual invocation of Bear::isA():
ZooAnimal name: cartoon Bear
        scientific name:        ursus cartoonus
```

This last example prints out a heterogeneous list of ZooAnimal pointers. It is implemented using the following nonmember print() function — because it must access the nonpublic ZooAnimal data member next, print() must be declared a friend to ZooAnimal.

```
#include <iostream.h>
#include "ZooAnimal.h"

void print( ZooAnimal *pz, ostream &os = cout )
{
    while ( pz ) {
        pz->print( os );
        os << endl;
        pz = pz->next;
    }
}
```

For our program example, we need a ZooAnimal pointer to head the linked list:

```
ZooAnimal *headPtr = 0;
```

main() is defined as follows:

```
#include <iostream.h>
#include "ZooAnimal.h"

extern ZooAnimal *makeList( ZooAnimal* );
ZooAnimal *headPtr = 0;

main() {
  cout<< "A Program to Illustrate Virtual Functions\n";
  headPtr = makeList( headPtr );
  print( headPtr );
}
```

makeList(), in turn, is defined as follows:

```
#include <iostream.h>
#include "ZooAnimal.h"
#include "Bear.h"
#include "Panda.h"

ZooAnimal circus( "circusZooAnimal" );
Bear yogi("cartoon Bear",BEAR,"ursus cartoonus");
Panda yinYang("Yin Yang",1001,"Giant Panda");
Panda rocky("Rocky",943,"Red Panda","Ailurus fulgens");

ZooAnimal *makeList( ZooAnimal *ptr )
{
    // for simplicity, hand code list
    ptr = &yinYang;
    ptr->link( &circus );
    ptr->link( &yogi );
    ptr->link( &rocky );
    return ptr;
}
```

When compiled and executed, the program generates the following output:

```
A Program to Illustrate Virtual Functions
ZooAnimal name: Giant Panda
        scientific name:        Ailuropoda Melaoleuca
        we call our friend:     Yin Yang
        Zoo Area Location:
        NorthWest: B1.P: area BrownSpots
        Room Location:   1001


ZooAnimal name: Red Panda
        scientific name:        Ailurus fulgens
        we call our friend:     Rocky
        Zoo Area Location:
        NorthWest: B1.P: area BrownSpots
        Room Location:   943


ZooAnimal name: cartoon Bear
        scientific name:         ursus cartoonus
        Zoo Area Location:
        NorthWest: B1: area Brown

ZooAnimal name: circusZooAnimal
```

Except for makeList(), the program is completely general, taking no account of the implementation details of the class objects, the member functions, or the inheritance hierarchy. Although simplistic, the example captures some of the spirit of object-oriented programming.

Exercise 9-8. Implement a nonmember `draw()` function which takes an argument of type `Shape*`. Have it draw a circle, a right triangle, and a rectangle.

□

Exercise 9-9. Implement a nonmember `reSize()` function which takes an argument of type `Shape&` (it will need a size argument as well). `draw()`, `reSize()`, then `draw()` a circle, an equilateral triangle, and a square.

□

Exercise 9-10. Add a virtual `draw()` instance which writes to a Screen class object.

□

Exercise 9-11. Implement the virtual functions `save()`, which writes an object of the Shapes hierarchy to an ostream, and `restore()`, which reads in the output of `save()`. □

Exercise 9-12. The list class implemented in Section 3.12 (page 150) is an unordered list. Derive an ordered list class, imposing an ascending order. □

Exercise 9-13. Derive an ordered list class with only one item of each value entered on the list. Each item contains a reference count of occurrences. Removal of an item decrements its reference count. When the count reaches 0, the item is actually deleted from the list. □

9.2 Virtual Base Classes

Although a base class may legally appear only once in a derivation list, a base class can appear multiple times within a derivation hierarchy. This gives rise to a form of member ambiguity.

   For example, there has been a debate, sometimes heated, within zoological circles for more than 100 years as to whether the Panda belongs to the Raccoon or the Bear family. From the computer science point of view, the best solution is to derive Panda from both families.

```
class Panda : public Bear, public Raccoon { ... }
```

Panda inherits a ZooAnimal base class from both Bear and Raccoon; that is, there are two base class parts to a Panda. Declaration of a Panda class object results in the invocation of two ZooAnimal constructors, in the following order:

```
ZooAnimal();   // base class of Bear
Bear();        // first Panda base class
ZooAnimal();   // base class of Raccoon
Raccoon();     // second Panda base class
Panda();       // derived class constructor is always last
```

For the purposes of this discussion, let's provide a simplified definition of ZooAnimal:

```
class ZooAnimal {   // simplified definition
public:
    void locate();
protected:
    short zooArea;
};


class Bear : public ZooAnimal    { /* ... */ };
class Raccoon : public ZooAnimal { /* ... */ };
```

Panda contains two sets of ZooAnimal data members: one `zooArea` data member inherited through Raccoon and one inherited through Bear. Figure 9.1 illustrates the class object layout of this Panda class.

`zooArea` cannot be directly accessed from within Panda. We must distinguish between the two instances of `zooArea`. The class scope operator can be used to disambiguate which instance is intended. Since the ambiguity rests in the multiple inclusion of the ZooAnimal base class part, however, writing `ZooAnimal::zooArea` is no less ambiguous than simply writing `zooArea`. To resolve the ambiguity, the qualification must indicate which of the two ZooAnimal instances is meant, either the one inherited through Bear or the one inherited through Raccoon; that is, either `Bear::zooArea` or `Raccoon::zooArea`. For example,

```
Panda::getArea()
{   // qualified reference to prevent ambiguity
    // BEAR is an enumeration constant
    return( (isA() == BEAR)
            ? Bear::zooArea : Raccoon::zooArea );
}
```

There is only one instance of `ZooAnimal::locate()`. Within Panda, both `locate()` and `ZooAnimal::locate()` access the intended inherited member function. Both, however, are flagged as ambiguous. Why?

Panda contains two ZooAnimal base class objects, one or the other of which must be bound to the function invocation. (See Section 5.4 (page 233)

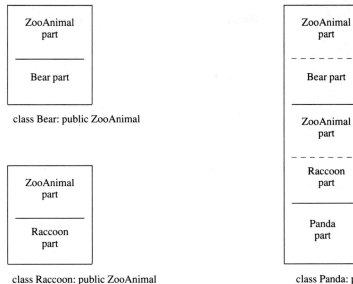

Figure 9.1 Multiple Inclusion of a Base Class

for a discussion of the binding of a member function and the invoking class object through the `this` pointer.) It is the programmer's responsibility to indicate which base class object, the one inherited through Bear or the one inherited through Raccoon. Once again, this is accomplished using the class scope operator. The programmer must indicate which class object: `Bear::locate()` or `Raccoon::locate`.

```
locate( Panda *p ) {
    switch( p->isA() ) {
        case BEAR:
            p->Bear::locate();
            break;

        case RACCOON:
            p->Raccoon::locate();
            break;
        }
    }
```

Under certain applications, the occurrence of multiple base class instances is desirable. In this case, however, it is not.

These are unnecessary ambiguities. The user has to know the details of the multiple derivations so as to make the disambiguating calls. In addition, the space required for the additional base class instances is wasteful.

Panda requires only one base class instance of ZooAnimal. Conceptually, Panda can be thought of as a directed acyclic graph (DAG) with a shared ZooAnimal base class instance. The default inheritance mechanism, however, defines a tree derivation hierarchy in which each occurrence of a base class generates a base class instance (see Figure 9.2).

It is necessary to find a way of overriding the default inheritance mechanism. It should be possible to specify a shared base class within a derivation hierarchy (that is, to define a DAG structure). Otherwise, a class of users (possibly quite small) will be penalized by its use of multiple inheritance.

Virtual base classes, a method of overriding the default inheritance mechanism, allow the class designer to specify a shared base class. Regardless of how often a virtual base class may occur in the derivation hierarchy, only one instance is generated. Panda, for example, would contain only one, shared ZooAnimal base class. Class member access would no longer be ambiguous.

Virtual Base Class Definition

A base class is specified as virtual by modifying its declaration with the keyword `virtual`. For example, the following declaration makes ZooAnimal a virtual base class of Bear and Raccoon.

```
// public, virtual keyword placement is not significant
class Bear : public virtual ZooAnimal    { /* ... */ };
class Raccoon : virtual public ZooAnimal { /* ... */ };
```

The definition of ZooAnimal need not be modified in order to specify it as a virtual base class. Here is the definition of ZooAnimal we will work with in our discussion of virtual base classes:

```
class ZooAnimal {   // simplified definition
public:
    ZooAnimal(){ zooArea = 0; name = 0; }
    ZooAnimal( char*, short );
    void locate();
protected:
    short zooArea;
    char *name;
};
```

The use of Bear and Raccoon class objects is unchanged. A virtual base class can be initialized in the same way as a nonvirtual base class:

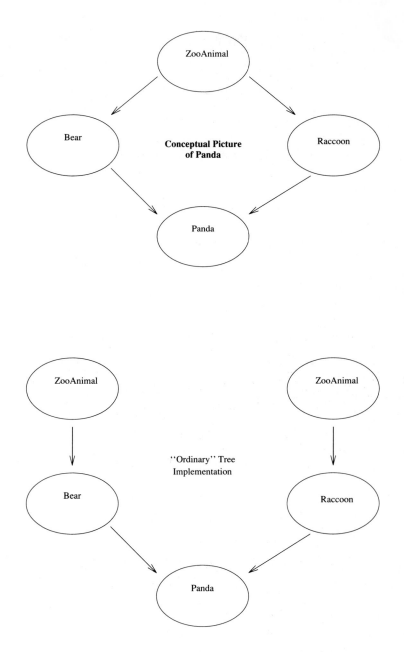

Figure 9.2 NonVirtual Multiple Inheritance

```
Bear::Bear( char *nm)
     : ZooAnimal( nm, BEAR ) { ... }

Raccoon::Raccoon( char *nm)
     : ZooAnimal( nm, RACCOON ) { ... }
```

The declaration of Panda looks the same as its nonvirtual instance:

```
class Panda: public Bear, public Raccoon { ... };
```

Because both Bear and Raccoon have declared ZooAnimal as a virtual base class, however, each Panda class object contains only one ZooAnimal instance.

Ordinarily, a derived class can explicitly initialize only its immediate base classes. In a nonvirtual derivation of ZooAnimal, for example, Panda could not name ZooAnimal in the initialization list of its constructor. Virtual base classes, however, are an exception. The reason why is as follows.

Panda contains a single ZooAnimal instance shared between Raccoon and Bear. Raccoon and Bear, however, both explicitly initialize ZooAnimal. The Panda instance cannot be initialized twice.

A virtual base class is initialized by its *most derived* class. Panda, in this case, is more derived than either Raccoon or Bear. Panda can explicitly initialize ZooAnimal in the initialization list of its constructor. If its constructor does not explicitly initialize ZooAnimal, the default ZooAnimal constructor is invoked. The ZooAnimal initializations of Raccoon and Bear are never applied to the ZooAnimal portion of a Panda class object.

A Panda constructor might be defined as follows:

```
Panda::Panda( char *nm )
     : ZooAnimal( nm, PANDA ),
     Bear( nm ), Raccoon( nm ) { ... }
```

If the Panda constructor is defined as follows,

```
Panda::Panda( char *nm )
     : Bear( nm ), Raccoon( nm ) { ... }
```

the default ZooAnimal constructor is invoked.

Virtual Base Class Member Access

Each Raccoon and Bear class object maintains its own set of inherited ZooAnimal members, which are accessed exactly like the inherited members of a nonvirtual derivation. An individual reading a program's code could not distinguish between the use of an object of a virtual and a nonvirtual base class derivation; the difference lies in the method of allocating the base class part.

In a nonvirtual derivation, each derived class object contains a contiguous base and a derived class part (Figure 8.4 in Section 8.6 (page 419) illustrating the object layout of a derived class object). A Bear class object, for example, has a ZooAnimal base and a Bear part. In a virtual derivation, each derived class object contains a derived part and a pointer to the virtual base class part. The virtual base class is not contained within the derived class object. The class model of a virtual derivation for the Bear, Raccoon, and Panda class is illustrated in Figure 9.3.

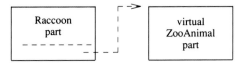

class Raccoon : public virtual ZooAnimal

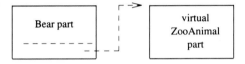

class Bear : public virtual ZooAnimal

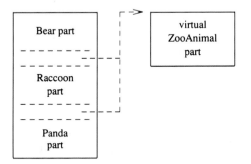

class Panda : public Bear, public Raccoon

Figure 9.3 Virtual Base Class Representation

A virtual base class obeys the same public and private rules as a nonvirtual derivation:

• The inherited members of a public virtual derivation retain their same public and protected access levels in the derived class.

- The inherited members of a private virtual derivation become private members in the derived class.

What happens when a once-removed derivation, such as Panda, includes both a public *and* a private instance of a virtual base class? For example,

```
class ZooAnimal {
public:
    void locate();
protected:
    short zooArea;
};


class Bear : public virtual ZooAnimal { ... };
class Raccoon : private virtual ZooAnimal { ... };


class Panda : public Bear, public Raccoon { ... };
```

Because ZooAnimal is a virtual base class, Panda inherits only one copy of `zooArea` and `locate()`. The question is whether Panda is allowed access to these members. Along the public path of the inheritance, Panda can access the two ZooAnimal members. These members, however, are not accessible to Panda along the private path of the inheritance. Which path predominates in a virtual derivation? Is the following call legal?

```
Panda p;
p.locate();
```

Yes, the call is legal. The public path always predominates. Panda can access both `zooArea` and `locate()`. The shared virtual base class instance always assumes the most accessible level of protection occurring within the set of its virtual derivations within the class hierarchy.

Dominance

Let's redefine our Bear class to provide its own instance of the ZooAnimal members `locate()` and `zooArea`.

```
class Bear : public virtual ZooAnimal {
public:
    void locate();
protected:
    short zooArea;
};
```

References to these identifiers through a Bear class instance now resolve to these members. For example,

```
Bear pooh;
pooh.locate(); // Bear::locate()
```

while references through a Raccoon class instance still resolve to the inherited ZooAnimal members:

```
Raccoon rocky;
rocky.locate(); // ZooAnimal::locate()
```

Ordinarily — that is, under a nonvirtual derivation of ZooAnimal — Panda, derived below,

```
class Panda: public Raccoon,
             public Bear {};
```

cannot directly reference either member without generating an error message:

```
// nonvirtual derivation

Panda tui_li;
tui_li.locate(); // error: ambiguous ...
```

Which locate() member is intended — the member inherited through the Raccoon base class or that inherited through Bear? The compiler has no basis on which to choose and so flags the reference as ambiguous.

Under a virtual derivation, however, the compiler does have a basis on which to choose — if, that is, the member in question is defined within a shared virtual base class. In this case, the most derived instance of the member (or nested type) is said to *dominate* the inheritance chain. There is no longer an ambiguity. The dominant member is chosen. In our example,

```
tui_li.locate(); // Bear::locate() dominates
```

the Bear instance dominates the Panda class hierarchy and therefore is the member selected.

Constructor and Destructor Ordering

Virtual base classes are constructed before nonvirtual base classes regardless of where they appear either in the base derivation list or the derived class hierarchy. For example, in the following TeddyBear derivation, there are two virtual base classes: the immediate ToyAnimal virtual base class and the ZooAnimal virtual base class from which Bear is derived.

```
class Character {...};
class BookCharacter : public Character {...};

class TeddyBear : public BookCharacter,
                  public Bear,
                  public virtual ToyAnimal {...};
```

```
TeddyBear pooh;
```

First, the constructor for the immediate ToyAnimal virtual base class is invoked. If a class has multiple immediate virtual base classes, the associated constructors are invoked in the order the classes appear within the base derivation list.

After that, the constructors for any virtual base classes occurring within the TeddyBear class hierarchy are invoked — in this case, there is only the ZooAnimal instance. Were Character, however, a virtual base class of BookCharacter, then its constructor, too, would be invoked. The class hierarchy is searched in the order of the base derivation list for the presence of virtual base classes. Therefore, if Character and ZooAnimal were both virtual base classes, the order of constructor invocations would be Character then ZooAnimal.

Once all the virtual base class constructors are invoked, the remaining base class constructors are invoked in the order of the base derivation list. The constructor order for TeddyBear, then, is as follows:

```
ToyAnimal();      // immediate virtual base
ZooAnimal();      // Bear's virtual base
Character();      // BookCharacter's nonvirtual base
BookCharacter();  // immediate nonvirtual base
Bear();           // immediate nonvirtual base
TeddyBear();      // derived class constructor
```

Following invocation of the base class constructors, member class constructors are invoked in the order the member class objects are declared. The order of destructor calls is always the reverse order from that of the constructor calls.

Mixing Virtual and Nonvirtual Instances

When a derivation contains both virtual and nonvirtual instances of a base class, one base class object is created for each nonvirtual instance and another base class object is created for all virtual instances. For example, if Endangered were modified to be a nonvirtual derivation of ZooAnimal, Panda would contain two ZooAnimal instances, the virtual instance from Bear and Raccoon and the nonvirtual Endangered instance.

Is this a good design choice? In general, it is hard to see how it might be. Ambiguity as to which member is being accessed is reintroduced into the design — in effect disabling the interface defined by the class. The complexity of the multiple instances, if it does not confuse the designer of the class, is likely to confuse those who later have to maintain the design.

Summary

The inheritance mechanism, by default, defines a tree derivation hierarchy in which each occurrence of a base class generates a base class instance. Virtual base classes provide a method of overriding this default mechanism. Regardless of how often a virtual base class may occur in a derivation hierarchy, only one instance of the virtual base class is generated. A virtual base class serves as a single, shared instance. In our example, ZooAnimal is a virtual base class of both Bear and Raccoon. Panda, derived from both Bear and Raccoon, contains a single shared instance of ZooAnimal.

9.3 Template Classes Under Inheritance

A template class can serve either as an explicit base class

```
class IntStack : private Array<int> {};
```

as a derived class with a nontemplate base class

```
template <class Type>
class Derived : public Base {};
```

or as both

```
template <class Type>
class Array_RC :
    public virtual Array<Type> {};
```

In the first example, the integer instantiation of the template Array class serves as a private base class of the nontemplate IntStack class. In the second example, the nontemplate Base class serves as the base class of each template Derived class instantiation. In the third example, each instantiation of the template Array_RC class has the associated template Array class instantiation as its base class. For example,

```
Array_RC<int> ia;
```

generates an integer instance of both the Array and Array_RC class.

When serving as a base class, a template class must be qualified with its full parameter list. Given the following template class definition, for example,

```
template <class T> class Base {};
```

one writes

```
template <class Type>
    class Derived : public Base<Type>{};
```

not

```
// error: which Base instantiation?
template <class Type>
    class Derived : public Base{};
```

In the next section, the template Array class defined in Chapter 7 serves as a virtual base class to a range-checking, sorted, and sorted, range-checking set of derivations. The original Array class definition, however, is not suitable for derivation:

- All its data members and auxiliary functions are private, not protected.

- None of the type-dependent functions, such as the subscript operator, are specified as virtual.

Does this mean that our original implementation was wrong? No. It was correct insofar as we understood it. At the time of the original template Array class implementation, we hadn't realized the need for specialized Array subtypes. Now that we do, however, we need to revise the Array class definition (the member function implementation remains the same). This new Array class definition is listed in Figure 9.4

A Range-Checking Array Class Derivation

In the try_array() function used to exercise our earlier implementation of the template Array class, there is the following two statement sequence:

```
int index = iA.find( find_val );
Type value = iA[ index ];
```

find() returns the index of the first occurrence of find_val, or −1 if the value does not occur within the array. This code is incorrect because it does not test for a possible return value of −1. Since −1 falls outside the array boundary, each initialization of value is potentially invalid; each execution of our program is potentially in error.

The programmer can defend against this by testing the index prior to its application and, if in error, raising a program exception. For example,

```
#ifndef ARRAY_H
#define ARRAY_H

#include <iostream.h>

// forward declaration for operator<<()
template <class Type> class Array;

template <class Type> ostream&
    operator<<(ostream&,Array<Type>&);

const int ArraySize = 12;

template <class Type>
class Array {
public:
    Array(int sz=ArraySize) { init(0,sz); }
    Array(const Type *ar, int sz) { init(ar,sz); }
    Array(const Array &iA) { init(iA.ia,iA.size); }
    virtual ~Array() { delete [] ia; }

    Array& operator=(const Array&);
    int getSize() { return size; }
    virtual void grow();

    virtual void print(ostream& = cout);

    virtual Type& operator[](int ix) { return ia[ix]; }
    virtual void sort(int,int);
    virtual int find(Type);
    virtual Type min();
    virtual Type max();

protected:
    void swap(int,int);
    void init(const Type*, int);

    int size;
    Type *ia
};

#endif
```

Figure 9.4 The Template Array Class

```
int index = iA.find( find_val );
assert( index >= 0 && index < iA.getSize());
Type value = iA[ index ];
```

Alternatively, the Array class itself can assume responsibility for testing the correctness of an index prior to each use. This has a number of impressive benefits:

- Array boundary errors are guaranteed not to go undetected for users relying on the public interface of the class.

- Array boundary exceptions are now handled uniformly across applications.

- The code for handling an array boundary exception is now centralized rather than scattered throughout user code.

This strategy has one significant drawback — range-checking can significantly impact the run-time performance of an application. Each subscript operation, for example, must now not only return the referenced array element, but must first compare the index against both a minimum and maximum bound. For some applications, the performance slowdown outweighs the safety benefits. For others, the trade-off between speed and safety is acceptable. To accommodate both user groups, we can abstract the range-checking facility into a specialized subtype derivation of Array. Here is its declaration (it is placed in a header file named Array_RC.h):

```
#ifndef ARRAY_RC_H
#define ARRAY_RC_H

#include "Array.h"

template <class Type>
class Array_RC : public virtual Array<Type> {
public:
    Array_RC(int sz=ArraySize)
        : Array<Type>(sz) {}

    Array_RC(const Array_RC& r);
    Array_RC(const Type *ar,int sz);
    Type& operator[](int ix);
};

#endif
```

Within the definition of the derived class, each reference of the template base class type specifier must be fully qualified with its formal parameter list. One writes

```
Array_RC(int sz=ArraySize)
     : Array<Type>(sz) {}
```

not

```
// error: Array is not a type specifier
Array_RC(int sz=ArraySize) : Array(sz) {}
```

The only specialized behavior of the Array_RC class is the range-checking performed by its subscript operator. Otherwise, the Array class interface can be reused without modification. However, since constructors are *not* inherited, the Array_RC class defines a set of three constructors that preserve the Array class interface for the initialization of objects. The virtual derivation anticipates a subsequent multiple derivation that we will look at later. Here is the full implementation (it is placed in a file named Array_RC.c):

```
#include "Array_RC.h"
#include "Array.c"
#include <assert.h>

template <class Type>
Array_RC<Type>::Array_RC(const Array_RC<Type>& r)
        : Array<Type>(r) {}

template <class Type>
Array_RC<Type>::Array_RC(const Type *ar,int sz)
        : Array<Type>(ar,sz) {}

template <class Type>
Type &Array_RC<Type>::operator[](int ix) {
        assert(ix >= 0 && ix < size);
        return ia[ix];
}
```

Each instantiation of Array_RC generates an associated Array class instance. For example,

```
Array_RC<String> sa;
```

generates both a String Array_RC and an associated String Array instance. The following program reruns try_array() (see Section 7.9 (page 385) for the implementation), passing it objects of the Array_RC subtype. If our implementation is correct, the boundary violation will be caught.

```
#include "Array_RC.c"
#include "try_array.c"

main()
{
    static int ia[10] = { 12,7,14,9,128,17,6,3,27,5 };
    Array_RC<int> iA(ia,10);

    cout << "template Array_RC<int> class" << endl;
    try_array(iA);

    return 0;
}
```

When compiled and executed, the program generates the following output:

```
template Array_RC<int> class

try_array: initial array values:
( 10 )< 12, 7, 14, 9, 128, 17
        6, 3, 27, 5 >

try_array: after assignments:
( 10 )< 128, 7, 14, 9, 128, 128
        6, 3, 27, 3 >

try_array: memberwise initialization
( 10 )< 128, 7, 14, 9, 128, 128
        6, 3, 27, 3 >

try_array: after memberwise copy
( 10 )< 128, 7, 128, 9, 128, 128
        6, 3, 27, 3 >

try_array: after grow
( 16 )< 128, 7, 128, 9, 128, 128
        6, 3, 27, 3, 0, 0
        0, 0, 0, 0 >

value to find: 5           index returned: -1
Assertion failed: ix >= 0 && ix < size
```

A Sorted Array Class Derivation

An array that is intended primarily for lookup is best stored in sorted order. The worst-case search time for a value in an unsorted array requires that the entire array be examined. On average, the search requires that half the elements be examined. When the number of elements in an array is large, this can be quite expensive. A better search time can be gained by using a binary search algorithm — if the array is guaranteed to be in sorted order. Both the average and worst-case time for a binary search is $log\ n$, where n represents the number of elements in the array. This is a significant gain provided that the array does not constantly have to be resorted. Figure 9.5 contains the template class derivation of Array_Sort (the code is placed in a header file named `Array_S.h`).

Each reference to the base Array class must specify the complete parameter list of the class.

```
Array<Type>::print(os);
```

invokes the base class `print()` function for the associated Array class instance of each Array_Sort instantiation. For example,

```
Array_Sort<String> sas;
```

instantiates both a String Array_Sort and a String Array class instance.

```
cout << sas;
```

instantiates the String Array instance of the output operator, to which `sas` is passed. Within the operator, the call

```
ar.print(os);
```

invokes the String Array_Sort virtual instance of `print()`. First, `check_bit()` is invoked. That done, the String Array instance of `print()` is statically invoked.

The member functions defined outside the class definition are placed in a file named `Array_S.c`. The declaration can look alarmingly complex due to the template syntax. However, except for the parameter lists, the declaration is the same as for a nontemplate class:

```
#ifndef ARRAY_S_H_
#define ARRAY_S_H_

#include "Array.h"

template <class Type>
class Array_Sort : public virtual Array<Type> {
protected:
    void set_bit()   { dirty_bit = 1; }
    void clear_bit() { dirty_bit = 0; }
    void check_bit() {
      if (dirty_bit) {
          sort(0,size-1); clear_bit(); }
    }

public:
    Array_Sort(const Array_Sort&);
    Array_Sort(int sz=ArraySize)
        : Array<Type>( sz )
        { clear_bit(); }

    Array_Sort(const Type* arr, int sz)
        : Array<Type>(arr, sz)
        { sort(0,size-1); clear_bit(); }

    Type& operator[](int ix)
        { set_bit(); return ia[ix]; }

    void print(ostream& os = cout)
        { check_bit(); Array<Type>::print(os); }

    Type min() { check_bit(); return ia[0]; }
    Type max() { check_bit(); return ia[size-1]; }

    int is_dirty() const { return dirty_bit; }
    int find(Type);
    void grow();

protected:
    char dirty_bit;
};

#endif
```

Figure 9.5 class Array_Sort Header File

```
template <class Type>
Array_Sort<Type>::
Array_Sort(const Array_Sort<Type> &as)
    : Array<Type>( as )
{
    // note: as.check_bit() does not work!
    if ( as.is_dirty() )
        sort( 0, size-1 );
    clear_bit();
}
```

Each use of the template name as a type specifier must be qualified with its full parameter list. We write

```
template <class Type>
Array_Sort<Type>::
Array_Sort(const Array_Sort<Type> &as)
```

and not

```
template <class Type>
Array_Sort<Type>::
Array_Sort<Type>( // error: not type specifier
```

because the second occurrence of Array_Sort serves as the name of the function and *not* as a type_specifier.

The reason we write

```
if ( as.is_dirty() )
    sort( 0, size );
```

rather than

```
as.check_bit();
```

is two-fold. The first reason is type-safety: check_bit() is a nonconst member function — it modifies its associated class object. The argument as is passed as a reference to a constant object. A call of check_bit() on as violates its constness and is flagged as an error at compile time.

The second reason is that the copy constructor is not concerned with the array associated with as other than to determine if the newly created Array_Sort object needs to be sorted. The associated dirty_bit data member of the new Array_Sort object is not yet initialized, remember: When the body of the Array_Sort constructor begins, only the array and size members inherited from the Array class have as yet been initialized. The Array_Sort constructor must both initialize its additional data members (clear_bit()) and enforce any specialized semantics of its subtype (sort()). An alternative implementation of the Array_Sort constructor might be the following:

```
// an alternative implementation
template <class Type>
Array_Sort<Type>::
Array_Sort(const Array_Sort<Type> &as)
    : Array<Type>( as )
{
    dirty_bit = as.dirty_bit;
    check_bit();
}
```

Here is an implementation of the grow() member function. The strategy is to reuse the inherited Array class instance to allocate the additional memory, then re-sort the array elements and clear the dirty_bit data member:

```
template <class Type>
void Array_Sort<Type>::grow() {
    Array<Type>::grow();
    sort( 0, size-1 );
    clear_bit();
}
```

Here is a binary search implementation of the Array_Sort instance of find():

```
template <class Type>
int Array_Sort<Type>::find(Type val) {
    int low = 0;
    int high = size-1;
    check_bit();

    while ( low <= high ) {
        int mid = (low + high)/2;
        if (val == ia[mid])
            return mid;
        if (val < ia[mid])
            high = mid-1;
        else low = mid+1;
    }
    return -1;
}
```

Let's try out the Array_Sort class implementation using the try_array() function. The following program tests both an integer and class String instantiation of the Array_Sort class.

```
#include "Array_S.c"
#include "try_array.c"
#include "String.h"

main()
{
    static int ia[10] = { 12,7,14,9,128,17,6,3,27,5 };
    static String sa[7] = { "Eeyore", "Pooh", "Tigger",
        "Piglet", "Owl", "Gopher", "Heffalump" };

    Array_Sort<int> iA(ia,10);
    Array_Sort<String> SA(sa,7);

    cout << "template Array_Sort<int> class" << endl;
    try_array(iA);

    cout << "template Array_Sort<String> class" << endl;
    try_array(SA);

    return 0;
}
```

The String instance output, when the program is compiled and executed, looks as follows — note that it fails during execution when it attempts to display an element using an index with an out-of-bounds value of −1.

```
template Array_Sort<String> class

try_array: initial array values:
( 7 )< Eeyore, Gopher, Heffalump, Owl, Piglet, Pooh
        Tigger >

try_array: after assignments:
( 7 )< Eeyore, Gopher, Owl, Piglet, Pooh, Pooh
        Pooh >

try_array: memberwise initialization
( 7 )< Eeyore, Gopher, Owl, Piglet, Pooh, Pooh
        Pooh >

try_array: after memberwise copy
( 7 )< Eeyore, Piglet, Owl, Piglet, Pooh, Pooh
        Pooh >
```

```
try_array: after grow
( 11 )< <empty>, <empty>, <empty>, <empty>, Eeyore, Owl
          Piglet, Piglet, Pooh, Pooh, Pooh >

value to find: Tigger    index returned: -1
Memory fault(coredump)
```

Notice that the display of the memberwise initialized Array class String instance is *not* sorted. This is because the resolution of a virtual function invoked for an actual object of a class is resolved statically at compile time (see Section 9.1 (page 461) for the discussion of the three cases in which a virtual function is resolved statically).

A Multiply Derived Array Class

Finally, there are a subset of users that wish for a sorted array class that also provides range-checking of each index. A sorted, range-checking array can be composed by inheriting from both Array_RC and Array_Sort. The full implementation is pictured in Figure 9.6 (the code is placed in a header file named Array_RC_S.h).

The class inherits two implementations of each Array class interface function: those of Array_Sort and those of the virtual Array base class inherited through Array_RC. In a nonvirtual derivation, a call of find() or min() is flagged as ambiguous — which instance is meant? In a virtual derivation, however, the Array_Sort set of instances *dominate* (see Section 9.2 (page 476) for a discussion). A call of find() is resolved to the inherited Array_Sort class instance, which is what the design depends on.

Since the subscript operator is redefined in both immediate base classes, neither implementation dominates the other — both are equally the most derived. Within the derived class, therefore, any call of the subscript operator is ambiguous. The class must provide its own instance in order to use the operator. Semantically, what does it mean to invoke the subscript operator for the Array_RC_S class? To reflect the sorted nature of its derivation, it must set the inherited dirty_bit data member. To reflect the range-checking nature of its derivation, it must provide a test of the submitted index. That done, it can return the indexed element of the array. Both these operations are provided by the inherited Array_RC subscript operator. The call

```
return Array_RC::operator[](index);
```

explicitly invokes this operator. Because it is an explicit invocation, the virtual mechanism is overridden. Because it is an inline function, its static resolution results in an inline expansion of its code.

```
#ifndef ARRAY_RC_S_H
#define ARRAY_RC_S_H

#include "Array_S.c"
#include "Array_RC.c"

template <class Type>
class Array_RC_S : public Array_RC<Type>,
                   public Array_Sort<Type>
{
public:

    Array_RC_S(int sz = ArraySize)
        : Array<Type>( sz )
        { clear_bit(); }

    Array_RC_S(const Array_RC_S& rca)
        : Array<Type>( rca )
        { sort(0,size-1); clear_bit(); }

    Array_RC_S(const Type* arr, int sz)
        : Array<Type>( arr, sz )
        { sort(0,size-1); clear_bit(); }

    Type& operator[](int index) {
        set_bit();
        return Array_RC<Type>::operator[](index);
    }
};

#endif
```

Figure 9.6 class Array_RC_S header File

Let's try out the implementation with an execution of the try_array()
function, providing it in turn with an integer and String class instantiation of
the Array_RC_S template class. Here is the program:

```
#include "Array_RC_S.h"
#include "try_array.c"
#include "String.h"
```

```
main()
{
    static int ia[10] = { 12,7,14,9,128,17,6,3,27,5 };
    static String sa[7] = { "Eeyore", "Pooh", "Tigger",
        "Piglet", "Owl", "Gopher", "Heffalump" };

    Array_RC_S<int> iA(ia,10);
    Array_RC_S<String> SA(sa,7);

    cout << "template Array_RC_S<int> class" << endl;
    try_array(iA);

    cout << "template Array_RC_S<String> class" << endl;
    try_array(SA);

    return 0;
}
```

Here is the output of the String instantiation of the template Array class. The out-of-bound index error is now caught.

```
template Array_RC_S<String> class

try_array: initial array values:
( 7 )< Eeyore, Gopher, Heffalump, Owl, Piglet, Pooh
        Tigger >

try_array: after assignments:
( 7 )< Eeyore, Gopher, Owl, Piglet, Pooh, Pooh
        Pooh >

try_array: memberwise initialization
( 7 )< Eeyore, Gopher, Owl, Piglet, Pooh, Pooh
        Pooh >

try_array: after memberwise copy
( 7 )< Eeyore, Piglet, Owl, Piglet, Pooh, Pooh
        Pooh >

try_array: after grow
( 11 )< <empty>, <empty>, <empty>, <empty>, Eeyore, Owl
        Piglet, Piglet, Pooh, Pooh, Pooh >

value to find: Tigger    index returned: -1
Assertion failed: ix >= 0 && ix < size
```

Template Class Summary

Template classes provide a type-safe mechanism through which class instances that vary only by type can be generated automatically as needed by the programmer. Once instantiated, each template class behaves the same as a nontemplate class. Should one or more of the template class member functions prove too general for a particular type, specialized instances can be hand-coded. If necessary, an entire class instance can be explicitly provided by the programmer.

Template classes cannot be overloaded based on their parameter lists. The following, for example, is an error:

```
// error: cannot overload template classes

// array class without bounded size
template <class Type> class Array;

// array class bounded by size
template <class Type, int size> class Array;
```

Nor can a template and nontemplate class share the same name.

Each instance of a template class is an independent class type. There is no special relationship between the following two instantiations of the Array template class:

```
Array<int> ia;
Array<String> sa = ia; // error
```

The special relationship between a derived and public base template class, however, still holds, provided both are of the same actual parameter types:

```
Array_RC<int> ia_rc;
Array_RC<double> da_rcda;

Array<int> *pia_1 = &ia_rc; // ok
Array<int> *pia_2 = &da_rc; // error
```

Each template instantiation behaves the same as if the programmer had hand-coded it. Any special relationship between particular instantiations of a template class must be explicitly provided by the class designer.

Templates: Implementation vs. Specification

The discussion of the template facility presented here (and in Chapters 4 and 7) reflects the Release 3.0 Bell Laboratories implementation. It conforms to the current ANSI C++ specification of the template facility except for two small extensions in its treatment of exact matches for template functions.

The first extension permits trivial conversions to be considered when searching for an exact match. This permits a template such as

```
template <class Type>
Type min(const Type*, int);
```

to exactly match a call such as the following:

```
const int size = 12;
int ia[ size ] = { ... };

// error: ANSI specification
// ok: implementation extension
int min_elem = min(ia,size);
```

(section 4.2 (page 198) discusses this example in detail).

The second extension permits derived classes to match their public base classes. Without such a relaxation, template functions *do not* support object-oriented polymorphism. For example, the following calls of `try_array()` each fail under a strict implementation of the template facility:

```
Array_RC<int> iarc;
Array_S<int> ias;
Array_RC_S<int> iarcs;

// without extension, each fails: no match
try_array(iarc);
try_array(ias);
try_array(iarcs);
```

Under a strict implementation of the template facility, the designer of each derived class needs to provide an inline "stub" such as the following:

```
// required by strict implementation
template <class Type>
inline void
try_array(Array_RC<Type> &rc)
{
    try_array( ((Array<Type>&)rc) )
}
```

These two extensions are intended to serve as interim solutions until the ANSI C++ committee proposes and votes on a full resolution of the issue of template function argument matching.

Does this mean the template facility is not yet ready to be used? No. Large application and production-quality libraries have already been implemented using this version of templates. Then why are small modifications and possible extensions still being considered? Feedback from these early users has suggested certain areas in which the template facility specification might be improved. It is the job of the ANSI C++ committee to consider each suggestion in turn.

Some Last Words on Instantiation

For single file applications such as the template programs in this book, the user can manage template instantiation simply by including the program text files. For example,

```
#include <iostream.h>
#include "Array_S.c"
#include "try_array.c"

// ... actual program goes here
```

Once the application grows beyond a single file, however, this method is likely to become unworkable. Multiple member function and static data member definitions are likely to be instantiated within the separate files of the executable, resulting in a link-time failure.

For small applications, management of the instantiations can be done by hand. One file is created in which all the instantiations are generated — think of it as an *implement* file. This file alone includes the template program text files. All the other program files include the template header files.

Beyond the small application, management of the instantiations is best managed by programming environment tools. As mentioned earlier (see Section 4.2 (page 197) for the discussion), there is currently no standard for such tools. The reader, therefore, should refer to the User Guide of his or her particular implementation for details.

Chapter 10: **Object-Oriented Design**

In the previous two chapters, we saw how to implement an object-oriented design in C++. The next step is actually the one that precedes implementation — that of providing the object-oriented design itself. This is the subject of this chapter.

The two primary steps of an object-oriented design are to identify the classes, or candidate abstractions, of the problem domain and to define the interfaces to these classes.

1. Identify the classes. These typically fall into two categories: the primary abstractions of the problem domain, and the supporting abstractions of the implementation.

A substep of class identification is to identify the relationships, if any, that exist between the classes. Once again, there are two typical categories:

*   An *is-a* relationship, denoting one class as being a subtype of the other — for example, a Panda is a kind of Bear

*   A *has-a* relationship, denoting that one class is composed of an object of the other — for example, a Stack has an Array class member.

2. Define the interface to the class or class hierarchy — that is, the set of operations provided by each class.

Some of the questions that need to be answered during this step of the design are the following:

*   Is an operation common to an entire class hierarchy, or specific to a particular subtype or subhierarchy? Feeding hour, for example, is common to the entire ZooAnimal class hierarchy; dancing, however, is peculiar to a subtype of Bear.

*   Is an operation common to an entire class hierarchy a type-dependent, virtual operation or one that can be resolved statically? The ability of a ZooAnimal subtype to draw itself, for example, is type-dependent; each subtype needs to define its own instance. Answering a query as to an animal's feeding hour, however, can be resolved statically. Although the feeding hour may vary with particular subgroups of animals, the information necessary to determine that hour is common to the entire hierarchy.

- Should the operation be available to the entire program (part of the public interface) or restricted to the class hierarchy (part of the protected interface)? An operation to highlight the location of an animal on a display map of the zoo, for example, is of general interest to the program; it belongs to the public interface. The operation to actually light up the appropriate portion of the display map, however, is of interest only to the class hierarchy.

Once these steps are completed and reviewed, a prototype implementation of the design can begin. Typically, this uncovers additional class abstractions and requires both additions to and modification of the interface. Occasionally, a design flaw is uncovered requiring part or all of the design to be reworked.

Designs in industry more often than not extend an existing application rather than start at ground zero to provide a new one. This offers a rich opportunity for the reuse of existing classes and class hierarchies. It can, however, also constrain and misshape a design. This chapter walks through portions of a design to extend an existing C++ compiler to support the template facility described earlier. See Section 4.2 (page 179) for a discussion of template functions, Chapter 7 for a discussion of template classes, and Section 9.3 (page 479) for a discussion of template classes under inheritance. The primary reasons motivating the choice of this design problem are the following:

- The process of developing a template design should further our understanding of the template facility. Therefore, before reading this chapter, the reader should become familiar with the template mechanism of the C++ language.

- The design of a template facility represents a real-world problem — unlike, for example, the pedagogical ZooAnimal hierarchy employed to guide us through the intricacies of class inheritance in the previous two chapters.

The following is an admittedly simplified problem specification:

Extend an existing C++ compiler to provide support for function and class templates.

Our first step is to identify the classes that will represent our problem domain. Okay, then, where do we start?

10.1 Identifying the Classes

A helpful first step in identifying the classes is to read through the problem specification underlining all nouns. These nouns represent possible class abstractions for our design:

```
C++ compiler
function
class
template
function template
class template
```

Before we can reasonably evaluate the merits of this list, the problem domain needs to be analyzed more closely. An analysis of the problem domain is the next step in the process of identifying the classes.

A template represents the definition of a class, function (a nonmember function or member of a template class), or static data member of a template class. For example,

```
template <class Type>
class Foo {
public:
    Type bar();
    Foo( Type t ) : val( t ) {}
private:
    Type val;
    static int Foo_count;
};



template <class Type>
Type Foo<Type>::bar() {
    return val;
}

template <class Type>
int Foo<Type>::Foo_count = 0;

template <class Type>
void do_Foo( Foo<Type> &ft ) {
    // ...
}
```

Our list of classes needs to be expanded to reflect the full set of possible types of template definitions:

```
member function template
static data member template
```

Are there other types of template definitions? What about friend template classes and functions? For example,

```
template <class Type> class Foo
{
    template <class T> friend Bar;

    template <class T>
        friend ostream&
        operator<<(ostream&,Foo<T>&);

    template <class T>
        friend void
        FooBar<T>::add(Foo<T>,Bar<T>);

    // ...
};
```

No. Although the word friendship is a noun, friendship is not an abstraction in our problem domain. Rather, it is a relationship between these abstractions. It is more effectively modeled as an attribute between abstractions rather than as an abstraction itself.

What about specialized instances of a template definition? Do these represent separate abstractions in our problem domain? For example,

```
#include <string.h>

class Foo<char*> {
public:
    Foo( char *str )
    {
        str = new char[ strlen(str)+1 ];
        strcpy(val,str);
    }
    const char *bar();
private:

    char *val;
    static int Foo_count;
};
```

```
int Foo<char*>::Foo_count = 0;

const char*
Foo<char*>::bar() {
    return val;
}

void do_Foo( Foo<char*> &ft ) {
    // ...
}
```

No. A specialized instance of a template definition does not introduce new template abstractions. An explicit instance of a template represents a hard-coded template instantiation. It does not extend our set of class abstractions — rather, it simply complicates our implementation.

At this point in our design process, the initial list of candidates to be made into classes within our application consists of the following:

```
C++ compiler             template
class                    class template
function                 function template
member function          member function template
static data member       static data member template
```

Let's try to make some sense of our list. One thing we can do is eliminate abstractions that fall outside our problem domain:

```
C++ compiler
```

Our assignment is to extend an existing compiler, not design a new one.

Do any of the classes in our list already exist? If so, it is likely we can reuse them rather than design them from scratch. An existing C++ compiler must already have designed and implemented the following abstractions on our list:

```
class
function
member function
static data member
```

This leaves us with the five template candidate abstractions. The next sections looks at the function and member function candidate abstractions.

The Template Function Representation

A template function can be a nonmember,

```
template <class Type>
    Type min( Type*, int );
```

or a member function of a template class,

```
template <class Type>
    Type Array<Type>::min() { ... }
```

Currently, we have

```
template function
template member function
```

listed as independent class abstractions. This cannot be correct — certainly they share a great deal of common functionality. What are the alternative design choices?

1. Factor out all common behavior and data into an abstract base class. Derive a member and nonmember subtype:

```
class Function {};
class NonMemFunc : public Function {};
class MemFunc : public Function {};
```

2. But is the behavior and implementation of a nonmember function different from that of the abstract function? The second design strategy collapses the nonmember derivation into the abstract function. The member function remains a specialized subtype.

```
class Function {};
class MemFunc : public Function {};
```

3. Alternatively, membership can be viewed as a conditional attribute of a function and not a subtype abstraction requiring a unique class. The third design strategy collapses the function and member function classes into a single class.

One purpose of a hierarchical design is to factor out the common state members and shared interface. Each subtype then need only program its differences. The differences between a member and nonmember function are the following:

- The this pointer.

Although both subtypes have the attribute of an argument list, only a member function contains a this pointer. However, not all member functions contain a this pointer — only nonstatic member functions. Should member functions be further subtyped into static and nonstatic abstractions?

No. The presence of the `this` pointer is simply an attribute that may or may not be present in a given function.

• *access* privilege.

A member function has access privilege to the nonpublic members of its class. This is different than for a nonmember function — except if the non-member function is also a friend to a class. Moreover, a member function (or all member functions) of one class can be made a friend to a second class. Are friend functions another function subtype? No. As we decided earlier, friendship is more effectively modeled as an attribute between abstractions rather than as an abstraction itself.

Both a nonmember and a member function can be represented by a single abstraction. Attributes such as membership, storage class, and friendship will need to be represented.

However comfortable we may be in our analysis, there is one constraint on our actual design choice: the design of the function abstraction in the existing C++ compiler. It would be difficult to justify two separate representations of functions within the same compiler. It would be even more diffi-cult to justify changing the existing, working implementation if that imple-mentation should differ from that of our design. As it happens, the existing compiler also chose to represent nonmember and member functions with a single class.

The Existing Compiler

One aspect of a compiler is that of generating an internal representation of a user's program. This internal representation is type-checked and possibly amplified to reflect C++ semantics. For example, if the user writes

```
X x = 10;
```

the compiler must verify that X is a type specifier and that 10 is a legitimate value with which to initialize X. If X is a class with a constructor defined requiring a single argument of type int, then the compiler must transform the definition. Here is one possible transformation, represented as C++ code:

```
// possible transformation by a C++ compiler

X x;   // uninitialized memory allocated
x.X::X(10); // constructor invocation
```

Moreover, if the constructor is defined as inline, the compiler must then expand it. Finally, if X defines a destructor, the compiler must insert a call to it at a point following the last use of x. Additionally, if the destructor is defined as inline, the compiler must then expand it.

Each user-supplied name is represented internally within the existing compiler as a `NameDef`. Each NameDef has an associated `TypeDef` member. TypeDef serves as an abstract base class for the internal type representation. Classes derived from TypeDef include those representing a *class* abstraction, a *function* abstraction, and an abstraction to represent program variables. The entire set of class abstractions defined within the existing C++ compiler is rooted by an abstract base class named `CNode`. Here is a portion of the hierarchy:

```
// abstract superclass of entire hierarchy
class CNode {};

// abstract base class of Type subhierarchy
class TypeDef : public CNode {};

// abstract base class for expressions:
// a, 1 + foo(), ix = xi
class Expression : public CNode {};


class ClassDef : public TypeDef {};
class FunctDef : public TypeDef {};

class ObjectDef : public TypeDef {
    // ...
protected:
    TypeDef *hasType;
};


class NameDef : public Expression {
    // ...
protected:
    TypeDef *typeof;
};
```

The definition

```
class X { ... };
```

is represented by a NameDef class object. Its `typeof` member points to a ClassDef class object. The definition

```
X x;
```

is also represented by a NameDef class object. Its `typeof` member points to an ObjectDef class object. That object's `hasType` member points to the ClassDef associated with X. Similarly, the definition

```
void doX( X *a, X *b ) { ... }
```

is represented by a NameDef. Its `typeof` member points to a FunctDef class object. The arguments a and b are represented as NameDefs. A special List class, ParamList, links the argument parameters.

The designers of the existing compiler considered providing an explicit parameter class but in the end chose not to. A parameter to a function, they argued, behaved essentially the same as a local object of the function.

Refining the List of Candidate Abstractions

The definition of a template consists of a list of formal parameters and the definition of either a function, class, or static data member. For example,

```
template <class Type, int size>
class Array { ... };
```

The existing compiler already knows how to handle the definition of the Array class. Our *template* abstraction must handle the list of formal parameters. These parameters can either be type parameters, such as Type, or expression parameters, such as size. This suggests three additional candidate abstractions

```
parameter
type parameter
expression parameter
```

where type and expression parameters are subtypes of an abstract parameter base class.

A template class definition *has* a formal parameter list. It can consist of either parameter subtype. As we indicated earlier, a *has-a* relationship is represented by a data class member, not by inheritance. For example,

```
class Class_Template {
public:
    // public interface
private:
    Parameter *params;
    // ...
};
```

What is the relationship of a template class definition to its associated class definition? Is Class_Template, that is, a kind of class? If so, it must be derived from the compiler's existing ClassDef implementation.

The answer, however, is no. A template class definition is not a kind of class. Objects of the class cannot be declared. Its name does not serve as a type specifier. For example,

```
// error: Array is not a class
Array *pa = new Array;
```

Rather, a template definition *has* an associated class definition.

```
class Class_Template {
public:
    // public interface
private:
    Parameter *params;
    ClassDef  *def;
};
```

What about a template function definition? It has an associated function definition. It also has a formal parameter list. Unlike a template class, however, a template function can only specify type parameters. Its private representation, therefore, might look as follows:

```
class Function_Template {
public:
    // public interface
private:
    Type_Parameter *params;
    FunctDef *def;
};
```

The template of a static data member could be defined as follows:

```
class Data_Template {
public:
    // public interface
private:
    Parameter *params;
    ObjectDef *def;
};
```

An essential step in refining our list of candidate abstractions is that of identifying relationships that exist between them. As we've seen, for example, a template class has a list of formal parameters. A function template and static data member template also have a list of formal parameters. What, then, is the relationship between these classes?

Each is a kind of template. Each shares a common set of attributes: a list of parameters, albeit a template function has a constraint on that list, and an associated definition in which the parameters appear. The *template* abstraction in our list can serve as an abstract base class to the three specific template classes. Moreover, the internal representation common to all three can be factored out and placed within that abstract base class. For example,

```
class Template {
public:
    // public interface of entire hierarchy

protected:
    Parameter *params;
    TypeDef   *def;
};


class Class_Template : public Template {};
class Function_Template : public Template {};
class Data_Template : public Template {};
```

Implementation-Dependent Abstractions

A template class definition is not a kind of class. Each instantiation of that template class, however, behaves exactly the same as a nontemplate class. Is a template instantiation a kind of class, or is it simply the same as a class? For example,

```
Array<int,512> ia;
```

The answer in this case depends on the person asking the question. For the user of ia, the instantiated template is exactly the same as a nontemplate class — no additional abstraction is necessary. For an implementor of ia, however, the instantiated template is a specialized kind of class — one containing a list of actual parameters and a pointer to an associated template definition. From an implementor's point of view, a template class instantiation is an additional domain abstraction. It behaves as a kind of class:

```
class Class_Template_Inst
        : public ClassDef
{
public:
    // public interface

private:
    Parameter *actuals;
    Class_Template *tdef;
};
```

The same holds true for a template function instantiation and the instantiation of a template static data member.

As was the case in the design of the template definition abstractions, shared attributes of these three instantiation classes can be factored out into a shared abstract base class:

```
class Template_Inst {
public:
    // public interface
private:
    Parameter *actuals;
    Template  *tdef;
};
```

The three template instantiation classes are now each a kind of Template_Inst *and* a kind of class, function, or static data member. Here is a sketch of the resulting class hierarchy:

```
class Class_Template_Inst
        : public Template_Inst,
          public ClassDef {};

class Function_Template_Inst
        : public Template_Inst,
          public FunctDef {};

class Data_Template_Inst
        : public Template_Inst,
          public ObjectDef {};
```

The Template class hierarchy is an abstraction representing the problem domain. A class or function template is an actual object occurring within user code. The Template_Inst class hierarchy represents an implementation-dependent abstraction. It serves an aspect of the problem domain viewed differently by the user and the implementor of a template instantiation. The following class represents a wholly implementation-dependent abstraction absent from the actual problem domain. The Templ_Buf class serves, that is, as an aid to our implementation rather than either as a direct or indirect support of the template abstraction. It provides a buffer area for the incremental parsing and verification of both a declaration and definition of a template. For example, given the following template class definition,

```
template <class T, double d, class T>
class parameter_list_in_error { ... };
```

Templ_Buf collects each parameter in turn, verifies it and, if valid, adds it to the list of parameters for this template definition. In this example, the second parameter is rejected:

```
expression parameter d of type double unsupported
```

The third parameter is also rejected:

```
reuse of T as a parameter name
```

The Templ_Buf object of a correct template definition contains a parameter list and the definition of the associated function, class, or static data member. The behavior of Templ_Buf is independent of the particular kind of template being defined. Function, class, and data Templ_Buf subtypes do not seem necessary. Templ_Buf, therefore, is designed as an independent, abstract data type. Here is a sketch of its implementation:

```
class Templ_Buf {
public:
    // public interface
private:
    TypeDef    *def;
    Parameter *params;
};
```

Summary

At the end of this phase of the design process, we have accomplished the following:

1. Identified a set of classes necessary for our application.

2. Defined the relationships that exists between them.

Is it complete? In terms of the classes that support the template abstraction, probably yes. In terms of the classes that support our implementation of that abstraction, most likely no. Additional implementation-dependent classes are likely to be uncovered during the definition of the interfaces and the implementation of the design. Is it a good design? It's hard to say at this point. Certainly, it seems a reasonable design.

10.2   Defining the Interface

In the next phase of the design process, we attempt to define the public interface required of each of our identified classes. The following is a short list of what we hope to accomplish:

- Identify the operations required by users of each class. These operations define the public interface of the class.

- Identify possible helping functions required by the class to support the operations of its public interface. These operations will either be private or define the protected interface of a class hierarchy.

- In the case of a class hierarchy, identify operations that are type dependent: these will be the set of virtual functions within the hierarchy.

- Identify the general representation of each class. This will likely determine access operations such as set() and get() functions. This could
be put off until the implementation phase of the design.

In the following sections, we'll consider first the Templ_Buf class and
then the Template class hierarchy.

Operations to Support the Abstraction

The Templ_Buf class encapsulates the process of collecting together and veri-
fying the correctness of a template definition (or forward declaration). What
are some of the operations it must perform?

As each formal parameter is parsed, we need to *add* it to the template's
parameter list. Before a parameter is added to this list, we must *verify* that
the name associated with the parameter is not a reuse of the name of a previously added parameter. Additionally, in the case of expression parameters,
we must *verify* that the type of the expression is supported by the template
mechanism. For example, expression parameters of type double are not
supported. Finally, for type parameters, each must somehow be *entered* into
the list of type specifiers recognized by the program. For example, in the following potential template declaration,

```
template <class T, int T::*pT> class TX;
```

T must be recognized as a type specifier by the parser prior to the analysis of
the second parameter.

One method of uncovering likely candidates for class operations is to
underline the verbs associated with a description of the behavior of the class.
Each of the verbs in italics in the above discussion represents a potential
Templ_Buf operation.

A certain level of syntactic correctness is necessary for the actual parsing
of the template to succeed. Syntactic violations, that is, in a sense are caught
for "free". For example,

```
template <class union> // ...
```

fails because the language grammar requires an identifier to follow the
class keyword, not another keyword such as union. The following illegal
declaration,

```
template <union U> // ...
```

however, does not fail because, although it is semantically wrong (a formal parameter cannot be designated as a union), its grammatical representation is correct. `verify_param()` provides semantic checks on each parameter:

```
void verify_param( const Parameter& );
```

Additionally, an operation is needed to manage the parameter list:

```
void add_to_param_list( Parameter& );
```

Finally, an operation is needed to enter the name of a formal type parameter into the list of type specifiers recognized by the program:

```
void register_type_formal( const Parameter& );
```

A Brief Digression: Type-Safety

Templ_Buf enforces information hiding. A public access function is therefore required to provide access to the parameter list for those who may wish to read it:

```
Parameter *get_params();
```

This definition, however, is problematic since it permits a user to gain access to the actual list of parameters. For example, although the following looks as if it enforces data encapsulation:

```
class Templ_Buf {
public:
    Parameter *get_params() { return params; }
    // ...
private:
    Parameter *params;
};
Templ_Buf curr_templ;

// error: direct access not permitted
Parameter *pt = curr_templ.params;
```

in fact, it does not enforce data encapsulation:

```
// oops: direct access of params
pt = curr_templ.get_params();
```

The solution in this case is to return a constant pointer to the parameter list:

```
const Parameter *get_params();
```

One might argue that this solution, although type-safe, is not type-secure, since constness can be explicitly cast away. The same can be said about the safety of a private derivation or, in fact, of privacy in general. A derived class can be explicitly cast to its private base class, violating the programmed intentions of the class design. Similarly, casting a class object to a char* allows the determined user to traverse the object's entire memory. For example,

```
class no_general_access {
    friend class permit_access;
private:
    int rating;
    double salary;
};

no_general_access my_record;

main() {
    // ok: explicit cast breaks type-safety
    char *p = (char*) &my_record;

    // grab access to the salary member
    double *pd = (double*)(p+sizeof(int));
    *pd = 250,000.00;
    return 0;
}
```

Explicit casts are an inherited characteristic of C++'s derivation from the C language. In certain program situations, without question, the use of a cast is necessary — to disambiguate an overloaded function call, for example, or to make some use of the generic void* pointer. Casts cannot be removed from the language. Does this mean that C++ cannot absolutely guarantee type-safety? Yes. A determined programmer can violate all the mores of type-safety through the use of an explicit cast. Should we then just give up all attempts to program in a type-safe manner? No. Our programs should be designed as if explicit casts did not exist in the language.

Operations to Support the Implementation

In order to support the template abstraction, Templ_Buf needs two members, one to address the formal parameter list, and one to address the associated class, function, or static data member definition. In order to support our implementation, Templ_Buf also requires a third member, one to address a Template defined (or declared) earlier in the program.

```
class Templ_Buf {
public:
    void verify_param(const Parameter&);
    void add_to_param_list (Parameter&);
    void register_type_formal(const Parameter&);
    const Parameter *get_params();
private:
    Parameter *params;
    TypeDef    *def;
    Template   *templ_def;
};
```

There are two situations in which the implementation needs access to a previously created Template object in order to successfully parse a current template definition. In one case, a declaration or definition of a previously declared template occurs. For example,

```
// forward declaration
// create a Class_Template
template <class T> class Foo;

// actual declaration
// retrieve previous Class_Template
template <class Type>
class Foo { ... };

// backward declaration
// retrieve previous Class_Template
template <class U> class Foo;
```

A second case in which the implementation requires access to a previously defined Class_Template object is during the definition of a template member function or template static data member. For example,

```
// in both cases, Templ_Buf must retrieve
// Class_Template associated with Foo

// member function definition
template <class Type>
void Foo<Type>::bar() { ... }

// static data member definition
template <class Type>
Type Foo<Type>::foo_bar;
```

In both cases, Templ_Buf needs the ability to *retrieve* a particular Template object, if it exists. The storage, look-up, and retrieval of objects are operations of an independent abstraction: a Table class. Table was not identified in our earlier design phase because it is not an element of the template problem domain but of our implementation. It is likely that additional implementation-dependent classes will be uncovered as the design process proceeds.

Refining the Templ_Buf Interface

Once the Template object is retrieved, the implementation needs to determine if it is the same as the current template definition being parsed. Let's call this operation

```
Boolean ???::is_same_template(???);
```

Two questions need to be answered with regard this operation:

1. To which class or class hierarchy does this operation belong?

2. What are the arguments necessary in order for the operation to determine if the two in fact are the same?

Template member functions and static class members are not involved in this issue — there cannot be a forward declaration of either outside the class definition. For example,

```
// error: can only define a class member
//    outside the definition of its class
template <class T>
void Foo<T>::bar();
```

For a template class, the two template occurrences are the same if the formal parameter list of the two are the same. For example,

```
// ok: the formal parameter lists match
template <class T, int sz> class Array;

template <class Type_of_element,
          int size_of_array>
class Array { ... };
```

A template function, however, can be overloaded. Therefore, two distinct template functions can share the same name and parameter list. For a template function, the two template occurrences are the same only if both the parameter list *and* the signature of the two are the same. For example,

```
template <class T> T min( T*, int );

// same parameter list, different signature
template <class T> T min( T, T );

// same parameter list and signature
template <class U> U min( U*, int );
```

To which class interface should is_same_Template() belong? The TemplDef class contains the validated template against which the current template is being compared. The Templ_Buf class contains the tentative half of the two templates — tentative because we are trying to determine if its declaration is valid.

A class interface implements the behavior of the class abstraction. is_same_template() is a predicate service the Templ_Buf class is client to. The operation is an aspect of the Template class abstraction. The operation should, therefore, be made a member function of the Template class. Moreover, its implementation is type-dependent on the kind of template being defined — a function template needs to compare not only the formal parameters but the formal arguments of the two occurrences. The operation, therefore, should be made a virtual function of the Template class hierarchy:

```
class Template {
public:
    virtual Boolean
        is_same_template(???) = 0;
    //  ...
};
```

The signature of the function still needs to be determined. A virtual function must have the same signature and return type for each member instance.

- For a template class, the parameter list of the second occurrence is needed.

- For a template function, the parameter list and the signature of the second occurrence are needed.

If is_same_template() is to be defined as a virtual function, its signature must be the most inclusive — that is, the signature supporting the comparison of the two template functions:

```
virtual Boolean
is_same_template( const Parameter*,
                  const TypeDef* );
```

The TypeDef object, constructed by the existing C++ compiler, contains the signature of the function.

Class Manager Functions

At this point in the design, an interface for the set of operations our Templ_Buf class is able to perform has been sketched. What remains to be defined are the class manager functions. The following questions need to be asked:

1. Is a constructor necessary? That is, is there anything that must be done prior to the first use of a Templ_Buf object?

   Yes. The data members of a Templ_Buf object should be initialized to zero since each is a pointer.

   ```
   Templ_Buf::Templ_Buf()
   {
       params = 0;
       def = 0;
       templ_def = 0;
   }
   ```

2. Is a destructor necessary? That is, is there anything that must be done subsequent to the last use of a Templ_Buf object?

   Yes. The associated Template object needs to be created and inserted into the table of Template objects recognized within the user's program.

   ```
   Templ_Buf::~Templ_Buf() {
       Template *pt = new Template(params,def);

       // don't know details of Table yet
       ???->insert(pt);
   }
   ```

3. Are the default memberwise initialization and copy operations sufficient?

4. Should the class take over its memory management?

   These last two questions are really implementation decisions — the interface is unaffected — and can therefore be deferred until later.

A Pure Static Class

The language restricts programmers to templates occurring at global scope — a template, that is, cannot be nested within a class or be made local to a function. If templates cannot be nested within one another, it would therefore seem to follow that templates are processed one at a time rather than recursively. This means that only one Templ_Buf object is required by our implementation.

A class that requires only one object and does not specify virtual functions can be defined as a pure static class — a class, that is, in which each of its data and function members is declared as static.

- One instance of each static data member exists independently of the definition of objects of the class. These members must be explicitly defined within a program file. For example,

```
// the static data members of Templ_Buf
Template  *Templ_Buf::templ_def = 0;
TypeDef   *Templ_Buf::def = 0;
Parameter *Templ_Buf::params = 0;
```

These members are able to be directly accessed by the Templ_Buf static function members. Access by the general program, however, is prohibited since each member is declared as a private member of the Templ_Buf class.

- Each static member function is invoked independent of any class object by using the fully qualified class syntax. This is possible, recall, because the static member function is without a this pointer.

A pure static class does not need a constructor since its data members are explicitly initialized. If start() and end() semantics are required, they need to be invoked explicitly. For example,

```
// about to begin a new template
// zero out all Templ_Buf members
Templ_Buf::start();

// handle user template definition

// completed parse of new template
// create a new Template object
Templ_Buf::end();
```

Summary of the Templ_Buf Class

This has been a first pass at defining the public interface to our Templ_Buf class. Is it cast in stone, final and complete? No. It is likely that during the implementation phase, additional necessary operations and data members will be uncovered. Later, after a prototype is available or a beta program has been initiated, particular elements of the template specification may be found to be incompletely implemented or implemented incorrectly. It may turn out that the specification itself is incomplete or in error and requires change. In correcting or extending our implementation, additional operations and/or data members may need to be defined. The design process is iterative and, unfortunately, often fraught with error.

For example, there is a design flaw in our Templ_Buf class — one that, for argument's sake, let's say is not found until near the end of an internal alpha program. It occurs when a user attempts to compile the following template definition:

```
template <class Type, int size>
class Buffer {
    template <class T>
        friend T min(T*,int) {}

    // ... compiler fails here
```

Our implementation (you might understandably wish at this point to assert, no, Stan, *your* implementation) fails to successfully parse the Buffer template class. Its Templ_Buf state becomes overridden by that of the min() friend function. This is a serious bug because the failure is not due to program logic, generally easy to fix, but to the logic of the design. What happened? The language specifies that templates do not nest. This is true. All template definitions must occur at global scope. Unfortunately, we — well, the designer — misinterpreted this to disallow syntactic nesting. A friend declaration, however, although occurring within the class definition, references an instance occurring outside the scope of the class. The definition of min(), that is, although syntactically nested within Buffer, is interpreted to occur at global scope. Its definition, therefore, is legal. The design is wrong. What are the available options for correcting this?

- Reengineer the original design to allow multiple templates to occur concurrently. Existing code is likely to require change — we don't know as yet the extent of the required changes. First, we need to determine how extensive is the design flaw, then sketch out a high-level alternative design. From that we can identify the nature and extent of the required code changes. The project schedule is likely to slip; meetings and explanations will be required.

- Patch the failure without, if possible, disrupting the current design, trying, of course, to minimize the number of new bugs introduced. The clarity of the design is compromised. It becomes more difficult to understand (the patch is unexpected and outside the logic of the design) and likely less able to accommodate change — that is, to modify or extend the design (or even to repair the next bug). This problem becomes more acute as time passes and the motivation behind the patch becomes obscured. The product schedule, however, is likely to stay on course.

How is the decision made? In theory, after careful analysis of the design flaw, alternative design, and proposed patch. In practice, product schedules or the needs of real users (if the problem is discovered out in the field) at times outweigh what otherwise would be the sound technical decision. Not that this is ever true of particular companies or individuals but of the industry in general. In his novel *Pierre*, Herman Melville observes, "Life breaks in on philosophy like morning." Paraphrasing this, we might say that product delivery pressures break in on the theory of software design....

Getting back to our — well, my design failure. Analysis shows the following:

- The syntactic nesting of templates is limited to that of a friend template declaration.

- The definition of a class is not permitted within its declaration as a friend. That is, the following is illegal in both a template and nontemplate class:

```
class Foo {
    // illegal: cannot define Bar
    friend class Bar { ... };
    // ...
};
```

- The only syntactic nesting of a template definition, therefore, is that of a template friend function, such as that of min(), above, that broke our implementation.

- Nesting within that friend template definition is not permitted — that would provide for local template definitions, explicitly disallowed by the language.

- The syntactic nesting level, therefore, is constrained to be no greater than one.

- A save() and restore() pair of operations are sufficient, therefore, to handle the Templ_Buf design flaw.

The Template Class Interface

The Template class consists of the following:

- A set of formal parameters.

- A class, function, or static data member definition.

- A set of 0 or more instantiations of the template.

Our design specified a Template class hierarchy — the abstract Template class and three subtypes: the Class_Template, the Function_Template, and the Data_Template. Our goal in this phase of the design are the following:

1. Identify those operations that provide the interface to the entire Template class hierarchy.

2. Identify which of those operations are type-dependent and, therefore, should be made virtual — for example, is_same_template(). Each of the three Template class derivations must provide an explicit instance of this function.

3. Identify operations unique to each specific derived subtype of the template definition class. These will comprise the extended interface of each subtype.

Our work on the Templ_Buf class interface has already sketched out a partial representation of the abstract Template class:

```
class Template {
public:
    Template( Parameter*, TypeDef* );
    virtual Boolean
        is_same_template( const Parameter*,
                          const TypeDef* ) = 0;

protected:
    Parameter *params;
    TypeDef    *def;
    Template_Inst *insts;
};
```

The primary purpose of an abstract base class is to provide a common interface for its subsequent subtype derivations. Although no actual objects of the abstract base class are ever expected to be created, it does not follow that the abstract base class must be stateless — that is, to be without data members. These members, if present, are shared attributes of the entire hierarchy. They are factored out and lifted up into the abstract base class in order that each subtype might contain these members without code duplication.

An additional attribute required by the entire hierarchy is that of a name. For example, given the following template definition

```
template <class T> class X{};
```

not only is the template class named X but also its associated internal Template class object. Within the existing compiler, a name is represented by a String object. We could, therefore, add an explicit name data member:

```
class Template {
public:
    String get_name() { return name; };
    // ...
protected:
    String name;
    // ...
};
```

However, since the Template name is the same as that of the template definition, an explicit Template data member is unnecessary. We can reuse the
existing compiler's public interface:

```
String Template::get_name() {
    return def->get_name();
}
```

Each nonpublic data member is likely to require a read access function.
These belong as Template members shared by the entire hierarchy.

```
const Parameter        *get_formals();
const TypeDef          *get_def();
const Template_Inst    *get_inst_list();
```

What about write access functions? In general, neither the parameter list
nor the definition of the template change over the lifetime of the program.
There is, however, a special case in which the Template of a class or nonmember function template needs to be rewritten. For example, the forward
declaration

```
// forward declaration
template <class T> class X;
```

creates an associated Template for X. The definition

```
template <class Type>
class X { ... };
```

requires that the compiler update the params and def members of the associated Template. One method of handling this is to define a pair of public set
functions:

```
class Template {
public:
    void set_formals( Parameter* );
    void set_def( TypeDef* );
    // ...
};
```

This is too permissive, however. The members are now able to be changed any time from anywhere within the program. These members, however, should be changed only once — and only in the case of a forward declaration preceding the definition of a template. Additionally, we know that they will be set only by the Templ_Buf class.

To handle the conditional setting of these members, a predicate function is required to test whether the template definition has as yet been seen. An is_defined() function is already provided as part of the type representation of the existing compiler. Our predicate function need simply return its value:

```
Boolean Template::is_defined() {
    return def ? def->is_defined() : false;
}
```

The two functions can now be implemented to turn on the result of is_defined().

```
if (is_defined() == false)
{
    // reset params or def
}
```

Separating the operation into two separate functions, however, leaves open a subtle order-dependency. For example, if set_def() is invoked first, then the test of is_defined() within set_params() evaluates to true and the parameter list is not updated. The mistake is in thinking of this rewriting of the template definition and parameter list in terms of the individual members rather than as an atomic operation on the Template object. The correct implementation is that of a single reset_template() member function:

```
void
Templ_Buf::reset_template( Parameter *p, TypeDef *t ) {
    if (is_defined() == false) {
        delete params;
        delete def;
        params = p;
        def = tn;
        return;
    }
    // perhaps issue warning or error here
}
```

What level of access should is_defined() and reset_template() be given? is_defined() is a helping function to reset_template() and is not intended to be part of the Template public interface. However, it may be of general use to the Template derived classes. It is therefore made a protected rather than private Template member — recall, a private member of the base class cannot be accessed by a derived class unless the derived class is made an explicit friend.

reset_template() is not intended to be called from anywhere within the program except within the Templ_Buf class. It, therefore, is made a private Template member. The Templ_Buf class is specified as a friend class in order that it may invoke reset_template().

Actually, this is still slightly too permissive. Our intention is not to permit all the member functions of the Templ_Buf class access to the nonpublic Template members. Rather, we wish to designate only the single Templ_Buf member function as a friend that needs to invoke reset_templ():

```
class Template {
    friend void
        Templ_Buf::update_template();
    // ...
};
```

This is legal provided the definition of the Templ_Buf class has previously been seen. Now, only this Templ_Buf member function is granted access to the nonpublic Template members.

Handling Instantiations of a Template

Template instantiations are added to each template definition throughout a user's program.

```
Array<int> ia;
```

instantiates an integer instance of a template Array class.

```
cout << Buffer<int>::size_val << endl;
```

instantiates an integer instance of the size_val static data member of a template Buffer class.

```
Array <int> ia;
ia[ ia.max() ] = ia.min();
```

instantiates three template Array member functions: the subscript operator, min(), and max().

```
cout << min(ia.min(),ia.max()) << endl;
```

instantiates the Array member functions min() and max() and an integer instance of the nonmember template function min().

The access function to add the new instantiation to the list of instantiations belongs to the template definition class:

```
void TemplDef::
     add_to_inst(const TemplInst*);
```

An instantiation of a template class announces itself somewhat dramatically. The declaration

```
T< mumble > id;
```

announces T to be a template class and mumble to be list of actual parameters. Before T can be *instantiated*, we must *verify* that it is in fact a template class and that mumble is an acceptable list of actual parameters. Once again, each verb placed in italics suggests a possible Template operation.

The process of recognizing a template instantiation, however, is type-dependent. For example,

```
int i, j;
Array<int> ia;
Buffer<int,512> *pbuf;

void display_some_globals() {
    cout << min( i, j+2 ) << "\t"
         << ia.max() << "\t"
         << pbuf->size_val << endl;
}
```

min() is a nonmember template function. max() is a member template function of the template Array class. size_val() is a static data member template of the template Buffer class.

Until now, our design has been noninvasive of the existing compiler implementation — that is, the implementation of the compiler has not been changed apart from changes to the grammar to recognize template syntax. In order to recognize these template instantiations, however, the *ClassDef*, *FunctDef*, and *ObjectDef* classes within the compiler need to be modified to support the following predicate query:

```
Boolean is_template();
```

Because these classes share a common abstract base class — TypeDef — this operation can be placed within that rather than duplicated within each subtype.

Handling a Template Function

Once the template definition is retrieved, the correctness of the actual parameters has to be verified. Much of the verification processing is dependent on the actual template type. For example, given the call

```
String SA[] = { "Neuromancer", "Count_Zero",
                 "MonaLisa_OverDrive" };
// ...
cout << max(SA,3) << endl;
```

and the following template declaration:

```
template <class Type>
    Type max(const Type*,int);
```

what are the actual parameters to the call of the template function max()?
At this point we don't actually know. If the template is a nonmember function, the first thing we need to do is *extrapolate* the actual parameter list:

```
class Function_Template : public Template {
public:
    Parameter *build_actuals( ??? );
    // ...
};
```

How is the actual parameter list built? The arguments to the call of the template need to be compared to the formal arguments. The argument to build_actuals(), then, must be the argument list representation. In the case of

```
max(SA,3)
```

the actual parameter list returned by build_actuals is a single parameter of type String.

Two attributes of a template function complicate the implementation of build_actuals(). The first is that the argument to a template function must be an exact match. (The original specification is even more exacting, disallowing even trivial conversions. During the process of designing and implementing a specification, it may happen that the specification itself is altered in some way. This is actually not uncommon. Not only designs but designers need to be able to accommodate change.) If the second argument to max() were either an unsigned int or short, for example, the call and formal definition of max() would not match. Since type-checking is an integral aspect of the existing compiler, we can presume both that functions exist to perform these operations and that we can use them. Our only concern is that these operations might have been declared nonpublic members. If so, we will need to declare the Function_Template class a friend of the class to which they are members.

The second complicating attribute of a template function is that it can be overloaded. Imagine, for example, the following set of template declarations:

```
template <class Type>
    Type min(Type*, int);

template <class Type>
    Type min(Array<Type>, int);

template <class Type>
    Type min(Type, Type);
```

The call

```
Array<int> *pIA = new Array<int>[10];
cout << min(pIA,10) << endl;
```

must resolve to

```
template <class Type>
    Type min(Type*, int);
```

with the actual parameter list being a single parameter of the template Array<int> class. The call

```
cout << min(pIA[0],pIA[0].getSize()) << endl;
```

must resolve to

```
template <class Type>
    Type min(Array<Type>, int);
```

with the actual parameter list being a single parameter of type int. The call

```
cout << min(pIA[0],pIA[1]) << endl;
```

must resolve to

```
template <class Type>
Type min(Type, Type);
```

with the actual parameter list being a single parameter of type Array<int>.

Our template function class needs an additional data member to hold the potential list of overloaded instances (This is unique to function templates — class and static data templates cannot be overloaded. Overloading is not based on the parameter list but, rather, the signature of the function.)

```
Function_Template *overload_list;
```

and a set of member functions to operate on it:

```
Boolean is_overloaded() {
    return overload_list != 0;  }

void add_overloaded( Function_Template* )
const Function_Template *get_overloaded();
```

build_actuals() needs to be called for each overloaded instance of the template. A successful call is one in which one and only one overloaded instance can build a parameter list of actual types. If two or more return a type list, the call of the template is ambiguous. If no type list is returned for any instance, the call of the template is illegal.

These actions are unique to the definition of a template function. Their general purpose, however, is to confirm the legality of the actual parameters. A general function invoking these actions might be called

```
Boolean is_legal_instance( ??? )
```

This function would serve as a common interface to the entire hierarchy. Its argument list, therefore, would be the most inclusive necessary to support the three Template class subtypes.

```
class Template {
public:
    virtual Boolean
        is_legal_instance( Parameter*,
                           TypeDef* ) = 0;
    // ...
};
```

Each derived class subtype will provide its own instance.

Summary

The process of defining a complete public interface is iterative. Through an analysis of the abstraction, a set of operations are defined — these primarily reflect the behavior of the class. A second aspect of an interface is to support the implementation of the class — often, these operations are nonpublic, of interest only to the class or class hierarchy. Included in these operations are operators new and delete and the memberwise initialization and copy functions (I am presuming, of course, that the reader is going to implement this design using C++). Users of the class or class hierarchy inevitably uncover further operations that are needed. (A user might be an actual programmer or another class in the problem domain that operates on or requires services from this class.)

Designs also change. For example, our Templ_Buf class is designed as an independent, abstract data type. At the end of processing a template definition, it needs to create some type of internal Template object. At the time, the following call seemed sufficient:

```
new Template( params, def );
```

This call is no longer workable, however, since each subtype defines additional data members that require initialization. Templ_Buf must each time invoke the constructor of the appropriate derived class.

The conventional method of handling a type-dependent operation is to declare it as virtual. However, neither operator new (which is a static member function, recall) nor the constructor of a class may be declared virtual. A virtual constructor can be simulated by defining a virtual function that is called in place of operator new. For example,

```
class Template {
public:
    virtual Template *new_Template( ??? );
    // ...
};
```

The argument list to new_Template() must be the most inclusive argument list for the constructors of the derived classes.

There is still a problem, however. A virtual call must be bound to a reference or pointer to a class object. Our Templ_Buf design does not provide a class object through which to invoke new_Template()! There are a number of design options at this point:

• We can go back and redesign Templ_Buf as an object-oriented hierarchy. new_Template() can then be made a virtual operation of this hierarchy.

• We can try to introduce new_Template() as a virtual function of the existing C++ compiler Type hierarchy.

• We can forgo the type encapsulation altogether in Templ_Buf and introduce a switch statement, providing some appropriate rationale for our decision in the implementation notes and comments in the source code.

```
/*
 * mumble ...
 */
switch( templ_def->typeof() ) {
    case class_template:
        return new Class_Template( // ...
    case function_template:
        // ...
};
```

10.3 Living in a Multi-Paradigm Universe

In the procedural programming paradigm, a problem is modeled to a set of algorithms. A library check-out system, for example, is represented as a series of procedures, the two central being the check-out and return of library material. Chapters 3 and 4 of this text focus on the support C++ provides for the procedural programming paradigm. Three prominent procedural languages are FORTRAN, C, and Pascal.

In the 1970s, the focus of program design shifted from the procedural paradigm to that of abstract data types. The problem now is modeled to a set of data abstractions. A library check-out system, for example, is represented as the interaction of library abstractions such as Book, Borrower, Due-Date (an object of Time), and the inevitable Fine (an object of Money). Chapters 5, 6, and 7 illustrate and discuss the support C++ provides for the abstract data type programming paradigm. Three programming languages supporting the abstract data type paradigm are CLU, Ada, and Modula-2.

Object-oriented programming extends abstract data types through the mechanisms of inheritance (a "reuse" of an existing implementation) and dynamic binding (a "reuse" of an existing public interface). Special type/subtype relationships between previously independent types is now provided. A book, videotape, recording, and children's puppet are each *a kind of* library material, although each has its own check-in and return policy. The shared interface and state information is placed in an abstract Library-Material class. Each specific class of library material need only program its differences; shared behavior is inherited. Chapters 8 and 9 illustrate and discuss the support C++ provides for the object-oriented programming paradigm. This chapter discusses the process of object-oriented design. Four prominent languages supporting the object-oriented paradigm are Simula, Smalltalk, CLOS, and, of course, C++.

Smalltalk is spoken of as a *pure* object-oriented language; that is, it supports a single programming paradigm — that of object-oriented programming. C++ is spoken of as a *hybrid* object-oriented language; while it supports the object-oriented paradigm, it does not require its use:

- Writing a program to determine whether an integral value is prime is perhaps best served by C++'s support of the procedural paradigm.

- Providing a Complex arithmetic class type is perhaps best served by C++'s support of the abstract data type paradigm.

- Implementing a template facility for an existing C++ compiler is best served by C++'s support of the object-oriented paradigm.

This hybrid nature of C++, depending on your background, is either one of its most attractive properties or the property most likely to be condemned.

For users of the language, of course, it is simply the universe we inhabit.

How does the multi-paradigm nature of C++ affect object-oriented design?

1. The programmer must explicitly declare a member function virtual. By default, it is resolved statically at compile time.

```
class Bar {
public:
    void print();   // nonvirtual
    virtual void display();
};

void foo(const Bar& b) {
    b.print(); // always Bar::print()
    b.display(); // cannot say which display()
}
```

A benefit of this behavior is that there is no unnecessary run-time overhead. If a class doesn't use dynamic binding, then it does not incur any of the overhead associated with it. A drawback is that a conservative design may at times guess wrong as to which function should be declared virtual. Thus, derivation can become invasive, at times requiring changes to the definition of the base class interface.

Some class designers suggest declaring virtual all functions of every class intended to serve as an object of derivation. This suggestion in general is a bad idea. In C++, the trade-off in run-time efficiency is not between nonvirtual and virtual functions calls. Rather, it is between *any* function call and the inline expansion of that function. A virtual function call cannot be expanded inline. A function, therefore, should not unnecessarily be declared to be virtual.

2. A class must be explicitly prepared for inheritance by specifying a protected access section. By default, an unlabeled section is treated as private.

The benefit is that the programmer cannot misuse inheritance as a means of gaining access to data intended to be private. The drawback, again, is that the class designer eventually is going to guess wrong. Encapsulation is too important, however, to do away with the `private` keyword and declare all nonpublic members `protected`.

Object-oriented programming is an evolutionary advance in the design and management of large software systems. It is not, however, the *deus ex machina* come forth to resolve the many ills of the software industry. Good code is difficult to produce under any paradigm and, once in production, bugs continue to be uncovered. This is unlikely to change for quite some time yet.

Appendix A: **The C++ I/O Library**

Input/output facilities are not defined within the C++ language, but rather are implemented in C++ and provided as a component of a C++ standard library. The I/O library described here is referred to as the *iostream* library. The ANSI C++ committee's work on defining a standard I/O library for C++ is based on this library.

At its lowest level, a file is interpreted simply as a sequence, or *stream*, of bytes. One aspect of the I/O library manages the transfer of these bytes. At this level, the notion of a data type is absent.

At the user level, of course, a file consists of a sequence of possibly inter-mixed data types — characters, arithmetic values, class objects. A second aspect of the I/O library manages the interface between these two levels.

The iostream library predefines a set of operations for handling reading and writing of the built-in data types. In addition, the programmer can extend certain of these operations to handle class types. These two components of the iostream library form the subject of this appendix.

Input and output operations are supported by the *istream* (input stream) and *ostream* (output stream) classes. The *iostream* class is derived from both istream and ostream; it allows for bi-directional I/O. The ostream output operation, referred to as *insertion*, is performed by the left shift or insertion operator ("<<"). A value is said to be inserted into the output stream. The istream input operation, referred to as *extraction*, is performed by the right shift or extraction operator (">>"). A value is said to be extracted from the input stream.

A useful way of thinking about the two operators is that each "points" in the direction of its data movement. For example,

        >> x

moves the data *into* x, while

        << x

carries the data *out from* x.

Four stream objects are predefined for the user:

1. `cin`, an istream class object tied to standard input.

2. `cout`, an ostream class object tied to standard output.

3. `cerr`, an ostream class object tied to standard error and that provides for unbuffered output.

4. `clog`, an ostream class object also tied to standard error but that provides for buffered output.

Any program that uses the iostream library must include the header file `iostream.h`.

File manipulation using the input and output operations is also supported. A user can tie a particular file to the program by defining an instance of one of the following three class types:

1. *ifstream*, derived from istream, ties a file to the program for input.

2. *ofstream*, derived from ostream, ties a file to the program for output.

3. *fstream*, derived from iostream, ties a file to the program for both input and output.

The iostream library also supports "incore" formatting within character arrays. There are two associated class types:

1. *istrstream*, derived from istream, that fetches characters from an array.

2. *ostrstream*, derived from ostream, that stores characters into an array.

File manipulation and the use of incore operations are discussed later in this appendix following a general discussion of output and input.

A.1 Output

The general output method is to apply the insertion operator ("<<") to cout. For example,

```
#include <iostream.h>
main() {
    cout << "gossipaceous Anna Livia\n";
}
```

will print as follows on the user's terminal:

```
gossipaceous Anna Livia
```

A predefined set of insertion operators are provided that accept arguments of any of the built-in data types, including `char*`. Later in this appendix, we discuss how to extend this set of operators to accept arguments of user-defined class types.

Any complex expression can be specified that evaluates to a data type accepted by an insertion operator. For example,

```
#include <iostream.h>
#include <string.h>

main() {
    cout << "The length of ``ulysses'' is:\t";
    cout << strlen( "ulysses" );
    cout << endl;

    cout << "The size of ``ulysses'' is:\t";
    cout << sizeof( "ulysses" );
    cout << endl;

    return 0;
}
```

will print as follows on the user's terminal:

```
The length of ``ulysses'' is:    7
The size of ``ulysses'' is:      8
```

endl (endline) is a predefined ostream operation. It both inserts a new-line and flushes the ostream buffer.

The insertion operator can be concatenated into a single statement. For example, the preceding program can be rewritten as follows:

```
#include <iostream.h>
#include <string.h>

main() {
    // insertion operations can be concatenated

    cout << "The length of ``ulysses'' is:\t"
         << strlen( "ulysses" ) << endl;

    cout << "The size of ``ulysses'' is:\t"
         << sizeof( "ulysses" ) << endl;
    return 0;
}
```

A predefined insertion operator for pointer types is also provided, allowing for the display of an object's address. By default, these values are displayed in hexadecimal notation. For example,

```
#include <iostream.h>

main() {
    int i = 1024;
    int *pi = &i;

    cout << "i:    " << i
         << "\t&i:\t" << &i << endl;

    cout << "*pi: " << *pi
         << "\tpi:\t" << pi << endl
         << "\t\t&pi:\t" << &pi << endl;

    return 0;
}
```

will print as follows on the user's terminal:

```
i:    1024        &i:      0x7ffff0b4
*pi: 1024         pi:      0x7ffff0b4
                  &pi:     0x7ffff0b0
```

To display an address value in decimal notation, an explicit cast of the value to type `long` is necessary. For example, the previous program could be modified as follows:

```
#include <iostream.h>

int i = 1024;

main() {
    int *pi = &i;
    cout << "i:    " << i
         << "\t&i:\t" << long(&i) << endl;

    cout << "*pi: " << *pi
         << "\tpi:\t" << long(pi) << endl
         << "\t\t&pi:\t" << (long)&pi << endl;

    return 0;
}
```

This version of the program will print as follows on the user's terminal:

```
i:    1024        &i:      2147479732
*pi: 1024         pi:      2147479732
                  &pi:     2147479728
```

The following program presents something of a puzzle. Our intention is to print out the address value `pstr` contains:

```
#include <iostream.h>

char str[] = "vermeer";
main() {
    char *pstr = str;
    cout << "The address of pstr is: "
        << pstr << endl;
    return 0;
}
```

When compiled and executed, however, the program unexpectedly generates the following output:

```
The address of pstr is: vermeer
```

The problem is that the type char* is interpreted not as an address value but as a string. To print out the address value pstr contains, we must override the default handling of char*. We do this with an explicit cast of pstr to type void*:

```
<< (void*) pstr << endl;
```

When compiled and executed, the program now generates the expected output:

```
The address of pstr is: 0x116e8
```

Here is another puzzle. Our intention is to display the larger of two values:

```
#include <iostream.h>

inline void
max_out( int val1, int val2 ) {
    cout << ( val1 > val2 ) ? val1 : val2;
}

main() {
    int ix = 10, jx = 20;

    cout << "The larger of " << ix;
    cout << ", " << jx << " is ";
    max_out( ix, jx );
    cout << endl;
    return 0;
}
```

When compiled and executed, however, the program generates the following incorrect results:

```
The larger of 10, 20 is 0
```

The problem is that the insertion operator has a higher precedence than the arithmetic if operator (it shares the same precedence as the bitwise left shift operator). (Section 2.10 (page 84) presents a discussion of operator precedence.) The expression

```
cout << ( val1 > val2 ) ? val1 : val2;
```

evaluates as

```
(cout << ( val1 > val2 )) ? val1 : val2;
```

In order to override the predefined order of operator precedence, the full arithmetic if expression must be placed within parentheses:

```
cout << (val1 > val2 ? val1 : val2);
```

The safest method of inserting an expression is to fully parenthesize it.

A.2 Input

iostream input is similar to output, except that the right shift operator (">>"), referred to as the *extraction* operator, is used. Predefined extraction operators for the built-in data types, including char*, are provided. The extraction operators can also be concatenated. For example,

```
#include <iostream.h>

main()
{
    int val1, val2;

    cout << "Please enter two integers: " << endl;
    cin >> val1 >> val2;

    cout << "Values read are: < " << val1 << ", "
         << val2 << " >" << endl;
    return 0;
}
```

will print as follows on the user's terminal:

```
Please enter two integers: 20 27
Values read are: < 20, 27 >
```

A more general method of reading from the input stream is to make the extraction operation the truth condition of a while loop. For example,

```
char ch;
while ( cin >> ch )
    // ...
```

reads a character at a time from standard input. When end-of-file is encountered, the truth condition evaluates as false and the loop terminates.

The character sequence

```
ab c
d        e
```

is treated by operator >> as a sequence of five characters ('a', 'b', 'c', 'd', 'e').
White space (blanks, newlines, and tabs) serve only to separate values on the
input stream and are not themselves read as characters. The member functions get(), getline(), and read() can be used when the programmer
wishes to also read white space characters. We will look at these later.

The extraction operator can also be used to read a sequence of strings
from the input stream. For example,

```
char inBuf[ wordLength ];
while ( cin >> inBuf ) ...
```

A string is treated by the predefined char* instance of the extraction
operator as being a sequence of characters delimited by white space. The
presence of quotation marks does not cause embedded white space to be
handled as part of an extended string. For example,

```
"A fine and private place"
```

requires five iterations of the preceding while loop to process. The
sequence of strings read are the following:

```
"A
fine
and
private
place"
```

A null character is appended to a string during input. The size of a character array necessary to hold a string, therefore, is the length of the string
plus one. For example,

```
char inBuf[ 4096 ];
while ( cin >> inBuf ) {
    char *pstr = new char[ strlen(inBuf) + 1 ];
    strcpy( pstr, inBuf );
    ...
}
```

The following program extracts a sequence of strings from standard input and determines which of the strings read is largest.

```cpp
#include <iostream.h>
#include "String.h"
#include <string.h>

char *msg[] = {
    "The number of words read is ",
    "The longest word has a length of ",
    "The longest word is " };

const bufSize = 24;
main() {
    char buf[ bufSize ];
    String largest;

    // hold statistics;
    int curLen, max = -1, cnt = 0;

    while ( cin >> buf ) {
        curLen = strlen( buf );
        ++cnt;

        // new longest word? save it.
        if ( curLen > max ) {
            max = curLen;
            largest = buf;
        }
    }

    cout << msg[0] << cnt << endl;
    cout << msg[1] << max << endl;
    cout << msg[2] << largest << endl;
    return 0;
}
```

The input to the program is the first few sentences of the novel *Moby Dick*:

```
Call me Ishmael.  Some years ago, never mind
how long precisely, having little or no money
in my purse, and nothing particular to interest
me on shore, I thought I would sail about a little
and see the watery part of the world.  It is a
way I have of driving off the spleen, and
regulating the circulation.
```

When compiled and executed, the program generates the following output:

```
The number of words read is 58
The longest word has a length of 12
The longest word is circulation.
```

In the program, each string is stored in buf, declared to be an array of length 24. If a string were read which equaled or exceeded 24 characters, buf would overflow. The program would likely fail during execution.

The setw() manipulator can be used to prevent the overflow of an input character array. For example, the previous program might be modified as follows:

```
while ( cin >> setw( bufSize ) >> buf )
```

where bufSize is the dimension of the character array buf. setw() breaks a string equal to or larger than bufSize into two or more strings of a maximum length of

```
bufSize - 1
```

A null character is placed at the end of each new string. Use of setw() requires that the program include the iomanip.h header file.

If the visible declarations of buf do not specify a dimension,

```
char buf[] = "An unrealistic example";
```

the programmer can apply the sizeof operator — provided that the identifier is the name of an array:

```
while ( cin >> setw(sizeof( buf )) >> buf );
```

Use of the sizeof operator in the following example results in unexpected program behavior:

```
#include <iostream.h>
#include <iomanip.h>

const bufSize = 24;
char buf[ bufSize ];

main()
{
    char *pbuf = buf;

    // each string greater than sizeof(char*)
    // is broken into two or more strings
    while ( cin >> setw(sizeof(pbuf)) >> pbuf )
        cout << pbuf << endl;
    return 0;
}
```

When compiled and executed, the program generates the following incorrect results:

```
$ a.out
The winter of our discontent

The
win
ter
of
our
dis
con
ten
t
```

setw() is passed the size of the character pointer rather than the size of
the character array to which it points. On this particular machine, a character pointer is four bytes, and so the input is broken into a sequence of strings
three characters in length.

The following attempt to correct the mistake is an even more serious
error:

```
while ( cin >> setw(sizeof(*pbuf)) >> pbuf )
```

The intention is to pass setw() the size of the array to which pbuf points.
The notation

```
*pbuf
```

however, yields only a single char. setw(), in this case, is passed a value
of 1. Each execution of the while loop will place a null character into the
array to which pbuf points. Standard input is never read; the loop executes
infinitely.

A.3   Additional I/O Operators

The put() member function provides an alternative method of inserting a
character into the output stream. put() accepts an argument of type char
and returns the ostream class object that invokes it.

The istream member functions get() and getline() can be used when
the programmer does not wish to skip over white space. There are two
forms of the member function get().

1. get(char& ch) extracts a single character from the input stream and
   stores it in ch. It returns the iostream object that invokes it. It serves as
   the inverse of the put() insertion function. For example,

```
#include <iostream.h>

main() {
    char ch;
    while (cin.get(ch))
        cout.put(ch);
    return 0;
}
```

2. get() extracts and returns a single value from the input stream, including EOF, the end-of-file value defined in iostream.h. For example,

```
#include <iostream.h>

main() {
    int ch;
    while ( (ch = cin.get()) != EOF )
        cout.put(ch);
    return 0;
}
```

To distinguish EOF from the character set values, its associated value most often is −1. ch is best declared to be of type int if it will hold both character values *and* EOF.

Seven iterations of get() are required to read the following sequence of characters:

```
a b c
d
```

Seven characters are read ('a', blank, 'b', blank, 'c', newline, 'd'). The eighth iteration encounters EOF. Operator >>, because it skips over white space, reads the character sequence in four iterations ('a', 'b', 'c', 'd').

The write() member function provides an alternative method of inserting a string into the output stream. It has the following function signature:

```
write( const char *str, int length )
```

where length specifies the number of characters to display, beginning with the character addressed by str. write() returns the ostream class object that invokes it and may be concatenated.

The signature of getline() is the following:

```
getline( char *Buf, int Limit, char Delim = '\n' );
```

getline() extracts a block of characters and places them in the character array addressed by Buf. The invocation of getline will extract at most Limit - 1 characters. getline() appends a null character to Buf. If either the end-of-file is reached or the `Delim` character is encountered, `getline()` will extract less than `Limit - 1` characters. By default, the delimiter for string termination is the newline. `Delim` is not placed within `Buf`.

The istream member function `gcount()` returns the number of characters actually extracted by the last call of `getline()`. Here is an example of using `getline()`, `gcount()`, and `write()`:

```
#include <iostream.h>

const lineSize = 1024;
main() {
    int lcnt = 0; // how many lines are read
    int max = -1; // size of longest line
    char inBuf[ lineSize ];

    // reads 1024 characters or up to newline
    while (cin.getline(inBuf, lineSize))
    {
        // how many characters actually read
        int readin = cin.gcount();

        // statistics: line count, longest line
        ++lcnt; if ( readin > max ) max = readin;

        cout << "Line #" << lcnt
            << "\tChars read: " << readin << endl;
        cout.write(inBuf, readin).put('\n').put('\n');
    }
    cout << "Total lines read: " << lcnt << endl;
    cout << "Longest line read: " << max << endl;
    return 0;
}
```

When run against the first few sentences of *Moby Dick*, the program generates the following output:

```
Line #1 Chars read: 45
Call me Ishmael.  Some years ago, never mind

Line #2 Chars read: 46
how long precisely, having little or no money

Line #3 Chars read: 48
in my purse, and nothing particular to interest
```

```
Line #4 Chars read: 51
me on shore, I thought I would sail about a little

Line #5 Chars read: 47
and see the watery part of the world.   It is a

Line #6 Chars read: 43
way I have of driving off the spleen, and

Line #7 Chars read: 28
regulating the circulation.

Total lines read: 7
Longest line read: 51
```

The inverse of the ostream `write()` function is the istream `read()` function, whose signature is defined as follows:

```
read( char* addr, int size );
```

`read()` extracts `size` contiguous bytes from the input stream and places them beginning at `addr`. `gcount()` will also return the number of bytes extracted by the last call of `read()`.

The user should be aware of three other extraction operators:

```
// push character back into the iostream
putback( char c );

// returns next character (or EOF)
//       but does not extract it
peek();

// discards up to Limit characters
// stop if encounters Delim character
ignore( int Limit=1, int Delim=EOF );
```

The following code fragment illustrates how these operators might be used:

```
char ch, next, lookahead;

while ( cin.get(ch) ) {
    switch (ch) {
```

```
case '/':
        // is it a line comment?  peek()
        // yes? ignore() rest of line
        next = cin.peek();
        if ( next == '/' )
            cin.ignore( lineSize, '\n' );
        break;

case '>':
        // look for >>=
        next = cin.peek();
        if ( next == '>' ) {
            lookahead = cin.get();
            next = cin.peek();
            if ( next != '=' )
                cin.putback(lookahead);
        }
```

A.4 Overloading Operator<<

There are no predefined insertion operators for user-defined class types. The designer of a class, however, can overload the insertion operator to define output for that class. For example,

```
#include <iostream.h>

class WordCount {
    friend ostream&
            operator<<(ostream&, WordCount&);
public:
    WordCount( char *, int = 1 );
    // ...
private:
    char *str;
    int occurs;
};

#include <iostream.h>

ostream&
operator <<( ostream& os, WordCount& wd ) {
    os  << "< " << wd.occurs
        << " > " << wd.str << endl;
    return os;
}
```

The WordCount instance of the insertion operator can now be intermixed freely with the predefined insertion operators.

```
#include <iostream.h>
#include "WordCount.h"

main() {
    WordCount wd( "sadness", 12 );
    cout << "wd: " << endl << wd << endl;
    return 0;
}
```

will print as follows on the user's terminal:

```
wd:
<12> sadness
```

The insertion operator is a binary operator that returns an ostream reference. The general skeleton of an overloaded definition looks as follows:

```
ostream&
operator << ( ostream& os, <ClassType>& )
{
    // ... any special logic for <ClassType>
    os <<  // ... output members
    return os; // ... return ostream object
}
```

Its first argument is an ostream reference; the second, a particular class type
reference. The return value is the ostream argument.

Because the first argument is an ostream reference, the insertion operator
must be defined as a nonmember function. (Section 5.5 (page 239) discusses
this in detail.) When the operator requires access to nonpublic members, it
must be declared as a friend to the class.

Loc is a class that holds the line and column number of each occurrence of
a word. Here is its definition:

```
#include <iostream.h>

class Loc {
    friend ostream& operator<<( ostream&, Loc& );
public:
    Loc( int l, int c ) : line(l), column(c) {}
    Loc *next;   // for simplicity of example
private:
    short line;
    short column;
};
```

```
ostream& operator <<( ostream& os, Loc& lc )
{
    // output of a Loc object:  < 10,37 >
    // deliberately leave off endl
    os << "<" << lc.line
       << "," << lc.column << ">";
    return os;
}
```

Let's redefine WordCount to contain both a Loc and a String class object:

```
class WordCount {
    friend ostream& operator<<(ostream&, WordCount&);
    friend istream& operator>>(istream&, WordCount&);
public:
    WordCount() : occurs(0), occurList(0) {}
    WordCount(char *s)
        : str(s), occurs(0), occurList(0) {}
    WordCount(char *s, int l, int c, int o=1)
        : str(s), occurs(o)
        { occurList = new Loc(l,c); }
    WordCount( String&, Loc&, int = 1 );
    void found( int, int );
private:
    String str;
    int occurs;
    Loc *occurList;
};
```

It now contains two class members, each of which defines an operator <<
instance.

found() inserts a new Loc object into the list of locations at which the
word has been found. Here is its implementation:

```
#include <assert.h>

void WordCount::found( int l, int c ) {
    Loc *tmp = new Loc( l, c );
    assert( tmp != 0 );
    ++occurs;
    tmp->next = occurList;
    occurList = tmp;
}
```

WordCount now contains two class members, each of which defines an
operator << instance. Here is the new definition of the WordCount insertion
operator:

```
ostream& operator <<( ostream& os, WordCount& wd ) {
    Loc *tptr = wd.occurList;

    os   << "<" << wd.occurs << "> "
         << wd.str << endl;   // os << String

    int cnt = 0, onLine = 6;
    while ( tptr ) {
        os << *tptr << " ";        // os << Loc
        if ( ++cnt >= onLine )
            { os << endl; cnt = 0;   }
        tptr = tptr->next;
    }
    return os;
}
```

Here is a program that utilizes the new definition of WordCount. For simplicity, the occurrences are hand coded.

```
#include <iostream.h>
#include "WordCount.h"

main() {
    WordCount search( "rosebud" );

    // for simpilicity, hand code 6 occurrences
    search.found(7,12);   search.found(7,18);
    search.found(14,2);   search.found(34,36);
    search.found(49,17);  search.found(67,51);

    cout << "Occurrences: " << endl << search;
    return 0;
}
```

When this program is compiled and executed, it generates the following output:

```
Occurrences:
<6> rosebud
<67,51> <49,17> <34,36> <14,2> <7,18> <7,12>
```

The output of this program is stored in a file named output. Our next effort will be to define an input operator (">>") to read this back in.

The overloaded insertion operators are not class members, and so they are not inherited. Moreover, they cannot be made virtual functions directly. An example of how to provide virtual output functions while retaining the iostream insertion syntax is presented in Section 9.1 (page 460) using the ZooAnimal class hierarchy.

A.5   Overloading Operator >>

Overloading of the extraction operator ("`>>`") is similar to overloading the insertion operator. Figure `A.1` presents an implementation of the extraction operator for WordCount.

This example illustrates a number of issues with regard to possible iostream error states. These are as follows:

1. An istream that fails because of a bad format should mark the state of istream as *bad*. The expression

   ```
   is.clear( ios::badbit|is.rdstate() )
   ```

   does just that.

   Here is what it means. The error state of an iostream is maintained as a bit vector. The member function `rdstate()` returns this vector. `clear()` resets the entire error state to `0`. `clear(ios::badbit)` sets the badbit flag, which is what we want, but it resets the other error bit flags to `0`. We want to retain the previous error state, whatever it is, while setting the badbit flag. We do this by *oring* `ios::badbit` with the previous error state — which is the reason we write

   ```
   is.clear( ios::badbit|is.rdstate() )
   ```

2. The insertion and extraction operations of an iostream in an error state are without affect. For example,

   ```
   while ((ch = is.get()) != lbrace)
   ```

   will loop forever if `is` is in an error state. This is why the condition of `is` is tested before each call of `get()`:

   ```
   // insure ``is'' is not bad
   while ( is && (ch = is.get()) != lbrace)
   ```

   `is` evaluates to `0` when its error state is set.

The following program reads in the WordCount class object previously written by the overloaded insertion operator defined earlier.

```
#include <iostream.h>
#include "WordCount.h"

istream& operator >>(istream& is, WordCount& wd) {
/* format of WordCount object to be read:
 * <2> string
 *    <7,3> <12,36> */

    int ch;
    if ((ch = is.get()) != '<' ) { // bad format
        is.clear( ios::badbit | is.rdstate() );
        return is;
    }

    is >> wd.occurs;
    while ( is && (ch = is.get()) != '>' ) ;
    const bufSize = 512;
    char buf[ bufSize ];
    is >> buf;
    wd.str = buf;

    // read in the locations; build list
    // format of each location: <l,c>
    for ( int j = 0; j < wd.occurs; ++j )
    {
    Loc *tptr;
    int l, c;

        // extract values
        while (is && (ch = is.get())!= '<' ) ;
        is >> l;

        while (is && (ch = is.get())!= ',' ) ;
        is >> c;

        while (is && (ch = is.get())!= '>' ) ;

        // build list
        tptr = new Loc( l, c );
        tptr->next = wd.occurList;
        wd.occurList = tptr;
    }
    return is;
}
```

Figure A.1 WordCount Extraction Operator

```
#include <iostream.h>
#include <stdlib.h>
#include "WordCount.h"

main() {
    WordCount readIn;

    if ( (cin >> readIn) == 0 ) {
        cerr << "WordCount input error" << endl;
        exit( -1 );
    }
    cout << readIn << endl;
    return 0;
}
```

The expression

```
if ( (cin >> readIn) == 0 )
```

checks that the WordCount extraction operator was actually successful in reading from standard input.

When compiled and executed, the program generates the following output:

```
<6> rosebud
<67,51> <49,17> <34,36> <14,2> <7,18> <7,12>
```

A.6   File Input and Output

A user wishing to connect a file to the program for input and/or output must include the fstream.h header file in addition to iostream.h:

```
#include <iostream.h>
#include <fstream.h>
```

To open a file for output only, an *ofstream* (output file stream) class object must be defined. For example,

```
ofstream outFile( "copy.out", ios::out );
```

The arguments passed to outfile specify, in turn, the name of the file to be opened and the mode under which to open it. An ofstream file can be opened in either output (ios::out) or append (ios::app) mode.

If an existing file is opened in output mode, any data stored in that file is discarded. If the user wishes to add to rather than write over an existing file, the file should be opened in the append mode. Data written to the file will then be added at its end. In either mode, if the file does not exist, it will be created.

Before attempting to read or write to a file, it is always a good idea to verify that it has been opened successfully. Our test of outFile is coded as follows:

```
if ( !outFile ) { // opened failed
    cerr << "cannot open ''copy.out'' for output\n";
    exit( -1 );
}
```

The ofstream class is derived from the ostream class. All the ostream operations can be applied to an ofstream class object. For example,

```
outFile.put ( '1' ).put ( ')' ).put ( sp );
outFile << "1 + 1 = " << (1 + 1) << endl;
```

inserts

```
1) 1 + 1 = 2
```

into the file copy.out.

The following program *gets* characters from the standard input and *puts* them into the file copy.out:

```
#include <iostream.h>
#include <fstream.h>
#include <stdlib.h>

main() {
    // open a file copy.out for output
    ofstream outFile( "copy.out", ios::out );

    if ( !outFile ) { // open failed?
        cerr << "Cannot open ''copy.out'' for output\n";
        exit( -1 );
    }

    char ch;
    while ( cin.get( ch ) )
        outFile.put( ch );
    return 0;
}
```

User-defined instances of the insertion operator ("<<") can also be applied to an ofstream class object. The following program invokes the WordCount insertion operator defined in the previous section:

```
#include <iostream.h>
#include <fstream.h>
#include "WordCount.h"

main() {
    // open a file word.out for output
    ofstream oFile( "word.out", ios::out );

    // test for successful open goes here ...

    // create and manually set
    WordCount artist( "Renoir" );
    artist.found( 7, 12 ); artist.found( 34, 18 );

    // invokes operator <<(ostream&, WordCount&);
    oFile << artist;
    return 0;
}
```

To open a file for input only, an *ifstream* class object must be defined. ifstream is derived from istream and inherits its nonprivate members. The following program reads copy.out and writes it to standard output:

```
#include <iostream.h>
#include <fstream.h>

main() {
    // open a file copy.out for input
    ifstream inFile( "copy.out", ios::in );

    // test for successful open goes here ...

    char ch;
    while ( inFile.get( ch ))
        cout.put( ch );
    return 0;
}
```

The enumeration constant ios::in specifies that copy.out is to be opened in input mode.

The following program copies an input file into an output file, placing each string on a separate line:

```
#include <iostream.h>
#include <fstream.h>
#include <iomanip.h>

char *infile = "in.fil";
char *outfile = "out.fil";

main() {
    ifstream iFile( infile, ios::in );
    ofstream oFile( outfile, ios::out );

    // verify both files are open ...

    int cnt = 0;
    const bufSize = 1024;
    char buf[ bufSize ];

    while ( iFile >> setw( bufSize ) >> buf ) {
        oFile << buf << endl;
        ++cnt;
    }

    // display count of strings processed
    cout << "[ " << cnt << " ]" << endl;
    return 0;
}
```

Both an ifstream and an ofstream class object can be defined without specifying a file. A file can later be explicitly connected to a class object through the member function open(). For example,

```
ifstream curFile;
// ...
curFile.open( filename, ios::in );
if ( !curFile ) // open failed?
// ...
```

where filename is of type char*.

A file can be disconnected from the program by invoking the member function close(). For example,

```
curFile.close();
```

In the following program, five files are in turn opened and closed using the same ifstream class object:

```
#include <iostream.h>
#include <fstream.h>

const fileCnt = 5;
char *fileTabl[ fileCnt ] = {
    "Melville","Joyce","Musil","Proust","Kafka"
};

main() {
    ifstream inFile; // not attached to any file

    for ( int i = 0; i < fileCnt; ++i ) {
        inFile.open( fileTabl[i], ios::in );
        // ... verify successful open
        // ... process file
        inFile.close();
    }
    return 0;
}
```

An *fstream* class object can open a file for either input *or* output. The fstream class is derived from the iostream class. In the following example, word.out is first read then written using the fstream class object `file`. The file word.out, created earlier in this section, contains a WordCount object.

```
#include <iostream.h>
#include <fstream.h>
#include "WordCount.h"

main() {
    WordCount wd;
    fstream file;

    file.open( "word.out", ios::in );
    file >> wd;
    file.close();

    cout << "Read in: " << wd << endl;

    file.open( "word.out", ios::app );
    file << endl << wd << endl;
    file.close();
    return 0;
}
```

An fstream class object can also open a file for *both* input and output. For example, the following definition opens word.out in both input and append mode:

```
fstream io( "word.out", ios::in|ios::app );
```

The bitwise OR operator is used to specify more than one mode.

All the iostream class types can be repositioned using either the `seekg()` or `seekp()` member function, which can move to an "absolute" address within the file or move a byte offset from a particular position. Both `seekg()` and `seekp()` take the following two arguments:

```
typedef long streampos;

seekg( streampos p, seek_dir d=ios::beg );
```

where `seek_dir` is an enumeration that defines three elements:

1. `ios::beg`, the beginning of the file.

2. `ios::cur`, the current position of the file.

3. `ios::end`, the end of the file.

A call with two arguments moves some offset. The following example positions the file at the ith Record entry for each iteration:

```
for ( int i = 0; i < recordCnt; ++i )
    readFile.seekg( i * sizeof(Record), io::beg );
```

A negative value can also be specified for the first argument. For example, the following moves backwards 10 bytes from end-of-file:

```
readFile.seekg( -10, ios::end );
```

If supplied with only one argument, the file is positioned n bytes from the beginning of the file. Thus, whenever the second argument is `ios::beg`, it can be omitted.

The current position in a file is returned by the member function `tellg()`. For example,

```
// mark current position
streampos mark = writeFile.tellg();

// ...
if ( cancelEntry )
    // return to marked position
    writeFile.seekg( mark );
```

A programmer wishing to advance one Record from the current file position might write either of the following:

```
// equivalent repositioning seek invocations
readFile.seekg( readFile.tellg() + sizeof(Record) );

// this is considered the more efficient
readFile.seekg( sizeof(Record), ios::cur );
```

Let's go through an actual programming example in some detail. Here is the problem. We are given a text file to read. We are to compute the byte size of the file and store it at the end of the file. In addition, each time we encounter a newline character, we are to store the current byte size, including the newline, at the end of the file. For example, given the following text file,

```
abcd
efg
hi
j
```

the program should produce the following modified text file:

```
abcd
efg
hi
j
5 9 12 14 24
```

Here is our initial implementation:

```
#include <iostream.h>
#include <fstream.h>

main() {
    // open in both input and append mode
    fstream inOut( "copy.out", ios::in|ios::app );
    int cnt=0;    // byte count
    char ch;

    while ( inOut.get( ch ) ) {
        cout.put( ch ); // echo on terminal
        ++cnt;
        if ( ch == '\n' ) {
            inOut << cnt ;
            inOut.put(' '); // blank space
        }
    }
}
```

```
        // write out final byte count
        inOut << cnt << endl;
        cout << "[ " << cnt << " ]0;
        return 0;
    }
```

inOut is an fstream class object attached to the file copy.out, which is opened in both input and append mode. A file opened in append mode will write all data to the end of the file.

Each time we read a character, including white space but not end-of-file, we increment cnt and echo the character on the user's terminal. The purpose of echoing the input is so that we have something to look at and measure in the off chance that our program does not work as expected.

Each time we encounter a newline, we write the current value of cnt to inOut. Reading end-of-file terminates the loop. We write the final value of cnt to inOut and also to the screen.

The program compiles. It seems correct. The file contains the first few sentences of *Moby Dick* that we have used previously in this appendix. When we execute the program, the output generated is the following:

```
    [ 0 ]
```

No characters are displayed and the program believes the text file is empty.

The problem is that the file, being opened in append mode, is positioned at its end. When

```
    inOut.get( ch );
```

is executed, end-of-file is encountered and the while loop terminates, leaving cnt with a value of 0.

We can solve this problem by repositioning the file back to the beginning before we begin to read. The statement

```
    inOut.seekg( 0, ios::beg );
```

accomplishes just that. The program is recompiled and rerun. This time, the following output is generated:

```
    Call me Ishmael.   Some years ago, never mind
    [ 45 ]
```

The display and byte count are generated for only the first line of the text file. The remaining six lines are ignored. Can you see what the problem is?

The problem is that the file is opened in append mode. The first time cnt is written, the file becomes repositioned at its end. The subsequent get () encounters end-of-file and once more prematurely terminates the while loop.

The solution this time is to reposition the file to where it was prior to the writing of cnt. This can be accomplished with the following two additional statements:

```
// mark current position
streampos mark = inOut.tellg();
inOut << cnt << sp;
inOut.seekg( mark ); // restore position
```

When the program is recompiled and executed, the output to the terminal is correct. Examining the output file, however, we discover another problem. The final byte count, although being written to the terminal, is *not* being written to the file. The insertion operator following the while loop is not being executed.

The problem this time is that inOut is in the "state" of having encountered end-of-file. As long as inOut remains in this state, input and output operations are *not* performed. The solution is to clear() the state of the file. This is accomplished with the following statement:

```
inOut.clear(); // zero out state flags
```

The complete program looks as follows:

```
#include <iostream.h>
#include <fstream.h>

main() {
    fstream inOut( "copy.out", ios::in|ios::app );
    int cnt=0;
    char ch;

    inOut.seekg(0, ios::beg );
    while ( inOut.get( ch ) ) {
        cout.put( ch );
        cnt++;
        if ( ch == '\n' ) {
            // mark current position
            streampos mark = inOut.tellg();
            inOut << cnt << ' ';
            inOut.seekg( mark ); // restore position
        }
    }

    inOut.clear();
    inOut << cnt << endl;

    cout << "[ " << cnt << " ]\n";
}
```

When the program is recompiled and executed, it generates the expected output — at last!.

A.7 Condition States

An iostream library object maintains a set of condition flags through which the ongoing state of the stream can be monitored. The following four predicate member functions can be invoked:

1. `eof()`: returns true if the stream has encountered end-of-file. For example,

```
if ( inOut.eof() )
    inOut.clear();
```

2. `bad()`: returns true if an invalid operation, such as "seeking" past end-of-file, has been attempted.

3. `fail()`: returns true either if an operation has been unsuccessful or if `bad()` is true. For example,

```
ifstream iFile( filename, ios::in );

if ( iFile.fail() ) // unable to open
    error( ... );
```

4. `good()`: returns true if none of the other conditions is true. For example,

```
if ( inOut.good() )
```

The iostream classes define an overloaded instance of the logical NOT operator ("!"):

```
if ( !inOut )
```

that provides a shorthand notation for the following equivalent compound expression:

```
if ( inOut.fail() )
```

The reason the truth condition of a `while` loop of the following form

```
while ( cin >> buf )
```

evaluates to 0 on encountering end-of-file is because of a stream member conversion operator which is generally equivalent to the following compound expression:

```
// predefined logical NOT operator
if ( !( cin.bad() || cin.fail() ))
```

It is also possible to test a file stream object explicitly to learn if it has yet been opened. For example,

```
ifstream ifile;
```

defines an unattached ifstream class object. Before writing

```
ifile << "hello, world\n";
```

it is a good idea to verify that ifile has been attached to some file. Since no operations have been attempted, the test

```
if ( ifile.good() )
    // ...
```

evaluates to true even though the file may as yet be unopened. The following predicate tests whether ifile is open:

```
if ( ifile.rdbuf()->is_open == 0 ) {
    // no file attached
    ifile.open( filename, ios::in );
    // ...
```

rdbuf() is a member function which accesses the internal buffer associated with the file stream.

A.8 Incore Formatting

The iostream library supports incore operations on arrays of characters. The ostrstream class inserts characters into an array while the istrstream class extracts characters from an array. To define objects of either class, the strstream.h header file must be included. For example, the following program fragment reads the entire file words into a character array dynamically allocated by the buf ostrstream class object:

```
#include <iostream.h>
#include <fstream.h>
#include <strstream.h>

ifstream ifile("words", ios::in);
ostrstream buf;

void
processFile()
{
    char ch;
    while (buf && ifile.get(ch))
        buf.put(ch);

    // ...
}
```

The `str()` member function returns a pointer to the character array associated with the ostrstream class object. For example,

```
char *bp = buf.str();
```

initializes bp with the address of the array associated with `buf`. The array can now be manipulated through bp in the same way as any "ordinary" character array.

Invoking `str()`, in effect, hands off the character array from the ostrstream to the programmer. Calling `str()` has the effect of "freezing" the array — subsequent insertions using the ostrstream operators are not permitted. `str()`, therefore, should be invoked only after character insertion is complete.

If the ostrstream goes out of scope and `str()` has not been invoked, the array is automatically deleted by the ostrstream destructor. Once `str()` is invoked, however, deletion of the array becomes the responsibility of the programmer. Before bp goes out of scope, therefore, the array it addresses must be explicitly deleted:

```
delete bp;
```

Let's look at an example. In the program pictured in Figure A.2, the ostrstream `inStore` is used to store the file `words`. (`words`, recall, contains the opening sentences of *Moby Dick*.) Unlike the previous example, however, the file is stored as a sequence of null-terminated strings. `ends` is a predefined manipulator that inserts a null character.

```cpp
#include <iostream.h>
#include <fstream.h>
#include <strstream.h>
#include <iomanip.h>
#include <string.h>

ifstream ifile("words", ios::in);
ostrstream inStore;
const len = 512;
main() {
    char inBuf[len];
    int wordCnt = 0;

    while ( inStore &&
            ifile >> setw(len) >> inBuf )
    {
        ++wordCnt;
        inStore << inBuf << ends;
    }
    char *ptr = inStore.str(); // grab hold of array
    char *tptr = ptr; // keep track of beginning

    // words is an array of character pointers
    // its size is the number of strings read from ifile
    char **words = new char*[wordCnt];
    wordCnt = 0;

    // initialize each element of words
    //   to address a string within inStore
    while ( *ptr ) {
        words[ wordCnt++ ] = ptr;
        ptr += strlen(ptr) + 1;
    }

    // print out the strings in reverse order
    // in lines of length lineLength
    const lineLength = 8;
    for ( int i=wordCnt-1, cnt=0; i >= 0; --i ) {
        if ( cnt++ % lineLength == 0 ) {
            cout << endl;
            cnt = 1;
        }
        cout << words[i] << " ";
    }
    cout << endl;
    delete tptr;
}
```

Figure A.2 Incore Formatting Program Example

When executed, the program generates the following output:

```
circulation. the regulating and spleen, the off driving
of have I way a is It world.
the of part watery the see and little
a about sail would I thought I shore,
on me interest to particular nothing and purse,
my in money no or little having precisely,
long how mind never ago, years Some Ishmael.
me Call
```

A second use of ostrstream is to provide the class object with the address of a preallocated character array. This instance of an ostrstream class object requires three arguments:

1. A character pointer, char *cp, to a preallocated array.

2. A long containing the size in bytes of the array.

3. An open mode, either ios::app or ios::out. If ios::app is passed, cp is assumed to be a null-terminated string; insertion begins at the null character. Otherwise, insertion begins at cp.

For example, let's define a format function to convert a set of arguments into a string. Note the use of seekp() to reposition the ostrstream to the beginning of the array.

```
#include <iostream.h>
#include <strstream.h>

char*
format(const char *name, int cnt) {
    const bufLen = 128;
    static char buf[bufLen];
    static ostrstream oss(buf,bufLen,ios::out);

    oss.seekp(ios::beg);
    oss << name << " is mentioned "
        << cnt << " times!" << ends;
    return buf;
}

main() {
    int val = 24;
    cout << format("Anna",24) << endl;
    cout << format("Daniel",val) << endl;
    return 0;
}
```

When compiled and executed, the program generates the following results:

```
Anna is mentioned 24 times!
Daniel is mentioned 24 times!
```

The istrstream class extracts characters from a character array. An istrstream class object takes two arguments:

1. A character pointer to a preallocated array.

2. The size, in bytes, of the array.

The istrstream object can be either anonymous or named. For example, in the following program, an anonymous istrstream object is used to transform a character string into an integer value:

```cpp
#include <iostream.h>
#include <strstream.h>

int str_to_dec(char *s) {
    int val;
    istrstream(s,sizeof(s)) >> val;
    return val;
}

char *tbl[5] = {
        "400", "10", "-5", "15", "1024" };

main() {
    int sum = 0;
    char *p = tbl[0];

    for (int i = 0; i<5; p=tbl[++i])
        sum += str_to_dec(p);
    cout << "Sum: " << sum << endl; // Sum: 1444
    return 0;
}
```

A.9 Format State

Each iostream library class object maintains a *format state* that controls the details of formatting operations, such as the conversion base for integral numeric notation or the precision of a floating point value. The programmer can set and unset format state flags using the setf() and unsetf() member functions. Additionally, a set of manipulators is available to the programmer for modifying the format state of an object.

By default integers are written and read in decimal notation. The programmer may change the notational base to octal or hexadecimal or back to decimal. To change the conversion base for a value, the manipulators hex, dec, and oct can be inserted between the stream object and the value to be handled. For example,

```
#include <iostream.h>

main()
{
    int i = 512;
    cout << "Default: " << i << endl;

    // applying oct changes base to octal
    cout << "Octal:    " << oct << i;
    cout << "\t" << i << endl;

    // applying hex changes base to hexadecimal
    cout << "Hex:      " << hex << i;
    cout << "\t" << i << endl;

    cout << "Decimal: " << dec << i;
    cout << "\t" << i << endl;

    return 0;
}
```

When compiled and executed, the program generates the following output:

```
Default: 512
Octal:    1000    1000
Hex:       200     200
Decimal: 512       512
```

The application of one of hex, oct, or dec changes the default interpretation to the specified notational base for subsequent integer values. The program illustrates this by printing the value a second time without use of a filter.

By default, a floating point value has a precision value of 6 (this prints out the decimal point and five digits of precision). This value may be modified by using either the precision(int) member function or the setprecision() stream manipulator (to use the latter, the iomanip.h header file must be included). precision() returns the current precision value. For example,

```
#include <iostream.h>
#include <iomanip.h>
#include <math.h>

main() {
    cout << "Precision: "
         << cout.precision() << endl
         << sqrt(2.0) << endl;

    cout.precision(12);
    cout << "\nPrecision: "
         << cout.precision() << endl
         << sqrt(2.0) << endl;

    cout << "\nPrecision: " << setprecision(3)
         << cout.precision() << endl
         << sqrt(2.0) << endl;
    return 0;
}
```

When compiled and executed, the program generates the following output.

```
Precision: 6
1.41421

Precision: 12
1.41421356237

Precision: 3
1.41
```

The setf() member function sets a specified format state flag. There are two overloaded instances:

```
setf( long );
setf( long, long );
```

The first argument can be either a format bit flag or field. Table A.1 lists the format bit flags.

The second argument is a format bit field associated with a particular set of format flags. Table A.2 lists two format bit fields.

For example, to have cout show the numeric base of integral values, one would write the following:

```
cout.setf( ios::showbase );
```

Similarly, to set the numeric base for integral values to octal, one would write the following:

Flag	Meaning
ios::showbase	display numeric base
ios::showpoint	display decimal point
ios::dec	decimal numeric base
ios::hex	hexadecimal numeric base
ios::oct	octal numeric base
ios::fixed	decimal notation
ios::scientific	scientific notation

Table A.1 Format Flags

Bit Field	Meaning	Flags
ios::basefield	integral base	ios::hex ios::oct ios::dec
ios::floatfield	floating point notation	ios::fixed ios::scientific

Table A.2 Format Bit Fields

```
cout.setf( ios::oct, ios::basefield );
```

setf(long,long) first resets the format field to 0, then sets the format bit of its first argument. It returns the previous state as a long integer value. This allows that state to be saved. We can restore it later by passing it as the first argument to setf(long,long). For example,

```
#include <iostream.h>

main() {
    int ival = 1024;
    long oldbase;

    cout.setf( ios::showbase );
    cout.setf( ios::oct, ios::basefield );
    cout << "ival: " << ival << endl;

    // save previous notational base
    oldbase = cout.setf( ios::hex, ios::basefield );
    cout << "ival: " << ival << endl;

    // restore previous notational base
    cout.setf( oldbase, ios::basefield );
    cout << "ival: " << ival << endl;

    return 0;
}
```

The reason we don't simply write

```
cout.setf( ios::hex );
```

is that this instance of setf() does not clear the previous state. Were ios::basefield previously set to decimal, it would now be set to *both* hexadecimal and decimal. If ios::basefield is set to more than one base, or if no base at all is set, output defaults to decimal notation.

By default, the trailing zeros of a floating point value are discarded when the value is displayed. For example,

```
cout << 10.70 << endl
```

will print on the user's terminal as

```
10.7
```

while

```
cout << 10.0 << endl
```

will print as 10 without either the trailing zero or the trailing decimal point.

In order to display trailing zeros and the trailing decimal point, the programmer must set the ios::showpoint flag. For example,

```
cout.setf( ios::showpoint );
```

The ios::floatfield format state controls the display of floating-point values. The programmer can explicitly set or unset it by using one of the following enumeration constants:

1. `ios::fixed`: display value in decimal notation.

2. `ios::scientific`: display value in scientific notation.

   For example,

```
#include <iostream.h>
#include <iomanip.h>
#include <math.h>

main() {
    cout << setprecision( 8 ) << "Precision:    "
         << cout.precision() << endl
         << "Default:    10.0: " << 10.0 << endl
         << "Default:    pow(18,10): "
         << pow( 18, 10 ) << endl;

    cout.setf( ios::fixed, ios::floatfield );
    cout << "\nPrecision:    " << cout.precision()
         << endl << "Fixed:       10.0: " << 10.0
         << endl << "Fixed:       pow(18,10): "
         << pow( 18, 10 ) << endl;

    cout.setf( ios::scientific, ios::floatfield );
    cout << "\nPrecision:    " << cout.precision()
         << endl << "Scientific: 10.0: " << 10.0
         << endl << "Scientific: pow(18,10): "
         << pow( 18, 10 ) << endl;
    return 0;
}
```

When compiled and executed, the program generates the following output:

```
Precision:   8
Default:     10.0: 10
Default:     pow(18,10): 3.5704672e+12

Precision:   8
Fixed:       10.0: 10.00000000
Fixed:       pow(18,10): 3570467226624.00012000

Precision:   8
Scientific: 10.0: 1.00000000e+01
Scientific: pow(18,10): 3.57046723e+12
```

A.10 A Strongly Typed Library

The iostream library is strongly typed. The attempt, for example, to read from an ostream, or to assign an ostream to an istream are both caught at compile time and flagged as type violations. For example, given the following set of declarations,

```
#include <iostream.h>
#include <fstream.h>
class Screen;

extern istream& operator>>( istream&, Screen& );
extern void print( ostream& );
ifstream inFile;
```

the following two statements result in compile-time type violations:

```
main() {
    Screen myScreen;

    // error: expects an ostream&
    print( cin >> myScreen );

    // error: expects >> operator
    inFile << "error: output operator";
}
```

Input/output facilities are provided as a component of the C++ standard library. Beginning with Release 2.0, they are supported by the library component referred to as the *iostream* library, the subject of this appendix. The ANSI C++ committee's work on defining a standard I/O library for C++ is based on iostream (although it looks as if the final version will be simplified somewhat from the full iostream implementation).

The appendix does not describe the entire iostream library — in particular, the creation of user-derived manipulators and buffer classes are beyond the scope of a primer. The author has chosen instead to focus on the portion of the iostream library fundamental to providing program I/O, and that portion of the library likely to remain in the ANSI C++ library standard.

Appendix B: **Exception Handling**

Exceptions are run-time program anomalies such as division by zero, arithmetic or array overflow, and the exhaustion of free store. Programmers generally develops their own style for handling exceptions. Here, for example, are a number of different ways they might handle the possibility of operator new returning 0:

```
// styles of handling free store exhaustion

// explicit test for exhausted free store
if ((pi = new int) == 0) {
    cerr << "program's free store exhausted\n"
    exit( -1 );
}



// just trust that it won't happen
pi = new int[ 10000 ];

// make use of new_handler facility
#include <new.h>
extern void freeStoreException()
set_new_handler(freeStoreException);



// use assert() macro facility
#include <assert.h>

*pi = new int;
assert (pi != 0);
```

Coding practices become even more diverse in the case of user-defined classes. Each user-defined class type introduces its own potential class-specific anomalies — a BitVector or Array that indexes a nonexistent element, a Screen class with a height or width less than 1.

Exception handling provides a standard language-level facility for responding to run-time program anomalies. A uniform syntax and style is supported, yet one that supports fine-tuning by individual programmers. The exception-handling facility can significantly reduce the size and complexity of program code by eliminating the need for testing anomalous states explicitly. By analogy, think of the amount of code reduction that results from the use of virtual functions and the elimination of explicit `switch` statements for determining the actual type of a class object.

An exception is raised at the point of a program anomaly. In C++, the raising of an exception is spoken of as *throwing* and is associated with a `throw` expression. A thrown exception transfers control from the point of the program anomaly to an exception handler, if there is one. In C++, the exception handler is said to `catch` an exception. Exception handlers are associated with `try` blocks. A try block groups together one or more program statements for which all or a subset of exceptions will be caught. The program terminates following the handling of an exception.

What, for example, are the possible exceptions for our template Array class defined earlier? Two that come to mind are the following:

- Free store exhaustion during allocation of the array.

- An out-of-bounds index array (raised by the range-checking array).

Code that we wish to handle these possible exceptions is placed in a try block.

B.1 The Try Block

The try block begins with the `try` keyword followed by a sequence of program statements enclosed within braces. Following the try block is a list of handlers (that is, `catch` clauses). The try block serves to group together a set of statements for which a set of raised exceptions are to be handled. For example,

```
#include "Array_RC.h"

template <class Type>
  extern void
  doit(Array<Type>&);

template <class Type>
  Array<Type>&
  sum_it(Type &sumval, Type *arr, int sz, int *ix)
  {
```

```
try {
    Array_RC<Type> array(arr, sz);
    doit(array); // whatever ...
    sumval = array[ix[0]]+array[ix[1]];
    return array;
}
catch(const char *string) { ... }
catch(RangeErr &re) { ... }
catch(ArrayErr &ae) { ... }
}
```

In our example, the try block catches three exceptions that might be raised during

(a) the construction of the Array class object `array`,

(b) the execution of the nonmember function `doit()` (and any subsequent functions it may call), and

(c) the assignment to `sumval` invoking the Array class subscript operators.

Each catch handler specifies the types of exceptions to be caught. A raised exception occurring during the execution of the try block is in turn compared to a `const char*`, `RangeErr`, and `ArrayErr` type. If there is a match, the associated catch handler is executed.

B.2 The Catch Handler and Throw Clause

What kind of exceptions could be of a `const char*` type? Something like the following:

```
template <class Type>
Type min(Type *array, int size)
{
    if (array == 0)
        throw "Panic: min(array==0 ...";

    if (size <= 0)
        throw "Panic: min(array,size<=0)";

    // ...
}
```

The set of catch handlers resembles a set of overloaded functions. The appropriate catch handler is determined by matching on the type of the thrown exception. The catch handlers are evaluated in the order of their appearance following the try block. If there is no match among the catch

handlers of a try block, the next enclosing try block is searched. This continues up through all the enclosing try blocks. If no matching catch handler is
found, the predefined `terminate()` function is called.

The ArrayErr and RangeErr exceptions are class types explicitly provided
to handle the set of run-time exceptions associated with the Array class hierarchy.

```
class ArrayErr {
public:
    ArrayErr(enum ErrOp,int);
    virtual void response();
protected:
    enum ErrOp {
        MEM_EXHAUST=1,
        BAD_VALUE,
        UNDERFLOW,
        OVERFLOW
    };
    // ...
};


class RangeErr : public ArrayErr {
public:
    RangeErr(enum ErrOp,int,int=0);
    void response();
protected:
    // ...
};
```

How are `throw` expressions matched to a catch handler? The actual
object of a throw expression is compared to the type of each catch handler in
turn. A match is effected if any one of the following three conditions hold:

1. Both types are exactly the same.

2. The catch handler type is a public base class of the object thrown.

3. The catch handler type, `Type`, is a pointer and the object thrown is a
   pointer that can be converted to `Type` by a standard pointer conversion.

Once a match is found, the subsequent catch handlers are *not* examined. No
priority is given to an exact match over a match requiring the application of a
standard conversion. Some care must therefore be taken when listing the set
of catch handlers for a try block. The following order of catch handlers, for
example, could never be correct:

```
void some_function() {
    try {
        // ...
    }
    // incorrect order of catch handlers
    catch (void*) { ... }
    catch (ArrayErr&) { ... }
    catch (RangeErr&) { ... }
    catch (const char*) { ... }
    catch (void (*pf)(const char*)) { ... }
    // ...
}
```

Every pointer exception matches on that of void* through application of a
standard conversion. The other instances, therefore, are never examined. (A
warning should be issued by the compiler.) Similarly, all exceptions derived
from ArrayErr match on the base class instance — the derived class instances
are also never examined. The following is a correct ordering of the catch
handlers:

```
// a correct order of catch handlers
catch (const char*) { ... }
catch (void (*pf)(const char*)) { ... }
catch (void*) { ... }

catch (RangeErr&) { ... }
catch (ArrayErr&) { ... }
```

A throw expression looks a great deal like a return statement. In the following example, throw expressions are associated with two possible Array
class anomalies: an invalid size parameter and the exhaustion of the the
program's free store.

```
template <class Type>
Array<Type>::Array( int sz )
{
    if ( sz < 0 )
        throw ArrayErr(BAD_VALUE, sz);

    array = new Type[ size = sz ];

    if (array == 0)
        throw ArrayErr(MEM_EXHAUST, size);
    // ...
}
```

In this next example, throw expressions are associated with Array boundary exceptions. Whether the program continues to execute following the

handling of an exception is for the most part determined by the catch handler. On completion of the catch handler, the exception is no longer considered raised. If execution of the program is allowed to continue, it does so at the point following the try block of the catch handler, *not* at the point following where the throw expression occurred. In the following definition of the subscript operator, if either conditional test is true, the remainder of the function following the throw expression is not executed. There is no need to conditionally tie the statements togethers with an else clause.

```
template <class Type>
Array_RC<Type>::operator[]( int ix )
{
    if (ix < 0)
        throw RangeErr(UNDERFLOW, ix);

    if (ix >= size)
        throw RangeErr(OVERFLOW, ix, size);

    return array[ix];
}
```

A catch handler need only specify a name to its exception if it needs to manipulate it within the body of its catch clause. Sometimes it is enough simply to know that a particular type of exception has been raised.

```
void foo()
{
    try
    {
        do_it();
    }

    catch (ArrayErr&)
    {
        // some kind of an Array exception raised
        // do whatever is necessary here,
        // then let the program continue ...
    }

    // execution continues following try block
    // ...
}
```

An ellipsis provides a kind of catch-all. For example,

```
try
{
    do_it();
}

catch ( ArrayErr & ) {
    // ...
}

catch ( ... ) {
    // catches everything that is not an ArrayErr
    // associated with this try block
    throw;
}
```

An empty throw expression simply passes the exception up to the enclosing try block. An empty throw expression can only occur within a catch handler.

B.3 The Function Throw List

A function can specify the set of exceptions it directly or indirectly will throw by providing a *throw list*. A throw list is a kind of contract the function makes with the rest of the program. For example,

```
extern void
do_it(int,int) throw(const char*, RangeErr);
```

A call of do_it() guarantees not to throw any exception other than a RangeErr and character pointer. If it should, a compiler-generated run-time exception occurs.

An empty throw list is a guarantee that the function does not throw an exception. For example,

```
extern void
no_problem(int,int) throw();
```

The throw list is not part of the function type. The following two declarations of foo(), for example, resolve to the same function:

```
// two declarations of the same function
extern foo(int) throw(const char*);
extern int foo(int bar=0);
```

Of course, without an explicit throw list, there is no way of determining, other than by inspection, whether a function does or does not throw an exception.

B.4 Summary

Exception handling provides a language-level facility for the uniform handling of program anomalies. It was officially accepted into the language at the November 1990 ANSI C++ committee meeting. Although there is no conforming implementation at the time of this writing, work is currently underway at a number of different locations.

Appendix C: Compatibility of C++ with C

An important factor in the rapid spread of C++ has been the ease of using C++ with the C language. There is language compatibility: The ability to use C++ with existing C-based systems; and there is what Andrew Koenig refers to as programmer compatibility: The ease with which C programmers can learn and make effective use of C++.

A C programmer first learning C++ can use it as C with strong type checking. (The function prototype introduced in C++ has been adopted by ANSI C.) Within a day, a C programmer can begin writing C-like C++ programs.

- The C standard I/O library can be used rather than the C++ iostream library. The programmer simply includes `stdio.h`.

- The C struct can be used in place of the C++ class. Associated functions may or may not be declared as member functions of the struct. The following two declarations are equivalent in C++:

```
class foo_1 {
public:
      /* ... */
};

struct foo_2 {
      /* ... */
};
```

- Under the UNIX operating system, all the C library and system calls can be invoked from a C++ program provided that the proper header file is included. The CC command by default includes `libc.a`, the standard C library. Additional C libraries are included by providing a `-l` option on the command line, the same as for the `cc` command.
The following program is both legal C and C++:

```
#include <stdio.h>

main()
{
    printf("hello, world\n");
    return 0;
}
```

The equivalent C++ program is written as follows:

```
#include <iostream.h>

main() {
    cout << "hello, world\n";
    return 0;
}
```

The C++ programmer relies less on the C preprocessor (cpp) than does the C programmer, using it primarily for conditional compilation and the inclusion of header files. C++'s support of templates, inline functions, and read-only symbolic constants has made the use of cpp #define macros largely unnecessary.

The primary difference between C++ and C is the support C++ provides for the following:

- Inlining and overloading of functions.
- Ability to provide default argument values.
- Argument pass-by-reference (in addition to the C language default pass-by-value).

- The new and delete free store operators (in place of direct calls of malloc() and free()).

- Support of template functions and classes.
- Support of abstract data types by providing for information hiding and the definition of a public interface.

- Support of object-oriented programming through the mechanisms of inheritance and dynamic binding.

C.1 The C++ Function Prototype

C++ is based on the C programming language as described by Kernighan and Ritchie's *The C Programming Language*. Nearly all of the changes to C specified by the ANSI C report have been adopted by C++. A program written in a subset of the language common to both C++ and C has the same meaning when compiled in either language. Most ANSI C programs are also legal C++ programs. The most visible difference between the original C language and C++ is in the declaration of external functions. For example, here are their respective declarations of the same function, min():

```
extern min(); // C
extern min( const int*, int ); // C++
```

In C++, the type and number of each argument must be specified in the declaration of the function, referred to as the *function prototype*. Because of the function prototype, C++ can flag both of the following incorrect calls of min() at compile time as errors. In C, both calls are accepted. The burden of finding the mistakes is left to the programmer.

```
int i, j, ia[10];
main() {
    min( i, j ); // illegal first argument
    min( ia );   // missing second argument
}
```

The main work in having a C program run under C++ is in converting the extern declarations of functions. For example,

```
extern foo();
```

will need to be rewritten to make its arguments explicit:

```
extern foo( const int* );
```

In C, a function can be invoked without first declaring it provided its return value is of type int. C++ requires an explicit declaration of a function prior to its use. Providing explicit declarations of implicit functions, then, is another aspect of getting existing C code to run under C++.

```
bar(10,20);
```

Finally, in C, a value-returning function is not actually required to return a value. In C++, a value-returning function must return a value at each exit point within the function.

Distributions of C++ provide a C++-style set of system header files with explicit function prototypes. In the C++ supplied stdio.h, for example, printf() is declared

```
int printf(const char* ...)
```

Because of the C++ function prototype, the following "typical" C program will *not* compile under C++:

```
struct node {
    int val;
    struct node *left, *right;
};
```

```
struct node*
get_node(val)
int val;
{
    char *malloc();
    struct node *ptr;

    /* C++ error: call of malloc() */
    /* C run-time error: wrong argument! */
    if ((ptr=(struct node*)malloc(sizeof(ptr)))==0)
        /* handle memory exhaustion error */ ;

    p->val = val;
    p->left = p->right = 0;
    return ptr;
}

main()
{
    struct node *p, *get_node();
    /* C++ error: call of get_node() */
    p = get_node( 1024 );
    /* ... rest of program ... */
}
```

This program fails under C++ because of these two declarations:

```
char *malloc();
struct node *get_node();
```

Why? Because both functions are declared with an empty argument list. In C++, an empty argument list means that the function does not take an argument. An attempt to pass an argument to either function, then, is flagged at compile time in C++ as a function interface error:

```
unexpected first argument of
    type int for get_node()
```

To C++-ify this program, each prototype needs to be given the explicit argument list. One might do well to view this conversion an an opportunity to clean up an application's interface specification — you'll be surprised at what you find, if experience is any indication.

The preferred conversion method is to rely on header files rather than on per-file or per-function declarations. This ensures that a function is declared consistently across all program modules. When a change in the interface needs to be made, it then needs be made only once. All modules dependent on the changed header file are updated automatically by the application's *makefile*. Actual program code need not be changed.

For example, since `malloc()` is a C library function, the programmer can simply delete its local declaration and instead include the standard header file `malloc.h`. However, since `get_node()` is an application-specific function, the programmer will need to define an applicable header file, perhaps `node.h`. This header is included, the local declaration is deleted, and the program now compiles under both C and C++. Unfortunately, since `malloc()` is being passed the wrong size value, the program will most likely *coredump* during execution. Rather than passing `malloc()` the size of a node structure, the programmer accidentally passed the smaller size of a pointer to a node structure.

This kind of memory allocation error is difficult to make using the C++ operator new. Here is the equivalent C++ program.

```
#include <malloc.h>

/* equivalent C++ version of program
 * class Node{} normally would be
 * placed in a Node.h header file.
 */

class Node {
public:
    // automatic initialization function
    Node( int i = 0)
    {
        left = right = 0;
        val = i;
    }
    int val;
    Node *left, *right;
};

main()
{
    Node *p = new Node( 1024 );
    // ... rest of program
}
```

The function `Node()` with the same name as the class tag name is referred to as a *constructor*. It provides for implicit initialization of each new Node object that enters scope. Operator new is the method of allocating memory from the heap in C++. It returns a pointer to the amount of memory necessary to hold an object of the named type, such as Node. The value in parentheses is passed to the Node class constructor.

C.2   Where C++ and C Differ

In a small number of areas, C++ and ANSI C diverge in their handling of a language feature. Stronger compile-time type checking and the greater functionality of C++ motivate the small number of differences between the two languages. These differences are the subject of this section.

Greater Functionality

The following are a list of differences between C++ and ANSI C that result from the greater functionality of C++ exhibited in its support of function name overloading, abstract data types, and object-oriented programming.

- C++ reserves additional keywords:

catch	inline	protected	throw
class	new	public	try
delete	operator	template	virtual
friend	private	this	

- In C++, the type of a literal character constant is char; in C, it is int. For example, on a machine with a four-byte word,

```
sizeof( 'a' );
```

evaluates to 1 in C++ and to 4 in C. This distinction is necessary in C++ in order to allow functions to be overloaded by an argument of type char.

- A side-effect of C++'s support for abstract data types is that each class, unlike the C struct, maintains both an associated scope and a mechanism to access or restrict access to individual elements within that scope. This extends to types (classes, enums, and typedefs) defined within the class.

```
struct Tree {
    struct Node { /* ... */ };
    enum status { fail, found };

    Node *tree;
};

/* The names
 *      Node, status, fail, found
 * C:   visible at global scope
 * C++: visible only within scope of Tree
 */
Node c_use; /* C++: error */
Tree::node cplus_use; /* C++: ok */
```

- A local structure name hides the name of an object, function, enumerator, or type in an outer scope. For example,

```
int ia[ iaSize ];
void fooBar() {
    struct ia { int i; char a; };

    /* C++: size of the local struct */
    /* ANSI C: size of ::ia */
    int sz = sizeof( ia );
    int ln = sizeof( ::ia ); /* equivalent C++ */
}
```

This is because structure names and identifiers occur in a single name space within C++. Note, however, that within the same scope, C++ handles the C-style reuse of identifier and type names. For example,

```
/* ok: C++ and C */
struct stat { /* ... */ };
extern struct stat *stat(char*, struct stat*);
```

- In C++, a goto statement cannot jump over a declaration with an explicit or implicit (that is, a class constructor) initializer unless the declaration is contained in a block and the entire block is jumped over. This constraint is not present in ANSI C.

- In C++, a variable declaration without an explicit extern is considered a definition of that variable. This is necessary for automatic invocation of class initialization functions. In ANSI C, the same declaration is treated as a "tentative" definition. The occurrence of multiple tentative definitions within one file is resolved to a single definition. For example,

```
struct Int { Int(); /* ... */ };

// ANSI C: ok.
// C++: error: two definitions of I,i,j
file a.c: int i; Int I; // apply Int()
file b.c: int i; Int I; // apply Int()
file c.c: int j; int j;
```

- In C++, the default linkage of a constant is static. In ANSI C, the default linkage of a constant is extern. Programs expected to run under both languages should always provide an explicit extern or static in the declaration. For example,

```
class Boolean { /* ... */ };

extern const Boolean TRUE(1);      // ANSI C default
static const Boolean FALSE(0);     // C++ default
```

Stronger Type Checking

The following are a list of differences between C++ and ANSI C that are due to stronger type checking within C++.

- C++ and ANSI C interpret the empty argument list differently. In ANSI C, the empty argument list suspends type checking. The declaration

  ```
  char *malloc();
  ```

  is interpreted to mean that malloc() takes zero or more arguments of any data type. This means K&R C programs will continue to compile without change. This also means that there is a *huge* hole in the type checking of ANSI C programs. For example, neither of the following invalid calls of malloc() are caught by an ANSI C compiler that has accepted the empty argument declaration:

  ```
  char ac[] = "riverrun"

  /* both these calls are invalid */
  malloc( ac );
  malloc();
  ```

  In C++, the empty argument list means that the function takes no arguments. In ANSI C, this is indicated by the keyword void.

  ```
  // ff takes no arguments
  extern ff( void );
  ```

  The argument list with an explicit void is also accepted by C++. Programs expected to run under both compilers should always use an explicit void in the argument list of a function taking no arguments.

- In C++, the use of an undeclared function is an error. In C, undeclared functions are permitted; type checking is suspended. For example,

  ```
  main() {
      // C++: error, printf is undeclared
      // C: ok, taken to mean: int printf()
      printf( 3.14159 ); // interface error
  ```

- In C++, the failure to return a value in a function declared as value-returning is an error. In C, this is permitted. For example,

```
// C: ok
// C++: error: no return value
double foo() { /* ... */ ;   return; };

main() {
    if ( foo() )
        // do something important ...
    return 0;
}
```

- In C++, the assignment of a pointer of type void* to a pointer of any other type requires an explicit cast since it is potentially very dangerous. In ANSI C, the conversion is implicit. For example,

```
main() {
    int i = 1024;
    void *pv = &i;

    // C++: error, explicit cast required.
    // ANSI C: ok.
    char *pc = pv;
    int len = strlen( pc ); // bad pointer
}
```

- C++ and ANSI C interpret differently the type of a string constant used to initialize a character array. In C++, the following initialization is illegal because it does not provide space for the null character that terminates a literal string constant:

```
// C++: error
// ANSI C: no error
char ch[2] = "hi";
```

In ANSI C, the string initializer is interpreted as a shorthand notation for the character elements 'h' and 'i'. A terminating null is supplied if the array has sufficient size to accommodate it. The following general form of array initialization

```
char ch[] = "hi";
```

creates an array of three elements in both C++ and ANSI C. Programmers are encouraged to use this form if they intend to move code between the two languages.

588   COMPATIBILITY OF C++ WITH C

C.3 Linkage Between C++ and C

C programmers can "escape" the C++ type system for argument declarations
by adding ellipses. This will "C++-ify" their C programs.

```
struct node *get_node( val )
int val;
{
    /* turns off C++ type checking */
    char *malloc( ... );
}
```

Although this program will now compile under C++, it will *not* link. This is
because all function names in C++ are internally encoded. The programmer
must explicitly inform the compiler not to encode the function name. This is
done by a linkage directive. (Section 4.4 (page 208) considers the linkage
directive in detail.) For example,

```
extern "C" char *malloc( unsigned );
```

The linkage directive informs the compiler not to encode the function name.
malloc() will now link with the libc.a instance. The recommended solution is to include malloc.h.

    If the programmer wishes to define the program so that it runs under *both*
C++ and C, the predefined __cplusplus (double underscore) can be used.

```
#include <stdio.h>
#include <stddef.h>

#ifdef __cplusplus
extern "C" char *malloc(size_t);
#endif

struct node*
get_node( val )
int val;
{
    struct node *ptr;
#ifndef __cplusplus
    char *malloc();
#endif

    /* ... */
}
```

__cplusplus allows for the intermixing of C-style and C++-style function
declarations through the use of the #ifdef and #ifndef conditional preprocessor directives.

C.4 Moving from C to C++

An important factor in the rapid acceptance of C++ has been the ease of using C++ with C. There are two aspects to this compatibility: the ability to use C++ with existing C based systems and the ease with which C programmers can learn and make effective use of C++. Typically, new users of C++ have been programming in C and often the initial use of C++ is to provide some new functionality to an existing program. Some of the lessons learned from the experience of melding C and C++ include the following:

- Keep the interface between the C and C++ parts clear and clean.

- "If it ain't broke, don't fix it" — that is, there is likely to be insufficient payoff to justify converting an existing system unless some substantial new development is undertaken at the same time.

- Use the new features of C++ gradually rather than all at once. You can get "spaghetti" classes just as you can have "spaghetti" code.

- Effective use of C++ comes with better design. You will get big payoffs from having some of the more experienced people spend the time to design a few classes that are fundamental to your application.

- Most users can start with a minimal knowledge of C++ and yet make effective use of general-purpose or application-specific class libraries.

Appendix D: **Compatibility with Release 2.0**

In this section, the primary changes in the C++ language introduced between Release 2.0 and Release 3.0 are detailed.† This appendix should be of primary interest to two categories of readers. For those without access as yet to a Release 3.0 implementation, the appendix notes those elements of the language described in the body of this book that do not apply to implementations based on Release 2.0. For those who have written code based on an implementation of Release 2.0 and wish to migrate the code to Release 3.0, this appendix can be used as a guidepost for making the transition.

The differences between Release 3.0 and Release 2.0 fall into two major categories:

- Language extensions introduced in Release 3.0. These include the template facility and the ability of a class to specify both a prefix and a postfix instance of the increment and decrement operators.

- Modifications to the language semantics of Release 2.0 introduced in Release 3.0. These modifications consist both of small refinements, such as the ability to implicitly inherit the pure virtual functions of a base class, and large changes, such as the introduction of nested types within classes.

D.1 Changes to Class Inheritance

The following language changes affect class inheritance:

- Introduction of protected base classes.

- Implicit inheritance of pure virtual functions.

- Extension of dominance to the data members and nested types of a virtual base class.

The subsections that follow consider these changes in turn.

The presence or absence of a particular change to the language may vary across implementations of C++. Our discussion is based on Releases 2.0 and 3.0 as implemented by Bell Laboratories, and the definition of the language as documented in the *Annotated C++ Reference Manual*.

Protected Base Class

Prior to Release 3.0, it was not possible to specify a derived `protected` base class. A derivation was either `public` or `private`. The following, for example, fails to compile under Release 2.0:

```
class ZooAnimal { ... };

// ok: 3.0: protected base class
// error: 2.0: illegal keyword: protected
class Rodent : protected ZooAnimal { ... };
```

Inheritance of Pure Virtual Function

Under Release 2.0, a derived class had to explicitly redeclare a pure virtual function of its base class if it did not wish to override it. With Release 3.0, a derived class inherits each pure virtual function it does not explicitly override.

```
class ZooAnimal {
public:
    virtual void draw() = 0;
    // ...
};

// ok: 3.0: inherits ZooAnimal::draw()
//      Bear is also treated as an abstract base class
// error: 2.0: Bear must explicitly redeclare draw()
class Bear : public ZooAnimal {};
```

Virtual Base Class Dominance

Under Release 2.0, dominance did not extend to the data members and nested types of a virtual base class. The following, for example, fails to compile under Release 2.0:

```
class ZooAnimal {
public:
    enum status { Not_Fed, Fed, On_Loan };
    void locate();
protected:
    status stat;
};
```

```
// inherits all members of ZooAnimal
class Raccoon : public virtual ZooAnimal {};

class Bear : public virtual ZooAnimal {
public:
    // 2.0: error: redefinition of status: type not nested
    // 3.0: ok: Bear::status and ZooAnimal::status distinct
    //      Bear::status dominates hierarchy ...
    enum status { Dances, Drives_Car };
    void locate();
protected:
    status stat;
};

class Panda : public Raccoon, public Bear {
public:
    void dances();

    // 2.0: error: illegal reuse of type name
    // 3.0: ok: Bear::status dominates
    status entertain;
};

void Panda::dances() {
    // 2.0: error: ambiguous: no dominance of data members
    // 3.0: ok: Bear::stat dominates
    stat = Dances; // not stat = Fed;

    // 2.0, 3.0: ok: Bear::locate() dominates
    locate();

    // ...
}
```

D.2   Changes to Classes

The following language changes affect the definition and use of classes:

- A class object of a class defining a constructor can now be passed to the untyped portion of a function signature — that is, the portion for which an ellipsis is specified.

- Truly nested types are introduced with access permission and an extended class scope operator.

- A non-fully-elaborated invocation of a class destructor is now permitted.

- Default constructors for arrays of class objects can now specify default arguments.

- The delete operator for an array of class objects no longer need specify the size of the array.

  The following subsections considers these changes in turn.

Argument to Ellipsis

Under Release 2.0, an object of a class defining one or more constructors or an instance of the memberwise copy operator could not be passed to an ellipsis function argument. This restriction has been lifted under Release 3.0. The class object is bitwise copied in its entirety onto the stack. For example,

```
class X {
public:
    X();
    X(const X&);

    // memberwise copy operator
    X& operator=(const X&);
};

extern void foo(...);

main() {
    X xx;

    // ok: 3.0: bitwise copied onto stack
    // error: 2.0: ''object of class X with
    //        constructor or = copied''
    foo( xx );
}
```

This untyped bitwise passing of a class object can be extremely dangerous if the class contains either a virtual function or a virtual base class. This practice, in general, should be avoided when possible.

Types Nested Within Classes

Prior to Release 3.0, type names (classes, unions, enums, and typedefs) defined within a class were exported to the enclosing scope. For example,

```
class Tree {
    class Node {};
public:
    // ...
private:
    Node val;
    Tree *left, *right;
};

// 2.0: ok: Node is visible and accessible
// 3.0: error:  ''Node a_dubious_use_of_node :
//      Node is not a type name''
Node a_dubious_use_of_node;
```

Under Release 3.0, a reference to Node outside the scope of Tree requires use of an extended class scope syntax unsupported within Release 2.0. For example,

```
class Tree {
public:
    class Node {};
    // ...
private:
    Node val;
    Tree *left, *right;
};

// extended nested class syntax:
// 3.0: ok.
// 2.0: error: ''syntax error''
Tree::Node a_dubious_use_of_node;
```

Note that under Release 3.0, Node also had to be moved to a public section of Tree in order to permit access. The name of a nested type not only is enclosed with the scope of the class it is defined in but assumes the access of the class section it is placed within.

Explicit Destructor Call

Under Release 2.0, the explicit call of a destructor required the explicit class scope syntax:

```
// ok: 2.0, 3.0
ptr->x::~x();
```

This meant that a virtual destructor could never explicitly be called — the fully elaborated class syntax overrides the virtual mechanism. With Release

3.0, the more direct invocation of the destructor is also supported:

```
// 3.0: ok.
// 2.0: error: ''syntax error''
ptr->~x();
```

Default Constructor for a Class Array

Prior to Release 3.0, an array of class objects without an explicit initializer for each element could not be declared unless the class either defined no constructor or defined a constructor taking *no* arguments. With Release 3.0, this constraint is relaxed to allow for a constructor specifying a full set of default arguments. For example,

```
class X {
public:
    // 2.0: not a vector default constructor
    // 3.0: ok: may be used with vectors
    X(int=2, int=4);

    // ...
};

// 3.0: ok.
// 2.0: sorry: ''default arguments for
//       constructor for array of class X''

X xa[10];
```

Vector Delete Operator

Under Release 2.0, it was necessary to pass operator `delete` the number of elements of the class array to be deleted. The destructor for the class, if defined, would then be applied to each element of the array.

```
X *px  = new X[10];

// 2.0, 3.0: ok.
delete [10] px;
```

Under Release 3.0, the user need only specify the empty bracket pair. Operator new itself keeps track of the number of allocated array elements.

```
X *px   = new X[10];

// 2.0: fails to compile
// 3.0: ok.
delete [] px;
```

D.3   Changes to the Basic Language

The following language changes affect the definition and use of the basic language:

- Nonconst references now must be initialized with an lvalue of its exact type. (A derived class can still be assigned to a reference to a public base class.)

- Reference arguments requiring temporaries are no longer treated as a special case in the resolution of an overload function call.

- The intersection rule for the resolution of multi-argument overloaded function calls has been refined.

- As part of the language support for templates, a number of class constructs can now be applied to non-class types.

- Restrictions on the use of local variables as default arguments have been clarified.

The following subsections considers these changes in turn.

Reference Initialization

Prior to Release 3.0, it was legal to initialize a nonconst reference with an rvalue or an object that was not of its exact type. The effect of such an assignment proved counter-intuitive and led to a number of subtle program errors. Here is a description of the problem as it was described in the first edition of this book.

A reference argument of a predefined integral or floating-point type can behave unexpectedly when passed an actual argument that is not of its exact data type. This is because a temporary object is generated, assigned the rvalue of the actual argument, *then* passed to the function. For example, here is what will occur when `rswap()` is invoked with an `unsigned int`:

```
int i = 10;
unsigned int ui = 20;
extern void rswap(int&,int&);

rswap( i, ui );
```

becomes

```
int T2 = int(ui);
rswap( i, T2 );
```

Execution of this call of rswap() results in the following *incorrect* output:

```
Before swap():   i: 10    j: 20
After swap():    i: 20    j: 20
```

ui remains unchanged because it is never passed to rswap(). Rather, T2, the temporary generated because of type mismatch, is passed. The result is a simulation of pass-by-value. (The compiler should issue a warning.)

Under Release 3.0, the compiler now will issue an error.

Argument Matching Algorithm Change

Prior to Release 3.0, the resolution of an overloaded function call took into account the possibility that a match might result in the generation of a temporary if the formal argument was a reference. Under Release 3.0, with the change to the rules in reference initialization described above, the presence of a reference as a formal argument is no longer considered as a special case. Here is a description of the behavior as it was described in the first edition of this book:

A temporary variable is generated whenever a reference argument is passed either an rvalue or an identifier whose type is not exactly that of the reference. In the case where two or more standard conversions are possible for the resolution of an overloaded function call, a conversion that does not require the generation of a temporary takes precedence over one that does.

In the following call, for example, a match requires the application of a standard conversion in both instances. The conversion of an int to short, however, does not require the generation of a temporary whereas the conversion to char& does. The conversion to short, therefore, takes precedence. There is no ambiguity.

```
extern ff( char& );
extern ff( short );
int i;

ff( i ); // ff(short), standard conversion
```

Under Release 3.0, this call is flagged as ambiguous: both matches have equal precedence.

The Intersection Rule

Prior to Release 3.0, the intersection rule for the resolution of an overloaded function with multiple arguments required that the function chosen be the one for which the resolution of each argument be as good as or better than for the other functions. Under Release 3.0, the additional constraint is added that the function provide a strictly better match than all other functions for at least one argument. This refinement prevents certain complex anomalies from occurring. (For a discussion of this addition, see *The Annotated C++ Reference Manual*, Ellis and Stroustrup, pp. 314 – 315.

Additionally, under Release 2.0, an overloaded function that required no user-defined conversions was automatically considered better than one that did. For example,

```
class X { public: X(int); };
extern void foo( X, int );
extern void foo( long, long );

main() {
// 2.0: ok: foo(long,long) chosen
// 3.0: error: ambiguous call
foo( 0, 0 );
}
```

Under the intersection rule, this call should always have been ambiguous. For the first argument of type int, the best match is the actual argument of type long — a standard conversion is always preferred to a user-defined conversion. For the second argument of type int, however, the best match is an exact match to the argument of type int:

```
          argument              best match

     #1   0 (int)               foo(long, long)
     #2   0 (int)               foo(X, int)
```

Under Release 2.0, foo(long, long) was preferred simply because calling it required no user-defined conversions.

Extended Non-Class Type Syntax

As part of the language support for templates, Release 3.0 permits non-class types to use class constructor and destructor syntax. For example,

```
// ok: 3.0: extended syntax for basic types
// unsupported: 2.0
int j( 10 );
char *q( "a string" );
int *pj( &j );

void foo() {
    int i = int();
    int *pi = new int();
    pi->int::~int();
}
```

Local Variables as Default Arguments

Local variables are not permitted to be used as default arguments. The following program, for example, is illegal under Release 3.0, although it was accepted by Release 2.0:

```
// ok: 2.0; error: 3.0
void foo() {
    int local_var = 10;
    extern void bar( int = local_var );
    bar();
}
```

The name of the formal argument enters scope immediately following its declaration, hiding global or class member names. Under Release 2.0, the reference to a in the following program resolved to the global a. The program compiled and when executed printed 10, 30. With Release 3.0, the reference to a resolves to the first argument of foo(), which is an illegal default value.

```
extern "C" void printf(const char* ...);
int a = 30;

// 3.0: error: illegal default argument
// 2.0: ok: b <== ::a -- generates: 10, 30
void foo(int a, int b=a) { printf("%d, %d\n",a,b); }
main() { foo(10); return 0; }
```

CODE DISK

A disk (in 5 1/4 inch format) containing the C++ code appearing in this book is available from Addison-Wesley. To order the disk, simply clip or photocopy this entire page and complete the form below. Enclose a check for $12.75 (includes shipping and handling) made out to Addison-Wesley Publishing Company, and mail to:

Addison-Wesley Publishing Company, Inc.
Attn: Order Department
Reading, MA 01867-9984

Please send me the code disk (0-201-56742-3) that accompanies *A C++ Primer* by Stanley B. Lippman. I enclose a check for $12.75 made out to Addison-Wesley Publishing Company.

Name _____

Address _____

City _____ State _____ Zip _____